Hope and Danger in the New South City

GEORGINA HICKEY

Hope and Danger
in the
New South City

Working-Class Women and
Urban Development in Atlanta,
1890–1940

THE UNIVERSITY OF GEORGIA PRESS
Athens and London

© 2003 by the University of Georgia Press
Athens, Georgia 30602
All rights reserved
Set in 10.5/13 Bulmer by Bookcomp, Inc.
Printed and bound by Maple-Vail
The paper in this book meets the guidelines for permanence
and durability of the Committee on Production Guidelines
for Book Longevity of the Council on Library Resources.

Printed in the United States of America
06 05 04 03 02 C 5 4 3 2 1

Library of Congress Cataloging-in-Publication Data
Hickey, Georgina, 1968–
Hope and danger in the New South city : working-class women
and urban development in Atlanta, 1890–1940 / Georgina Hickey.
p. cm.
Includes bibliographical references and index.
ISBN 0-8203-2333-0 (alk. paper)
1. Working class women—Georgia—Atlanta—History.
2. Atlanta (Ga.)—History.   I. Title.
HD6096.A7 H53 2003
305.4'09758'23109041—dc21
2002009367

British Library Cataloging-in-Publication Data available

CONTENTS

ACKNOWLEDGMENTS

WHEN I STARTED as a graduate student, I would read the acknowledgments in all my course books and wonder why it took people a decade to finish a single book. One husband, one dog, two kids, seven moves, two jobs, and very nearly ten years later, I finally get it. This book began as my dissertation and has traveled significant personal and professional ground with me since then—and I think it is much better for it. I will forever feel a special affinity for and interest in Atlanta because of this long association. Over the course of researching and writing this book, my work has been nurtured by many different communities—Ann Arborites; ballet dancers on the big island of Hawaii; musicians, artists, and old friends in Atlanta; colleagues in Statesboro; and family and friends across the country—and I thank them all for the sorts of contributions that do not wind up in footnotes.

On the professional side, I owe many debts as well. I had the good fortune to be a graduate student at the University of Michigan during the early 1990s, when the place was teeming with scholars who shared and nurtured my particular historical interests. In addition to David Scobey, Earl Lewis, and Carol Karlsen, who served as my dissertation committee, I thank Elsa Barkley Brown, Alice Echols, Susan Johnson, and Robin Kelley for their interest and encouragement. My graduate student cohort was also top-notch, and Robin Bachin, Erik Seeman, and Victoria Wolcott remain generous colleagues and good friends. My colleagues at Georgia Southern University, especially Jonathan Bryant, Peggy Hargis, Annette Laing, and the members of the Social Science Research Network, provided crucial intellectual and moral support during my five years in Statesboro. Returning to the North to take up a position at the University of Michigan—Dearborn during the final stages of revising has provided me with yet another group of incredibly supportive colleagues. Outside of my home institutions, Nan Enstad, Glenda Gilmore, Elna Green, Nancy Hewitt, Sarah Judson, Cliff Kuhn, and Gretchen Maclachan, Clay McShane, Mary Odem, Peggy Pascoe, and especially Susan Cahn offered enormously helpful feedback and support at crucial stages of the revision process.

As a dissertation, this project received financial support from the University of Michigan History Department, Rackham Graduate School, the Mellon Foundation, the Atlanta History Center, the American Historical Association (the Albert J. Beveridge Grant for Research in the History of the Western Hemisphere), and my parents, who gave me a car and a place to live rent-free. Since then, I have also been fortunate to receive a sabbatical and two grants from the Faculty Research Committee at Georgia Southern University and a National Endowment for the Humanities Summer Grant. The librarians and archivists at all the institutions I visited proved invaluable, but I thank in particular the staff at the Atlanta History Center (for making me feel so at home), Aloha South and Bill Creech (for unlocking the mysteries of the National Archives), and the Interlibrary Loan staff at Georgia Southern. Portions of the text were previously published by and are reprinted here with permission of the Georgia Historical Society and courtesy of Garland Publishing; portions of this text appeared previously in: Copyright 2000 from *Blacks in the Industrial City: Historical Roots of the Contemporary Urban Crisis, 1900–1950* by Henry Louis Taylor and Walter Hill, eds. Reproduced by permission of Routledge, Inc., part of The Taylor and Francis Group.

The most personal debts are the hardest to put into writing: they are so much deeper because they come purely from love—there are no professional obligations to balance them out. My family, in-laws, and a handful of good friends have always been supportive and never once (directly) asked me why it was taking a decade to finish this book. My husband was around before this project began, and I am happy to say that it looks like he will be around well after it. He made midnight runs to the copy shop, read all the drafts, gently ridiculed my jargon, praised the odd turn of phrase, and even drew me hilarious cartoons of a fame-hungry police chief routing out prostitutes and other stories from the book, all to keep me moving forward on the project. He also created for us a delightful world of music and friends outside the academy that I count as invaluable. This one is for him; the next one will be for the kids.

Hope and Danger in the New South City

Introduction

IRMALEE DAVIS ignored her husband's complaints and frequented Atlanta's dance halls at all hours of the night. Hattie Harper publicly accused the city relief officer of demanding sexual favors and threatening to ruin her reputation. Flossie Nealy won fifty dollars from the city council for undisclosed "damages." Annie Parr and Mae Parkman wore overalls and caps and visited the bars of Decatur Street disguised as men. Nellie Busbee told Atlanta Chief of Police James Beavers to "go to hell." Mrs. Allen demanded that her social worker not return unless she brought pain medicine for Allen's aching back and a new hat for her to wear.

In many ways, these are the vibrant, outspoken, working-class women of early-twentieth-century Atlanta that I had hoped to find when I began my research. I wanted to tell their stories—how they thought of themselves as urbanites and how they used the opportunities and the anonymity of the city to their benefit or at least for their own defense. I assumed that I might find, much like Christine Stansell did in her research on women in early national New York City,[1] that these women carved out a life for themselves uniquely suited to their urban surroundings. Although my research would obviously differ from hers in time, region, and race, I fully expected to focus on women and how they constructed a place for themselves within their urban environment. What I discovered about Atlanta's women both surprised me and compelled me to tell a somewhat different story. Working-class women did indeed profess urban identities, but more importantly the city at large recognized their significance to the community, though not necessarily in ways that benefited the women. City residents were acutely aware of the working-class women among them, often speaking about them publicly and using their images and experiences (whether imagined or real) as symbols within crucial civic debates. In the early decades of the twentieth century, Atlanta's working-class women not only served the "better classes" in their homes and factories but provided city boosters, politicians, and reformers with a common set of images, issues, and language that would help bring seemingly disparate problems into focus. Residents' public "concern" for the welfare of working-class women became

1

a means for creating an illusion of social and moral order in a city experiencing chaotic growth. Working-class women's lives and the discussions surrounding them provides a window through which to observe how city residents negotiated new social boundaries during a period of rapid urban development.

Women have more to tell us about the history of cities than we often realize. By the end of the nineteenth century, women not only fulfilled most of the domestic and reproductive tasks of urban life, but they increasingly reshaped the cities in which they lived. In the decades surrounding the turn of the twentieth century, middle-class women "saved" the city from the "strangers" who overwhelmed already crowded neighborhoods and strained urban services.[2] Club women, social workers, and suffragists carved out a space for themselves in the public discourse of the nation's cities long before women had won the right to vote.[3] Plans for suburbs, parks, and department stores began to provide for the presence of genteel women and were in some cases developed by women or to attract women.[4] Middle-class women constructed a network of female spaces in the urban environment where they could safely travel and work, laid the groundwork for many women's professions, created an accepted public presence for themselves, and "shared" at least some of these things with the city's working-class women.[5]

Working-class women, for their part, developed strong communities within nineteenth- and twentieth-century cities, usually bounded by neighborhood, race, ethnicity, and class but also reflective of emerging peer cultures and new shop floor relationships.[6] These communities proved resilient and uniquely suited to the urban environment, and from them working-class women pioneered new forms of urban leisure, sexual standards, family patterns, and activism.[7] Working-class women at times allied themselves with sympathetic women of the middle class but also resisted many of the moralizing efforts of settlement house women and social workers. These responses varied according to the working-class women's needs and perceptions of respectability, possibility, and independence.[8]

American cities have themselves proven to be remarkably durable but in a very different way. An overwhelming desire for economic growth attracted new businesses to U.S. cities around the turn of the century.[9] The growth brought with it disorder, most notably in the form of new populations that competed for housing, jobs, and city services. The irony of this process was that city officials, business leaders, and established urban residents had a distinct distaste for disorder, yet their boosterism and priorities had invited it.[10] Hierarchies of class, race, and ethnicity had been the traditional way cities gave order to urban space, and those who had already made their way up the ladder, especially if it were only a rung or two, resented the intrusion of newcomers whether they were southern blacks flooding into Milwaukee or Polish immigrants overwhelming Chicago's stockyard district.[11] In the decades surrounding the turn of the century, women were also perceived as urban newcomers, not because they were literally just arriving in the city (though many of them were) but because, as women's historians are discovering, women began to use the cities in new ways. The competition became one for public space, urban citizenship, and independent identities.

The lives of urban women and the competitive environment of Progressive-era cities came together in a public discourse that often highlighted working-class women. Women became symbols of public order and disorder, not just for issues relating strictly to women or even gender but for far more than that. What has been lacking in the historiography of women and cities is a wholehearted analysis of the connection between gender and urban development.[12] A consideration of the iconography and public discourse of a city—essentially, its cultural history—pushes us to understand urban development outside of economic realms and get at issues of respectability, morality, and social order that are bound up with a city's women and with what it has meant to live in and be a part of a city.

ATLANTA took great pride in its triumph over the ravages brought by the Civil War and in the city's progress toward its goal of being the premier "New South City." By 1880, the city's population had nearly doubled its wartime total to reach thirty-seven thousand. By century's end, the city's population stood at more than ninety thousand, and it would reach two hundred thousand by 1920. As Atlanta grew, new businesses, new neighborhoods, new populations, and less familiarity between the races and classes strained the old circumscribed styles of interaction. New institutions, particularly in the realm of commercial leisure, and new residents crowded Atlanta in the first twenty years of the century. Despite this growing diversity and the conflicts it engendered, the city remained remarkably united in its "Atlanta spirit," a shared commitment to continued growth and faith that the city could overcome the challenges associated with rapid urban growth. When a stylish young "city-as-woman figure" looked into the mirror, as an advertisement for the Chamber of Commerce showed, she saw overcrowded schools, dirty streets, congested traffic, and other urban problems. The ad copy, however, cheerfully urged citizens to "restore Atlanta's powder puff to her and with one application of the old 'Atlanta Spirit' her complexion will take on a different hue."[13] Such optimistic city boosterism generally depicted growth as good, but residents rarely agreed on what form that growth should take, what institutions and social mores should ground and govern the city, what new residents the city should try to attract, or who would control the direction of the city's development in the modern age. Who would wield the puff, and what powder would they use?

During the 1900s and 1910s, crusades to save women from the perils of the city as well as to save the city from immoral and dangerous women became a means for setting circumscribed social boundaries along class, racial, and gender lines for all of Atlanta's residents. Controlling women's access to dance halls and theaters would protect public morality. Limiting women's paid labor would result in more jobs and better pay for men and would leave women at home for their families. Keeping white women away from black men—and, perhaps surprisingly, black women away from white men—would cause racial harmony, or at least silence, to prevail. During these early decades, Atlantans wanted the city's economic prosperity to be recognized far and wide, but they also prized a reputation as a moral, hardworking, and well-ordered community.

A broad, diverse group of women appeared in the cultural debates of the first two decades of the twentieth century. I have found, for the sake of clarity, that it is useful to refer to them collectively as working class, but that is hardly their sole or definitive identity. The working-class women who found themselves at the heart of controversies and debates surrounding such diverse public issues as dance halls, industrial growth, welfare policy, and political maneuverings were both black and white, married and single, young and old. At times their class position and gender overshadowed other identities uniting them—but not always. Some women labored outside of their homes in industry, the service sector, or the informal economy, while others worked primarily inside their homes. Some of these women were financially independent and some were not, but none could make a claim to middle-class status. More often than not, they all experienced the hardships of having a poor education, low income, and little personal property.

While images of white women predominated in Atlanta's cultural debates of the 1900s and 1910s, both the white and black communities expressed concerns over changes in the city through representations of working-class African American women as well. Race almost always divided the women who appear in this study into separate groups in their daily existence, but there are moments when race does little to explain the similarities that existed between black and white women, especially in the day-to-day battles in which women engaged. [14] On the whole, the social and cultural visibility of black women paralleled that of white women in three significant ways. First, images of white and black women produced by whites, and sometimes even by the black elite, portrayed women as threatening or dangerous elements in the civic body. This suggests that race was not always the most salient feature of public discourse. Blacks were not always the demons for white fears; whites were not always the sole source of oppression in black minds. Second, the black and white middle classes constructed similarly positive images of women of their respective races. For example, the hope attached to motherhood dominated imagery on both sides of the color line. Third, new economic opportunities for women after the turn of the century provided a new understanding of citizenship and encouraged particular kinds of activism that led to greater public visibility for women of both races. This is not to say that race did not matter in Atlanta—it did. Rather, race was not necessarily the sole or most salient identity of southerners. Sometimes, gender and class position mattered even more.

There is no simple or singular explanation for the visibility of working-class women in the early twentieth century; rather, the phenomenon resulted from a combination of factors. Because questions relating to race seemed so "settled" to whites "protected" by the elaborate Jim Crow system and so dangerous to blacks, who faced both the legal threats and extralegal violence that maintained discrimination, gender became a much more useful construct in public discourse in the first two decades of the twentieth century. Women were often equated with social order, morality, family, purity, innocence, and fragility. Thus, women could also be associated with anything that might undermine virtue. Working-class women posed a special threat to moral order and social hierarchies because such women often frequented the newest parts of the city, the spaces that had fewer traditions and rules to give them order—the streets, the dance halls, and many new shop floors. At a time when Atlanta's overwhelming desire to project a positive reputation made the city uncomfortable with directly confronting divisive or confrontational issues, working-class women made an easy scapegoat since they, unlike their middle-class counterparts during the Progressive era, had no sustained, organized voice in the city. In isolation and combination, these factors help us to understand the ways in which working-class women were represented symbolically and used by the "better classes" in their discussions of rapid urbanization during the first two decades of the twentieth century. These factors also shaped the way real women negotiated the city on a daily basis.

While the specifics of the story are rooted in the history of one city and region, this tale is not unique to Atlanta or even to the South. There are striking parallels among cities just coming to terms with the impact of industrialization. Cities struggled to provide adequate services for burgeoning populations, wrestling with a host of political, economic, and social upheavals when established forms of moral and social order were threatened. During the Progressive era, at least twenty-five cities experienced racially motivated violence against African Americans similar to Atlanta's race riot of 1906. Fifty cities tried to close their red-light districts, much as Atlanta did in 1912. Los Angeles, Sacramento, San Francisco, Dallas, Charlotte, New Orleans, Minneapolis, Cincinnati, and even Butte, Montana, grappled with many of the same issues as Atlanta and sought to sanitize amusements, hire female police, investigate workplaces, eliminate red-light districts, expand welfare services, and incorporate women—and by extension men, children, families, classes, races, and ethnicities—into stable social structures, all in the midst of impressive urban growth.[15]

The story of Atlanta, and perhaps of these other cities, teaches us that a city obsessed with its economic growth might also remain concerned with its moral, physical, and social order, at least during times of relative prosperity. Exploring the images of women, both textual and visual, that were circulated during the first two decades of the twentieth century can bring the city's political contours and power struggles into sharper focus. For a brief moment, the washerwomen, cooks, secretaries, store clerks, box makers, bag folders, poor mothers, dance hall girls, and prostitutes functioned as the ideological territory for the contested work of city building. Women represented both the city's best hope and the greatest threat to its future.

The themes illuminated by an examination of both women and gender in these events, therefore, map much of the social and cultural terrain of the city. The cultural richness of these moral dilemmas also illustrates the texture of day-to-day life and the place of women in the development of the city. While public debates often included calls for the protection of working-class women, women's actions usually demonstrated that they neither needed nor desired the protection often imposed on them but instead had distinct demands of their own. Ultimately, crusades to protect innocent and virtuous women and those designed to protect the city from immoral and dangerous women resulted in circumscribed social boundaries along class, racial, and gender lines for all of Atlanta's residents.

The chapters that follow explore the shape and meaning of the visibility of Atlanta's working-class women. What makes this a story worth telling is the range of arenas in which working-class women's images were produced and debated. Between 1905 and 1909 alone, the city saw the founding of the first citywide charity organization, a brutal race riot, a tuberculosis scare, and an economic downturn that left many Atlantans out of work. Each of these developments connected to and encouraged increasing attention toward the city's working-class women. This visibility peaked in the 1910s, before the U.S. entrance into World War I, as issues of public health, welfare, public morality, and the excesses of a capitalist economic system dominated public discourse in Atlanta. Consequently, during the first two decades or so of the twentieth century, gender crises fluctuated to accommodate shifting populations, competing interests, new opportunities, and old prejudices.

To set the stage for this story, the first chapter briefly traces Atlanta's nineteenth-century economic development. The foundations of the city's zeal for growth are clearly evident in the history of Atlanta's earliest days, but this does not mean that city residents lived harmoniously. The expansion that so many in the city actively courted also created dissension, diversity, and competition. Most evident during these years were class tensions and racial strife. By century's end, however, a cultural change took hold, and gender moved center stage in debates over the city's future, not eliminating conflicts rooted in race and class but often absorbing them.

The next three chapters cover the development of working-class women's visibility in the realms where it emerges the earliest: paid labor, city streets and public spaces, and social welfare. Chapter 2 analyzes the dialogue that developed among city residents over the meaning of women's paid employment in the 1900s and 1910s. City boosters, middle-class reformers, and organized labor all debated the merits of women's employment, trying to reconcile the economy's increasing reliance on female laborers with desires for strong urban families by focusing almost exclusively on the labor of young single white women. The need to protect these workers, and by extension the city, from the worst effects of industrialization became an oft-repeated theme but a rarely applied concept. The discussions created vastly different pictures of women's work and women workers than those produced by working-class women themselves.

Opening with a discussion of the 1906 race riot, chapter 3 focuses on the ways in which the city also became obsessed with how working-class women spent their hours away from work and the presence of large numbers of women in the city's public spaces. In many cases, working-class women were on the frontier of urban growth through their increased use of city streets, transportation, parks, and commercial amusements as sites of leisure, places of employment, and arenas of protest. Both the newness of these institutions and the presence of working-class women engendered numerous debates over the regulation of streets, streetcars, and "cheap amusements." The regulation of women's behavior in these venues by the 1920s and beyond ultimately provided city officials and reformers with the key to establishing ground rules for the types of amusement trades and patron behavior that would be tolerated without stunting the profitability of the city's new leisure industry.

The next two chapters focus on the shifting class structure of the city during the early twentieth century and the emergence of a community of middle-class reformers. Focusing on the growth of the city's social welfare network starting shortly after the turn of the century, chapter 4 analyzes how working-class women of both races became the central target of welfare efforts while simultaneously being offered up as both the best hope and the worst danger for the city. Chapter 5 focuses on the later but related development of the public health movement in the 1910s. By this time, much of the city had become obsessed with the idea of "protection." Working-class women, as in so many other cases, appeared at the center of these discussions as both the primary agents of contagion and the most vulnerable population, representing the desire to protect Atlanta and its residents from the diseases of urban America.

Chapter 6 focuses specifically on the relationship of working-class women to formal politics and the legal system. The chapter contrasts the ways in which white women's bodies were used as potent political symbols in the 1910s with the political actions of the city's working-class women themselves, both black and white. This chapter is organized more around a particular set of related venues—elected offices, legislatures, courts—than around a distinct set of issues. The text of the debates and the substance of the issues raised in relation to the city's political and legal structures built on ideas about women, womanhood, and protection developed in other realms.

The decline in working-class women's visibility forms the core of chapter 7. Cultural change is amorphous and does not happen in one moment, but between the end of World War I and the early 1920s, the city's focus profoundly and permanently shifted away from concerns over order and discipline that had promoted working-class women as significant cultural symbols. Only during the Great Depression, the subject of the final chapter, does a new coherent set of cultural symbols emerge. In the 1930s, the figure of the black washerwoman who threatened white families with tuberculosis and the white streetwalker spreading venereal disease gave way to male thieves and bootleggers who turned to crime out of desperation. Gangs of men without the discipline of steady employment congregated on street corners, provoking concern formerly reserved for unescorted women seeking out the city's theaters and dance halls. In the end, the economic downturn, racial tensions, and fears of radicalism fostered a new sense of hope and danger that was better represented by the symbol of the unemployed male.

CHAPTER ONE

Rising, Ever Rising

IN 1887, Atlanta adopted a new city seal. The city council voted in that year to replace the old city seal, a locomotive engine, with the image of a phoenix rising out of the ashes of destruction, symbolizing the triumphant revival of a city virtually destroyed at the end of the Civil War. Beyond that, the phoenix also symbolized Atlanta's expansion beyond an economy based merely on commerce and transportation to a more diverse economy that by the turn of the century would include industry, finance, administration, service, and tourism. With a population of only twenty-one thousand at the close of the Civil War, the city grew to nearly one hundred thousand by 1900 and would surpass two hundred thousand by 1920.[1]

Railroads

ATLANTA is where it is and is shaped as it is because of railroads and Georgia's commitment to supporting the building of railroads. When, in 1842, a stake was driven into the north Georgia soil seven miles from the banks of the Chattahoochee River to mark the terminus of the Western and Atlantic rail line from Chattanooga, Tennessee, the future center of Atlanta was also marked. Originally called Terminus, Atlanta started as a railroad town, a place where transportation lines from the South's coastal cities converged with connections to the upcountry, midwestern, and northern markets. The Georgia Railroad from Augusta, Georgia, and the Macon and Western line from Macon, Georgia, soon came to meet the Western and Atlantic, linking Georgia's seacoast and farmlands with markets in the North and Midwest in the 1850s. The junction created by these railroads drew people and businesses to the area as a town—and eventually a city—evolved around the tracks. Even as Atlanta's focus and energy embraced the world beyond commerce in the decades surrounding the turn of the century, the city would remain closely tied to the economic foundations that underlay its success.

Samuel Mitchell, a planter from west-central Georgia, owned most of the land around the Western and Atlantic terminus. At the urging of Governor Wilson Lumpkin, Mitchell donated five acres to the state to support railroad development. In return, the state provided an engineer to divide Mitchell's remaining property into town lots. Unlike other planned cities, Atlanta's city plan did not follow a single, coherent pattern, and downtown Atlanta traffic still suffers today from its haphazard early development. Under Lumpkin's guidance, the state engineer laid out the town lots perpendicular to the rail lines of the Western and Atlantic, ignoring the existing highways running through the area. Other local landowners sold lots in conflicting grids, built off different sections of the rail lines, without easy transition points between the various patterns. As the town outgrew the early lots, development shifted to follow the north-south and east-west pattern of the older highways, which soon became the major road arteries of Peachtree, Decatur, Whitehall, and Marietta Streets. Triangular blocks and complex intersections, such as Five Points in the heart of downtown, resulted where the different development patterns met.

Hoping to shed the image of a rough-and-tumble railroad town while honoring the daughter of the governor who had committed Georgia to railroad development, the city changed its name to Marthasville in 1843. This change did little to improve the reputation of the town, and into the 1850s it was known "as a wide-open town, where there was said to be one saloon for approximately every 50 inhabitants."[2] In 1847, just as the first through rail lines opened, the city was incorporated under the name Atlanta (after railroad officials complained about the length of *Marthasville*). The 1850 census noted a population of two thousand, pushing Atlanta into a class with other new cities of the mid–nineteenth century, including Los Angeles, St. Paul, and San Antonio.

From the beginning, the town growing up around this intersection of rail lines had an uneasy relationship with the railroads that fueled its development. Atlantans did not own the rail lines, and local leaders had virtually no control over the commerce that passed into and through the city. The railroad owners, for example, only poorly maintained their buildings in the center of town. When local officials asked the Macon and Western to remove its freight depot so that traffic could better flow away from the center of downtown (where a passenger depot was to be built), they were met with indifference. Even railroad schedules fed local frustration: most trains arrived in Atlanta in the middle of night, discouraging excursionists and shoppers from visiting the town. Although the railroads had created the town and were the reason for its continued existence, they were also Atlanta's first great challenge.[3] This helps to explain the boosterism of many business leaders, who even before the Civil War worked to expand and secure for Atlanta an economic base beyond commerce by attracting northern capital and industry.[4]

Antebellum Atlanta and its promoters capitalized on the town's location between cotton-producing and food-producing regions. The city built a public
market to draw farmers from northern Georgia and consumers from the rest
of the state, thus encouraging goods to be sold in Atlanta rather than merely
transported through to other locations. The market encouraged local farmers to
bring produce to the city, where they not only would receive a higher price but
could also purchase needed manufactured goods at a significantly lower price
than in rural areas. The plan worked well, and Atlanta's newspapers boasted tales
of consumers traveling up to 150 miles to make their purchases in Atlanta.

During the middle of the nineteenth century, in the years leading up to the Civil
War, Atlanta struggled to build public order alongside the new town's growing
economic elements. During the 1840s, however, the town commission could
not collect enough revenue to enforce its laws. Atlanta's "respectable" citizens
elected Jonathan Norcross mayor in 1851 largely because he promised to clean
up the streets by putting an end to prostitution and cockfighting. Norcross and
his followers were soon labeled the Orderlies, and their opponents, who shot a
cannon into the mayor's store in an attempt to get him to resign, were dubbed the
Rowdies. The Orderlies held their ground, however, and the next mayor, John
F. Mims, took these law-and-order efforts further by cleaning out the gamblers
and criminals from the town's roughest neighborhoods. The challenge for these
early Atlantans came mostly from the newness of the settlement and the railroads
that brought a variety of travelers drifting through the city. Once the town grew
roots—public schools, churches, and a volunteer police force were all established
in the 1850s—the permanent settlers' cries for order subsided.

The Civil War

SECTIONAL TENSIONS and the coming of the Civil War, however, disrupted
Atlanta's profitable northern and western trade. During the war, the city adopted
new roles in the region, first serving as an essential supply line for the Confederate
Army and then later developing industries to supply the war effort, especially after
the war began to disrupt commercial trade. The war created more than economic
disruptions for Atlanta, pushing a wealth of new residents into the city. The
population nearly doubled during the war years, taxing the local government's
insufficient resources as the demand for city services increased. White Atlantans
funneled much of the anxiety created by this wartime expansion into an overwhelming fear of slave insurrections. They increasingly saw the potential for
urban disorder in the growing presence and decreasing supervision of the city's
enslaved African American population. Labor strikes, desperate and continually
unmet demands for skilled laborers, and an alarming crime rate added to the

sense of crisis that pervaded the city during the war years and ignited latent class tensions in a city that had fancied itself, as did much of nineteenth-century America, a classless society. While local officials struggled to deal with these challenges, trying more cases of disorderly conduct and paying out more in poor relief than ever before, Atlanta learned little from these experiences.[5] Indeed, when the city was faced with similar problems during the early twentieth century, the government and business leaders appeared as ill equipped to deal them as the Civil War generation had been.

Considering Atlanta's rail connections and growing wartime importance as a manufacturing center, it is not surprising that the Union targeted Atlanta for attack late in the war, when General William Tecumseh Sherman made his famous march through Georgia. During the 1864 Battle of Atlanta, fleeing Confederates, wasting ammunition and weapons lest they fall into enemy hands, and the advancing Union Army destroyed much of the city. Thousands of homes and businesses lay in ruins, including most of the city's fledgling industrial concerns. Atlanta's entrepreneurs immediately set about rebuilding, starting with the railroads, which ran again as early as 1867, and the city's commercial enterprises. These priorities left the city's residents to suffer for many more years with inadequate housing and few city services. Focused on economic recovery, Atlantans accepted Reconstruction policies without much complaint, hoping that this stance would encourage northern capital to flow into Atlanta. The city's boosters also set about recruiting migrants to provide the physical labor for Atlanta's rebuilding efforts and new industries, inviting immigrants and rural blacks in particular to lend themselves to Atlanta's "spirit of enterprise."[6]

Most nineteenth-century Atlantans eschewed the ideals, values, and markings of Georgia's planter class. Many were laborers, both black and white, who under the postwar free labor system drifted in and out of the city, working for wages. Wealthier residents, who were likely to have lived in Atlanta for longer periods of time, usually worked their way up to success in the entrepreneurial world with assistance from colleagues, family, or a good marriage.[7] The city's residents, whatever their class standing, generally believed, as did most nineteenth-century Americans, that hard work would offer plentiful rewards, especially in an up-and-coming setting such as Atlanta. Outsiders and residents usually agreed: Atlanta was "a home-made city by self-made men."[8]

In the years following the Civil War, Atlanta recovered quickly, with its expanding population and now firmly rooted industrial mind-set.[9] While port cities such as Charleston and Savannah languished, Atlanta's real estate values rose steadily during Reconstruction. In 1868 the city successfully lobbied to serve as the state capital, in 1875 Atlanta was rewarded with a federal customhouse, and in 1879 the first cotton factory opened in the city. Throughout the 1870s Atlanta hosted the Georgia State Agricultural Society's annual fairs and saw five new railroad associations and two new rail lines pass through the city. The city's first opera house, De Give's, and luxury hotel, the Kimball House, also opened during this postwar building frenzy. The city nearly doubled its wartime population, and by 1880, Atlanta once again boomed with businesses catering to railroad freight and passengers. The city now stood ready to build a great industrial economy.

Postwar Prosperity

THE TURNING POINT in Atlanta's economic diversification and its nineteenth-century building boom came in the closing decades of the nineteenth century. Starting in the 1880s and continuing into the 1890s, the city welcomed a wealth of new industry and financial concerns that quickly eased "the scars of war within the city proper."[10] The wealth of new buildings and businesses built in these decades led one observer to comment that "the Atlanta that rose like the fabled phoenix from the ashes [had] been obliterated . . . [n]ot [by] the red hand of war, but [by] the nervous, irreverent hand of progress."[11] The city's appeal for new economic concerns continued to grow out of its fine rail connections, its cheap and plentiful labor force, and the active recruiting done by Atlanta's business leaders. Municipal services, including streetcars and electrification, expanded in an attempt to keep pace with this growth and technological advancements. "The so-called 'Elegant Eighties,'" in the words of the city's historian, "saw the transformation of Atlanta from an unpaved, gas-lit and largely wooden town into an electric lighted, partially paved brick city."[12]

The International Cotton Exposition of 1881, modeled on the Philadelphia Centennial Fair of 1876, augured this shift from a commercial economy to an industrial one. The fair, the first of its kind in the South, drew the attention of industrialists, particularly New England textile manufacturers, to Atlanta's excellent transportation system and proximity to the region's cotton belt.[13] The northern capitalists who invested in the exposition hoped to use the fair to teach new methods of growing and harvesting cotton that would improve the raw materials shipped to northern textile mills. Atlanta's business community, including *Atlanta Constitution* editor Henry Grady and hotelier H. I. Kimball, however, saw the opportunity to convince the world of the advantages of manufacturing textiles in the South. The fair did indeed promote cotton manufacturing in Atlanta, and immediately after the closing of the exposition the fair's main building was converted into the Exposition Mills for the production of textiles. Perhaps more important to the future development of Atlanta, however, the International Cotton Exposition was "crucial in galvanizing the city's business leadership," providing a "rush of confidence" that would persist through the heady days of growth in the closing decades of the nineteenth century.[14]

The 1881 fair and a smaller 1887 exposition encouraged Atlantans to find ways to expand the city's industrial base beyond textiles. Spurred by the success of the earlier fairs and the depression of the 1890s, local leaders again embraced the idea of an industrial exposition to stimulate the local economy. The International Exposition of 1895, which sought to ignite "old-time enthusiasm" in the city, announced to the world Atlanta's expansionist intentions for the twentieth century.[15] Moving beyond the 1881 fair's focus on cotton production, the 1895 exposition advertised Atlanta's advantages to a wealth of industries and sought to encourage migration from across the country. The image of the city created at the fair emphasized "the grit, the dash, [and] the enterprise" of Atlanta's growing industrial base while trumpeting the more civilized side of the city with cultural and artistic exhibits that had been missing from earlier expositions.[16]

By end of the century, and the end of Atlanta's great expositions, the city had in many ways attained the economic goals articulated by the nineteenth-century fairs. Atlanta could boast more than four hundred businesses and production houses. The list of goods manufactured in the city included items from baking powder and overalls to sawmill machinery and boilers.[17] These industries created a wealth of jobs, and more than 70 percent of Atlanta's workforce found employment as skilled, semiskilled or unskilled labor.[18] Among the city's working classes, white males tended to concentrate in the skilled trades, while African American males generally held unskilled or service positions. Women comprised approximately one-third of Atlanta's workforce. Black women filled the ranks of domestic and personal service jobs, and the largest concentration of white women worked in semiskilled positions.[19] While male labor built the nineteenth-century industrial and transportation economy, women's domestic and semiskilled work outside the home served the city's commercial efforts and growing population, especially the increasing number of transients, by supplying and supporting visitors and the predominantly male labor force with clothing, room and board, and leisure activities.[20]

Social and Economic Relations

THE GLORIOUS RECOVERY embodied in the new symbol of the phoenix and the success of the international expositions captured only one aspect of the city's economic growth during the nineteenth century, however. As Atlanta launched itself as the center of the New South, the city struggled to control race and class relations within its rapidly expanding population. The process of industrialization challenged much of the city's economic structure, forcing residents to renegotiate and reshape the order of the city's workforce. Moments of crisis, particularly in the form of labor strikes and small-scale rioting, erupted in these years, revealing the fissures of class and race that challenged the city's pace of progress. The white business elite in most cases remained committed to putting a good face on these types of incidents, downplaying them in the promotion of the city and refusing to interrupt the script of progress Atlanta had adopted. Hannibal Kimball, the pro-Atlanta hotel owner, claimed that after the success of the expositions, "There will be no sectional controversies in our land, we are one people, rejoicing in common heritage, hopeful of a glorious destiny."[21]

Many Atlantans, particularly the city's economic leaders, clung to the notion that Atlanta was a wide-open town where virtually any industrious individual might make his fortune. The spectacular wealth of some residents who had started out in low-level white-collar positions and climbed the ranks seemed to attest to the validity of this story. But as the wealthy class of the city grew, so did the animosity between the haves and have-nots. Class tensions among whites flared during the Civil War, exacerbated by the inflation and food shortages that ravaged the city. Scandal erupted in 1862 when the local press revealed that "wealthy ladies were doing the government work, and making money rapidly" in the Quartermaster's Depot, in spite of the fact that the depot's commander had promised to employ the poor wives and daughters of Confederate soldiers.[22] Tensions escalated further in the spring of 1863 when war widows rioted against high prices, looting stores on Whitehall Street for basic foodstuffs, and numerous strikes threatened to disrupt war production.[23]

Class antagonism continued to plague Atlanta in the second half of the nineteenth century, despite claims that the city's "wealth and comfort" came in large measure from "the harmony of all classes."[24] In 1871 wealthy Democrats successfully overturned ward-based elections, which offered political power to predominantly black and working-class neighborhoods, in favor of at-large municipal votes. Two years later Atlanta's working classes of both races suffered another blow when a new city ordinance required that all municipal taxes be paid before an individual could vote. The national Panic of 1873 caused something of a local panic as well. Fearing that the privations caused by the depression would set off the working classes of both races, Atlanta's elite maneuvered for a new city charter in 1874, hoping that removing the police from direct control by the city council and reining in municipal spending would eliminate the party machine's major organizing issues and undercut the power of the working-class-supported Democratic Party regulars in Atlanta. In this instance, these leaders wagered correctly, and the resulting charter created a city government that "had to cut back on services to the city's less prosperous citizens."[25] The city's working classes had success in 1887, however, during a campaign to lift the county's two-year-old Prohibition regulation. Heated arguments enlivened mass meetings and street corner rallies as well as the city's press. "Antis" complained vociferously that "no mechanic or laboring man was invited to speak at any of the prohibition meetings" and challenged the city's working classes to see the restriction on alcohol as a class issue, arguing that "the 'kidgloves,' who have money enough to keep private barrooms want to deprive the poor man of the same privilege."[26] Despite early returns that gave the drys a substantial lead, the city's working classes turned out later in the day, and afternoon returns handed the wets a clear victory on this issue.

Racial tensions similarly took center stage during much of the nineteenth century as African Americans flooded the city, more than doubling the percentage of blacks in Atlanta's overall population in the years following emancipation. The number of blacks in Atlanta grew from 1,939 in 1860 (20 percent of the total population) to 9,929 by 1870 (46 percent). By 1880, 16,330 blacks called the city home, and ten years later, the African American population reached 28,089, 43 percent of Atlanta's total.[27] The city's business community had, intentionally or otherwise, encouraged African American migrants by downplaying incidents of racial tension and violence, a strategy perhaps meant more to promote the city in the eyes of northern capitalists than to attract more blacks. After the war, what drew most blacks to southern cities was not only the safety from racial attack provided by the presence of federal soldiers or the appeal of a growing African American community but also economic opportunities.[28] These pulls were particularly strong for older widowed, deserted, and never-married African American women. Lone black women often faced increased racial violence and found few opportunities in the rural South, where landowners preferred to deal with men.[29] Black women far outnumbered African American men in Atlanta throughout the nineteenth and early twentieth century as a result of these forces.[30]

The shift from a slave labor system to one based on free labor was not necessarily a peaceful or easy transition for Atlanta—or, indeed, for the South as a whole—and the growing presence of African Americans in the urban South emerged as a "persistent source of instability" during the late nineteenth century.[31] For all of Atlanta's claims that its "negro population is mainly made up of as high a class of negroes as can be found anywhere," the city remained in its opportunity and power structures very much "a white man's city."[32] Severe housing shortages forced the city's African Americans into temporary camps on the outskirts of the city, where diseases like smallpox ravaged the population. Federal troops clashed violently with camp residents, with the worst incident occurring in the Shermantown settlement in the fall of 1867.[33] Vagrancy laws and apprentice acts provided legal means for white Georgians to force blacks to labor, while the judicial system regularly meted out longer and harsher sentences to African Americans than to whites.[34]

Race relations seemed to have improved only somewhat as the immediate postwar crises passed. Blacks found residences in every ward of the growing city, and the massive influx kept the boundaries of segregation present but fluid.[35]

While the patterns of racial separation may have been shifting during these years, extralegal segregation or exclusion of blacks altogether from the institutions of public life was very much the bedrock of urban race relations long before the drafting of Jim Crow legislation.[36] The city's growing African American presence symbolized danger for many of Atlanta's whites, but for blacks seeking to escape the terrors and abuses of the rural South, these burgeoning nineteenth-century African American communities represented hope, freedom, and a physical space removed from the world of whites. Out of these communities came, in the words of one historian, "a flourishing urban resistance campaign" across the South in which blacks organized strikes, lobbied for better police protection, protested lynchings, and threw their political support behind the Republican Party. In the midst of the 1895 exposition, for example, the black congregants of Atlanta's Big Bethel Church urged African Americans to boycott the segregated fair, where "Negroes have not even a dog's show inside . . . unless it is in the Negro Building" and blacks were made "to feel inferior to other American citizens." Any African Americans who did visit would only "see on all sides: 'For Whites Only' or 'No Niggers or dogs allowed.'"[37] This kind of African American activism in the closing decades of the century would be, according to historian Howard Rabinowitz, a driving force behind the construction of Jim Crow segregation, particularly in urban areas.[38]

One Atlanta incident that exemplified African American desires and willingness to challenge the economic order of city occurred in the summer of 1881, when three thousand of the city's washerwomen struck for better pay. While Atlanta's blacks were largely powerless to challenge their confinement to racially specific work such as domestic service or unskilled labor, they did not passively accept the conditions and tenets of that work: hotel waiters refused to enter the city's dining rooms, laborers lobbied for employment on state railroads, and washerwomen organized for a decent pay standard. Indeed, the city's washerwomen used their virtual monopoly in laundry as the basis for their attempts to form protective associations and raise pay levels in 1877, 1879, and 1880. The city's black female laundry workers then formed the Washing Society and launched a strike in July 1881. Hoping to establish a citywide pay standard of one dollar per dozen pounds of laundry, the strikers formed groups that traveled door to door, recruiting women to lobby for improved and uniform wages and encouraging other washerwomen to honor the strike.

With the 1881 Cotton Exposition set to open in September, Atlanta's white community balked at the strikers' demands. The police arrested members of the strikers' recruiting committee, accusing them of harassing and intimidating other laundry workers. The *Atlanta Constitution* cautioned strikers to give up their cause lest they "find house rent going up so rapidly that they will have to vacate."[39] Other whites promised that contributions to relief organizations would cease, leaving the strikers without any source of assistance during the winter months. The city council got involved at the behest of wealthy whites, considering both a plan to exempt a new commercial laundry from taxes for a period of ten years and a licensing measure that would require washerwomen to pay twenty-five dollars to the city each year. The washerwomen responded with bravado, claiming that they would pay the fees "for licenses as a protection so we can control the washing for the city."[40]

The end result of this face-off between the city's white population and its black service workers is unknown.[41] The city council ultimately did not pass the licensing ordinance, but the strike petered out anyway. Threats and intimidation from city leaders and the local press seem to have had their intended effect, as washerwomen returned to work. Historian Tera Hunter suggests, however, that the laundry workers prevailed, not so much by raising pay but rather by "heightening the city's awareness of laundry workers' role in the New South economy."[42] The city's African Americans exploited the racial coding of Atlanta's labor landscape for their own ends as much as they could. The washerwomen and the other domestic workers they inspired could hope to wage successful strikes precisely because whites would not take over these jobs. The women also used the city's desire for growth in plotting their actions. The 1881 strike had great potential since it threatened to disrupt vital services during the South's first world's fair as well as to counter the message southern boosters hoped to send to the nation: southern workers were compliant and "utterly unacquainted" with striking.[43]

As the washerwomen's strike attests, women played important roles in the economy of nineteenth-century Atlanta. As service workers and the primary caretakers of working-class homes, women provided crucial labor to the industrializing city, but their lack of representation in industry meant that the city as a whole paid them little heed. In the heady years toward the close of the century, Atlanta's focus rested solidly on its economic growth. But economics dominated not only the city's hopes but also many of its problems. The competitiveness of the city and the uneven distribution of the benefits of its growth appeared most readily in the clashes between the city's working classes and its business leaders and, to a lesser extent, in the efforts of Atlanta's blacks to create a meaningful place for themselves in the city.

1897 Race Strike

LATE in the summer of 1897, white women employed as bag folders at the Fulton Bag and Cotton Mills walked off their jobs when management hired twenty black women to fill similar positions, thereby violating the familiar patterns and practices of the city's labor market. Women's activism formed the core of the strike, as the white bag folders attempted to reinforce gender and racial boundaries in the workplace through their walkout and black women attempted to gain a foothold in industrial employment. Male textile workers and the union local rallied to the defense of white womanhood, shifting the focus of the strike away from white women's rights as workers and toward a defense of working-class respectability and economic self-determination. The mill owner insisted on his right to hire any workers he saw fit, but he ultimately appeased his white workers by firing the black women. The press followed the story avidly for the four days of the strike, placing reports sympathetic to the strikers prominently on the front page of every edition. The strikers became the heroes of the city's white working classes and led the Labor Day parade that September.

Although it is easy to read this as merely one more example of white working-class Atlanta's familiar nineteenth-century racial animosity, the strike also pointed to a newer cultural trend taking hold in the city.[44] Clashes between labor and management over the following two decades increasingly focused on issues related specifically to women. This gendered component of labor conflict provided the means for workers to assert their respectability as well as to make claims for workplace rights. The inclusion of women, however, did not diminish the significance of race—indeed, Atlanta's early-twentieth-century industrialists and workers inextricably linked gender with race. The city's female paid laborers, such as those involved in the 1897 strike at the Fulton Bag and Cotton Mills, often displayed a conception of their lives and their work that differed markedly from the images produced by employers, middle-class observers, and even working-class men. The themes that emerge from this incident, then, encompass much of the breadth of women's visibility in Atlanta's labor market during the early twentieth century and can serve as a useful point of entry for the emerging visibility of working-class women.

The mill's owner insisted that the African American women hired in August 1897 had been employed only when efforts to find white women to take the positions proved fruitless. He realized some of the potential difficulties this change in hiring policy might represent and confined the new black employees to their own department on a floor apart from white women performing the same tasks. Nevertheless, white bag folders interpreted the presence of black women as a threat to white jobs and status. The white male mill hands who soon joined the striking women viewed the situation quite differently, arguing that by employing black women, management diminished white womanhood.

Blacks and whites in turn-of-the-century Atlanta most often encountered each other in the realm of work, but rarely did they meet on equal terms. The labor market functioning at the behest of employers, unions, and senior white workers consistently routed African American workers into positions inferior to those given to whites. Only when mill management altered the usually well-scripted and white-advantaged relations between workers did mill operatives go on strike. Even at the Fulton Bag and Cotton Mills, blacks had been employed for years as firemen and scrubwomen. Mill owner Jacob Elsas repeated this point during the strike, claiming that "no objection had ever been made to these colored people being employed by the mill."[45] Strikers, however, perceived the situation in August 1897 as different because blacks had been hired to fill positions equal in both status and pay to those held by whites. Even the spatial segregation between black and white women workers could not mitigate this. While "[s]ome of the men said that it did not make any difference about the negro women because they would be on a different floor," the women claimed that it would indeed make "a good deal of difference because we are all there together and the negroes would be considered as employed with us just as much as if they were on the same floor."[46]

On the first day of the strike, the bag folders left their stations in the mill and urged all operatives to follow. Other women workers soon joined the strikers outside the factory gates. Ella Brooks and Dovey Andrews emerged as early leaders of the strike, confronting Elsas and talking with the press. Men started leaving their posts in the hours that followed, essentially idling the mill by lunchtime. The police arrested several in the crowd as the men grew rowdy and confrontational. By the time of the mass meeting on the evening of the first day of the walkout, male strikers had taken over much of the leadership. Two all-male committees were formed to acquire legal counsel for the arrested men and publicize the strike. The local textile workers' union joined the cause as well and formed a committee to present the strikers' demands to mill management. Although the women strikers, male supporters, and the union held somewhat divergent views on the reasons for the strike, the issues of respectability and economic self-determination united the participants and resonated with the public following the story in the local press.

Respectability appeared repeatedly in this strike, but defining the meaning of this concept for the working class is difficult. Bourgeois respectability was largely codified by the late nineteenth century—through advice and etiquette manuals, finishing schools, and popular magazines—and focused primarily on standards of behavior and deportment.[47] Working-class respectability, however, revolved more around economic independence, self-determination, and protection than around manners and morals. And even within the working class, no clear consensus existed about the meaning of these elements.

During the 1897 strike, the white women created a dialogue concerning their status as workers and fought to protect their status in the mill. Job security was particularly important to women, since they, unlike their husbands, sons,

and fathers, had virtually no access at this time to the labor market outside the
mill.[48] "We are running this part of [the mill]," Brooks declared, "and if you
are going to employ the negroes we are not going to work."[49] Illuminating the
hierarchy and racial coding of textile jobs, one woman argued, "No negroe[s]
have ever been employed in the factory. . . . They had negro women to do th[e]
scrubbing and cleaning up and such work as that, but none were employed a[s]
regular hands."[50] "It is all piece work and so far as we were informed all woul[d]
be paid the same price," complained another female bag folder, who objected [to]
the implied equality between workers paid at the same rate rather than fearir[g]
that cheaper black workers would take over her job, an argument articulat[ed]
primarily by the union.[51] The women took the strike beyond the issues of rac[ial]
solidarity and expressed a larger critique of mill management, which chose to le[ave]
white men idle, instead hiring white wives and children and blacks. The wom[en]
asserted their power to use their labor to influence mill policy. While attempting [to]
preserve their jobs, the striking women also expressed white workers' frustrati[on]
over their precarious economic position in an industry that used low wage[s to]
limit men's ability to be their families' sole breadwinners.

Male strikers invoked very different reasons for the walkout, justifying t[heir]
position in the racialized language of protection for white womanhood. The [men]
asserted their perceived right to guard white women against encroaching bla[cks.]
The men postured as protectors, threatening with rocks to "fix them niggers w[hen]
they come out."[52] Only an issue that affected white women's status as deep[ly as]
the threat of hiring black women could have galvanized workers and the ge[neral]
public.[53] In contrast to the issues raised by female strikers about job sec[urity]
and status, the male strikers reemphasized their role as the protectors of [white]
women under the guise of working-class respectability.[54] Because of the low w[ages]
offered male mill operatives, men were often unable to fill this role econom[ically]
and turned to violence against both black workers and the police, who threa[tened]
to intervene during the strike.

Expanding on the sentiments of male strikers, the textile union local adv[anced]
a third interpretation of the significance of African American women being [used]
to perform tasks traditionally done by white women. Organizers appealed [to]
racial solidarity of whites and blacks alike, describing the hirings as "indign[ities]
would meet [with] the condemnation of every loyal white citizen of Atlant[a and]
also of the majority of self-respecting black citizens."[55] In lobbying for job s[ecurity]
for all textile workers, the union used the embattled symbol of the woman [being]
threatened by the encroachment of black women to represent the explo[itation]
of the producer at the hands of capitalists. The union also criticized mi[ll man]-
agement for adopting methods that "degrade manhood, prostitute wom[en,]
and debauch childhood," in the name of profit. The union ultimately ex[pressed]

the strike's issues beyond the experiences of the women workers. Through the lens of capitalist exploitation, union organizers cast the strike as a "fight for self-preservation for the right to life and liberty and against the iniquitous treatment" by mill management.[56] The 1897 strike in many ways was an opening salvo in a two-decade discussion of the relationship of economic growth to moral and social order.

In 1897, however, Elsas repeatedly refused to engage any of these arguments about worker status, gender definitions, or worker respectability. He defended his decision to hire black women as solely a response to economic need. Claiming that he had "no desire to oppress any of the people," Elsas meticulously explained that the black women "were downstairs, and up above them on the next floor were the [white] girls who quit work. Except for that back stairway there is no connection between the two departments and there could be no communication between the operatives in the two places."[57] Elsas either missed or intentionally avoided the point the strikers and union organizers were trying to make. He tirelessly defended his decisions as nonthreatening to white workers by pointing to the physical segregation of workers, overlooking entirely the issues of social and economic stratification that mattered most to the strikers.

The racial and gender messages encoded in the mill strike were not lost on the city's press or its white readership, which generally supported mill workers' fight for respectability. Echoing the strikers' sentiments, a local painters' union passed a resolution insisting that Elsas accept blacks as his social equals if he insisted on hiring them in positions equal to white mill operatives. Invoking both his class and racial positioning, Elsas replied that blacks were acceptable only as servants at his table, implicitly reminding strikers that he was rich enough to afford such luxuries. Despite the divergent language and tactics used by white bag folders, male strikers, and the union local, these groups united around the issue of respectability. They were battling for the respectability—the independence and sense of honor—Elsas and other white Atlanta elites assumed solely on the basis of economic class. To maintain a sense of respectability and to elevate their status, poor whites turned to the denigration of blacks. To work with African Americans in similar positions and for similar pay, argued the strikers, degraded the whites and threatened their social and economic self-determination.

Nowhere in the written accounts of the strike were recorded the voices of the twenty black women hired as bag folders. This phenomenon certainly speaks to how white unions, mill owners, and the daily newspapers normalized white privilege and disregarded the interests of Atlanta's black residents. Yet we can assume at least a few things about the women who so readily took the jobs Elsas offered: in a city where most black women had to work for wages to survive and where tradition, education, and experience generally confined African American

females to undesirable domestic work, positions inside a textile mill must have been enormously appealing. Even without explicit proof, it is worth considering that the African American women who took these jobs did so in part out of their own conception of respectability. The financial stability and the independence it offered, so important to the white textile workers, probably also motivated Atlanta's working-class blacks.

Whatever similarities might have existed across the racial divide in the city's working class, white strikers and union organizers prevailed in their racialized arguments for protection and job security. Elsas capitulated and fired the African American bag folders. Black workers remained in the mills, but only in the dirty and despised jobs that they had occupied prior to the strike. The centrality of white women to issues raised by the 1897 race strike brought to the surface deeply embedded fears of blacks encroaching on the domain of whites through access to white women. These anxieties included fears of racial mixing, moral breakdown, sexual chaos, and declining status for poor whites.[58] Working-class men's declining economic and political power escalated the tensions that erupted during the strike, not because the new workers hired were black women but because they were black. For women involved in the strike, however, the fact that the new workers were female appears as the crux of the issue. In sex-segregated textile mills, black women posed more of a threat to white women's position than men of either race ever could. White workers of both genders and mill management never envisioned men taking jobs as bag folders, but crossing the racial divide and bringing black women into the mill did seem an all-too-real possibility.

In September 1897, workers from Fulton Bag and Cotton Mills led the Labor Day procession. At the head of their contingent marched the women who had initiated the July walkout. All alike in blue shirtwaists and white skirts, they were the first women ever to march in a public parade in Atlanta. Whatever else it had accomplished, the strike initiated women into the city's larger white trade union movement. Suggestive of larger trends to come, women found some opportunities in the events surrounding this strike to advance their interests and perspectives. However, neither the black women who lost their jobs as bag folders nor the white women whose claim to status as workers was overwhelmed by the male strikers and union officials could transform women's centrality to the events at the mill in the summer of 1897 into a clear victory. The focus on women in this instance, as in debates to come, was so intertwined with class sentiments and racial stratification that attention did not easily translate into power. In the two decades following this strike, working-class women would try repeatedly in both individualistic and collective ways to capitalize on their newfound visibility, with similarly limited success.

Attempts by Atlanta's poor to maintain their often tenuous economic positions

as well as to define themselves as respectable workers would also appear repeatedly
in the early twentieth century. The Fulton Bag workers struck again in late 1897,
in 1913, and in 1914. Many of these struggles were inextricably bound up with
notions of womanhood and gender propriety, protection, and self-determination.
And as the summer 1897 strike suggests, arguments about and by women rarely
escaped a racial and class coding in which definitions of womanhood often stood
for ideas about race and class relations. Within this complex of meanings, the
city's wage-earning women of both races sought the means to make a living,
struggling to apply their own notions of "respectable" or at least "acceptable"
labor to the options before them.

AS THE CITY moved into the twentieth century, the maturation of Atlanta's industrial economy, growth in white-collar employment, and the emergence of
modern metropolitan Atlanta would create new debates and crises. These would
focus increasingly on issues of gender, with race and class in close attendance.
White women gradually moved into industrial jobs before the turn of the century,
but the pace of this change increased dramatically in the early 1900s. Black women
continued to work predominantly in the service sector, although opportunities
there also expanded enormously with the pace of urban growth. Tensions shifted
from antagonisms driven explicitly by class and race to disruptions where gender
often took center stage. In some cases, gender represented racial and class conflict; in other instances, the moments of crisis and attention given to working-class
women represented new issues emerging in the urban environment. This process
began in the world of paid labor and the formal economy, but it quickly spread
to other realms: city streets and services, amusements, welfare, and politics.

CHAPTER TWO

Laboring Women, Real and Imagined

In 1903, Atlanta's *Journal of Labor*, a weekly newspaper and the premier voice of organized white labor across the state, began a celebration of women connected to the city's federated white trade unions. Two images of white women appeared in these photographs and stories: the union wife and the working girl. The former were a part of "a body of noble women, who have thrown their consecrated efforts with their husbands, brothers, and fathers, in the great labor movement."[1] Not paid laborers themselves but instead the backbone of the working-class family, these married women directed their efforts toward maintaining a home, organizing union auxiliaries, and directing "buy union" campaigns. The union wife carried "an abiding faith in the equity and justice of unionism" and, with almost "religious zeal," taught "her children accordingly."[2]

The second image, that of the working girl, generally received praise in the pages of the *Journal of Labor* first for her popularity or beauty and second for her skill as a worker.[3] Descriptions of the working girl characterized her as loyal, energetic, "lovely and lovable," with the underlying message that she was available for marriage: "we can hear the wedding bells already."[4] The local labor press encouraged union men to "abolish female competition in the work room" by marrying "the competition" and celebrated a 1907 shortage of hat trimmers resulting from a spate of marriages during the preceding year.[5] Union leaders urged women who worked for wages to become union members and celebrated these women as wage earners in their own right, at least as long as they were single. Yet it was hoped and expected that the working girl's greatest aspiration in the early twentieth century would be to become a union wife.

Following the turn of the century, the union wife would increasingly find herself surrounded by growing numbers of working girls. She might even find herself becoming one of them as the employment of women shifted to include many more older and married women. Organized labor's focus on women's relationship to work would be continued by businessmen, middle-class reformers, and local newspapers over the next fifteen years. Arguments over the fate of young, white, and single workers predominated in this dialogue, however. For as much as this narrow exchange revealed about the city's fears about greedy capitalists, shifting race relations, and disintegrating families, it reflected little of the realities of working women's lives and resulted in no widespread actions to protect workers from extremes of the capitalist labor market. The developing divide between women's experiences in the workforce and the discussions of the meaning of women's paid employment ultimately revealed that the boosterish attitude of many Atlantans, residents' concerns about the city's reputation, and the limited social change the city was willing to exchange for economic growth reverberated far beyond the immediate realities of women's work in the first two decades of the twentieth century.

Women's Paid Labor

THE TREMENDOUS economic growth Atlanta experienced at the turn of the twentieth century created numerous new employment opportunities for women. Gender and racial segmentation, where whole categories of work went to a particular group, continued to shape the growth of the city's workforce and molded women's wage-earning experiences by opening some opportunities while closing the door to others. Most black women continued to earn their income as domestic workers—maids, child nurses, cooks, and laundresses—just as in the nineteenth century.[6] However, Atlanta's blossoming population and growing middle class meant that there were more of these positions to be had. Expansion in business and trade drew large numbers of women into manufacturing starting in the 1890s and 1900s, and by 1919, women made up more than a quarter of all factory operatives.[7] White women predominated in the garment, candy, and box-making industries, while commercial laundries and textile mills hired women of both races. As Atlanta's business and commercial economies matured in the 1910s, clerical and sales positions started opening up to white women, employing 40 percent of white female workers by 1930. A notable minority of African American women found similar employment in the thriving black businesses created when Jim Crow segregation closed the doors of white-owned businesses to black patronage.[8] Some women of both races also generated income through their labors in the city's informal economy. Only a quarter of Atlanta's female population over the age of ten worked for wages in 1890.[9] By 1920, however, more than 40 percent of Atlanta's women over the age of sixteen toiled in the city's formal economy, a milestone the nation as a whole would not reach until fifty years later.[10]

Beyond the increase in the number of women working, significant shifts in the racial composition and marital status of the female labor force occurred between 1890 and 1920. In 1890, African American women accounted for three-quarters of the city's female paid laborers. In contrast, by 1920, almost half of the city's wage-earning women were white. Black women continued to work in numbers greater than their counterparts in other southern cities and in the nation as a whole, so the shift to an almost evenly split female workforce resulted from the increasing employment of white women and the declining percentage of blacks in the city's overall population. Where African Americans had once accounted for more than 40 percent of the city's residents, that figure had fallen to 33 percent by 1910 and 31 percent by 1920.[11] Married women also joined the labor force in new and surprising numbers. Between 1900 and 1910, the percentage of employed white women who were married jumped from 12.6 to 21.3. The percentage of married women in the African American female labor force increased from 25.7 in 1900 to 43.2 in 1910.[12] Thus, the early twentieth century witnessed both an increase in the number of women working for wages and a shift in the composition of the female labor force to include more married women and white women who worked for wages.

Imagining Women's Work

IN RESPONSE to rapid changes in the female workforce, an often narrow and revealing dialogue developed among city power holders—elected officials, business leaders, reformers, and unions—over the meaning of women's paid employment. The bulk of this attention focused on the employment of single white women, even though one of the most dramatic changes in women's paid labor during this period was the increasing participation of married women in the industrial and service workforce.[13] African American women's work also received only tangential treatment even though such women made up between half and three-quarters of the city's female workforce throughout the period.[14]

The focus on single white women reveals the larger concern of the city's white organized labor community, middle-class reformers, and city boosters with the impact of continued growth on moral and social order.[15] In its own way, each group reinforced a model of the white urban family in which women's role as mother and caretaker of the home was central. The ideal supported the illusion that male paid labor was the norm and reinforced a racial order that privileged whites and downplayed racial tensions by virtually ignoring the existence of African Americans. White men could earn enough to support their families, and white women, safely ensconced in tidy homes, would not encounter the city's African American population, except for the black women who did the family's washing, cooked the meals, and made the beds. Despite these sectors' varying interpretations of the meaning of women's paid labor, most endorsed similar themes: motherhood, family, and the temporary nature of women's paid employment.

The city's response to the growth and changes in women's employment after the turn of the century was most noticeably articulated by progressive reformers from Atlanta's middle classes, the city's business elite, and the organized labor community. Wage-earning women contributed to this dialogue on the working girl, but the language of victimization and control that reformers and labor leaders employed effectively silenced women's voices. Commentators expressing concern for "future motherhood" denied the possibility that women might have positive experiences in the world of paid labor. Relying on images that emphasized the vulnerability of female workers, particularly their sexual vulnerability, middle-class reformers, organized labor, and the white business elite expressed a variety of responses to the changing composition of the city's workforce. Ultimately, however, these reactions worked to incorporate women into a stable, sex-segregated, and racially specific labor system.

Atlanta's urban boosterism, the name given to the unbridled promotion of the city in the pursuit of economic growth, reached its peak following the turn of the century and was one of the driving forces behind the discussion of women in the labor market. The city's new class of businessmen actively promoted the city as the capital of the New South, portraying Atlanta as a site of cheap labor and pleasant race relations. Key to these messages was a particular imaging of the female workforce. Business leaders created the common perception that women were "more tractable than men, . . . less apt to organize, and . . . cheaper than men" to attract new industry.[16] Even Atlanta advertisers built on the image of the working woman, although they tended to portray all women workers as young, beautiful, single, and white. For example, the wholesomeness of Atlanta's industry was promoted in an advertisement picturing pretty young women in white caps and aprons sitting in the bright, airy workrooms of a local bakery. The advertising copy touted not the quality of the product but the "health and comfort" the company provided for its employees as well as the tidiness and orderliness of the "dainty girls in white caps" who wrapped the cakes.[17] Employers, customers, and boosters actively fostered the implication that these women and other female workers like them would add feminine attributes of cleanliness, purity, and a kind of wholesome sexuality to any firm interested in doing business in Atlanta. This advertisement cast the female employees at this bakery as women first and workers second, a prioritization many service-oriented businesses echoed.[18]

Within the city, however, a larger dialogue on the place of women in paid employment also included negative images of female workers. Women moving into the workforce and particularly into clerical jobs, which brought them into regular contact with male employees, became sexual objects to be avoided or flirted with—competitors for male affections but not for men's jobs.[19] The popular press played up the dangerous moral aspects of working-class women's sexuality in the workplace. A cartoon series in the *Atlanta Constitution*'s Sunday magazine, for example, followed the fictional adventures of working girl Kitty Cobb. A clerical worker in an office filled with men, Kitty represented the potential for uncontrolled sexuality, whether as the prey or the predator of the male workers around her. Responding to this threat in one story, an executive's wife successfully maneuvers to have the youthful and beautiful Kitty fired and replaced by a dowdy older woman. The caption for this story declared that "the hand that wears the wedding ring rules these United States." The message to wage-earning women was clear: paid labor should be considered only temporary, and marriage offered the only road to security and power for women.[20] Perhaps more deeply encoded in this cartoon, however, was an illustration of the threat that wage-earning women, especially those in male-dominated spaces such as offices, posed to family stability.

The business elite sought to distract attention from these potentially disruptive aspects of working-class women's lives. In addition to presenting glowing reports on the state of labor, boosters sought to suppress negative and potentially damaging descriptions of the city's industries. When rumors surfaced during the 1908 recession that some Atlanta industries mistreated their female employees, the city council commissioned a study of the conditions of women's wage work in the city. Council members, many of them intimately involved in the city's boosterism and industrial economy, expected that the study's findings would contradict the rumors and clear Atlanta's name. When the final report apparently supported allegations of poor working conditions in concerns that relied on female labor, the council, which had ordered the report, suppressed the results.[21] Despite expressions of concern over the conditions encountered by working-class women, no widespread regulation of female employment ever materialized for fear that a frank discussion of industrial conditions for women workers would too greatly damage the city's reputation.

The focus on young, white, and never-married workers generally kept the ideological complications presented by married or older wage-earning women out of the public discourse. African American women also presented problems to the city's boosterism. Atlanta's white businesses referred to black women only in their relatively despised though widely accepted role as household workers, implying erroneously that their position in the city's economic structure was limited to domestic work. Playing on tensions between black domestics and white employers, the Troy Laundry ran advertisements in the 1910s declaring the "washerwoman problem solved" to promote their commercial laundry services.[22] The laundry offered not a white-only shop (since commercial laundries employed both black and white women) but the service of relieving white patrons from dealing directly with black workers. This advertisement is telling in its portrayal of industrialization as a solution to racial tensions, but advertisements of this kind were rare. Instead, boosters actively sidestepped or entirely overlooked racial segregation when promoting the city as the industrial and financial capital of the New South. Business leaders generally chose to keep the discourse centered on young, single, white women and to avoid altogether the troubling issue of black workers.

Whether black or white, women remained a part of the unskilled masses throughout the early twentieth century and consequently had little job security during economic downturns. When the city's industrial economy slowed in 1908, for example, hundreds of women lost their positions.[23] Manufacturing recovered in the following year, however, and employers once again sought to fill their empty positions with the city's women. Nunnally and McCrea, manufacturers of overalls, advertised in the local labor press, hoping to attract "girls who desire secure positions" by offering "the best wages" in a "well lighted and well heated" factory where "the work is light and where . . . short hours are required."[24] Even as women were increasingly pulled into the industrial workforce, they acted as a fluid pool of cheap labor to be drawn on when circumstances dictated. This trend relegated women to the lowest-paying and least-secure jobs, and this structure was further refined by race, with African American women occupying positions below those of white women in terms of desirability, pay, and working conditions.

In contrast to the pretty picture of white women workers generally promoted by urban boosters, Progressive middle-class reformers and the local press responded to changing patterns of female employment by focusing on the need to protect wage-earning women. These groups of ministers, club women, church members, social workers, and liberal newspaper editors did not argue that young women should cease wage work altogether but instead contended that they needed to be protected from its dangers. The black and white middle classes focused, not surprisingly, on young female wage earners of their particular races. The black elite, including newspaper editors and settlement house workers, instructed young African American women to seek skills and education as a means of increasing their marketplace value and improving their job security. African American reformers more readily accepted paid labor for women than did white reformers, and the issue consequently received far less attention from blacks than it did in white circles. As part of the broad-based movement for "racial uplift" driven by the black middle class in the early 1900s, discussion of women's work outside the home quickly shifted to an emphasis on the respectability of black women, a focus on character over occupation, and the hope that women of the race would find "home-making . . . the best paying profession of all" as well as the source of "wisdom, love, reverence, and happiness."[25]

Atlanta's white middle class focused much of its attention on young, single, white women. The reformers consistently told women and the city at large that home and a primary role as wife and mother offered the only true security and respectability for women. Much in this message dovetailed with that sent by the black middle class to African American women. White reformers often portrayed Atlanta's white female workforce as migrants from the countryside, innocents unschooled in the ways of the city and easily duped. This particular view was no doubt shaped by growth in the city's white female population that outpaced that of white males.[26] But the characterization of female migrants as greenhorns from the rural South also excused some women's forays into prostitution and stealing. According to reformers, rather than the product of some inevitable decline in the morals of the city precipitated by continuing industrialization, women's illicit behavior was as the product of ignorance and youth and could be erased with the proper supervision. The Evangelical Ministers Association, for example, passed a 1913 resolution "recognizing the close relation between prostitution and the living wage."[27] Similarly, in 1910 the Men's Club of the Central Congregational Church requested that the city council hire a woman probation officer to "aid in the protection of working girls, and to assist them in leading clean, upright lives, to assist in the suppression of the white slave traffic and to investigate the conditions that surround our girls in the stores, workshops and factories."[28] Middle-class reformers challenged the city government to protect women workers and the employer "to treat the women in his employ as he would have his own daughter treated by another man."[29]

The Young Women's Christian Association held the most sympathetic views of working-class women's lives, yet it too reflected the views of the larger reformer community and focused on the victimization of women workers. A group of young middle-class YWCA women from colleges in Virginia, North Carolina, South Carolina, Georgia, and Florida ventured to Atlanta to better understand the lives of working-class women by working in industry during the summers of 1922 and 1923. The women were surprised at the conditions they found: "It seemed that I walked from one end of Atlanta to the other and the world was such a cruel one which cared little whether I got a job or not," reported one disheartened participant. Describing the city's industrial sections and working-class neighborhoods, she continued, "the entire atmosphere created by rough, dingy streets walled by factories between which were crowded fruit stands, bill boards and old stores and traversed by the working men and women, sickened me." "The weakening of one's morale," she concluded, "is a most certain outcome of continued unemployment. The discouragements and temptations which a girl experiences are enough to weaken one whose home background has been conducive to the highest and biggest things in life."[30]

Supporters of YWCA work demanded that the city protect the "faithful and earnest young women struggling for a livelihood for themselves or some other."[31] A local minister urged that "greater reverence be shown to women than the mere

doffing of hats in elevators and tendering of seats in street cars: . . . give better
wages to working girls, that they may live decently."[32] The YWCA employment
secretary urged the *Journal of Labor* to warn "country girls" against coming to
Atlanta without a "bona fide offer" of work. The newspaper's editors apparently
agreed, running the letter in full and adding, "if fortunate enough to secure a
place, [the country girl] becomes a mere piece of machinery; that beautiful and
attractive personality possessed in her country town is lost forever."[33] Underlying
these calls for protection was the image of the white working girl as innocent
and morally pure; any deviation from these standards was thus attributable to
outside forces.

With the sensationalized 1913 murder of Mary Phagan and subsequent trial of
her accused killer, Leo Frank, tensions over women's changing roles in the city,
class politics, and regional conflicts found a prominent place in public discussions
of the case. The moral—especially sexual—and social dangers of women's paid
labor predominated over reports of poor working conditions, long hours, and
low pay. Phagan's murder and the Frank trial crystallized many southerners'
fears about the pace of industrialization in the South and the encroachment of
northern capital.[34] The image of a brutally murdered young white woman rallied
many elements in the city, bolstering middle-class reformers' arguments and
temporarily dampening the city's booster atmosphere.

Almost fourteen at the time of her death, Phagan worked for twelve cents an
hour at Atlanta's National Pencil Company. On April 26, 1913, she left her home
in Bellwood, a mill village just outside the city, traveling downtown to pick up
her pay envelope at the factory and to watch the Confederate Memorial Day
parade. Shortly after receiving her wages, Phagan was murdered. Her beaten and
strangled body was discovered early the next morning in the basement of the
factory. Blame quickly fell on the factory's manager, Frank, a Jew.[35]

In the telling and retelling of her story, Phagan eventually became a potent
symbol for the dangers of the urban environment. Popular songs and local press
coverage portrayed the slain factory worker as the quintessential victim, killed not
so much by "one lustful Jew" as by the indifference of a city that had not protected
her from harm. She became one embodiment of the host of fears generated
by and about women who worked for wages and traveled freely through the
city. Accusations that Phagan had been raped before she was murdered, rumors
that she had died to protect her "virtue," and even more shocking stories of
promiscuous young women employed in the factory alongside Phagan created
anxieties over changing norms surrounding sexuality and the sexual vulnerability
of the city's young women.

When Phagan's body was discovered, police initially arrested Newt Lee, the
African American night watchman who found her. Shortly thereafter, Frank and

Jim Conley, a black janitor, were also arrested. Claiming that Frank was the murderer, Conley admitted to being an accomplice by disposing of the body in the basement. He became the prosecution's star witness in the trial against Frank. The trial riveted the state's attention. Frank was eventually convicted and sentenced to hang. When all appeals were exhausted two years later, the conviction remained intact. Governor John Slaton, considering the pleas of elite and Jewish citizens from across the country as well as the recommendation of the original trial judge in the case, commuted Frank's sentence to life in prison.[36] Shortly after the commutation, a mob angered by the governor's decision removed Frank from prison and lynched him in Marietta, Georgia, Phagan's birthplace. In subsequent examinations of the case, evidence clearly suggested that Conley had murdered Phagan, and Frank received a posthumous pardon in 1985.

Following the murder, Phagan's image was rewritten and retold in ways that reveal the reasons behind the widespread fascination with the case. Phagan's qualifications for the role of martyr are obvious: she was young (thirteen), pretty, white, and dead. The last factor was critical, for it meant that she could not tell her own story, and her actions could not complicate the picture of innocence and passivity that came to symbolize both her life and death. Once dead, Phagan became, according to historian Joel Williamson, "the very child of the New South."[37]

Mary Phagan was the daughter of tenant farmers who had migrated to a textile mill just outside of Atlanta when cotton prices fell. To help support her family after her father's death, she took a factory job in the city. Many fears of the dangers associated with the ever-increasing number of wage-earning women could be found in Phagan. A young woman who worked for wages and traveled the city unescorted represented the potential for sexual expression unchecked by the restraining presence of family as well as economic independence that might lead her to shun marriage and family altogether. Typical of middle-class reformers' arguments, however, the most frequent images of Phagan represented the moral danger these shifting social and economic patterns posed to wage-earning women. Concerned observers pointed to Phagan's murder as an extreme example of employers' almost unlimited control over their female employees. Focusing on the alleged rape attempt by Frank, sexual dangers took center stage over reports of poor wages and miserable working conditions. The story of Phagan's fated trip from the watchful eye of her mother into the heart of the city became a metaphor for the dangers of the city. Unions and most of Atlanta's working classes united in the message that independent women were in danger. The resulting cries for protection reinforced the desired position of many men as respectable breadwinners, able and willing to protect their families from abuses at the hands of the capitalist elite. Sexual conservatism also triumphed in descriptions of

Phagan that denied that she might have been an independent—potentially sexually active—young woman and reduced her to a mere child.[38] Shortly after the murder, for example, the *Atlanta Constitution* reported, "Mary Phagan's life was one of such beauty and purity that when the world knew of her memory [she] instantly became the fondled child in the heart of every parent and the playmate of every little girl in the city."[39]

The mythology attached to Phagan surfaced repeatedly between 1913 and 1915 in song, speech, and picture. Newspaper drawings of Phagan increasingly imaged the victim as prettier, happier, and more childlike in the weeks and months following her death.[40] Former populist leader Tom Watson provided some of the most fiery and frequent renditions of Phagan in his anticommutation speeches and writings. Watson posed the question not as much to the governor as to the state's white working-class and middle-class communities, "How much longer is the innocent blood of little Mary Phagan to cry in vain to Heaven for vengeance?"[41]

Fiddlin' John Carson, Atlanta's foremost white folk musician, eulogized Phagan in three separate songs written to please the crowds outside the courthouse and at other working-class gatherings. The profits Carson made from performing these songs are a testament to the resonance of the images of Phagan he called into play.[42] In the earliest of these, "The Ballad of Mary Phagan," Phagan appears as "little" and a "poor child":

> Little Mary Phagan
> She left her home one day;
> She went to the pencil factory
> To see the big parade.
>
> She left her home at eleven
> When she kissed her mother good bye;
> Not one time did the poor child think
> She was going there to die.
>
> Leo Frank met her
> With a brutely heart we know.
> He smiled and said; "Little Mary,
> Now you go home no more."[43]

Carson's description grew more detailed in a later song, "The Grave of Mary Phagan":

> Little Mary Phagan was just fourteen
> She was pretty as a queen

Her hair was dark and curly
A sweeter child never was seen.[44]

"My Little Irish Rose," written in 1915, reveals the most pervasive image of Phagan as well as the hatred attached to Frank:

She died for her virtue.
We all know that's true.
Before she would give her honor
To that brutal Jew.[45]

Beyond these representations, the incidents surrounding Phagan's death and Frank's trial provide a window to some of the least organized yet most visible activism of white women. From the time of Phagan's funeral to the viewing of Frank's body after he was lynched two years later, many Atlanta women showed an intense interest in the issues raised by the Frank case. In other instances, Atlanta women signed petitions for commutation of the Frank sentence: judging by their addresses and husbands' professions as listed in the 1915 Atlanta city directory, most of these women were middle class.[46]

Working-class women participated in the events surrounding the Frank case most commonly through their presence at the trial and in the crowds that gathered in the streets around the courthouse. Most historians of the Frank case have either dismissed or ignored the significance of women in the crowds. Historian Nancy MacLean, who emphasizes the critical role of gender in understanding the uproar created by the trial, denies the role women played because they "wrote only a handful of the myriad letters against [Frank] and rarely signed the many petitions."[47] As newspaper accounts of the proceedings reveal, however, "women of every class and age" followed the trial with great interest.[48] Indeed, women's participation may have produced counternarratives to historians' previous explanations for the popularity of the Frank affair, which stressed the hostility many southerners felt toward northern capitalists.[49] The women who followed the case demonstrated no such easily categorized interest in the case. They came to be a part of the event, to hear witnesses' lurid tales of sexual deeds, to catch a glimpse of the major players, and to mingle in the crowd. The women who testified sought their moment in spotlight and wanted to fulfill their civic duty, and most seem to have been trying to protect their jobs and defend their respectability as workers.

The defendant's lawyers used testimony by wage-earning women to defend Frank against accusations that he regularly brought female employees and other women into his office on Saturday afternoons for clandestine meetings. Virtually all of the female supervisors from the pencil factory and many of the women employed there as machinists testified to Frank's "good" character during the trail. By and large, these twenty-one witnesses spoke in Frank's defense and denied reports that the factory supervisor met women alone in his office, drank beer with them, and engaged in other unspecified "immoral" acts. Even if these women had known these stories to be true, it is doubtful that they would have admitted to it in court. Defense attorneys carefully tied general questions about Frank's conduct with women to questions of the witnesses' own conduct, implying that if the women knew of clandestine meetings, it must have been because they had participated.[50] Not surprisingly, the women protected their reputations by denying any knowledge of unscrupulous behavior on Frank's part. As a few witnesses suggested, so many women may have willingly appeared to defend their boss after factory officials promised that "if [the women] would stick by the company during the trouble . . . they would not lose anything by it."[51] It is worth at least considering that a desire to protect their reputations and to keep their jobs compelled many women to testify glowingly about their former supervisor's character.

A smaller number of women took the stand to criticize Frank. These women suggested both disturbing images of sexual exploitation by male employers and shockingly free sexual expression on the part of working women. Irene Jackson, the daughter of a local policeman, grudgingly told the court of Frank entering the women's dressing room without knocking. The prosecution tried to use the pronouncement to suggest that Frank regularly took sexual liberties with his female employees, but the young woman on the stand offered a plausible, if equally troubling, explanation for Frank's behavior: Frank entered the second-floor dressing room only to stop the women from flirting through the windows with men on the street below.[52] Two other female employees testified that they had seen a forewoman and Frank visit the empty dressing room together and spend fifteen to thirty minutes in there at a time. Another young woman stated that Frank called the murder victim by her first name, visited her several times a day, put his hand on her shoulder, and "leaned over in her face" when he spoke to her.[53] This kind of testimony raised serious challenges for the all-white, all-male jury. To find Frank guilty of Phagan's murder would mean taking the word of Jim Conley, the African American janitor who first introduced stories of licentious behavior on Frank's part, over that of white women who worked in the pencil factory. To find Frank not guilty might mean admitting that half-dressed women flirted with male passersby and that female workers might willingly visit their bosses for afternoon trysts.

There is at least suggestive evidence that some women may have even seen an opportunity for personal gain in the events surrounding the trial. Images of the attractive young factory operatives adorned the front pages of the newspapers throughout the trial. The Franks' cook may have gotten a raise, bonus money, and a new hat for withholding information on conversations held in the Frank home, but the police arrested and held her until she produced a damning affidavit against her employer.[54] A woman who testified to lascivious behavior on Frank's part, lawyers for the defense successfully revealed, had recently been arrested for "immorality," and an attorney friendly to the prosecution had gotten her released from jail.[55] The opportunity for a moment of fame, material rewards, legal services, or other bounties may have shaped the testimony and actions of the working women involved in the Frank case, though the press coverage and the court did not necessarily research or record these motivations.

The individuals in the crowds that gathered to mourn Phagan and follow the trial, like the women who testified, undoubtedly had a variety of reasons for being there. The women who appeared in the courtroom and on the street took an active role in choosing to participate in these events, even if they did not leave behind a written record of their views on the case. By filling the streets outside the courthouse on their lunch breaks and during their off hours, the chorus girls, waitresses, and factory operatives who followed the trial demonstrated a desire to demand protection for themselves. Women complained noisily when the judge in the Frank case cleared the courtroom of women during the "revolting" testimony of Conley, Frank's key accuser. The 150 or so women forced to leave "displayed the keenest resentment that they were not permitted to remain."[56] One woman managed to talk her way into the courtroom by posing as a reporter (the *Atlanta Constitution* doubted her credentials), while another gained admittance by claiming to know of potential witnesses the prosecution had not yet identified.[57] On the last day of the trial, after women had demanded to be allowed back into the courtroom, court officers seated 175 women as soon as the doors opened, leaving only 50 seats for men.[58]

Protection arose as one of the central issues in the Frank case and appeared repeatedly in discussions of wage-earning women shortly after the turn of the century. In the South, the protection of white women had long served as the underlying justification for the often violent racism that characterized the region, particularly following the Civil War. With the dramatic rise in female wage labor and its economic necessity for family survival, the portrayal of white women as passive beings in need of male protection became commonly tied to white women of the working class. Here a class and religious script of female victimization placed Frank, the "capitalist Jew," as villain. Phagan served as the cultural symbol of the virtuous young woman, ripe for victimization in the world of industrial work. While the working-class women who gathered to follow the trial may have agreed that Frank represented employers' exploitation of female workers, these women showed themselves to be far from passive victims. Whatever the issues at stake, however, it is important to remember that the murder of Phagan and Frank's trial made for a good story, complete with shady men, innocent virgins, and suggestions of illicit sex. This kind of "folk pornography" was hyped by the newspapers competing for circulation and loved by the crowds who followed the trial. [59]

Much of the interest in Frank's fate stemmed from the potential and realized sexual dynamics of the workplace. Many observers chose to believe that Phagan's life bore "no stains from a spotted past to shriek their shame to the world." [60] Tom Watson, the aging Populist leader, assumed Phagan's virginity and used the alleged assault by Frank as an analogy for the destruction of southern society at the hands of northern capitalism. But most of the women who swelled the ranks of the courthouse crowds or even those who took their turn on the witness stand certainly would not fit this noble picture. Just by virtue of participating in the "veritable honeycomb of humanity" that filled downtown Atlanta on trial days, women challenged notions of southern womanhood that conservatives such as Watson were trying so hard to maintain. The leaders of Frank's opposition reinforced "the paternalism of white supremacy" by demanding " 'protection' of women by men rather than measures which might enable young women to protect themselves." The reactionary factions led by Watson cried for Frank to hang, maintaining with "staunch insistence [that] Phagan died to preserve her chastity." [61] The subtext of these arguments upheld the notion that some women were worthy of protection and others were not.

Real working-class women, however, blurred the lines of respectability not only by appearing in public but also by voicing their impressions of the hearing. Newspapers reported women whispering, taking notes, laughing, and applauding throughout the trial. The trial judge repeatedly threatened to clear the courtroom of spectators because of women's rowdy behavior. [62] Women did not necessarily disagree that society owed them some sort of protection, but their presence in the crowds insisting on Frank's guilt demonstrated their desire to participate in their own protection and defy gender conventions that painted women in the streets, courtrooms, and shop floors as morally suspect, wholly innocent, or potential victims. [63]

Southern white paternalism, which Frank apparently threatened for many in Atlanta, did not allow for "windows crowded with women and girls and children" waiting to hear the verdict. And on hearing the trial results, women "wept and shouted by turns" as they passed the information through the crowd. [64] On the verge of Governor Slaton's commutation of the sentence, women as well as men stormed the Slaton's Buckhead neighborhood, threatening violence and forcing the governor to declare martial law in the area. [65] And after Frank's lynching, newspapers reported that men, women, and children alike grew "threatening when refused permission to see [his] body." [66] In the face of a judge who removed them from the courtroom, police threats to disperse the crowd, and the state militia, women refused to be silenced or erased from the events surrounding Phagan's death and Frank's trial.

The trial and its aftermath demonstrate the dual nature of working-class women's visibility. Women's actions often clashed with the highly symbolic images of Mary Phagan created by politicos such as Tom Watson as each advanced different ideals of protection. Many Atlantans advocated an end to women's wage work as the only means by which women could be safe from the sexual exploitation of employers. The ideal of protection circumscribed social boundaries for women within the changing urban economy by casting paid labor as morally dangerous and therefore undesirable unless absolutely necessary. Management at the National Pencil Factory, for example, replaced the white women who had worked alongside Phagan with black men. [67] Wage-earning women, for their part, focused on the respectability and intangible rewards of their work and work environment. They testified to protect their positions and perhaps enhance their job opportunities. They also reveled in the lurid details of the case revealed in the courtroom.

A white mob avenged Phagan's murder by lynching Frank, but no new regulations on conditions in industries employing women materialized in the wake of the sensationalized case. White middle-class club women eventually succeeded in their campaign to raise the age of consent in Georgia from ten to fourteen, but this 1918 bill officially established only the age at which a girl might legally consent to sexual relations and did nothing to ameliorate low wages, long hours, and the adverse work conditions so many women found on shop floors and in wealthier homes. [68] The local Women's Christian Temperance Union, the City Federation of Women's Clubs, and the Atlanta Woman's Club endorsed raising the age of consent, as did the Associated Charities, an umbrella welfare agency, and most local labor unions. This widespread support for the measure relied on an unstated connection between controlling sexuality and protecting girls by keeping them out of paid labor, suggesting that the biggest threat working women faced was predatory sexual behavior of supervisors and male employees. This certainly had been a major theme in much of the publicity surrounding the Frank case, and that discourse both shaped and limited the reforms middle-class Atlantans and organized labor sought to deal with the problems presented by the working girl.

Aside from the continuing age-of-consent initiative, most reform organizations contented themselves not with lobbying for new legislation but with running night schools designed to give women access to better skills, boardinghouses meant to give them a safe and respectable refuge in the city, and social and religious uplift clubs in some of the larger factories. In the end, these programs may have done more to reinforce the image of women workers as white, young, single, and vulnerable than for the women who attended the classes or lived in the homes. Reformers' narrow focus, especially in the early 1910s, helped to create the illusion of an ideal social order in which women worked for only a brief period between adolescence and motherhood. Ultimately, this particular sense of order allowed poor working conditions and low wages to continue. When the public at large perceived women's paid labor as only temporary, much of the sense of urgency to improve working conditions evaporated.

The white organized labor community's focus on the women in its midst contributed to the dialogue about white women workers in the city in ways remarkably similar to those of middle-class reformers. A rich dialogue on women developed in the local labor press of the 1900s and 1910s, although images of the union wife promoted by the Atlanta Federation of Trades ultimately dominated, emphasizing women's role as figureheads for Atlanta's union movement and testaments to the organized labors' respectability. In the 1900s, the working girl and union wife had been compatible images, one merely the younger version of the other. By the 1910s, however, labor leaders and journalists had begun to play the roles against each other: rather than assuming that the working girl would become the union wife, the white labor aristocracy fought to create a world in which women had no other option. Messages told women that the only road to security was through a strong marriage and actions supporting a labor market where a man would be the sole breadwinner for his family. These images formed the bedrock of local trade unions' larger vision for urban order. A city having "women of pure thoughts, lofty ideals[,] and community pride" would be key to preserving the "progress, enterprise, and thrift" of Atlanta as well as the "high moral standard" of the community.[69]

While the images created around white wage-earning women were less universally positive than the images of the union wife, laboring women still appeared as valued unionists, although the Atlanta Federation of Trades had only one predominantly female union in the early twentieth century, Local 29 of the United Garment Workers.[70] By the late 1900s and 1910s, a few of the women who wrote for the *Journal of Labor* strove to create a positive image of wage-earning women and to argue for improved rights and respect for the working girl. In particular, O. Delight Smith's columns sang the praises of women's hard work in the city's industries. Smith became a proponent of unions while working as a telegrapher, an occupational category shared by men and women. A series of moves and a difficult marriage brought her to Atlanta, where she immediately joined the local organized labor movement. Taking advantage of the growing interest in working women, Smith began her newspaper column under the pen name Athena but in 1906 began using her real name in her byline. Smith recommended equal pay for women and encouraged, even harangued, women to join unions. She touted paid labor as a cure for "the blues" and source of empowerment and self-worth for women.[71] Unlike most of the paper's other columnists, Smith also seemed uniquely sensitive to the hazards working women encountered as they traveled to and from their jobs: the columnist recommended leash laws to restrain the city's dogs and shelters at streetcar stops.[72] Women took advantage of the hospitable atmosphere, organizing strongly in the garment trades, in the candy industry, and among telephone operators in the 1910s.

As the number of women working for wages increased throughout the decade, however, the local union leadership increased its praise of the union wife, valuing her role over that of the wage-earning women. Less positive images of wage-earning women as cheap workers and fickle unionists crept into union language. Male unionists perceived employed women as threats to men's employment status.[73] Since women generally earned less than male workers, men feared that employers would choose the cheap labor of women over that of relatively expensive unionized men. Arguments focusing on the capitalist exploitation of labor stressed that industry "forced [women] to leave the home," thus "lowering wages, crowding men out of positions and creating fiercer and ever fiercer competition for jobs."[74] Increasingly in the 1910s, however, women also received much of the blame for dragging down male wages. Commentators also often explained women's low unionization rates and poor working conditions as the product of women's vanity and "false pride" in refusing to organize for fear that "joining a labor union would tend to lower them socially."[75] A Kansas City editorial reprinted in Atlanta echoed these sentiments by arguing that it was not unions that had failed the working girl "but the almost absolute indifference with which the girl looks at the trade union."[76] Even positive messages encouraging women workers usually included clear pronouncements on the dangers presented by women who remained in the workforce after crossing the line into marriage, insinuating that married women kept wages low for all women by accepting this low pay because "they know they always have their husband's earnings to fall back on."[77]

Beyond sending gendered messages to the labor community, Atlanta's unions also used references to the working girl to challenge poor working conditions generally and industrialists' control of the work process. The Atlanta Federation of Trades often used the case of women who worked for wages as an example of the capitalist exploitation of the working classes. "The only consideration the employer is willing to accord" a woman seeking a job, labor leaders accused, "is a consideration of how little he can induce her to work for."[78] Women workers' low wages also raised fear among Atlanta's unions that women would drag down men's wages. Organized labor's arguments for an increase in women's wages often paralleled those of middle-class reformers.[79] For unions, equal-pay arguments served as a means to counteract the feared negative impact of women's wage work on men's earning ability. Focusing attention on the poor pay most women received as part of the city's industrial workforce, the issue became a "battle cry in the war to protect men's jobs."[80] Rather than arguing for an increase in women's wages, unions tended to encourage women to leave the workforce altogether.

Trade organizations' concerns over the plight of the working girl, a question that "caused unions more thought and consideration than any other one issue," often focused on the morality and purity of working-class women. [81] While many union leaders celebrated the woman who strove through wage work "to save herself from dishonor in the midst of the burdens and trials of our complex civilization," others echoed the victimization tales promoted by middle-class reformers and challenged industrial and municipal leaders to enact protective labor legislation by pointing to the "moral suicide" (meaning prostitution) some women chose in the desperation of "semi-starvation."[82] "Wages that will enable a female to live decently" became a popular solution to keeping women out of prostitution. [83] Another labor activist repeated the themes of defenselessness and innocence when he wrote of wage-earning women, "They are as helpless as the dove before the hawk, and are pushed forward into the hands of the cadet by conditions they could not control."[84] Much of the function of these images was the same for unions as it was for the reformers: to cast wage-earning women as young and single, to elevate the role of married women in the community, and to paint women's paid labor as temporary. "The woman in industry," proclaimed labor leaders, "is not an economic question. It is far more vital. It simply is that the woman in industry means the uprooting of the home."[85] By denying many women's very real need to support themselves and their families, trade union leaders' arguments reinforced low pay and limited opportunities for women workers but did little, because of sex segregation in the labor market, to secure jobs or better wages for the city's men. This approach further associated women's work with issues of morality and directed attention away from equality with men.

While organized labor directed considerable rhetoric toward the problems of the working girl, local unions consistently avoided claiming a role for themselves in changing the conditions of women's employment. Challenging the city of Atlanta to address the role of women in the city's economy, the *Journal of Labor* pointedly asked, "You may build your great viaducts, your imposing buildings, have fine schools, wonderful parks and playgrounds, immense churches, but what avail will all these be when the women and girls of our city, foundation of our future citizens, the mothers of the next generation, labor and toil try[ing] to eke out an existence on [inadequate] wages?"[86] When discussing better pay for women, trade union arguments stressed either the need for wages that would protect morality by keeping women from turning to prostitution or the need to protect mothers. Motherhood played a key role in the social order unions envisioned, helping to define the value of the union wife, to remind the working girl of the temporary nature of her paid labor, to reinforce women's role in maintaining stable working-class families, to soothe men's fears over female encroachment on male work domains, and to reinforce the Atlanta Federation of Trades' power to speak for the city's white working class.

Concerns over the potential harm women could suffer in low-paying jobs represented a larger movement by organized labor to maintain stable working-class families with the union man solidly cast as breadwinner. A 1908 report produced by an economics class for local labor organizers concluded, "The general opinion among . . . physicians [is] that the injury to motherhood was not so great in farm work as factory work and other industrial pursuits." One class participant further stated, "If our mothers are weakened, the future of our sons will likewise be weakened . . . physically, mentally, and morally."[87] "O God," labor leaders prayed for wage-earning women, "Grant them strength of body to bear the strain of unremitting toil and may no present pressure unfit them for the holy duties of home and motherhood which the future may lay upon them. Give them grace to cherish under the new surroundings the old sweetness and gentleness of womanhood, and in the rough mingling of life to keep the purity of their hearts and lives untarnished."[88]

The net effect of these arguments was twofold. In addition to aligning the interests of organized labor with middle-class reform efforts, cries for the protection of motherhood allowed unions to take a paternalistic view of working-class women. Such efforts stressed women's youth and inexperience and advised them to seek marriage as a means of obtaining security. Union men were also encouraged to see marriage and support of a stay-at-home wife as the most important form of protection for working-class women, valuing it above efforts to unionize female workers. Moreover, like the images promoted by Atlanta businesses and middle-class reformers, union ideology contributed to a heightened visibility of young, single, and white wage-earning women while obscuring the growing sectors of the female work force that were black, older, or married.

What Work Meant to Women

THE EXPERIENCE of Atlanta's women in domestic work, independent enterprises, industrial jobs, and clerical positions entailed a complex array of experiences often overlooked by union leaders, reformers, and newspapers. Despite the variety of work settings, women of both races generally expressed great pride in their skills as workers, even if they were classified as unskilled by their employers,[89] and in their ability to help support their families. Persistent, if not always collective or organized, activism on the part of wage-earning women attests to the centrality of a worker identity for many of Atlanta's women. Consequently, paid labor often functioned as a battleground for workers' control over labor conditions for both white and black women.

Segregation and the usually unskilled or solitary nature of domestic work performed by most African Americans during this period effectively closed collective union activism to black women, although they proved themselves adept at using individualistic techniques to control their work environment. Individual and often spontaneous acts of worker resistance served to combat the most demeaning aspects of domestic work by conveying the "worker's determination to make her occupational role personally meaningful and socially acceptable."[90] Domestic workers' protests, while appearing somewhat random, drew on a culture of protest familiar to women in Atlanta's black communities and to generations of domestic workers.[91]

Domestic workers—overwhelmingly black women in Atlanta—were particularly proficient in their protest tactics and small-scale negotiations to alter the balance of power between employer and employee. African American women and their white employers frequently clashed over the methods and goals of domestic work as each struggled to control the work. Domestic workers employed a variety of techniques to advance their workplace interests, including refusing to do specific duties, removing items from employers' homes, borrowing clothes and other items, and otherwise asserting their independence. Willie Mae Cartwright, who worked a variety of service jobs in Atlanta in the 1910s, lied to one employer that her cousin was ill so that she could have time off to try out another job that paid higher wages without jeopardizing her original position.[92] Domestic worker Mary Morton wanted to attend church and so refused to work on Sundays, claiming, "I'm poor but I know how to live."[93] Many African American women also chose to limit white employers' control by moving to "independent" (live-out) day work or by taking in washing.

One of the most effective techniques through which workers could control their work experience was to change jobs. With the expanding job market of the early twentieth century, finding a new employer was the easiest way to better working conditions. Workers continually sought new positions, hoping to improve wages and hours, shorten the distance to work, or find a more lenient employer.[94] Annie Alexander, a nurse, changed jobs frequently so that she could always "get to church on Sunday."[95] In general, wage-earning women of both races resisted conforming to the work discipline advocated by their employers, even if that meant finding a new job. Worker transience plagued many industrial, domestic, and business employers. Atlanta's mills complained incessantly of "repeaters," workers who would quit and then later return.[96] Nannie Leah Young had worked in twelve different mills by the time she was thirty years old.[97] Atlanta's female paid laborers were rarely the docile workers touted by boosters or the easy victims imagined by reformers.

Some women chose to increase their skills and thus their wage value as workers. They could then change jobs, negotiate wages with employers, and hold walkouts or slowdowns to protest changes. Leola Young's experiences were not uncommon among industrial women: she started work in a bag factory, then proceeded to work in a shoe factory, a candy company, an overall factory, and a general store.[98] When a candy factory tried to decrease the piece rate, one worker recalled, "all the girls with one accord struck; the firm after vainly trying to find other workers, was compelled to meet the girls' terms."[99] Mrs. Smith, a packer at the Georgia Preserving Factory, needed to increase her wages to support a sick husband, so she threatened to quit unless she could make more than $8.50 a week. The supervisor, according to Smith, "didn't want to do it but he had to as I'm a good worker and he didn't want to lose me. He said a woman didn't have to work, that if I'd just sit down, my husband would get up and support me. The overseer don't understand. I tell you I can't leave my old husband; he's been mighty good to me."[100] While survival for female factory operatives was often tenuous, the confidence of women such as Smith in their own abilities may have provided a sense of job security that was not inherent to or generally recognized for these factory positions.

Despite the harsh experiences of many female industrial and service workers, wage-earning women often stressed positive aspects of their work. Women took great pride in their skill, even though most of the jobs they held were classified as unskilled. Contradicting reformers' views, these women did not think of themselves as victims and found dignity in their ability to survive on the money they earned. A worker in an overall factory and her sister, a sales clerk, supported their family of six. She claimed to have "never wanted people to help me in a financial way," and she proudly paid for her and her family's expenses.[101] According to an interview conducted by the U.S. Department of Labor's Women's Bureau, Mrs. Campbell was a "courageous, energetic widow with four children" who owned her own home and supported her family by working as a chocolate dipper.[102] Lucile Reynolds, who described herself as "a first-class box maker," also supported her family after her older sister married and moved out.[103] Even women who lived alone or were not the sole support of their families emphasized the necessity of their work and the defining role it played in their lives. Indeed, women workers may have needed to stress their sense of accomplishment and make demands for equal pay to counteract negative and devaluing assessments of their work.[104] According to Alice Kessler-Harris, women's demands for equal pay may also have been an "expression of self-confidence and self-worth that belied the contemporary image of women workers as impermanent or unwilling to invest in their own training; and it offered a statement of female commitment to the labor force."[105] The obvious difficulties and perils involved in paid work in the formal economy and the messages of boosters, reformers, and union leaders deterred few of Atlanta's potential female workers, as women of both races flocked to these jobs in the early twentieth century.

Aligning Images and Activism

WHILE African American women relied mainly on noncollective means to negotiate for control of their work in the early twentieth century, the relationship between white women and Atlanta's white organized labor movement allowed some women to launch a variety of workplace protests and strikes.[106] The early 1900s appear to have been a historical moment in which the goals of male-dominated trade unionism overlapped with the concerns of many white working-class women. The 1914 textile worker strike at the Fulton Bag and Cotton Mills exemplifies this connection. The gulf between women's experiences in the world of paid labor and the rhetoric of reformers and unionists shrank somewhat during the strike as women became an important symbol the workers used to justify their cause to a wider audience.[107] This, in turn, gave women the opportunity—in front of cameras, the press, and government investigators—to tell their stories and, in some cases, to advance their interests as workers and community members.

On May 20, 1914, several hundred employees of the Fulton Bag and Cotton Mills walked off the job. Tensions between employees and mill owners over union recognition, a repressive contract policy, and excessive fines had grown increasingly intense during the preceding year.[108] Following an unsuccessful 1913 walkout, the Textile Workers Union had been steadily organizing in the Atlanta mills. When Fulton Bag management began firing union organizers, operatives again struck in the spring of 1914, this time staying out of the mill for almost a year despite being evicted from their homes. Mill owner Oscar Elsas hired industrial spies to infiltrate the mill village and union leadership. Elsas used these undercover agents to discredit union representatives and plant seeds of dissent among strikers. In the face of Elsas's tactics, most mill operatives stood firm in their demands for respectability and better working conditions.

Women played a vital role in the 1914–15 Fulton Bag and Cotton Mills strike. Women, both mill operatives and community members, filled the ranks of strikers, forming a crucial base of support for the strike and the United Textile Workers' local. The strike provided an arena in which women were encouraged to participate by both the union and the mill community, and, in turn, their activism lent a particular character to the conflict with mill owners. Definitions of labor solidarity advanced during the strike included the community as a whole and women in particular. The union responded by engaging the mill owners in a battle over the respectability of mill workers, particularly females. The divisions among mill management, striking operatives and mill village residents, and interested middle-class reformers were drawn in gendered terms. Publicity surrounding the conflict created by strikers and reformers painted strikers as almost exclusively female. Attacks on the strikers' positions by mill management sought to discredit the union by sexualizing women's actions and portraying male strikers as weak and unmanly. The discussions of women, womanhood, and gender relations in the strike represented both the more latent tensions in the strike, class relations and social positioning and the overt battle lines between capital and labor.

In an attempt to gain sympathy for their cause, strike leaders consciously positioned women mill operatives to receive media attention. Union organizers planned regular parades, rallies, and marches in addition to daily pickets to publicize the strike and garner public support. During these demonstrations, union organizers moved women to prominent positions in the front of the crowds and marchers, hoping to use the women as symbols of the innocent victims of industrialism. A march from the union hall to a mass meeting in the White City amusement park next to Grant Park, for example, was carefully orchestrated so that "the women will walk down and the men after."[109] Leaders also encouraged crowds to gather around the homes from which strikers were being evicted to draw attention to women and children being thrown out on the street by mill management's hired thugs. The union leadership intended the images produced during these scenes to create a particular racist resonance among Atlanta's whites when the employer used African American laborers to evict white families.[110]

Probably the most visible woman in the strike was O. Delight Smith, who in addition to writing a column for the *Journal of Labor* was a blacklisted telegrapher and president of the National Ladies Auxiliary of the Order of Railroad Telegraphers. Once tensions at Fulton Bag erupted, she secured a position as a paid organizer for the textile union. Through her activism, Smith continually challenged gender boundaries, demonstrating great physical strength, a confrontational style, and aggressive organizing tactics. Realizing the power good press could play in the outcome of the strike, Smith recruited film crews to shoot the evictions of strikers from their company-owned homes. She also carried a still camera, photographing strikers, evictions, and people she suspected of being management spies. Smith's photographs of labor spies hired by the mill fundamentally altered the relationship between spy and striker, as the spy became the object to be observed instead of the observer.[111]

The photographs and film clips of the strike served as one of the main sources of publicity. Images of striking women fill the pages of the photo albums Smith compiled. Many of the photographs were also displayed in the windows of Atlanta shops as a means of showing the city the deplorable conditions in the mill village, rallying a sense of community among strikers and garnering public support.[112] Women, often posed with children but without a husband or male breadwinner, faced the camera squarely. Margaret Dempsey, a particularly vocal and active local striker and a thirty-seven-year veteran of the mills, played up her unwillingness to bow to the wishes of the mill management that was evicting her from her home. Her eviction was filmed as a moving picture that captured part of the drama of the day as Dempsey threw her arms up in the air, obviously disgusted with management tactics. Even the women who worked in the tent camp's kitchen, which fed the strikers after the evictions, turned away from their traditional and private tasks turned public during the strike and toward the camera focused on them. Their erect posture and unsmiling faces convey the seriousness with which they addressed their strike work. Another image circulated through the city showed a striking woman with her three children, one of them severely crippled, standing in front of the tent that had become their home after their eviction from company housing. Through these stories and images of women, union leaders emphasized the greedy nature of mill owners, who not only forced women and children to work for pitiful wages but also were not above removing them from their homes. Union organizers ultimately used images of wage-earning women to stake out a political position that effectively cast their employer as exploitative and cruel.

Sara Conboy, a leading union organizer sent south by the United Textile Workers Union of America, used her experience in the Boston Women's Trade Union League and talents as a fiery public speaker to further the issues of the strike. She commonly compared the cause of the strikers to a religious crusade and drew her audience at the strikers' mass meetings together by reminding them that their faith in God would get them through this ordeal. Industrial spies for the mill management, whom the strikers referred to as pimps, regularly attended the daily union meetings to record the proceedings. Conboy often intensified her speeches, knowing that her words would eventually reach the ears of mill manager Oscar Elsas, the owner's son. Typical of her style, Conboy reportedly "went on to say the 'Pimps' were annoying her all the time . . . and said one was in the hall at the time, and she wanted him to go back to the mill [and] tell them she was a freeborn American, and she would go where she liked."[113]

Strikers, however, were not the only ones to appeal to the emotional and political resonance embedded in representations of working-class women. Union leaders and middle-class reformers also avoided the central issue of the strike, the workers' attempt to gain more control over the work process, to raise public sympathy for the strikers by focusing on the alleged mistreatment of women dependent on the mill. The Men and Religion Forward Movement (MRFM), a local evangelical organization, proved the most aggressive practitioner of this tactic.[114] The MRFM's frequent bulletins, printed in the local press, emphasized the "human degradation" created by mill management tactics of family employment, long hours, and low wages. The movement supported the textile union and urged mill owners to accept mediation in an effort to end the strike and the suffering of the mill operatives. The MRFM's arguments, much like mill management's rhetoric, used feminized references to strikers as "weak mentally, spiritually, and bodily."[115] Fresh from a battle against vice in the city, the MRFM also deployed images of women and girls to represent worker exploitation. "A little girl not over twelve, her pink dress fluttering against the grime, run[ning] through a forbidding door to work," came to symbolize the stolen youth and health of the city's respectable working classes.[116] By focusing on female workers and using feminized terms in reference to all strikers, MRFM members structured the relationship of middle-class reformers to working-class mill hands along patriarchal lines, positioning the reformers as both class and sexual protectors and ignoring the issues of control for which workers were striking.

The MRFM's efforts to influence the strike's outcome often ranged far beyond the immediate issues raised by the walkout. MRFM members also attacked the mill district as a hospitable atmosphere for saloons, brothels, and gambling houses, using the crisis at the mill to advance the movement's evangelical agenda. Images of women played an important role in the organization's reform efforts, which sought to stabilize shifting social relations, particularly those of family, in the face of the city's rapid growth. Rather than being solely a reactionary movement, a MRFM campaign to remove liquor and prostitution from Atlanta represented one position among many in the larger debates over how to control social order in the expanding city.

The criminalization and sexualization of the mill village and its residents advanced by the MRFM echoed the management and its spies' perceptions.[117] Criticizing Fulton Bag and Cotton Mills for not paying a living wage to male operatives, the MRFM described the slow descent of workers into the "social evil[s]" of liquor, gambling, and prostitution.[118] The actions of women who worked in the mill or lived in the village became a litmus test for the moral atmosphere for all textile workers in the city. Middle-class observers considered women drinking, dancing, or engaging in sex as drunk, disorderly, or prostitutes. Mill management similarly used the industrial spies' reports in an attempt to portray strikers as immoral and lazy. In the process, management tactics painted the Elsases as benevolent employers who cared about their workers and justified the owners' rough handling of the strike leaders.

Spies' hostile reports often attacked and sexualized strikers' places of recreation, the tent city where strikers lived after eviction, and female strikers' activism. One restaurant popular with mill workers was described as having a room "fixed

up as a bed room and . . . used for immoral purposes."[119] Another local establishment, according to spies, was "a place where plans are made to holdup,
burglarize, [and] blow safes."[120] Rumors of white slavery also furthered these
images of vice and immorality, with both male and female strikers accused of
luring young women to the nearby saloon district to have "their lives ruined."[121]

Other reports sought to discredit the female union leadership by pointing to
the presence of female organizers in these establishments. Oscar Elsas and his
industrial spies attempted to neutralize strike leaders' effectiveness with what
Jacquelyn Hall has referred to as "the tawdry mudslinging directed at female tres-
passers who disrupt the hierarchies of the public sphere."[122] O. Delight Smith's
evenings in a local beer garden, for example, became fodder for management
attempts to neutralize her success as a union organizer. Spies also tracked her for
weeks in an unsuccessful attempt to uncover an illicit relationship between Smith
and another union leader, Charles Miles. The mill finally enlisted the support of
Smith's estranged husband, Edgar, who attempted to divorce her on the grounds
of infidelity but eventually dropped the suit. Smith stood up to these attacks,
denying the charges, fighting the divorce, and confronting the spies of whom she
was aware, photographing them and reporting them to the police.[123]

Strikers and the union hierarchy realized the destabilizing effect charges of
immorality could have on the perceptions of city residents and the federal officials
who were investigating the strike. Organizers countered allegations of immoral
behavior by drawing up strict rules for conduct and sanitary conditions in the
tent city: tents had to be clean, everything from eating to picket duty happened
on a schedule, telephones could not be used for courtship, profane language
would not be tolerated, and a curfew of 10:00 P.M. was enforced each night
except Saturday.[124] Prominent female leaders such as Smith and Conboy took
a different approach toward the threat posed by charges of immoral behavior,
directly confronting mill management by threatening to expose the industrial
spies' identities, thereby exposing them to violence at the hands of frustrated
strikers if the rumor and innuendo continued.[125]

The large-scale direct participation of female operatives and women of the
mill village in the strike reshaped the meaning of the confrontation with mill
management. While Smith and Conboy were prominent women in traditional
union organizing positions, hundreds of other women formed the backbone
of the strike.[126] Josie Sisk, Dora Davis, Margaret Dempsey, and Alice Carlton all
actively recruited and picketed early in the strike. Industrial spies singled out these
women for aggressively trying to stop nonstrikers from reporting for work. These
female picketers usually, though not always, targeted other women in attempting
to keep workers out of the mill. Spies reported that some women occasionally
offered sexual favors or otherwise used their sexuality to convince male workers

not to scab.[127] In December 1914, a spy posted in a saloon on Decatur Street reported, "In the rear of this place are several small rooms, to which the lewd women from the camp come constantly, drink beer and whiskey, and tempt those now at work in the Mill to drink with them and quit work, if they can succeed in so doing."[128] Groups of women also canvassed the mill village, going to each home to convince their neighbors to join the strike.

In an attempt to document the poor working and living conditions at Fulton Mills, union leaders, especially Smith, encouraged women to provide affidavits describing their experiences as workers and village residents. Smith started taking the testimony of women shortly after the strike began. Inis Weed of the U.S. Commission on Industrial Relations and investigators from the Federal Mediation and Conciliation Service also recorded the stories of mill women. The women who volunteered to be interviewed documented a host of problems, many of which ranged far beyond the scope of the official reasons for the strike, and articulated their own reasons for the confrontation. The striking women used the opportunity presented by the investigations to attack mill management, other workers, the mill village settlement house, and neighborhood housing conditions.

Having captured the attention of union leaders, mill management, and the federal government, mill women freely aired their grievances, opinions, and fears. "I worked in the bag department sewing sacks," Alice Carlton told federal investigators. "These sacks are put through a process of wetting with salty water before they are given to us to sew and the salt is so bad in them that my fingers would be so sore that I would have to get some of the other women to thread my needle, who was not working on this kind of work." A thirty-six-year veteran of the mill, she reported having to "lay off every few days" so her fingers could recuperate, though she received no pay for these days. Like numerous other workers, Carlton revealed disagreements with floor managers over time worked and goods produced, concluding that in the end most workers were "compelled to take what ever the forelady would put down on the book and be satisfied."[129]

Margaret Dempsey, one of the women company spies singled out as a "very active and offensive picket," told her story to Weed.[130] Dempsey reported that she had been working in cotton mills, mostly in Georgia, for the eighteen years since her husband died. Responding to Weed's inquiries about the forty cents a day Dempsey made as a spooler, she replied, "no ma'm, I aint made a living wage and I don't never expect [to]." Dempsey also testified to the numerous diseases she had suffered as a result of the poor conditions in the mill, including pellagra and rheumatism. The main issue Dempsey addressed in her deposition, however, concerned workers' treatment by management. "The thing I wish they could stop in the mills," Dempsey explained to Weed, "is the unkind talk—they talk to us just as if we was dogs; order us around. They threaten to take out some of our pay and talk to us just awful if we stop a minute. They are unkind to us when we get sick. If you get sick and want to go home they won't let you until noon or night."[131]

Blanche Prince, another worker who had started in the mills as a child, laid out her reasons for participating in the strike without hesitation. "I came out on strike," she told Weed, "because I think the rules and regulations were oppressive. The rules are just too tight, and that is all there is to it—then they hold back our money." Prince also demonstrated her strong sense of community solidarity, claiming that even though she made good wages and was never fined, she wanted to strike anyway. Describing the hardships she and other women had to endure in the mill, Prince testified that women struggled to remain on their feet all day in a room with little ventilation. Management refused to open the windows, claiming, according to Prince, that "it made the work run bad." Prince, like other women interviewed, noted, "Lots of the women has tuberculosis, pellagra and female trouble." "I think one of the hardest things for us poor people," she concluded, "is having our money held back when we are sick."[132]

Both Josie Sisk and Addie Camp focused their testimony on the difficulties of being mothers working in the mills. Camp, who had worked for the mill for two years prior to the strike, had twin babies whom she left in the care of the Wesley House nursery, a Methodist missionary organization located next to and partially supported by the mill. Camp claimed that one of her children died during a convulsion caused by a blow to the head. She testified, "I know that it did not receive this lick at home and must have received it at the Wesley House the day I left him there." Camp also accused the nursery of neglecting her children, claiming that when she went to pick them up, she found that "they had never been tended to at all, they were wet from head to foot, and their little long dresses were drenched, their diapers not having been changed." She concluded her deposition by stating forcefully, "I attribute the death of my child to the treatment he received at Wesley House, and also attribute the sickness of the other twin to the same treatment."[133]

Sisk, a single mother of three children, also attacked the mill owners, focusing on the treatment of children in the day nursery on which so many mothers depended. "I have come to the nursery," she reported, "and found my children bruised up very bad; seems like they had been beat by the nurses or by the other babies or children. I went there one day at dinner and found my baby's lips all sealed up, and it was a little thing not [yet] walking. Once I found my little girl's head with a skinned place on it, just like it had been shaved off."[134] Sisk and the other women who testified to investigators revealed a host of reasons for the strike that included and expanded on union leaders' demands. In these depositions, women appear active and aware, critical of their situations and willing to hold employers responsible for the deprivations of the women's lives. These women also carefully asserted their respectability, implying that they were more honest than mill supervisors and better mothers than the middle-class women from the Methodist outreach program who ran the mill nursery.

In the almost yearlong strike against the Fulton Bag and Cotton Mills, working-class women played a crucial role at all levels of union organization. These textile workers, often considered pariahs of the labor community, embodied many of the qualities of both the good union wife and the working girl supported by the city's trade unions. While male union leaders and middle-class reformers often emphasized women workers as the worst victims of mill management's greed, female mill operatives used this attention to add their own grievances to the official reasons for the strike. Women crossed lines between community organizers and striking workers, providing critical support in the lengthy, though ultimately unsuccessful, strike.

FOR ALL OF the drama involved in the strike against Fulton Bag, and for as much as the strike's history reveals the centrality of working-class women to public discourse in the city by the 1910s, the strike also demonstrates how rarely the discussions of women's work and the experience of working women aligned during these years. Dialogues among Atlanta's business leaders, middle-class reformers, and even union officials embodied far more than issues pertaining directly to wage-earning women, explaining why the voices of working women so rarely received attention. These debates over the meaning of women's employment reveal the vision many residents had for the city, an Atlanta in which economic growth could be sustained within a moral atmosphere, an Atlanta that would maintain clearly distinct gender roles and racial order while embracing breakneck industrial and financial development, an Atlanta in which the city's working-class women in many cases represented the best hope for and worst threat to these visions of growth. As the next chapter demonstrates, parallel efforts to control women in urban and public spaces were also under way on Atlanta's streets and in its developing commercial recreations.

CHAPTER THREE

Public Space and Leisure Time

ACCORDING TO press reports, a black man raped Annie Laurie Poole on a rural road near her home south of Atlanta on the last day of July 1906. In the middle of August, Mrs. Richard Hembree claimed to have fended off a different black man's aggression using her hat pin. In another rural community outside of the city limits, Ethel and Mabel Lawrence alleged an encounter with a "tall, slender and very black negro," who beat the young white women severely. Mittie Waits supposedly met a would-be attacker in a wooded area nine miles from Atlanta but scared him off with her screams. Throughout the late summer of 1906, Atlantans read in their local newspapers these stories of white women attacked by African American men. The themes of the tales remained remarkably constant throughout the summer and into the fall: women living outside of the city, women who by virtue of their rural location (and their race) should have been safe, found themselves facing the worst elements of the city: "prowling and idle Negroes," emboldened by gambling, drink, and drawings of naked white women on liquor bottles, seeking to establish their political equality through the sexual domination of white women.[1] Even alleged attacks on white women that occurred closer to the city's center in August and September happened in spaces that white Georgians imagined to be safe from the disorders of the city, the women's own homes. While most of the stories were later proved false,[2] repeated tales of rape and incendiary cries from the yellow press to "Protect Our Women!" coincided with blatantly racist efforts to close city establishments selling liquor to African Americans and an inflammatory gubernatorial campaign in which African American disfranchisement became a major rallying point for white voters. The furor these three trends created among whites culminated in four days of violent rioting in Atlanta in late September 1906.[3] At least twenty-five Atlantans died in the violence, and more than a hundred suffered injuries.

The calls to defend white women from black men and, by implication, from the supposed depravity of the city, left Atlanta's African American women vulnerable once white mobs began their rampage. Mattie Adams, a black woman who ran a small eatery near downtown, suffered a brutal beating at the hands of the white mob on the first night of the riot. In addition to assaulting Adams, her daughter, and her grandson, the mob broke dishes, tables, chairs, and other tools of Adams's trade—punishment for someone who crossed both gender and racial boundaries by running her own business.[4] Seven African Americans riding a streetcar bound for Grant Park found themselves facing an angry white mob when the car arrived downtown. As rioters entered the trolley, one black woman used her umbrella like "a savage wildcat" to fend off the mob.[5] Another wielded her hat pin as a weapon, but the women had little success against the mob. The white attackers meted out their cruel treatment to the African American riders of the car regardless of gender, and three of the trolley's black passengers died of their injuries. On another streetcar, white rioters taunted black men by ripping the clothes off black women and then beating with barrel staves any men who tried to protect the women.[6] Scenes such as these were repeated on as many as fifteen other streetcars before the company finally halted service to downtown. African Americans fled the city's center for their neighborhoods and homes, but white mobs and bands of police looking to disarm the city's black population followed them, and sporadic violence persisted for three more days.

As was the case with the 1897 race strike at the Fulton Bag and Cotton Mills, women of both races played important roles in the racial conflicts that turned violent in September 1906. White women functioned in a largely symbolic capacity, providing the sexualized image of white supremacy for newspapers and political candidates. For black women, the four days of violence proved much more real. Their gender afforded them none of the protection offered to white women. Even though white mobs pursued black men in supposed retribution for a rash of sexual assaults on white women, black women's race—and their presence in the city's public spaces—left them open to attacks as well. The 1906 race riot proved the single most pivotal event in the ordering of Atlanta's race relations for the first half of the twentieth century; it also played a significant role in shifting public discourse toward working-class women. White mobs lynching and beating African Americans in full view of the police, blacks arming themselves in self-defense, and four days of property destruction helped to create a new set of priorities in an effort to keep future violence at bay and restore the city's reputation as a progressive and well-ordered community. Following the riot, Atlanta's middle classes of both races strove to mute racial conflict over public space, thus clearing the way for images built around other identities to become more explicit in discussions of the city's future.

Race Riot

BEYOND reporting stories of rape, local newspapers in many cases encouraged and condoned the action of vigilante mobs formed to exact retribution from "the brutes who are bent on ravishing defenseless white women."[7] The local reporting produced both "sexual hysteria" and a "climate of fear" in Atlanta in the months leading up to the September violence.[8] All aspects of contact between blacks and whites, especially those between black men and white women, became sensationalized in press coverage and editorials run in the weeks before the riot. The *Atlanta Evening News* attacked the practice of white women riding next to their black drivers: "To see a big black negro sitting alongside of and touching the body of a white woman makes the blood in every white man's veins boil. [Women] get in these narrow seated buggies and take a big black buck up by their side, and it is utterly impossible for the woman to keep from touching the body of the negro. This is a horrible sight for white people to witness."[9] Prohibitionists painted lurid scenes of black men wasting their days away inside saloons.[10] Anxieties abounded that without the restraining effect of full-time employment, these men threatened Atlanta's social and racial order as well as the surrounding rural communities. The city's main saloon district, the *Atlanta Journal* concluded, "should undergo a thorough physical and moral cleaning" to rid the city of "loafers, vagrants, and criminals."[11] To accomplish this, the paper even advocated arming women and deputizing every white man in Fulton County "with all the deputies' rights and authorities, and with the will and power to make every suspicious negro character give an account of himself."[12]

The panic over the sexual threat of black males to southern womanhood (meaning white women) barely disguised the riot's political and economic undercurrents.[13] Walter White, a future civil rights advocate, witnessed the riot as a child. Years later he explained, "No matter how low a white man fell, he could always hold fast to the smug conviction that he was superior to two-thirds of the world's population for those two-thirds were not white."[14] This was an important conviction to many working-class white men, whose economic and political position in the city was precarious at best. Elite blacks had also been pressing hard for political inclusion since the closing years of the nineteenth century. Many whites in the state concluded that the "political equality being preached to the negro in the ring papers and on the stump" encouraged blacks to see "no distinction between political and social equality." During the summer of 1906, this type of rhetoric also linked black political ambitions to the alleged series of rapes. The *Atlanta Journal* explained the apparent rash of attacks on white women as a product of the black man, emboldened by talk of political equality, growing "more bumptious on the street, more impudent in his dealing with white men; and then, when he cannot achieve social equality as he wishes with the instinct of a barbarian to destroy what he cannot attain to, he lies in wait . . . and assaults the fair young girlhood of the south."[15] In the fall of 1906, gubernatorial candidate Hoke Smith used similar language and calls for black disfranchisement to draw in supporters. Smith won the Democratic white primary that fall (assuring him the governorship in one-party Georgia), demonstrating the popular appeal of his racist rhetoric. The inflammatory political campaign, stories of rape circulating through the newspapers, and an antiblack campaign against local dives finally erupted in widespread violence on September 22, 1906. Remembering the riot decades later, Atlanta resident Ethel Meyers provided the oversimplified explanation that many Atlantans, both black and white, adopted immediately following the violence: "Word got around that some white woman had been raped and, of course, that just stirred up great trouble."[16]

Many of the complex causes of the riot came from the nature of the city itself. White Atlantans were accustomed to having blacks in the city's public spaces; indeed, whites relied on the African American population to carry bags, clear tables, sweep streets, deliver goods, drive cabs, pick up garbage, and transport laundry. Even areas of the city devoted to leisure for whites usually included black laborers, janitors, and service workers. The riot disrupted this relationship, and for three days whites moved their own baggage, drove themselves or took streetcars, watched piles of garbage and dirty laundry grow, and cooked their own meals. As one newspaper noted with uncommon humor in the midst of the crisis, "The spectacle of the young man of the family peeling the potatoes and the mater and sisters cooking the meals was quite the thing Sunday."[17] With white mobs and police roaming the streets looking for blacks, the city's African Americans stayed home, and the city's whites went without many familiar services. If life were to return to normal, a compromise of sorts had to be reached so that whites and blacks could share the city's public spaces.

The violence of 1906, as many in the city understood even before the riot had begun, also represented a significant threat to Atlanta's reputation. When the crowd of white men on Decatur Street began to grow threatening on Saturday evening, the city's mayor mounted a box and asked those assembled to consider how violence might become a "blot on the fair name of our most beautiful city." "What you may do in a few minutes of recklessness," he continued, "will take Atlanta many years to recover from."[18] By Monday, newspapers whose editorials had helped feed the racial frenzy two days earlier with reports of alleged rapes became concerned with "defend[ing] our city and our state against the disgrace that has come to us."[19] Calculations of the riot's cost to the city ran as high as one million dollars, but business leaders also noted that no dollar amount could be placed on the "stigma" the city would now carry.[20] Attorney Charles Hopkins lamented, "The reputation we have been building up so arduously for years has been swept away." Alluding to the myth white Atlanta chose to believe about itself, he continued, "up until Saturday night we had a city famous for its fairness and freedom from race issues and known as the most prosperous and safest city in the South."[21] The Fulton County Grand Jury, expressing the feelings of white business leaders as well as many in the black elite, worried about what else Atlanta might lose if it did not restore and maintain order. "This city is on trial before the world," the jury told the mayor and city council, "and your safety and the safety of this city depends on the result."[22]

The concern over the city's reputation brought most middle-class and wealthy Atlantans together in a push for law and order. Segregation, already developing in the city in the 1890s and early 1900s, appeared as a rational solution to the racial tensions expressed so violently during the riot. Business and community leaders on both sides of the color line embraced or at least accepted the further separation of the races. Some even came to think of Jim Crow as a "progressive" reform on par with building playgrounds for children or eliminating urban vice.[23] After the riot, the city council approved liquor licenses only for establishments that restricted their business to one race or the other.[24] Theaters, elevators, parks, and virtually all elements of the city's public spaces similarly became subject to the rules of segregation, which demanded black deference to whites. In many ways the riot closed the door on the racial tensions that had loomed so large for the city in the nineteenth century, not because the issues had necessarily been solved by segregation but because fears of more violence and for the reputation of the city kept both the black and white elites from directly discussing the tensions.

Following the riot, black-owned businesses abandoned Peachtree Street and their white clientele for the safer confines of the black neighborhood surrounding Auburn Avenue. Black political activism also became increasingly subsumed under "home sphere" and noneconomic reforms, since post-riot organizing on overtly political issues might have provoked another round of violence against the city's blacks.[25] The riot pushed the African American community further into itself and greatly restricted, though by no means eliminated, efforts to achieve social justice in subsequent decades. Atlanta's black leaders embraced a political agenda that sought to improve race relations by "uplifting" the black masses. Promoting respectability within the African American community led to an increased focus on the homes, children, work, and the behavior of the working-class women of the race. Many in the black elite came to believe that black women's activities in the city's public spaces represented the morality—and therefore the fate—of the whole race.

The riot sharpened the process of building a racially segregated city already underway by the first decade of the twentieth century. Whites intended segregation to erase blacks' troubling presence by confining them to certain spaces and forcing a constant performance of subordination through segregation customs—stepping out of the path of whites, entering through marked doorways, filling the back seats of trolleys but the front cars of trains, and using back doors and stairways. The creation of racial segregation, baffling as its logic often was (blacks had to ride up in freight elevators but could come down in any car, for example), allowed whites to feel that the race problem had been solved and that the place of blacks and whites in southern urban society was secure. This sense of security, however false it may have been, helps to explain why the city's middle-class whites so readily turned their attention to the activities of young women in Atlanta's new and numerous commercial amusements. Separating the races could ward off the possibility of continued racial violence and therefore protect an orderly image of the city as a whole. But in the early twentieth century, in the midst of substantial urban growth, the morality of the city, and therefore its respectability, also depended on controlling the behavior of Atlantans in public. Controlling the behaviors of working-class women became the means through which the city's middle-classes attempted to do so. The policing of women's behavior in public—particularly at commercial amusements—under the guise of protection set the stage for many of the debates over the use of urban space that would play out through the 1910s.

Public Space and Urban Order

AT THE BEGINNING of the twentieth century, calls for restoring order in the midst of rapid growth gained prominence in Atlanta. The riot did not create the desire for order but instead shifted the way in which Atlantans would pursue that elusive goal. Between 1900 and 1910, the city's geographic boundaries expanded at a fantastic pace, and streetcar lines crisscrossed the city, opening its whole range of attractions to all for only a nickel. The population jumped from just over 65,000 in 1890 to well over 150,000 in 1910 as rural southerners, black and white, fled the declining prospects of farm life for the lure of urban wage labor. Economic growth had brought a wealth of people and substantial physical growth but also escalated tensions among the city's population. The rapid expansion of work, leisure, and travel opportunities—and the threat of disorder built into the 1906 race riot—placed working-class women, particularly those who were young and single, in positions of high visibility in Atlanta's public spaces. Urban growth shifted the rhythms of work and leisure, challenged the racial etiquette of the late nineteenth century, tipped the delicate class balance, and introduced controversial commercial amusements to the city. Dance halls, cheap theaters, and amusement parks—frequented by working-class youth of both genders— joined the formerly male-dominated saloons and flophouses of the rough-and-tumble railroad town era. These changes offered Atlanta's working-class women in particular new possibilities for paid labor, friendships, and entertainment and increased women's geographic mobility. In addition, these innovations brought increased attention to the city's women.

Atlanta's business districts became increasingly distinct from its residential areas. Growing wealth allowed the city's elite and even many in its expanding middle classes to move away from the bustle of downtown and the poverty of many working-class neighborhoods.[26] Residential segregation ordinances passed regularly beginning in 1913, and although they were consistently struck down by the U.S. Supreme Court, they governed development in the city long enough that racial residential patterns followed lawmakers' intent.[27] Economic development and a growing disparity in residents' wealth further encouraged the growing distinctions between residential and commercial spaces in the built environment. The meanings and uses of urban space also shifted in this period with the increasing availability of cheap transportation, commercial amusements, and growing leisure time. These changes were tied less to work and family, both thought of as stabilizers in early-twentieth-century cities, and more, at least in the minds of parents, ministers, and many social workers, to the unrestricted behavior of young people, consumerism and consumption, and other similarly destabilizing trends. While Atlantans could convince themselves that orderliness prevailed in the city's economy and its increasingly segmented residential patterns, they tended to see real and potential threats of disorder in the city's many amusements.

The efforts of the Atlanta City Council, middle-class reformers, police, public health officials, and even working-class parents combined during the first two decades of the twentieth century to control working-class women's use of public spaces in an attempt to establish rules and boundaries for Atlanta's emerging commercial amusements, new norms for social interaction in public, and a well-ordered image for the city. Atlanta's youth—young working-class women in particular—resisted many of the behavioral boundaries middle-class reformers tried to erect, instead embracing the wealth of new attractions the city offered for their leisure hours. While attention frequently focused on working-class women, the dialogue over their behavior helped to establish codes of conduct for both genders and all races and classes. In a blossoming city such as Atlanta, the intense scrutinization and even criminalization of women's behavior in the city's public spaces—particularly its streets, trolleys, theaters, restaurants, parks, and dance halls—became vehicles for larger negotiations of the pattern and pace of urban development.

In large part, the controversies produced around women in cheap theaters and dance halls represented the negotiated process of creating social codes for behavior in these new institutions, even those in which racial segregation had already been established through law and practice. Even in cases where battles over class positioning and relations between the races did take precedence over defining gender boundaries, however, working-class women often represented the most pervasive argument for regulation and vehicles through which the conventions and distinctions of class and race would be sorted out. The uncontrolled yet highly visible participation of young single women signaled the potential social chaos of the business of leisure, as what was considered most pure became openly impure through the presumed free association with men, intoxication, frivolous spending, and generally risqué behavior. In attacking the most corrupting aspects of cheap amusements—their effect on women—African American leaders battled for the moral reputation of their community while white middle-class reformers and businessmen endeavored to portray Atlanta to the nation as a well-ordered and wholesome city.

Downtown, the area surrounding the Five Points intersection and encompassing the city's burgeoning commercial district and transportation hub, served as the most important area of the city for promoting a progressive and harmonious image. Here, the best of the city's white businesses, shops, theaters, and restaurants thrived. African Americans who had owned businesses downtown moved their shops away from this area after the violence of 1906, but blacks continued to work in the area surrounding Peachtree Street and to travel through downtown on a daily basis. In the first decade of the twentieth century, the city government encouraged the expansion of the Five Points area by turning downtown into a kind of promenade. In 1909 the city council approved funds to start construction on its own "Great White Way" in the center of the city. The project created corridors of streets and sidewalks around Peachtree Street and Five Points that were lit by electric lights and that connected downtown stores and theaters, making them attractive to evening consumers. In later years, the city and local businesses poured more money into the White Way, lighting more streets and adding restrooms for women along the way. The project continued until 1914, when the city finally declared it complete.[28] Along these downtown streets the city's elite encouraged all classes of whites to mingle, stroll, and shop, no doubt hoping the style of the upper classes would provide a positive influence on wage laborers. Department stores and a shopping arcade drew elite and middle-class white women downtown, while the headquarters of the Young Women's Christian Association and secretarial schools attracted the city's white working-class women. With the expansion of downtown's attractions beyond the realm of business, women gained a strong foothold in what had traditionally been a male domain.[29]

Downtown Atlanta also served as the site for numerous expressions of civic visions in the form of parades. Unlike the mobs that gathered during the Leo Frank trial, these public events were highly organized and carefully orchestrated to appeal to a broad cross section of the city's population, including working-class women. The day before the 1909 mayoral election, for example, the Citizens' Committee commanded Atlantans to "fall in, citizens, fall in" and support candidate Robert Maddox. Thousands apparently heeded the order, including "the

cheers of tens of thousands of the best women in the world." Publicized as the
"greatest civilian parade ever seen in the South," factories across the city closed
so that employees could attend the parade.[30] Organizers constructed parades
to convey particular messages, including civic and regional pride, patriotism,
political goals, and labor solidarity, and depended on large crowds for success.[31]
Across the board, the city's parades escaped the controversy that surrounded
other types of public amusement during these years. The civic and patriotic
nature of most of these demonstrations and their sanctioned use of the center of
town rendered parades as wholesome and culturally uplifting entertainment.

For many of the city's African American residents, Auburn Avenue provided
much of the same cross-class entertainment and civic pride as the Five Points area
did for whites. In the era of segregation, the western section of Auburn Avenue,
which adjoined Peachtree Street just north of Five Points, became the center of
the black business and social world. The street's reputation extended well beyond
Atlanta, attracting black visitors from across the South. "Auburn Avenue used to
be like white folks' Peachtree," recalled one domestic worker. "We just enjoyed
Auburn Avenue. That's why you dressed up and put on [your] good clothes
and go to the show on Auburn Avenue and you were going places. . . . When
you walked down Auburn Avenue you'd better be well dressed because it was a
beautiful city—beautiful street."[32] It became the undisputed center of black life,
supporting the Prince Hall Masonic Temple and a variety of stores, churches,
offices, and nightclubs. Blacks from all walks of life crossed paths on Sweet
Auburn, and although members of different classes attended different churches
and frequented different meeting halls, an air of "pride and joy" permeated the
street.[33] Particularly for the young people, Auburn Avenue became the social
center of the black community, as a local barber recalled, "You had to go there
for real decent social entertainment . . . and if you didn't take your girl over there
back in those days, why you were a cheapskate. The girls . . . wanted to go to
Auburn, if you didn't go down and buy anything but an ice cream cone, just take
them to Auburn; that was their evening, that was their glory."[34] For many blacks
whose economic fortunes did not allow them to wholly isolate themselves from
the hostility of whites or the insults of segregation, the street became the mecca
of black life, far removed from the eyes of white employers, coworkers, police,
and streetcar conductors.

Auburn Avenue and Peachtree Street stood as models of the best the city's
black and white communities had to offer. Black Atlantans pointed to Sweet
Auburn's thriving businesses, fine homes, and well-dressed pedestrians with
understandable pride. For the city's whites, Peachtree Street was the centerpiece
of both business and leisure in the city where whites of different classes peacefully
mingled under the electric lights of urban progress. Five Points and Auburn

Avenue stood as segregated middle-class ideals, not just of recreation but also of city life in general, even as debates over the morality of cheap amusements flourished for other sections of the city.

While downtown and Auburn Avenue glimmered in the distance, most of the recreations catering to Atlanta's working classes operated in other parts of the city. Underground, illegal, or just inexpensive entertainments could be found in many sections of the city, but by far the largest concentration of saloons, brothels, and gambling houses was located on Decatur Street, adjacent to downtown and only two blocks from the train station. Decatur Street was one of the few areas where races and ethnicities mixed freely. "Decatur Street is the home of humanity as it is," noted a writer for the *Journal Magazine* in 1913, "where the negro is found in his element of fried fish and gaudy raiment, and characters which might have walked through the pages of Dickens or O. Henry, have their joys and their sorrows, and laugh and cry, make love and die. . . . Life hums here, for Decatur Street is a kaleidoscope of light, noise and bustle from dawn to dawn."[35]

Many of Atlanta's elite did not share that author's enthusiasm for this "melting pot of Dixie." Black and white leaders alike shunned the entertainments and services available on the street and the working-class populations who took advantage of these offerings.[36] Despite fairly rigid social and geographical segregation, this one neighborhood just blocks from the city's business center existed as a kind of borderland where Atlanta's social divisions blurred. Most other settings that brought different races and classes together were governed by established social codes that regulated interaction. Black women, for example, appeared in white homes but only as servants. Working-class mill hands shared a shop floor with middle-class supervisors, but here again, job classifications and pay provided clear divisions even when physical space did not. Decatur Street defied both physical and social distinctions, creating an infamous neighborhood where many "cultures edge[d] each other," in Gloria Anzaldúa's words, "where people of different races occup[ied] the same territory, where under, lower, middle and upper classes touch, where the space between two individuals shrinks with intimacy."[37]

The Decatur Street area functioned as a physical buffer between Five Points, Auburn Avenue, and surrounding Jewish, black, and working-class white neighborhoods. The businesses and residences represented the variety of the communities surrounding the area. On one particular block, between Ivy and Collins Streets, a white-run shooting gallery sat two doors away from a beer house and a black-owned theater. African American entrepreneurs Lina Richardson, Martha Jones, and Ella Jackson provided rooms for lodgers and sold lunches next to white jewelry stores, Chinese laundries, a Jewish shoe store, and several brothels.[38] Other areas of the Decatur Street neighborhood mixed businesses with recreation and sponsored the illicit services of bootleggers and prostitutes. Because of

Decatur Street's transitional status, however, the reputation of the area and the people who spent time there were often criminalized and exoticized.

Many of the most sensationalized stories of white slavery—young women doped and tricked into prostitution by unscrupulous foreigners—and other tales of the perils the city held for women emerged from Decatur Street. Rumors of opium dens where "Chinamen" doped young women and prominent Atlantans went to "hit the pipe" circulated with great alarm.[39] Black ministers and local newspapers called for the area's bars to be closed. The police consistently raided the area for bootleggers and gamblers, but many on the city's all-white force also spent their off-duty hours enjoying Decatur Street's amusements. Supernumerary Walter Davis, for example, was dropped from the force after being found in a Decatur Street room with an African American woman.[40] Other officers received reprimands for drinking and carousing with women on the street and in the cafés. The crowded sidewalks and variety of businesses that catered to limited budgets for both goods and recreation also attracted many working-class women of both races seeking fun, anonymity, or a bargain.

Beyond the shops and vendors, Decatur Street offered some of the few saloons in the city that welcomed women. Despite the prohibition ordinance of 1908, "dives" and saloons selling both legal near beer and illegal alcohol were common in the poorer sections of town. The popularity of drinking as a recreation among working-class women appeared repeatedly in divorce suits. Wilborn O'Connor, for example, accused his wife, Janie May, of drinking whiskey, complaining she would "come home late at night in an intoxicated condition."[41] Industrial spies for the Fulton Bag and Cotton Mills often discovered women strikers drinking near beer with their male counterparts on Decatur Street. At one point, mill management even tried to use reports of married strike leader O. Delight Smith drinking in the German Café with fellow organizer Charles Miles to suggest an illicit affair and to discredit Smith's leadership.[42] The charges carried little weight with strikers and Atlanta's working classes, many of whom also frequented these establishments.

What appealed to some city residents about Decatur Street frightened others away. Undeniably, this could be a rough part of town, where no one might want to travel alone late at night, but the stories generally exceeded the danger because they touched on so many of the fears of middle-class businessmen, city officials, ministers, and working-class parents. Relying only on what relatives had told her, domestic worker Alice Adams declared, "Decatur Street used to be rough, [it] wasn't safe for walking. . . . [M]y peoples told me when I came to Atlanta 'Stay off Decatur Street.' And I did just that."[43] Stories of women being doped and kidnapped reverberated through the white and black communities and became the central trope through which the entire Decatur Street area was criminalized.

Even legitimate businesses and law-abiding residents felt the results of this process as young people were warned away from the street and police regularly raided the area. Decatur Street's businesses and amusements probably attracted only a small portion of the city's working-class women, yet the "social and sexual anarchy" this area symbolized tainted by association almost all other sites of commercial recreations that catered to the city's working classes and wage-earning women in particular.[44] Downtown and Auburn Avenue, as the most lauded areas, and Decatur Street, as the most despised, represented two ends of the spectrum of Atlanta leisure and public space. Working-class women appeared across this continuum, and their leisure-time pursuits and urban travels both fueled and served debates over the character, purpose, and accessibility of Atlanta's public spaces.

Commercial Amusements

COMMERCIALIZED RECREATIONS provided the most popular and many of the newest diversions for working-class women in Atlanta, but their presence in these venues also generated the most controversy. In fairs, circuses, and fiddle contests as well as movies, vaudeville theaters, and amusement parks, entrepreneurs provided the city's working classes with a variety of ways to spend their wages and leisure hours. And working-class women, increasingly mobile in the early-twentieth-century city, flocked to these commercial amusements. In these sites, physical representations of the growing moral stratification between social classes became evident. Because of the public nature of these amusements, the behaviors of women who frequented them were highly visible to and thoroughly critiqued by observers—middle-class reformers, ministers, city officials, and working-class parents. The actions of the city's women, particularly those who were young and single, became the focus through which Atlanta's residents negotiated the boundaries of social participation in the burgeoning world of commercialized leisure.

Consequently, commercialized amusements received the most concentrated opposition from middle-class reformers concerned with the plight of the working woman and the moral atmosphere of the city. Atlanta's new dance halls, saloons, cheap theaters, and amusements parks usually bore the brunt of organized attacks on the respectability of Atlanta's inexpensive sites of recreation and the patrons who frequented them. Similar to the "victim" approach reformers took to women's paid labor, working-class women were often cast as the innocent casualties of wage slavery and unscrupulous businesses that played on their desires to be released from the "drudgery and monotony of their narrow, hopeless lives."[45] Starting in the 1900s and peaking in the 1910s, reformers set out to create the "right sort of environment" in which the city's working-class women could learn "how to enjoy and what to enjoy, and through wholesome pleasure and innocent gaiety these girls will reach a degree of development that will insure them against the temptations of coarse dissipation."[46] White reformers focused most of their attention on the victimization of white women, but that concern sometimes brought these reformers into the city's more racially integrated sections, such as Decatur Street. Producing a moral image of Atlanta's African American community in the wake of the 1906 riot became a priority for black civic leaders. These elites, worrying over the reputation of the race, often imaged black working-class women, much like their white counterparts, as sexually vulnerable and morally dangerous in the public sites of urban leisure.[47] The sanitizing of Atlanta's commercial amusements, then, was not strictly a movement to control the actions of women in these venues but also an effort to regulate the behavior of the crowds in general and govern the city's image.

Of all the city had to offer working-class women during their leisure hours, drinking establishments, dance halls, vaudeville theaters, amusement parks, and, later in the 1910s, movie houses, proved to be the most attractive to the women and the most alarming to parents, the middle-class, and some city officials. Women drank in the streets and alleys surrounding Decatur Street, in annexes to men's saloons, or at restaurants, sometimes referred to by reformers as "women's bars."[48] Women danced the night away—often for free—at rooftop pavilions, in crowded halls, and under the stars on dance floors in the city's public parks. Dances were so popular among the city's working-class women that some enthusiasts would even skip work to attend. Lula Turpin, a mill operative, gained a reputation for staying "out one day a week—not because she is sick but because she goes to dances and doesn't get home until late, and then does not feel like going to work the next morning."[49] Two amusement parks catering to the city's working classes also appeared after the turn of the century: White City, for the city's whites, and a small storefront version called Luna Park for African Americans. For black and white youth alike, the city's growing number of theaters, including the Star, the Imperial, the Famous, the Arcade, and the American, also offered an appealing range of entertainments from the extremely popular and generally considered more "decent" vaudeville shows to risqué burlesque performances.[50] Describing the lives of young wage-earning women, a sympathetic YWCA worker concluded, "homes are . . . regarded by the girls as merely a place to eat and sleep and do it cheaply. They dress and live for the streets and the shows where they live their real life after the day's work is over."[51]

New commercial recreations also promoted consumption as a form of recreation in which part of the fun was to indulge in souvenirs, food, and other treats as well as to "put on the style" to impress members of the opposite sex. Twentieth-century production techniques also helped to make many new items available to the masses at relatively cheap prices. Working-class women of both races actively participated in the developing consumer culture whenever their wages would allow. As historian Kathy Peiss has noted, young working-class women expressed their desire for social freedom, played with their identities, and created new images and roles by "appropriating cultural forms around them," particularly those of clothing styles.[52] And Atlanta merchants, eager for business, sought to attract young female wage-laborers with advertisements, sales, and the latest fashions.

Beyond the basic necessities of room, board, and transportation, many of Atlanta's wage-earning women poured their wages into the purchase of stylish clothes. Cheap ready-made garments and costume jewelry brought the styles of the middle class within reach of the working-class women. Even thirty years later, Willie Mae Cartwright recalled vividly the clothes she wore as a young domestic worker in Atlanta in the 1910s and 1920s. She took obvious pride in her ability to put together outfits, even when many of her items were only from the five-and-ten store or borrowed from employers and friends. Describing the night she met her future husband, she recalled, "I was fit to kill, too. I had on a mustard-yellow georgette dress with plaid on the bottom. . . . And tan patent-leather slippers and my good dropstitch stockings. . . . I had a bright comb in my hair that night too. It was nothing but Kress stuff, but it sparkled."[53] Many women took jobs in department stores to obtain the employee discount on store merchandise. As sales workers frequently and carefully noted to government investigators, Rich's, the largest department store in Atlanta, offered its sales staff a "10 percent discount on everything, and a larger discount in the millinery."[54]

As many cultural theorists have noted, style often functioned as an indirect challenge to social order.[55] In the case of working-class women in the early twentieth century, dressing up often evoked disdain from the middle classes, which believed that some women were trying to pass for a higher social class. In other instances, women's dress, especially if colorful and flamboyant, was interpreted as the mark of a prostitute. Even the committee charged with investigating vice in the city in 1912 criticized "extreme fashions, tight skirts, and the like, as a stimulation to sensuous desire" and a contributing factor to the growing number of prostitutes in the city.[56] Cartwright, a domestic worker, discovered different interpretations of her style one night in downtown Atlanta when she borrowed some items from her employer to "put on the dog" for a date. A white police officer, suspicious of a black woman dressed in such finery, took her into the station house and called her employer to ascertain whether the items were stolen. The officer eventually released her, but only after she had been humiliated. Certainly aware of the violence blacks often suffered at the hands of the police force, she recalled that even after her release, "I was still so scared I was weak."[57]

That Cartwright had been on her way to meet a young man when the police accosted her is also quite telling. Atlanta's young women increasingly spent their leisure hours with peers of both genders. The peer cultures developing on the shop floor and in neighborhoods spilled over into a relatively new form of social interaction, dating—a means of leisure that often centered on not only commercial amusements but also neighborhood streets and the community drugstore.[58] In Atlanta, dating often included trips to parks, soda fountains, or movie houses. Remembering a favorite hangout for African American youth, Dan Stephens recalled, "That's when the boys and girls would gather at the drugstore [of] Mr. Yates and Mr. Milton and the boys would set the girls up to a banana split and a chocolate ice cream and all those things."[59] With the rise in public amusements and the growing congestion in urban housing, working-class youths sought privacy within public spaces in courtship and in introductions to potential lovers.[60] As one woman explained her frequent visits to Atlanta's theaters, "I am going fishing and I go where the fish are."[61]

Inherent to this style of courtship was consumerism. The men were expected to treat their dates, making dating an especially appealing means through which working-class women who earned low wages could participate in commercial amusements. There was another side to this arrangement, though. "Financially unable to reciprocate in kind," historian Kathy Peiss notes, "women offered sexual favors of varying degrees, ranging from flirtatious companionship to sexual intercourse, in exchange for men's treats."[62] Ola Hinton, for example, was having an affair, rumored to be sexual in nature, with Otis McClutchin. Both were mill workers at Fulton Bag and residents of the mill village, and Hinton's "very friendly" attitude toward McClutchin was well known in the small community, as were his gifts to her of, among other things, a new suit and coat.[63] Laying bare the economic realities of dating for a young male friend, Slim Clemmons, another Atlanta mill worker, promised to arrange a date anytime his friend "wanted to put out three bucks."[64]

In some cases, women became quite adept at manipulating this system of treating to their own advantage. Lillie Priest, also a textile worker, frustrated the advances of one male companion by continually bringing a friend along when she met her date. He was then forced to treat both women to a night out. As this discouraged suitor reported, "I had to take the two of them out and we went to a dance on Hunter St. also a movie show [and] I escorted them home at 10:30 P.M. During the evening there did not develop much opportunity for conversation with Miss Priest on account of the third party's presence."[65] Priest gained not only for herself but also for a friend an evening of entertainment, without providing much in return.

The free and easy interaction of young men and women in Atlanta's commercial amusements fueled middle-class apprehensions over the city's moral environment. Attacks on working-class women's leisure activities and use of public space continually emphasized the sexual vulnerability of women set adrift from family relationships and neighborhood observation. This sexualization of subordinate groups often functioned as a mechanism for legitimizing intervention in maintaining divisions along racial and class lines.[66] In Atlanta, racial and class divisions translated into both social and spatial boundaries. Repeated images of women forced into prostitution by low wages and unregulated social settings appeared as justifications for reformers' attempts to limit women's paid labor, access to working-class amusements, and ability to travel freely in the city as well as to restrict interaction between genders and races in the city's public spaces.

Atlanta's new commercial amusements represented an array of dangers for women and for the city's moral atmosphere. Common were the sentiments that unregulated amusements, particularly cheap theaters, might serve as "feeders," funneling young women into the city's brothels. John J. Eagan, a local businessman and founder of the evangelical Men and Religion Forward Movement, crusaded to warn women new to the city of the dangers of the "light that leads to bewilder and dazzles to blind."[67] He and many reformers like him feared that young working-class women were susceptible to being pulled into "a life of vice" where they would be "constantly diseased, frequently beaten by their so-called lovers or keepers, and often drunk and sick."[68] "One of the greatest evils" of Atlanta's commercial amusements, concluded a 1912 commission charged with investigating vice, was "the fact that many young girls, having no proper places of amusements and naturally seeking pleasure in the evenings, are lured to these places, frequently by companions of their own sex, who are not known to be immoral. Friends are introduced who take them to places of amusement frequently of doubtful character, and in this manner form a familiarity that leads to ruin."[69] Chronicling both the threat of cheap amusements and the typical middle-class reaction to these dangers, one newspaper columnist noted, "There is a wave of proper revulsion against girls in their teens displaying themselves in cheap theaters, of incurring, on the streets or public places generally, those incitements to temptation that lead toward the primrose path and that, in turn to the brothel or perhaps to an early end the sickening details of which we do not discuss in polite society."[70]

Many African American community leaders feared that women's attraction to the city's public amusements threatened morality, but black leaders demonstrated just as much concern for the potential impact of women's actions on the reputation of the race as a whole. Elite blacks, who generally avoided the segregated local theaters, scoffed at the behavior of the patrons at these shows, where, in the words of one disdainful observer, "you couldn't hardly sit in [these] theaters from [people] throwing peanuts [or] something down on you."[71] Working-class blacks' affinity for segregated and rowdy entertainments frustrated African American elites, leading them to target women as the key to ending segregation or at least

uplifting the behavior of working-class blacks in the city's amusements. As one
newspaper columnist argued, "If the Negro women will just stay in their places,
it will be an easy matter to control the men, and soon or late we will have an opera
house [where] you can go and not be molested or criticized."[72]

The important economic role that African American women filled also fed fears
that black women's patronage of commercial amusements might threaten the white
community. In one representation of these concerns, the often antiblack *Atlanta
Georgian* ran a cartoon in which a white housewife toiled in her own kitchen
while her "wandering cook" pretended to be sick so that she might enjoy herself
out "in sassiety."[73] Even the African American elite periodically echoed these
sentiments, arguing that too many domestics, in the words of conservative black
minister Henry Hugh Proctor, "tried to work all day and dance all night" only
to shirk their job duties and feed the image of blacks as lazy, reluctant workers.[74]
The morality and respectability threatened by working-class women's fondness
for the dance hall, then, crossed out of the realm of sexuality and into the worlds
of work and politics.

Middle-class reformers, mostly white but also some African American, strove to
ameliorate the potential disorder they saw in the city's commercial amusements
through regulations on the leisure venues, with limited success. Progressives
succeeded in getting the city council to pass a 1910 ordinance that prohibited
women from entering saloons and insisted that establishments be designated for
one race or the other in an attempt to end racial and gender mixing in barrooms. By
1918, the city also required dance halls to register all persons present to facilitate
public inspection.[75] In the early 1920s the city government moved to further
restrict dance halls catering to working-class youth by closing the dance pavilions
at Lakewood, Washington, and other city parks. Beyond this, however, the city
government did little to curb the prosperity of commercial leisure.

Consequently, middle-class Atlantans, boosters concerned with the city's reputation, and some municipal officials focused much of their efforts in the 1900s
and 1910s on creating alternatives to what entrepreneurs offered or on pressuring
the leisure industry to raise the standard of conduct for patrons. The Men and
Religion Forward Movement, the Atlanta Woman's Club, and city social workers came to believe that "young girls are generally attracted to the motion picture
shows and cheap vaudeville by a lack of proper amusement and recreation in their
homes," and these reformers sought to provide more proper amusements.[76] Emphasizing working-class women's ignorance, the Atlanta Woman's Club blamed
commercial amusements for the "so-called 'fall' of these young women" and for
taking unwholesome advantage of "nature's demand for the free, joyous social
life."[77] Reformers naturalized the desire of youth for amusement but hoped to
channel such desires through culturally uplifting venues that would "transform

these young women into the mothers, the leaders, the directors of a substantial race."[78]

Echoing the sentiments of Jane Addams and other national leaders of the organized play movement, Atlanta reformers recommended "the establishment of civic recreation centers, where [girls] could get the amusement they crave, but in an uplifting instead of a degeneration atmosphere."[79] The Georgia Federation of Women's Clubs, for example, lauded employers' attempts to provide "proper recreation" for their female workers. In particular, the organization singled out programs at Southern Bell and Fulton Bag and Cotton Mills that provided sitting rooms, magazines, and sewing classes for women workers while ensuring "no danger in interference of men" during work or rest periods.[80] The women's department of the Chamber of Commerce began offering dance classes, hoping to counteract the new working-class dance styles of the early twentieth century, which were beginning to spill over into the youth cultures of the middle classes. Girls' High School, fearing that middle-class teens would emulate dance styles from the city's racier halls, banned students from engaging in "zoo" dances like "the 'Turkey Trot,' the 'Boston Dip,' the 'Bunny Hug,' and other freak dances." "[H]ereafter," the administration admonished, "students of the institution will confine themselves to the simplest of two-steps and waltzes when tripping the light fantastic."[81]

Reformers who had supported closing burlesque theaters at the turn of the century remained suspicious of even the more sanitized vaudeville shows offered at lowbrow theaters with such suspect names as the Peekin and the Idle Hour. Shows with many entertainments—singing, dancing, and rowdy skits that encouraged audience participation—received the most pressure from reformers to clean up their acts, but by the 1910s, most Atlantans had come to accept vaudeville and women's presence in theaters. The city's middle classes supported a fairly strict set of gender conventions to govern women's behavior in the theaters, and these standards help illustrate the ways in which proscriptions for women's behavior created social and moral boundaries in the world of commercial leisure. White women were not to sit in the gallery, where they might be side by side with African Americans. Women were also not to attend shows at night without a male escort, but matinee audiences contained almost exclusively women and children.[82]

At the city's working-class amusement parks, as historian John Kasson noted for Coney Island, the attractions usually appeared "in a less earnest cultural mold" than middle-class reformers might have preferred.[83] White City intentionally blurred the line between spectator and performer, as part of the appeal became not just the rides but also the interactive participation of the parkgoers themselves. The park featured rides that threw people off balance and against one another in thrilling, if fleeting, moments of physical contact. Dimly lit adventures also offered the possibility of brief erotic encounters. Even the park's layout encouraged crowding, viewing, and mingling with strangers through the open pavilion, closely placed rides, and narrow walkways.

Middle-class Atlantans countered the bawdy behavior of White City's pleasure seekers by patronizing the far more sedate amusements to be found at Ponce de Leon Park. Upon its opening in 1906, the local press declared that the park would be "the mecca for the many pilgrims who will journey there to find relief from the din and confusion of the city during the long, hot summer."[84] Ponce de Leon Park contained more sanitized and less active amusements than its working-class cousin. Even nature was "reproduced" and re-created by the park's builders in "all the beauties of a landscaped garden."[85] Patrons could ride the Ferris wheel or merry-go-round, or swim and boat in the lake. Band concerts were also held daily. Much of the park's activity centered on strolling through the midway, enjoying the serenity of nature, or riding amusements that provided patrons with individual seats and thus maintained both dignity and distance. Those who frequented the park were expected to be of a higher social class and refined in their conduct. A sign greeting visitors as they entered the park declared, "Ponce De Leon is a Private Park under city police regulations. No disorderly characters tolerated. Colored persons admitted as servants only."[86] The city's middle classes demonstrated sincere concern for the morality of Atlanta's working class but also demonstrated a clear desire to keep the perceived immorality of that class out of middle-class leisure-time pursuits.

The lack of municipal regulations on commercial amusements can be explained largely by influential businessmen's commitment to maintaining and expanding this profitable industry. The city council and owners of local "sporting houses," beer saloons, boxing clubs, pool rooms, restaurants, and soft drink parlors publicly supported crackdowns against prostitution in Atlanta's red-light districts. These business leaders drew the line, however, at restricting legitimate enterprises, warning the police that to "go too far" in closing amusements would "retard the growth of the city."[87] When an overly ambitious group of plainclothes detectives assigned to investigate commercial amusements began interfering with profits, the police committee disbanded the force. The city council placed few restrictions on vaudeville theaters, and the regulation of movies was left entirely up to the National Board of Censorship until 1913, when it was then given to a local board consisting of businessmen.[88] The municipal court appointed one of its officers to censor local theater productions in the winter of 1913–14, but even that move was met with a threat of legal action from a city council member who owned a portion of the Columbia Theater. In the words of an Atlanta real estate developer, many businessmen were concerned that press coverage of overly moralizing and virulent attacks on commercial leisure would cause the public to become "disgusted" and ultimately "hurt our town" by discouraging tourists and investors.[89] Mayor James Woodward noted that amusements provided a key element of Atlanta's status as "a modern, cosmopolitan city."[90]

Considering the fears attached to the city's commercial amusements and the resistance of many businessmen and urban boosters to closing or even too closely regulating most of these profitable ventures, the solution on which interested parties generally agreed was the policing of unescorted women's behavior on the streets and in these venues. Municipal officials essentially hoped that policing the behavior of women in hotels, boarding houses, theaters, and the like would mean "the saving of many young girls and young men from destruction in the future, [as well as] the reformation and salvation of many women who already had fallen into the meshes of vice," without hurting the business of leisure too severely.[91] Consequently, when Chief of Police James L. Beavers decided to wage "war" on "loose living hotels . . . and cheap soda water joints" in 1912, he chose the path of least political resistance by opting to do battle with the young single women who frequented these establishments rather than the profitable businesses themselves.[92]

The policing of women's behavior in Atlanta's public spaces ultimately served a myriad of political, social, and moral purposes. It became the rational response to a growing recognition that women had become a permanent part of the city's public spheres.[93] The efforts of the Atlanta City Council, middle-class reformers, police, public health officials, and working-class parents combined during the first two decades of the twentieth century to essentially criminalize some of working-class women's use of public space, thereby establishing rules and boundaries for Atlanta's newest commercial amusements and social trends. While public portrayals and patterns of arrest focused on working-class women, the boundaries created through these means helped to establish codes of conduct for both genders and all races and classes. In a blossoming city such as Atlanta, this intense scrutinization of women's behavior served as a vehicle for larger negotiations of the pattern and pace of urban development without unduly harming the prospering leisure industry.

Sensationalized tales of young women saved from the immorality of commercial amusements by police intervention circulated through local newspapers, helping to feed this approach to preserving Atlanta's moral atmosphere. In 1907, for example, Atlanta police arrested a young woman named Bertie Owens at a local dance. Typical of the approach then developing in the city, the police removed the sixteen-year-old Owens despite her "screaming defiance[s] and declaring that she would kill herself before she would return home," but they did not shut down the dance.[94] The grounds for her removal are unclear from press accounts. The *Atlanta Georgian* suggested that the police motivation was "protection," but just as in the world of paid employment, the term embodied a host of divergent meanings.[95] Were Owens and other young women like her being protected from the unrestricted atmosphere of Atlanta's "tawdry boarding houses . . . and motion picture shows?"[96] Or were they part of the "serious menace" created by a "class of young women who frequent . . . prominent streets accosting men and young boys, inviting them to a life of shame and degradation"?[97] Whether *protection* meant saving young women from temptations created by a precarious economic position and unregulated social spaces or guarding the rest of the city from predatory behavior of morally suspect women, working-class women's presence in Atlanta's most public spaces was increasingly criminalized in the late 1900s and 1910s by the city council, urban boosters, middle-class reformers, and the police.

Much of the responsibility for regulating working-class women fell to the city's police force, meaning that women's behavior was inevitably associated with crime even though their actions rarely seem to have involved offenses against persons or property and were generally crimes against the social order. Hattie Campbell, for example, was remanded to the care of the probation officer for drinking on a Saturday night.[98] The police matron plucked fourteen-year-old Vessie Bostwick out of a traveling theatrical company, believing that either the theater or the company might have been a front for prostitution.[99] Other women attracted police attention by moving out of their homes, quarreling with their husbands, being too familiar with other residents of their boardinghouses, frequenting dance halls, keeping company with a "woman of poor reputation," or being "on the street without money and without a place to go."[100] Women could also be arrested for several crimes reserved exclusively for them: immoral conduct, indecent dress, or being a "lewd woman on the street."[101]

To deal specifically with the suspected female criminal, Atlanta's police department started hiring matrons to handle women in custody and allowed a private organization to employ a public probation officer to deal with female prisoners. Following the lead of such cities as Portland and Los Angeles, Atlanta eventually recruited policewomen to investigate the city's amusements and their female working-class patrons.[102] Starting in 1912, Beavers, the ambitious police chief, made a series of bold and often unauthorized policy moves that intensified police interest in the public activities of young, working-class women. After closing a red-light district with much fanfare from the local press, Beavers launched his campaign against the "woman of the streets," creating a squad of plainclothes detectives to patrol the streets and the city's cheap amusements. According to newspaper reports, women would "be tailed by relentless 'shadows' of the detective force. They [would] be watched at every moment."[103] Officers had orders to "inspect all cheap hotels and boarding houses" for women suspected of prostitution, who were not to be "allowed on the streets at night."[104] In "motion picture show[s] where patrons in skirts sit hour after hour, caring nothing for the picture," female officers ensured order and high moral conduct by arresting women who behaved objectionably, charging them with vagrancy, disorderly conduct, and the like.[105] Beavers publicly denied that he was using his arrests and shadowing tactics to punish women for their actions. His policies were, he insisted, "a movement calculated to lift the women to their feet."[106] Like many other Atlantans, Beavers argued that the double standard of morality should be abolished and that men should be held accountable for their immoral behavior in the same way as women. It is hard to put much stock in Beavers's professed commitment to locking up men and hauling them into court, considering the arrest rates surrounding prostitution. In only two years between 1893 and the 1930s did the number of men arrested for soliciting sex equal or even approach the number of "lewd women" or "occupants of houses of ill fame" arrested.[107]

This campaign was not the lone crusade of a power-hungry police chief: middle-class reformers, like those who hired the probation officer, and the city government generally endorsed this criminalization of women in public spaces as a means of controlling public morality. The city council's 1912 vice commission explicitly blamed women's presence on the streets as the cause of men's moral downfall, suggesting that the city needed to be protected from women.[108] The commission endorsed the policing of women as a means of protecting the city and of protecting "young girls" from meeting immoral "companions of their own sex" and "form[ing] a familiarity that leads to their ruin." Along with calling for better provisions for the treatment of venereal disease, the committee suggested that the city should construct a home for "wayward girls," discourage rural girls from venturing to the city, end women soliciting on the street, and, in a demonstration of the connection between moral order and the ordering of physical surroundings, build separate parks for whites and blacks that would prevent women from being approached on the street by forces desiring to lead them astray.[109]

Civic leaders of both races sought to curb the relatively free social interaction encouraged by cheap amusements, thereby protecting women and preserving the city's moral reputation. Restrictions on women's access to or behavior in these venues became the most popular and effective means of overseeing commercial leisure. Once the amusement park, dance hall, saloon, and vaudeville theater were under control or on the wane, many of Atlanta's middle-class reformers turned their attention to the censorship and regulation of motion pictures. Movie houses boomed in the late 1910s, and by 1920 Atlanta boasted more than twenty such theaters. This growth heralded the decline of other, more interactive amusements because, according to Kasson, movies killed the illusions created in amusement parks, dance halls, and theaters and offered cheaper entertainment.[110] Movies also became more accessible as theaters were built in most working-class neighborhoods, such as Little Five Points, and around downtown.

Both the theaters themselves and the content of the movies shown encouraged working-class amusement seekers to be spectators rather than actors during their leisure hours.[111] All of Atlanta's movie houses, from its great movie palaces such as the Fox and Loew's Grand to its smallest neighborhood theaters, shared similar spatial characteristics. With the screen at the front of the room, all seats faced forward in orderly rows. The "theater of action" itself in part determined the actions acceptable in that venue, as behavior and space are mutually dependent. While sexes and even classes could often mix in these theaters, the placement of the screen and the seating arrangement restricted their integration by not allowing patrons to face each other, share seats, or otherwise mingle too freely.[112] Movie theaters also reflected the social realities of segregation through practices that kept the races separate either by restricting African Americans to the balcony or by segregating particular movie showings by race.[113] The social reality and behavioral expectations built into Atlanta's theaters in the 1920s and 1930s reinforced both sanitized social interaction and the racial segregation so prized by many wealthier residents.

The growing convergence of Hollywood movies around themes of love, traditional gender roles, and morality also made regulating the movies themselves less of an issue in the 1920s. Messages inherent in these films told women they must choose between pursuing careers and creating solid and lasting families.[114] Through happy and fulfilling images, these films reinforced the primacy of family and marriage. In contrast, low-wage jobs with few prospects for advancement must have looked bleak and unrewarding. It is precisely at this point that developments in commercialized recreations and in women's paid work converge. Both trends ultimately served to maintain working-class women in dependent relationships of marriage and family, denying in popular culture the validation and rewards women may have gained from their wage labor. By the 1910s and 1920s, Atlanta could claim a vibrant, though well regulated, amusement industry. The city sought this kind of balance in the early decades of the twentieth century. A profitable economic endeavor had not been excluded, yet racial, gender, and moral order would still be enforced by the city's middle classes.

ATLANTA'S GROWTH in the early twentieth century challenged many of the traditional patterns of social interaction and deference that had governed the behavior of the city's races and social classes in the nineteenth century. Racial tensions exploded in the fall of 1906 in the form of a brutal riot that demonstrated, at least in the minds of many whites, the vulnerability of white women in the city. The underlying causes of the riot went much deeper and pointed to increasing anxiety among whites over the economic success of the African American community and the loosening of the ties that had bound and regulated the growing town. The church, for example, which had been a source of class and racial stability in the nineteenth century, found itself increasingly isolated in the twentieth century. [115] Atlanta's burgeoning status as the region's premier city brought with it many changes: new businesses, new populations, less familiarity between the races and classes, and the diminishing power of old institutions to oversee these changes. New middle-class civic organizations, the police, and an increasing municipal bureaucracy stepped in to control this growth and create a reputation of moral order as well as economic prosperity, a move that again pushed working-class women to the forefront of the city's attention.

The close association of women with morality and Atlanta's moral order served as the basis for incorporating the leisure industry into the larger social structure of the city while reinforcing racial, class, and gender boundaries within the growing city. Arguments for regulation frequently built on familiar stories of prostitution and white slavery. At issue for most civic leaders and middle-class reformers of both races was the necessity of developing new social mores concerning peer interaction between the sexes. Black and white leaders diverged, however, as whites also fought to maintain racial segregation, fearing that all commercial amusements would become as socially mixed as Decatur Street. For some middle-class blacks, the closing of cheap theaters and regulation of dance halls formed a piece of a larger effort to improve the image of the city's African American community. By sanitizing the cheap amusements many working-class women frequented, the regulation of public amusements ultimately facilitated the incorporation of Atlanta's burgeoning young female workforce into social patterns acceptable to the middle class.

This process was one of negotiation, however, and while the city's reformers and civic elite closed or regulated many of Atlanta's dance halls and cheap theaters, their efforts did little to change the picnics, house parties, and dates that filled the leisure hours of most working people. Many commercialized amusements appealing to the city's working classes suffered in the face of reform efforts, but the negotiation between classes and generations over control of leisure hours and the use of public space did not cease with the policing or closing of commercial leisure venues. Working-class women continued to use public transportation and appear on the streets, and their middle-class sisters even joined them as the presence of women in the city's downtown became more common. Some commercial amusements did not survive the era, but many more thrived with the general prosperity of the early decades of the twentieth century.

At almost the same moment that the city's middle classes were struggling to rein in the behavior of young women on the streets, attention also settled on the plight of older and married women living in poverty. If the abundance of commercial amusements threatened to create a reputation of the city as immoral, the growing numbers of urban poor threatened the image of the city as an economic success. Consequently, a movement in many ways paralleling the efforts to control women's behavior on the streets developed in the growth of a social welfare network. This network focused on Atlanta's poor women, as class stratification in the city became more pronounced in the decades following the turn of the century.

CHAPTER FOUR

Class, Community, and Welfare

IN THE WINTER of 1905, a brutal storm hit the Southeast. Snow and ice, a rare oc-currence in Atlanta, blanketed the city for a full week. While a few cheery ice skaters enjoyed themselves in Piedmont Park, the storm forced businesses and schools to close; downed communication, electrical, and transportation systems; and caused widespread misery among Atlanta's poorer populations, whose shabby housing and meager incomes offered few resources for dealing with the storm.[1] Joseph Logan, a young Atlanta lawyer, hoped to organize the various and often overlapping charity efforts being extended to storm victims through the creation of a citywide clearinghouse for relief. Logan was disturbed that "there had been little or no cooperation, no intelligent investigation, [and] no system of records."[2] The work of Logan's new Associated Charities to remedy this disorganization was part of a growing trend toward "scientific charity," a movement designed to bring efficiency and standardization to philanthropic efforts that began in the Northeast in the 1870s but reached Atlanta only in the winter of 1905.[3]

The Associated Charities' goal of orchestrating and coordinating relief never fully materialized in these early years. The dire need of a growing number of people seeking aid and the lack of other organizations able to take on new cases forced the Associated Charities into the business of direct relief. Labeled by a contemporary as the "mother of most of the social work in Atlanta," the Associated Charities became the city's largest source of direct relief.[4] Most important for this book, however, is the way in which this middle-class dominated agency went about giving relief. The Associated Charities, and essentially all Atlanta relief organizations run by the middle classes of both races, had developed by 1909 or so a set of welfare practices focused almost entirely on poor married women. Charity officers and, later, social workers primarily conceived of these women as mothers, caretakers of the family home, and the mainstays of working-class neighborhoods. Even as Atlanta's social welfare network began to professionalize in the 1910s, female clients still dominated in black and white agencies alike.

Women proved a useful, if not ideal, vehicle for reaching and reshaping the city's poorest residents, but women's prominent position as the focus of welfare work in the first two decades of the twentieth century went further than that. Besides promoting respectability among the working classes, extensive welfare services (at least considering the paucity that had been available before the turn of the century) could help protect Atlanta's reputation by projecting an image of a caring city, protecting and rehabilitating its least-fortunate residents. Welfare campaigns of the 1900s and 1910s helped to solidify local social workers' authority and more broadly shored up the rapidly expanding middle classes' status. The middle classes would be the city's experts, solve the city's problems, lead the race (in the case of blacks), and strengthen the institutions of family and neighborhood that maintained order and stability. Thus, at much the same time that single working-class women became central to dialogues on work and leisure, married poor and working-class women became central to the relationship between classes and discussions of family and home in the bustling city.

Class Structures

THE SOCIOECONOMIC stratification of Atlanta's population, on both sides of the color line, became increasingly pronounced during the nineteenth century, as only a handful of people made their way to society's top levels. A large and shifting transient population continued to move into the city, swelling the ranks of the poor and working classes. Perhaps the most significant change in class structure, however, was the emergence of a powerful and discrete middle class. The city's development in commerce, finance, and industry in the 1880s and 1890s opened the door for the formation of this class and for a distinct bourgeois identity for its members. Most of the men in this rising middle class made their money in business, and they quickly became the most prominent voices of economic boosterism. White families of this class organized the Gentlemen's Driving Club (later the Piedmont Driving Club), the Capital City Club, and other exclusive social institutions. African Americans formed similar institutions, such as the Negro Driving Club, indicative of the economic success of black entrepreneurs such as Alonzo Herndon, a barber turned insurance mogul.[5]

While not as clear as the city's racial divisions, social and geographical boundaries between classes became increasingly distinct after the turn of the century. White commercial and industrial entrepreneurs moved their homes north of downtown, away from Atlanta's African Americans and laboring classes. Developers created the city's first suburbs, Inman Park and Ansley Park, just after the turn of the century, offering affluent whites spacious homes with direct streetcar service to downtown. The wealthiest blacks owned fine homes along Auburn Avenue. Other well-to-do African Americans inhabited the Summer Hill district south of downtown, and African American intellectuals clustered around the black colleges on Atlanta's west side. As significant as changes in neighborhood composition, however, was the array of institutions developed by Atlanta's bourgeoisie, which drew them together as a class, although they remained divided by race, and marked boundaries between middle-class families and the city's laborers. Such organizations as the Men and Religion Forward Movement, the Neighborhood Union, and the Atlanta Woman's Club, in addition to the social clubs mentioned previously, highlighted Atlanta's middle classes' concerns with civic improvement, education, citizenship duties, and moral order.

Within early-twentieth-century Atlanta's increasingly stratified environment, gender—in particular, notions of womanhood—often represented distinctions between classes. Atlanta's bourgeois men and women became particularly concerned with the direction and character of the city's development and strove to control that growth according to their own class-bounded values. Judging by the numerous organizations and reform efforts launched by members of this class, their vision for the city featured strong families able to withstand the destructive forces inherent in industrialization and urbanization. Especially among middle-class Atlantans interested in providing for the destitute, working-class mothers represented the best hope against a failing social order; consequently, welfare agencies generally funneled the bulk of their assistance to working-class families through interactions with poor married women.[6]

The way in which the activist middle class went about enacting its ideas for urban order, however, reveals that the agenda's specifics were far from universally agreed on, even among reformers themselves. Women clashed with men over how to fund aid to poor women and their families, private agencies battled with public institutions for control of the city's burgeoning social welfare network, and black reformers faced off against the dominant white culture in an effort to restore and elevate the image of the African American mother and her family. Dichotomies frequently appeared in social workers' imaging of their female clients as either virtuous or vicious, the hope of a family's survival or its most dangerous threat to happiness. Married women also received different treatment than the single women whom social workers generally understood to be young and only temporarily unmarried. Caseworkers' assumptions that all women would marry (and would refrain from having children until they were married) allowed reformers largely to overlook the plight of destitute single women when designing programs for direct assistance to the poor. Images of welfare clients varied most markedly along racial lines, since black and white women represented different challenges to the urban community's social order. White middle-class reformers and social workers produced images that reinforced black women's identity as workers and white women's role as mothers. African American civic and benevolent associations, however, promoted more complex and broad-based images of black women that tended to put motherhood first.[7]

The way welfare organizations viewed their clients and promoted their relief work provided both opportunities and restrictions in the daily lives of working-class women of both races. In part, relationships with social workers and visiting nurses empowered working-class women, because social welfare agencies used them as an entrée into the world of the city's laboring classes. Poor women, however, rarely acted as passive clients for charity workers, as organizational records clearly demonstrate. These women used the attention focused on them to create a space in which to bargain for care and support that more closely met their own values and needs. Poor women, both black and white, often defined their lives in ways similar to each other during their dealings with social workers and public health nurses. These definitions contradicted the evaluations of social workers and friendly visitors, who often overlooked the expressions of autonomy and definitions of family and work advanced by their clients. This fissure highlights the class stratification between middle-class reformers and poor women, a social distance de-emphasized by relief agencies in the descriptions of poor women but readily apparent in the daily dealings of social workers and their clients.

Aiding the Poor

PRIOR TO 1900, only a few Atlanta organizations aided the poor, and even fewer dealt specifically or significantly with working-class women. Those that did provide substantial aid to women included the Home for the Friendless, which took in destitute women's children; the Florence Crittenton Home, which housed unwed pregnant women; and Grady Hospital, which provided health care, including gynecological and obstetric services, for the indigent. These institutions opened their doors in the late nineteenth century, and by the early twentieth century they formed the core of the city's charitable work.[8] The agencies that appeared in the early 1900s incorporated and expanded on the groundwork laid by these earlier organizations.

Aside from the citywide Associated Charities, a host of religious and benevolent agencies emerged in the first decade of the twentieth century to provide direct relief and other types of assistance (groceries, clothing, rent and fuel vouchers, and so forth) to certain neighborhoods and groups within the city. The poor of Atlanta's Jewish community secured assistance from the Federation of Jewish Charities, founded in 1906, and the Jewish Education Alliance, chartered in 1909.[9] Textile workers in the mill villages in and around the city could turn to settlement houses run by the Methodist women of the Board of City Missions. Along with a host of other programs, these Wesley Houses provided food, fuel, child care, and rent money to destitute community members.[10] Some African Americans received aid from the city warden's office or other citywide charities, but the bulk of the assistance this community received came from churches, such as Big Bethel and First Congregational, and similar institutions, such as the Neighborhood Union, supported by local middle-class African Americans.[11]

A few public institutions aided private social welfare agencies in their efforts. Beyond prisons and similar institutions, virtually no state or county programs supported indigent residents. The city, however, did sponsor limited work with the needy through the city warden's office, the police department, and court system. The city warden provided food and fuel to people of both races who needed only basic economic assistance. This office worked closely with private agencies, often providing direct relief to clients they recommended, though the warden's relationship with its private counterparts often proved adversarial. The Associated Charities, for instance, repeatedly complained that the city warden gave out relief indiscriminately, without first checking to see if applicants were receiving assistance from other agencies. Joseph Logan, head of the Associated Charities, concluded that the city warden's methods displayed a "serious lack of appreciation of almost universally accepted methods of charitable relief."[12] As Atlanta's largest welfare organization, the Associated Charities used such attacks to bolster its already powerful position. The organization wanted to control public funds earmarked for welfare and expected the warden's office to bow to the Associated Charities' "scientific" procedures.

The police department and local court system also functioned as an integral part of the larger network that aided and "rescued" the poor, particularly women. Mounted police investigated relief applicants for the city warden.[13] Police also commonly took women into custody, sometimes without formally arresting them, as a means of removing them from the street. Arrested women who did go to court faced Judge Nash Broyles, who had a reputation for meting out large doses of moralizing advice along with his rulings.[14] Others did not go to court but were released to a private agency, usually the Associated Charities, that would find them housing and work or return them to their families.[15] Common were stories like those of Tommie Hall and Ollie Jones. According to newspaper accounts, Hall, age nineteen, had come to Atlanta to marry her boyfriend and brought Jones along. The boyfriend left them in a Decatur Street boardinghouse, where the police found them and took them into custody. The police held the women until their families sent instructions about what to do with them.[16]

The police often provided the initial intervention that brought poor women into the social welfare system, a function the police did not fulfill for men. Women who were charged and appeared in Recorder's Court were often released to probation officers who worked for private organizations. Between 1913 and 1915 the Men and Religion Forward Movement (a private organization that also ran a home for former prostitutes) hired a woman to act as probation officer for women released from the Recorder's Court. This woman kept track of probationers, often arranging living spaces and employment for them as well as reporting legal and moral violations committed while on probation. This probation work also included trips to the city stockade to visit female prisoners and providing aid to women whose husbands were imprisoned. In 1914, funds were raised to hire a black probation officer to perform essentially the same work with arrested African American women.[17]

This network of private and public agencies had a widespread impact on the lives of the city's poor women in particular, influencing everything from their living situations and family structures to diet and health care. Organizations often shared staff, case files, and resources, but more importantly, they shared a vision of welfare that brought women to the forefront of discussions of poverty. The progressive elements of Atlanta's middle classes that drove the development of a social welfare network feared the disintegration of the working-class family and chose to address these perceived threats through poor mothers. While none of these organizations claimed to help poor women exclusively, the policies and practices developed over the first two decades of the century did almost that. As agencies' case files, reports, and committee meetings readily reveal, reformers channeled their interest in children, fathers, and the family as a social unit through interactions with women in three main ways: the means of determining need, the giving of relief, and the programs and policies agencies supported to better the lives of the city's poorest residents.

Private welfare agencies, with the assistance of public institutions, generally relied on the home visit as the primary means for reaching and aiding the city's poor. Through this procedure, social workers evaluated potential clients and surveyed homes for cleanliness, morality, and needs before providing any material relief. Social workers, visiting nurses, and volunteers conducted interviews with the women who kept these homes. Based on these women and the physical evidence present in the living space (for which the women were usually responsible), decisions were made about financial and medical support. Betty Lewis went to the Associated Charities in early 1907, requesting patent medicines for her mother and offering to pay for the supplies in washings. Following agency policy, the caseworker sent the girl home to await her visit to the family's house the next day. After meeting with the mother, the case worker determined there was no pressing need in the household and offered no material support to the family. Her report of the visit states that she found the house in "decent order," and Mrs. Lewis stated that the rent was paid regularly.[18] In this case, a well-kept home worked against the Lewises' request for aid; in other instances, however, orderliness was the prerequisite for receiving aid. Families were often accepted as clients only after reformers reported, "They have conditions as to tidiness and care, showed some good traits in woman upon visitor."[19]

The Methodist women who ran the Wesley Settlement House at the Fulton Bag and Cotton Mills also placed particular importance on visiting the homes of petitioners for aid. These encounters rarely embodied the objective tone promoted by "scientific" organizations such as the Associated Charities. One Wesley House worker reported after a visit to a needy mother, "The woman was not living right. I tried to show her there was a way of escape for her. I read the Bible to her, I prayed with her, I talked with her and tried to get her to give up her sinful life so she could keep her children with her." In the end, the visitor offered this woman no material aid and instead had the children remanded to the Georgia Industrial Home in Macon "where the mother could not easily reach them."[20]

Almost all varieties of direct support offered by these agencies and institutions to both black and white women depended on working-class women's efforts to translate that support into "the actual giving of nurture."[21] From the Associated Charities, women most often received aid in the form of grocery and fuel orders that then had to be filled at particular stores. Agencies offered poor women used clothing, much of which had to be repaired and altered for the family's use. Before the 1920s, women usually took on the role of seeking aid from local organizations, which often meant a trip downtown and then a lengthy wait in an office, only to be sent home to wait for a social worker's visit before relief would be approved. In cases of both poverty and disease, the welfare workers depended on the work of women in the home and as family caretakers to bring destitute families to the agency's attention as well as to carry out reformers' and doctors' instructions.

The practice of distributing direct relief in Atlanta, then, translated into a focus on women—as caretakers of the home and providers of most home-based services—as a means of reaching the larger working-class community. While creating a direct link between social workers and poor women that often allowed these women to advance their own demands, this direct assistance also required great amounts of work on their part. Nancy Fraser also cautions against finding this situation empowering for poor women: "A significant portion of their benefits is 'in kind,' " she writes, "and what cash they receive comes already carved up and earmarked for specific, administratively designated purposes. These recipients are therefore essentially *clients,* a subject-position that carries far less power and dignity in capitalist societies than does the alternative position of purchaser."[22] However, despite the work required and restrictions on use, food and coal orders did place the form of support firmly in the realm of women, so the women controlled the distribution of aid to family members. Poor women actively sought this aid and often worked hard to meet social workers' expectations to continue to receive relief.

Following the turn of the century, the social welfare network offered other forms of assistance beyond direct relief to Atlanta's poor. Like direct relief, though, these programs brought social workers into contact with poor women, most but by no means all of whom were mothers. In some ways, these forms of aid benefited working-class women even more substantially than aid given through home visits. Poor women used programs such as day nurseries and night schools to maintain a sense of self-sufficiency, which they often had to modify to receive direct relief as well as improve skills and take advantage of opportunities for wage work.

Between 1890 and 1920, day nurseries were established across the city to care for the children of working mothers, both African American and white. The reformers who ran these programs demonstrated a keen understanding that divorced, widowed, deserted, and never-married mothers "have no real income and they must work for the necessities of life for themselves and their children."[23] The Sheltering Arms Association operated six day nurseries in and around Atlanta that catered to the white children of "worthy working mothers," teaching both "some of the valuable lessons of regularity, punctuality and cleanliness . . . and interest in and kindness to others, love of nature and God indirectly taught by the various plans in the kindergarten during the year."[24] The Gate City Free Kindergarten, organized in 1905, consisted of five free nurseries operated in various black neighborhoods.[25] Both the First Congregational Church of Atlanta and the Neighborhood Union also operated day nurseries for the children of African American mothers as part of a larger set of programs designed to aid the black working poor. The Woman's Board of City Missions ran similar nurseries for whites in mill villages. Much of this work was encouraged by the mill owners, since women tended to be more consistent workers when they did not have to worry about their children's well-being.

While mothers were required to pay only a small fee for the child care offered by these nurseries, the women usually had to meet rigorous standards of morality and hygiene. Not surprisingly, then, many working-class women did not find these arrangements favorable. A Wesley House kindergarten teacher reported the following response when trying to enroll children from the mill community: "One mother said she could not be washing and scrubbing all the time to keep her children clean to send to that kindergarten, where they only kept them half a day and turned them out at 12 o'clock to wallow in the dirt the balance of the day, she did not see that they could learn them much in three hours, why did they not keep them all day?"[26] In part, these institutions allowed middle-class reformers and social workers to assert motherhood as a science and revalue it as a full-time and exacting job. Day nurseries and free kindergartens institutionalized support for women who were the economic providers for their families, but the importance of motherhood was reinforced when civil society's resources were used to fulfill the role of mother only under circumstances that forced biological mothers out of the home. Despite disagreements over how to care for children, day nurseries brought together middle-class reformers and working-class mothers through shared assumptions about the necessity of children being mothered (as opposed to being left alone while the female parent worked), momentarily suspending class differences and supporting working-class women in their efforts toward economic self-sufficiency.

Educational, recreational, and health care programs were also frequently a part of the assistance offered by Atlanta's social welfare network. In addition to running a day care program, for example, the First Congregational Church of Atlanta operated a community center that housed an auditorium, a library, a gymnasium, a kitchen, and showers. The church also offered cooking and business classes for African American women. [27] The Neighborhood Union, founded in 1908 by Lugenia Burns Hope and other elite black women in the community surrounding Atlanta University, operated a settlement house that offered a health clinic, mothers' meetings, and industrial training and cooking classes. [28] The lines between civic organization and social welfare agency blurred in the work of the Neighborhood Union. In addition to running community-oriented recreation and educational programs, the organization advocated for improved city services in African American neighborhoods, including better lighting, sanitation, police protection, and schools. The Neighborhood Union was unique in that it approached clients as part of a community, encouraging them to aid their neighbors before letting them turn to charity, but the organization also followed the general pattern of the city's social welfare network in focusing substantially on mothers.

The three settlement houses run by Methodist women in white mill communities combined home visiting and direct relief with programs that included a kindergarten, night school, club meetings for mill workers, mutual aid societies, and health clinics and medical dispensaries. Open daily at the settlement houses were a library and penny savings club. Monday through Saturday the houses provided a day nursery, kindergarten, and dinners for mothers. On Mondays, there was a clinic for children, gym classes for boys, and showers. On Tuesdays, the night school met. On Wednesdays, the children's clinic was again open, and meetings were held for the Happy Afternoon Club (a young women's group), the House Council, and the night school. On Fridays, the Woman's Club met, as did the Fulton Mutual Aid Society and other social clubs. Saturdays were filled with clothing sales, sewing school, girls' gym, and more open shower time. [29] While direct relief took up many of the resources of the city's welfare agencies, most also included in their work educational and recreation programs designed to uplift and moralize Atlanta's poor while attending to their physical needs.

Prior to the 1920s, the city's welfare network generally filtered aid through mothers, but some support was also offered to young, single working-class women as the future mothers of the city's working classes. Direct aid usually came in the form of new living options and educational programs. Around the turn of the century, more and more young women migrated to Atlanta without families, and there was a critical lack of housing for these workers. Many took up residence in the boardinghouses that sprang up around downtown and the mill districts. Others found room and board in homes built by reform and benevolent organizations—the Young Women's Christian Association, the Churches Business Home for Girls, the First Congregational Church, and the Men and Religion Forward Movement. Social welfare agencies and civic organizations from both races also created numerous small night schools and training programs for women, particularly in the 1910s. Courses ranged from mothering and nursing classes for married women to industrial, craft, and business courses for single women looking to improve their employment opportunities. In 1910, the Night School for Girls opened after a number of working-class women convinced an Associated Charities visitor that they "were anxious for an education, but had no way to get it."[30] Run by the Woman's Exchange, a white middle-class club, the Night School for Girls offered segregated courses in basic English and other subjects to women of both races. The school was scheduled to receive women directly from work and to end class shortly before the 9:00 P.M. streetcars left downtown. Students arrived while it was still daylight and made their way home after dark in groups. A free supper was also furnished to all who attended class. The Night School for Girls, like many similar programs in the city, offered a convenient place for working-class women to meet and socialize, and a free meal could help women stretch small budgets.

Legal aid offered by the Associated Charities and affiliated organizations and legislative campaigns supported by Atlanta's welfare organizations also reflect an intense focus on working-class women. Many of the women found by social workers had been abused and deserted. Caseworkers, especially those from the Associated Charities, encouraged and helped secure divorces if such action would improve conditions for the mothers and children. In situations where husbands had deserted or contributed only irregularly to the family, the Associated Charities helped women sue for alimony. A case that demonstrated the agency's willingness to use the court system on behalf of women involved a morphine-addicted husband and a destitute wife. The Associated Charities "tried several plans to keep the family together, but finally ordered the man arrested for vagrancy." The case history triumphantly reported that, after receiving treatment, the man could again support his family and was grateful for the agency's intervention.[31] By the 1910s, the Associated Charities had also worked to create other legislation supporting strong working-class women in family relationships. In conjunction with other civic and state groups, the organization fought to raise the age of sexual consent for girls. The Associated Charities also supported the passage of a liberalized divorce code that would expand the grounds for granting divorce, making it easier for women to extricate themselves from nonsupporting husbands. Finally, the 1919 "Wife Desertion Bill" also received the support of welfare workers who understood "the serious burden of deserting and non-supporting husbands on societies like ours and on the charitable people of Atlanta generally."[32]

Despite prizing the role of mother for working-class women, most of the charity and assistance agencies in Atlanta also became quite active in training women and securing employment for them when no male breadwinner could support the family. One white woman with a sick husband and no income borrowed a small sum of money to buy supplies so she could take in washing, a job that would allow her to care for her husband while earning money. In recording this woman's case history, the Associated Charities social worker noted with pride that her client had proved worthy of the assistance she had received: "Her husband finally died, but the wife paid back the forty dollars."[33] Since many of Atlanta's social workers hoped to prod poor women into adopting a strong work ethic that would encourage them to sacrifice for their children, this woman received praise for repaying the money she had borrowed. Typical of welfare agency policy, she was encouraged to support her family through a gender-specific occupation. Other agencies ran educational programs that trained women for employment in clerical and domestic trades. Black churches, such as the First Congregational Church of Atlanta and Big Bethel AME, the YWCA, and several of the boardinghouses for young women also served as employment bureaus for their clients. In some instances, however, this support of women's employment crossed the line of helpfulness into coercion. In cases where women without male breadwinners proved reluctant or unwilling to work, agencies often removed children from the home until the women would work steadily and support their families without assistance.[34]

Working the System

WITH THE EFFORTS of social welfare agencies, both public and private, focused so keenly on them, poor women often found a means for expressing their needs and desires. Social workers and reformers complained of the incessant demands from female clients. Stories of women who asserted themselves during the relief process rarely appeared in annual reports or newspaper accounts, but such tales pepper relief agencies' private records. Less-than-compliant women undermined social welfare organizations' image of professionalism and authority by refusing to defer to social workers on issues related to home, work, family, or health. Poor women of both races often articulated in no uncertain terms what they expected from relief agencies. Social workers commonly found their clients to be "stubborn and felt that rather than do something she didn't want to do it was the duty of the public to supplement her wages to meet family expenses."[35]

Demands for aid ranged from requests for specific jobs to new housing. When one woman approached the Associated Charities for assistance in finding a rental home, she specified that she needed a house in which she could take in washing, sell lunches and drinks to railroad men, and be near her friends.[36] One of clients' most successful means for obtaining desired relief was playing agencies off one another. Social welfare agencies complained bitterly about this practice and worked hard to eliminate it, but poor women still found it a useful way of meeting their needs. Georgia Moore requested aid from both the Associated Charities and the North Avenue Presbyterian Church on the same day. She told each organization that the other had refused her aid and that she "did not have anything at the house to eat." Even though the organizations discovered her duplicity, the Associated Charities issued her a grocery order in the amount of $2.50.[37] The Associated Charities found contrary clients to be an almost constant presence on their relief rolls. The agency understood that "a few of them do not come to us anymore because we will not aid them in the way they *wish* to be aided."[38]

While not all poor women were successful in their quests for material and medical aid, they employed similar strategies in making their demands. In many cases women flatly refused social workers' advice and promises of aid. At other times, women threw demands back at the social workers or made false promises. Mrs. Allen, for example, reported that her tuberculosis was not worsening and did not require more treatment. Instead, she insisted that the visiting nurse supply her with something to "relieve her back" and bring her a new hat. The nurse ignored Allen's requests. Believing she still needed treatment for her TB, however, the nurse did bring milk and eggs, recommended for the diets of tubercular patients and valuable commodities in their own right.[39] Jennie Lewis repeatedly demanded and received rent money from the Associated Charities by promising to look for a cheaper rental. She avoided her social worker at times by sending her children to make requests. The exasperated social worker finally found a less expensive house for the family with the aid of Lewis's daughter.[40] Women also commonly lied about their other means of support, including relief from other agencies, gifts from relatives, and income from wage work or taking in boarders. Interestingly, these techniques seem to have varied little across racial lines: black and white women alike were vocal and active in articulating their needs. Whatever strategy women employed, it appears that few of them were docile vessels for the lessons and lifestyles advocated by Atlanta's social workers.

While most women's demands involved material support in the form of food, shelter, or medical treatment, working-class women could also be quite vocal in their desire to maintain dignity and respectability or to defend their families. In the mill villages, women were often reluctant to send their children to the day nursery, fearing it "was only a trick to get their children away from them and give them away or put them in homes."[41] Indeed, this theme appeared prominently in female mill workers' testimony before government investigators during the 1914 strike at the Fulton Bag and Cotton Mills. Some women refused assistance and resented the intrusion of presumptuous social workers. When an agency sent a social worker to visit a woman purported to be in need, the visitor reported that the woman "seemed outraged at my visit, and said to please tell . . . anyone else interested she was not in need, and did not care for a visitor of the Associated Charities to be coming to her house," with the neighbors watching.[42] When advising a group of church women on Anti-Tuberculosis Association clients they might visit, Secretary Rosa Lowe cautioned that one client in particular, Mrs. LeRoy, was "very sensitive, and if the ladies visit her it will be necessary to bear that in mind and not allow her to know that her name was suggested by this office." Mrs. LeRoy apparently was "very proud and wants to pay for everything that she gets," and the visitors were instructed to help LeRoy maintain her dignity by letting the woman read their palms in exchange for any assistance offered.[43] Social workers generally appeared surprised at their clients' desire for secrecy or control over the relief process, but as was the case with LeRoy, the agencies encouraged working-class mothers' attempts to retain dignity by respecting their wishes for privacy and reciprocity.

Welfare and Social Order

POOR WOMEN'S INVOLVEMENT in the development of Atlanta's social welfare network ran deeper than the programs directed at these women and the relief they received. Charity and benevolent agencies' heightened focus on working-class women's bodies and lives reveals anxieties prevalent in the city shortly after the turn of the century. These agencies' practices and policies functioned in concrete ways to maintain women in stable family relationships (at least to their children, if not to their husbands), to encourage women in accepted occupations, and to create morally safe living spaces. The increased welfare activity during the Progressive era also assured "the maintenance and reproduction of the working class," according to Mimi Abramovitz, by providing an alternative to women's employment since typical "low pay, long hours, and poor working conditions not only diminished women's physical capacity at work but risked interfering with reproduction."[44] The client images that white reform agencies promoted, however, also sought to maintain the ideological structures that supported a stable social order while garnering support for social work and the professionalization of the field. In contrast, black benevolent and civic associations and the women who sought assistance produced competing sets of images and, therefore, competing understandings of social order.

White-run social welfare and reform agencies turned individual case studies and generalizations about working-class women into cultural symbols. These images reinforced gender, racial, and class hierarchies in which white women functioned primarily as mothers and black women were primarily workers. Both roles also reinforced positions of dependency for women. Motherhood placed women in a dependent family relationship that required a breadwinner (either the husband or welfare agencies) to provide the material necessities of life.[45] White agencies positioned black women as servants and as dependent on or at least controlled by their white employers. The promotion of these images, in turn, reinforced an obscured script in which white men functioned as workers and black men were rendered essentially useless or even irrelevant to black families. While U.S. welfare systems encouraged male individualism primarily through employment programs, welfare methods actively cultivated dependency for white women and paternalism to govern African American women.[46]

The Associated Charities led the way in deploying images of white women as mothers, but it was not alone. The executive committee of the Wesley Settlement House at the Fulton Bag and Cotton Mills, for example, was furious when it learned "the mill was sending children to Day Nursery who had fathers to support" them instead of encouraging "the mother [to] stay at home and care for" the children.[47] Despite the assistance many organizations offered women in securing employment, social workers understood wage work to be an option for white women only in cases of absent or nonsupporting husbands. Consequently, social workers quickly withdrew the resources that supported women's wage work if they believed that individual women had the ability to stay home and care for their children. As historian Linda Gordon has noted, however, the definition of which women could afford to stay home often differed according to race.[48] White reformers were more likely to encourage and even force white married women to stay home, while black clients were encouraged to work. In Atlanta, however, many social workers so feared that direct relief would demoralize the poor that they encouraged white women's paid employment over long-term material support as long as the job was in a gender-specific occupation such as sewing or laundry work.

The images of white women recorded in organizational case studies tended to reinforce the fine line between danger and protection that mothers represented. A mother who was honest, moral, and hardworking could ensure a bright future for her family. A woman who did not embody these qualities could easily destroy her family. While many cases of the latter type were discussed at board meetings and among social workers, only the more positive images of women struggling to keep their families together generally appeared in annual reports and newspaper articles produced by the organization. Not surprisingly, the organization chose to publicize models of client compliance and what social workers deemed desirable working-class respectability. Typical was the case of an immigrant couple and their three children that the Associated Charities labeled as "pitiful." As the case history explained, "The man was a good workman but he did not earn enough to employ a servant, and the woman almost literally crawled around the house doing her work and caring for the children."[49]

As was common in the Associated Charities publicity, the 1910 annual report alternately described female clients as "honest and industrious" or "industrious and a good mother."[50] Virtually all black women with whom the agency dealt (a very small number before 1917) and white women who did not at least appear to put motherhood first in their lives received no such praise. The agency applied negative images to women who surrendered their children to the care of others, exploited their children by allowing them to beg or to work for wages, or neglected their children because of alcoholism or other vices. One settlement worker reported a new mother, deserted by her husband, had asked to have her baby placed in an orphanage. The appalled visitor replied that "there were many mothers who made their living with many more little children and never think of giving them away."[51] In another case, the Associated Charities convinced the Juvenile Court to remove the children of one woman who "did not scruple to send them out to beg on the streets when the meal got low in the bag."[52] Also reinforcing the controlling and stabilizing effects of motherhood as a primary role for working-class white women was the portrayal of single women as potential infectors of "our young men with the diseases of the street."[53] In these notions of danger, the lines blurred between women adrift and mothers who did not meet middle-class standards.

Social workers and reformers promoted the image of women as the key to a family's survival; men appear only peripherally in these stories. This may result in part from the practice of case workers using the home as the site of intervention, evaluation, and assistance. Mothers then became the brokers through which welfare agencies reached other family members. Case histories ranged from the deserted wife who "with true mother instinct" worked to support her three tubercular children to a woman who, with the help of the Associated Charities, moved her family to a farm that she worked single-handedly so that she could care for her sick husband and two children.[54] In 1916 the city warden stressed the economic significance of working mothers to family survival, reporting that "there are generally two and more [children] in the average family and it is estimated that women workers in industrial lines will lose ⅕ of their time from employment, from sickness or other causes, it will thus be seen that there is bound to be a deficit in the family's living."[55]

Two dominant messages were imbedded in the case studies distributed by

Atlanta social welfare agencies in local newspapers and annual reports prior to
World War I. First, the city's more prosperous residents were called on to hear
the "constant cry for help . . . from the hearts of women and children" and to
act on a sense of duty by contributing to the organized relief of the poor. Because
working-class women were so frequently used to promote this message, their
images became a symbol for middle-class civic duty toward the less fortunate.
Second, the message aimed at the laboring classes of the city was industriousness.
These case studies reminded wage laborers and their families that only hard
work stood between them and absolute poverty. This message also targeted the
women of poor families, sanctioning their wage work as the last bulwark between
respectable poverty and destitution and immorality.

In the name of protecting and encouraging this kind of proper, self-sacrificing
motherhood and what Abramovitz has referred to as the "family ethic," reformers
justified their intervention into poor women's lives. This ethic cast women as
homemakers, consumers, and caretakers, becoming "the basis for distinguishing
between deserving and undeserving women" and "helping to meet the economy's
need for women's unpaid labor in the home and . . . low-paid labor in the market."[56] One of the most notorious proclamations on the position of working-class
women in society appeared in the Supreme Court's 1908 decision in *Muller vs.
Oregon.* Justice Louis D. Brandeis reinforced public viewing and intervention
in the lives of poor women when he wrote, "as healthy mothers are essential
to vigorous offspring, the physical well-being of a woman becomes an object of
public interest and care in order to preserve the strength and vigor of the race."[57]

Beyond brokering images of working-class women distributed to the city at
large, the relationship of poor women to the social welfare network also reinforced
social and economic class relations. As new, usually poor migrants poured into
the city after the turn of the century, social distance between classes was in part
maintained by the activities of social welfare agencies in working-class neighborhoods. The predominance of private agencies that relied heavily on volunteers
from the city's middle class and the invocation of civic duty as a reason to aid
the poor reinforced class lines. Both the middle class and the organized labor
community were encouraged to contribute to welfare work. By invoking this sense
of duty, however, welfare agencies allowed these groups to presume themselves
distant and safe from the forces that brought the destitute into a state of poverty.[58]
Social workers never meant for the respectability they encouraged in their poor
clients to erase class distinctions and privileges, and the messages to charitable
donors repeatedly communicated this point.

Social workers encouraged respectable poverty by pushing the needy, especially women, into wage work. In seeking to remove women from the city's relief
rolls, social workers often had to support women in searching and training for

work. The types of wage work encouraged by these agencies, however, was telling. The few black women with whom white welfare organizations dealt were uniformly pushed into domestic work, either in the homes of whites or in laundries. White women were also encouraged in these professions. The Martha's Home, which housed reforming prostitutes and women on probation, regularly received and fulfilled middle-class families' requests for white servants, for example. Settlement houses and some churches also taught women sewing in hopes of outfitting them to work as seamstresses, an occupation that would allow them to remain in their homes and care for their children. As the demand for clerical workers grew in the 1910s and 1920s, agencies such as the Associated Charities increasingly supported young, single women while they attended business school to qualify for these occupations.

The dealings of visiting social workers with poor women rewarded evidence of respectability while punishing those clients whom welfare agents felt were too ostentatious in their living conditions, dress, or actions, although acceptable behavior was rarely explicitly defined. Social workers expected poor white women to dedicate themselves to the maintenance of their families without resorting to begging, prostitution, or other illicit or suspect behavior. Day nursery workers, for example, investigated all mothers who requested child care through an "interview with the mother at the nursery, a visit to the home . . . and consultation with other agencies knowing [if] the family is desirable." These workers hoped to offer "the constructive service which the poor may properly expect" after determining the "true" reason why the mother could not care for the children.[59] Social workers took great pride in finding that families with whom they had worked had become able to provide for themselves. One teacher from an industrial school that worked with mill girls reflected, "After eight years of constant labor in these schools I began to see improvement. Many of the girls, now grown up, are making their living sewing, some have married and are sewing for their own little family. Many have come in to the church and Sunday school, and are living good and useful lives."[60]

Social workers rarely hid their contempt for poor white women who did not share middle-class notions of respectability. Early in its existence the Associated Charities stated its unwillingness to help those deemed to be living beyond the means of their station, like the young woman who "dressed better than her hardworking neighbors" or the family that "had ice cream every other day in the summer."[61] The antagonism that existed between private welfare organizations and the city warden's office hinged, in part, on this issue. Led by the Associated Charities, private agencies critiqued the warden for giving aid indiscriminately to all those who applied, claiming that "material gifts alone, instead of helping others to help themselves, . . . have resulted in maintaining many people in misery of body and soul."[62] The warden's relief efforts also undermined private organizations' decisions by providing assistance to families who had refused to restructure their lives according to social workers' recommendations. [63]

The distance social workers enforced between themselves and their clients was often most evident in the language of pity and contempt employed in case studies. Caseworkers described female clients as "lazy," "heart broken," and "feeble-minded." [64] A Wesley House worker considered her clients "ignorant of the details of any life different from their own, unacquainted with the usual comforts and pleasures that may belong to any one and above all they were contented to live in filth, endure ill-health and suffered for a wholesome, social and spiritual expression." [65] Social workers' sympathy for and desire to assist the impoverished were embedded in language that reinforced social aspects of economic class divisions.

Racial Uplift

ATLANTA'S black benevolent and civic organizations participated in this larger process, offering much of the same moralizing assistance to the poor while promoting images of African American women as mothers. The descriptions that appear in the records of these organizations are at times remarkably similar in tone, language, and content to the descriptions of white mothers created by the white social workers. Both white welfare agencies and black organizations reinforced a specifically gendered social order by endorsing the role of motherhood while maintaining distinctions in class between reformers and clients. The images produced by black agencies, however, also promoted a political strategy designed to improve race relations and based on the ideologies of racial uplift and respectability. [66]

Founded in 1908, just two years after the city's race riot, the Neighborhood Union quickly became the most active black organization waging this struggle and promoting poor black women in their role as mothers. Even the story of the founding of this group used the image of women as the caretakers of the family to justify the necessity of the organization. This often-invoked story focuses on a woman whom neighbors often saw but did not know. She usually sat on her porch in the afternoon, and after not seeing her for a several days, neighbors went to investigate. They found her critically ill, but it was too late to do anything for her, and she died shortly thereafter, leaving three children. On hearing this story, Lugenia Burns Hope called together other elite black women in the neighborhood to form an organization to "build the sort of ethnic pride that would take delight in constructive citizenship and happy family life" and would not allow neighbors to grow ill without anyone noticing. [67] The organization quickly grew strength and scope until it was, in the words of one historian, "the strongest and most visible community-controlled agency for Blacks in Atlanta." [68]

The Neighborhood Union's programs included mother's meetings, free clinics, recreational activities, and classes in nursing, home hygiene, sewing, and cooking. While many of these programs appear to resemble those run by other social welfare agencies, this organization did not embrace the standard social worker–client relationship. Although run by elite black women, the Neighborhood Union also incorporated working-class women into its organizational structure. Drawing from both the middle and working classes, "a woman was appointed to visit each home, acquaint the people with the plan for the neighborhood improvement and solicit their cooperation. So willing were they to cooperate that the neighborhood improved very rapidly."[69] In this sense, the Neighborhood Union functioned as a civic organization even though many of its programs were designed to provide relief to impoverished neighborhood residents.[70] Working-class and elite black women of the Neighborhood Union, however, never met on entirely equal ground.

Neighborhood Union organizers sought to "elevate the moral, social, intellectual, and spiritual standards of each neighborhood" as a means of both improving the community in which these women lived and earning the cooperation and respect of white communities.[71] Just as white relief agencies understood poor white women to be the key to family survival, the Neighborhood Union emphasized black working-class women as critical to community improvement in African American neighborhoods. Neighborhood Union workers hoped to rally the forces of "purity, virility and aspiration of the home" against the "problems of disease, vice, crime and inefficiency, if the Negro race is ever to solve its own problems."[72] Consequently, most of the organization's efforts were directed toward the caretakers of these homes, African American mothers.[73] Programs encouraged cleanliness, efficiency, and morality, values that middle-class reformers hoped mothers would pass on to their children. Understanding that "the parents of these children are poor but hard working people—[standing] over the wash tub all day and the ironing board most of the night," the Neighborhood Union also offered material relief and child care to weary mothers. Organizers unabashedly equated money with morals and offered direct assistance to protect the latter in poor families whenever possible.[74] In black reformers' minds, poverty did not exempt one from moral striving, but material resources made achieving or maintaining respectability far more likely.

Like other voluntary organizations, the Neighborhood Union promoted its work through newspaper accounts and annual reports. Case histories and reports of the Union's work prominently featured accounts of selfless women striving to save their families and consequently improving the neighborhood and the race. A 1916 case that received much promotion involved three women and eleven children living in one house. Reportedly, the women set to "cleaning, airing, and burning of rubbish as you had never seen before," when they learned that the

Neighborhood Union was going to call on them. Neighborhood Union workers looked sympathetically on this group because one of the women had "rescued these two other women from adulterous lives" and helped them improve the sanitary conditions of their living arrangements. [75]

As Deborah Gray White persuasively argues, however, the cost of a focus on morality was a widening of class divisions. In White's words, middle-class black women "opened a gulf between a small circle of club leaders and the masses" by insisting that most black women lacked moral character as a result of the sexual exploitation suffered during slavery. [76] The elite black women of the Neighborhood Union reinforced and at times actively cultivated this gulf. The organization may have taken the necessity of women's wage work for granted and instead promoted motherhood as African American women's primary role, but this did not mean that they saw working-class women as social equals. Elite members, for example, blended descriptions of training children "to be little helpers in their own homes" with similarly diminutive references to "little housekeepers' clubs" and "little mothers' leagues." [77] While black neighborhoods, especially those surrounding black colleges, were more socioeconomically mixed than were white areas, social distance between classes remained an important component of racial uplift ideology because the black elite, as Kevin Gaines notes, used clear distinctions between classes, as well as "the very existence of a 'better class' of blacks, as evidence of what they called race progress." [78]

Class superiority and an emphasis on morality consistently colored the Neighborhood Union's commitment to promoting black respectability through motherhood. The Union even incorporated its ideals of motherhood and homemaking into a favorite fund-raising event, the carnival. The homes of working-class women were opened up to the whole community to display proper housework techniques, wholesome entertainments, and appropriate play, institutionalizing the kind of observant neighborliness the Union practiced and encouraged on a daily basis. Peter Stallybras and Allon White suggest that fairs and similar events functioned as sites at which discourses and tastes were shaped, relaying the values of the center to other groups. [79] In the case of the Neighborhood Union, the carnivals contained highly scripted portrayals of the ideal community valued by the organization. These carnivals provided a space for poor women to try on middle-class respectability, if only for a day. In most cases, the Neighborhood Union provided appropriate furniture for the homes and clothing for the women on display, as well as assistance in cleaning and organizing, for which many working-class women would not regularly have had time. In one extraordinary case, a poor woman who desperately wanted to participate in the carnival was "loaned" the husband of a Neighborhood Union organizer. The woman could then open her home as a "Health House" since her "husband" was a dentist. [80] Appearances mattered to elite blacks in the 1900s and 1910s, and carnival organizers hoped that looking respectable would lead working-class blacks to be respectable. Almost more important, however, would be to have that respectability noticed by the city's white community.

The connection in racial uplift ideologies between morality and the physical environment meant that the Neighborhood Union often sought to raise moral standards by altering the physical state of black neighborhoods.[81] In the 1910s, the Neighborhood Union began annual "Clean-Up Campaigns" that soon became a citywide movement in black areas. Efforts focused on removing rubbish from under and around homes; scrubbing floors, walls, and windows; and transporting sick residents to clinics and hospitals for treatment.[82] As with direct relief, much of the responsibility for this clean-up work fell to mothers. During this intense weeklong campaign every spring, as well as in classes offered by the Neighborhood Union, women were pressured to change their housekeeping standards and practices, reinforcing the Union's long-standing belief that moral status could be judged by "the general external appearance of the several communities and their inhabitants."[83] Neighborhood Union members took great pride in the success of these campaigns as well as in the National Silver Cup the National Negro Business League awarded the Union for its efforts in the 1910s.[84] This claim to success provided ample validation of the significant difference made by the Neighborhood Union's work. Changing the physical state of black communities supported the organization's arguments about also changing the moral atmosphere. Neighborhood Union workers received some acknowledgment of their success from the white press and from white-run organizations that instituted similar clean-up programs on the other side of the color line.

In trying to raise moral standards, Neighborhood Union workers did not hesitate to attack women who refused to fit the model promoted in reformers' middle-class conceptualization of motherhood and neighborhood. The organization's earliest records include requests to the city council and the police department for the removal of specific women and families. The Neighborhood Union justified its actions by arguing, "We were not helping our neighbor when we failed to tell the mother of the evil company her daughter was keeping while she was away trying to make a living. Blind tigers, houses of ill repute, dance halls, and loud and disturbing gatherings are among the cases which come before the Union frequently." Members found support for these campaigns among many in the white community, reporting, "The police department has backed us when we have called on them. They say they are glad to assist us in our efforts to have a clean community."[85] District directors were encouraged to report neighbors believed unable to reform. In most cases, the reports list the reason for undesirability as questionable character. Once again, prostitutes (who were portrayed as single women) and prostitution were positioned in opposition to mothers and motherhood.

The black middle class appears to have been more sympathetic than white reformers to the demands placed on working-class women. "It is a daily experience," noted Atlanta University researchers in 1897, "to find a child of tender years left to tend the baby with but a scant meal of meat and bread, while the widowed mother is out at work, who returns at night tired and exhausted to feed and care for the children. Such a state of constant activity exhausts her vital force and she dies at an early age leaving little children in the hands of chance, to be brought up among the weeds of vice and sin."[86] Despite this empathy, however, the end result of the moral degradation of those who should be under her care remained the mother's responsibility.

In promoting working-class black women as mothers, Neighborhood Union organizers not only created a competing narrative to that promoted by the primarily white social welfare and public health movements but also furthered a vision of social order for the black community. This vision included a strong sense of mutual cooperation among a community of moral and law-abiding families. Consequently, motherhood meant more than caring for one's own family. The Neighborhood Union encouraged a kind of community mothering, accepting that because most parents worked for wages, the whole neighborhood took responsibility for all the children and made the neighborhood safe in the way a mother would make a home safe.

This enlarged conception of motherhood also provided a justification for the expanding role many elite black women claimed for themselves and helped them to establish their race leadership relative to men.[87] Black women, like their white counterparts, argued under the guise of "social housekeeping" that women should attend to society's needs in much the same way that they looked after those of their families.[88] By promoting poor women's crucial community role, black social housekeeping arguments, however, included a political distinction not found among white Progressive women. The imaging of African American working-class women as mothers played a central role in the "politics of respectability" asserted by black middle-class women as a means of improving race relations.[89] Improving the image of blacks, especially women, in white minds served as the primary means through which the African American elite battled segregation and racial discrimination following the race riot of 1906.

The members of the Neighborhood Union defined themselves in part through their relations with the population the organization served. They expressed their commitment to "self-respect, self-sufficiency, racial pride and solidarity, and a strong sense of noblesse oblige" by both living their lives as examples to the rest of the community and working to instill like values in others.[90] As a result, these women "mothered" black working-class mothers in the same way that reformers wanted these women to deal with their children. The way the Neighborhood Union cared for the community served as an example and metaphor for how working mothers should care for their own homes and families. This model of a involved community directly challenged negative images of black women—from the oversexed jezebel to the subservient mammy—popularized in mass culture during the early twentieth century.[91]

Organizers also used the women they imaged as mothers as a rallying point for middle-class women. The story of the founding of the Neighborhood Union, in which a working-class mother plays the central role, became something of a rallying cry, calling middle-class and elite women to the duty of serving their race. By emphasizing the need to teach poorer women to care properly for their homes and families, the Union's women further established their authority. Outlining the particular role she felt women fulfilled in the uplift of the race, Lugenia Burns Hope argued that in "the prevention of crime—training and reformation of law breakers—who knows more about the beginning of crime than a mother—who can better train and reform than a woman. What does a father know about the need of play grounds and recreation centers—when he is away from the children all day—what does he care about child labor and the exploitations of women—so long as he is a successful business man. He is perfectly willing to make her do a man's work and pay her half his salary."[92] Union members' efforts to define the role of women in relation to men spread beyond arguing for dominance in the work of reform and racial uplift. Reflecting back on these years before women could vote, Hope contended that black men had used the vote only "from their point of view." A black man "thought very little about the women's view point in fact he just naturally thought that his viewpoint was hers. A woman thinks from a domestic viewpoint, she thinks from what she knows—the things she comes in contact with each day in the home."[93] Arguments emphasizing women's distinct perspective reinforced the importance of work done by organizations such as the Neighborhood Union as a necessary complement to the more overtly political organizing expected of elite black men.

Neighborhood Union organizers' efforts to create a virtuous working class resembles historian Evelyn Brooks Higginbotham's description of black Baptist women and their attempts to counter contemporary racial discrimination. Higginbotham's analysis of middle-class women's moves toward establishing respectability illuminates the key role working-class women, promoted as competent and moral mothers, played in undermining white supremacist arguments. By living clean, moral, and temperate lives, female African American reformers believed that black communities could contradict the stereotypes that maintained racial divisions in the South. With this understanding, the Neighborhood Union's emphasis on manners and morals—in particular, those of poor black women— can be read as resistance similar to other more traditional forms of protest.[94] "By privileging respectability, and particularly the capacity and worthiness of poor, working-class black women for respect," these race women also promoted the ideals of self-esteem and self-determination.[95]

Having invested themselves so fully in this "strategy for reform of the entire structural system of American race relations," elites' efforts to make working-class women embody respectability could be quite intense. Retribution against those who refused to meet these standards often took the form of ostracism or exile. In other cases, those deemed lazy by reformers received almost constant pressure to change their lifestyles. The class biases and assimilationist tendencies embedded in the notion of respectability created new divisions in black communities as women allied themselves with the respectable working poor against "an unproductive lower class."[96] The Neighborhood Union's particular imaging of black motherhood reinforced the advantages to family, community, and race offered by respectability in an attempt to reform less desirable community members and to contradict racist images promoted by whites. Poor and working mothers, then, became the model for all black women as well as for the community at large. The Neighborhood Union's organizers created and reinforced images of black women as mothers in contradiction to their dominant images as domestic workers that primarily white social welfare organizations presented. For middle-class black women, the issues at stake involved not only material relief to the poor but also community reform and the reorganization of race relations.

Professionalization

THE ISSUES at stake for the white social workers and reformers, who also relied heavily on the images of white women as mothers, were quite different. Policies and practices of agencies dealing primarily with female clients furthered the professionalization of social work in the 1910s and early 1920s.[97] Historians have, for the most part, approached the professionalization of social work in terms of the meanings for its middle-class practitioners.[98] For Atlanta's social workers, the rise of professionalism meant consistency, efficiency, authority building, new forms of rigorous training, and, by the 1920s, centralization. Organizations centralized record keeping, transferring case history onto forms in which a standardized language of scientific diagnosis replaced the lengthy impressionistic descriptions that had characterized client records in the earlier decades of the twentieth century. The organizations that led the movement toward professionalization purged volunteers from their ranks and raised requirements for minimum training, and many private benevolent organizations left the field of welfare work entirely by the early 1920s.[99]

The move toward professionalization, begun in earnest in the 1910s, fed the growing visibility of working-class women, particularly white women, by promoting solutions to poverty that directly involved Atlanta's poor women, but new standards and practices would eventually shift attention away from women by the 1920s. Atlanta's poor women played a central role in white social workers' efforts to define themselves as experts and to build the standards of welfare as a profession; consequently, the shift to new standards and methods profoundly affected impoverished females. In the 1900s a clean home, a prominently placed Bible, and well-mannered children (at least during the visit) might have convinced home visitors that a mother was worthy of aid. Over the next two decades, however, social workers increasingly turned toward standardized "mental tests" to gauge the intelligence, emotionality, and worthiness of clients. Tests judged Lois Vancott, for example, to have mental age of less than twelve and the reasoning ability of a thirteen-year-old. The social work student analyzing this case concluded, "to overcome her weak points Mrs. Vancott must have constant supervision and training."[100] As Regina Kunzel notes in her study of aid to single mothers, social workers' struggle for professional recognition often "stigmatized" welfare clients as "pathological and criminal," whereas they had previously been pitied.[101]

The role poor women played in the professionalization of social work among the city's whites is clearest in welfare organizations' attempts to control access to the poor as a means of establishing social workers' authority as experts on the causes of and solutions to poverty. During World War I, the Associated Charities attacked day nurseries, a significant source of assistance for employed women, for not following standardized methods of investigation when accepting mothers' requests for child care. "In no nursery is the preliminary inquiry more than superficial," argued the Associated Charities. This organization also deemed child-care workers unqualified to "decide if the family difficulty is economic, domestic or temperamental." Finally, the Associated Charities admonished the nurseries to "familiarize themselves with the underlying principles of constructive family relief."[102]

Other attempts to control access to the poor and create a script of expertise and authority in dealing with them were aimed at benevolent organizations, particularly those run by local churches. Professional social welfare organizations bristled at other groups' attempts to work directly with client populations. In one case, the Associated Charities upbraided a church group that had passed out Christmas baskets of food to poor families in a neighborhood that the Associated Charities considered its territory. The Associated Charities insisted that the church group was trying to draw distinctions between worthy and unworthy poor among families already approved and assisted.[103]

The newspapers served as one of the most influential media through which social workers could articulate their new professionalism. In this realm, too, the stories of working-class women conveyed messages proselytizing the harm of individual or untrained giving to the poor. Newspapers also allowed welfare agencies to combat negative images of social workers as "officious meddlers" that began to appear in the media during this period.[104] In 1915 the *Atlanta Journal* gave the Associated Charities space in which to run a weekly "Column for the Needy," describing select cases and explaining the methods used to relieve their suffering. The most popular script that appeared in these columns told the story of a woman begging on the street: a well-meaning resident gave her change, but she spent it frivolously and then sank into even darker circumstances when it was gone. The solution to this woman's problems was always provided by an "efficient" social worker who would locate the woman's missing husband, contact her long-lost family, or place her children in an institution so she could go to work—all without directly passing a dime into the beggar's hand.[105]

Besides regularly publishing social welfare organizations' annual reports, newspapers also frequently printed letters to the editor that defended scientific social work. Even as late as 1920, social workers saw the need to justify their practices. In that year a piece appeared in the *Atlanta Constitution* decrying the lack of hospital care for the poor and recommending that anyone doubting this fact visit a particular ill woman who had been turned away from every hospital in the city.[106] R. C. Dexter of the Associated Charities wrote an emphatic letter to the editor defending his organization's work with the woman in question and denying that anyone could understand or assist her case without consulting his office.[107] This "technical and cultural gatekeeping," with its appearance of objective and rational expertise so often demonstrated through the cases of poor women, was largely effective.[108] Throughout the 1910s and into the 1920s, the Associated Charities held the foremost position in Atlanta's social welfare network, guiding both private and public relief. What the Associated Charities accomplished through professionalization, the Neighborhood Union achieved through its practices of racial uplift. Both strategies brought significant power and recognition to the organizations, and both relied heavily on the production, control, and distribution of images of respectable motherhood.

PROVIDING WELFARE became a crucial part of creating and shaping Atlanta's image in the early twentieth century. At the center of emerging welfare policies in the 1900s and 1910s stood the image of the virtuous mother. For a multitude of Atlantans, mothers represented a stable social order, not just for the families they created but also as a metaphor for the civic body as a whole. Mothers served ceaselessly the interests of others, imparted discipline and morality to their charges, and submitted to the will of their husbands. Mothers had a clear place in the family structure, just as the races and classes were meant to have a clear place in

SCENES IN THE DISTRICT WHERE THE FACTORY STRIKERS RESIDE.

One of the earliest indicators of the shift to a public discourse that would include the images and actions of the city's working-class women came when white female hands at a local textile mill launched a successful strike to protest the hiring of twenty African American women in jobs that had traditionally been filled by white women. *Atlanta Constitution,* August 8, 1897.

Images of attractive white women at work in Atlanta's factories helped to build a positive industrial image. City boosters—primarily politicians and businessmen—hoped that the implied docility of the female workers would help draw investors interested in cheap, plentiful, and pliant labor. From *City Builder,* June 1918; photo courtesy of the Metro Atlanta Chamber of Commerce.

Dainty Girls in White Caps and Aprons Wrap STONE'S Cakes

BRIGHT, cool and cheery is the wrapping-room of the F. O. Stone Baking Company, at the corner of Highland avenue and Dunlap street. ¶ Adjoining the wrapping room is a big, airy rest-room for the wrapping girls. Every provision is made for the health and comfort of the Stone employees.

Visitors are always welcome.

A trip through this spotless sunlit CAKE BAKERY will be both interesting and educational.

Initial images of Mary Phagan, a young factory worker murdered at her workplace in 1913, depicted the victim as somber, doe-eyed, and even seductive. *Atlanta Constitution*, May 4, 1913.

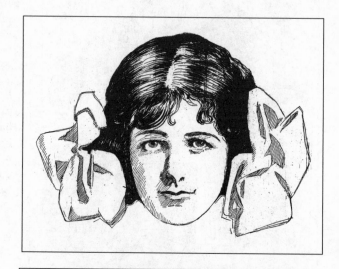

During her employer's trial for murder, Mary Phagan became the symbol for the dangers posed by the city's rapidly expanding industrial economy. Descriptions and images of Phagan became more innocent, happy, and childlike as she came to embody innocence destroyed at the hands of greedy capitalists. *Atlanta Constitution*, August 26, 1913.

MARY PHAGAN, THE VICTIM

Scenes in Courtroom Monday While Conley Was on Stand

"JIM, CAN YOU PUT THIS CORD AROUND YOUR NECK LIKE YOU FOUND IT ON MARY PHAGAN'S BODY?"

—SOLICITOR DORSEY—

WOMEN SPECTATORS.

JIM CONLEY— On the STAND.

Women from across the socioeconomic and age spectrum attended the trial of Mary Phagan's accused murderer, Leo Frank, and protested bitterly when the judge removed them from the courtroom during the salacious but key testimony of Jim Conley. *Atlanta Constitution*, August 5, 1913.

More than twenty female supervisors and workers from the pencil factory where Mary Phagan worked testified in defense of their boss, Leo Frank. Many of these women found themselves fleeting local celebrities when their pictures made the front page of the local newspapers. *Atlanta Constitution*, August 7, 1913.

Their Testimony Will Have Direct Bearing on Leo Frank's Case

While the proportion of women employed in domestic work declined in the early twentieth century, Atlanta's African American women remained heavily concentrated in this sector of the economy. Laundry work, the most arduous of the domestic labor jobs, also provided the most autonomy and, therefore, appeal, as washerwomen generally performed their work in their own yards and away from the eyes and control of whites. Courtesy of the Georgia Department of Archives and History.

During a 1914–15 textile strike, women played key organizing and symbolic roles. Union leaders placed women prominently at the front for publicity photographs and public events so that observers could not fail to see these victims of the mill owner's greed. Courtesy of the George Meany Memorial Archives.

Within the photograph (text on the image):

TO.BY
LSON

A.WIDOW.HOLDING
HER.EMACIATED
IMBECILE,NINE
YEAR.OLD.CHIL
THE.RESULTS.O
THE.MOTHERS HA
LABOR.IN.THE.MIL
PRIOR.TO.THE
BIRTH.OF.HER.
CHILD.XI.
THIS CHILD.HAS
DIED.SINCE.PHOT
WAS.TAKEN.

FULTON. BAG.AND
COTTON. MILLS CO.
STRIKERS.

Strike leaders made some of the images of female mill hands into postcards to be mailed to supporters and government officials. The handwritten note on the back of this postcard reads, "Mrs. Taylor—Supt. of mill ordered her continue at work altho. she told him she was about to be delivered of a baby. He sd he cd continue anyhow for another [hour]. She obeyed. [Before the] close of the hour she became so ill that she had to leave without permission. She had scarcely reached her home but 8 minutes, when she gave birth to her baby who as a result suffered from infantile paralysis. It died a few days ago." Courtesy of the National Archives.

When government officials arrived in Atlanta to investigate the textile strike in the summer of 1914, women added their own grievances to the official causes of the strike, most frequently citing the challenges faced by mothers who worked in the mill. Courtesy of the George Meany Memorial Archives.

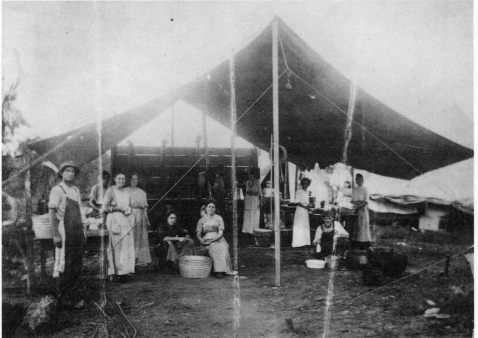

When mill officials evicted strikers from their homes, women's domestic roles merged with their strike efforts, and tasks such as cooking for the residents of the newly erected tent city became community endeavors. Courtesy of the George Meany Memorial Archives.

Middle-class concerns over many African American women's fondness for "sassiety" crossed racial lines. Whites feared losing their access to cheap domestic labor, and elite blacks feared that the popularity of commercial amusements reflected badly on the morality and respectability of the race as a whole. *Atlanta Georgian,* July 6, 1919.

City boosters' unbridled promotion of Atlanta in the early twentieth century often included reference to the city's good health. Also in these years, however, the city launched its first significant public health campaign in an effort to eliminate tuberculosis. *Atlanta Georgian*, July 12, 1919.

White women generally received sympathetic attention from the white-run Atlanta Anti-Tuberculosis Association. In photographs accompanying the records of white women, caseworkers posed the women away from their usually dismal lodgings. The women faced the camera directly and, as in this photograph, often held cherished objects. Courtesy of the Atlanta History Center.

Public health nurses considered this African American woman, Sallie Pride, a danger to the city not because she had tuberculosis but because she took in washing for ten different white families despite having a tubercular daughter in the house. Her profession—and the source of health workers' disdain—is clearly evident from the washtubs and laundry lines that appear in this 1909 photograph. Courtesy of the Atlanta History Center.

Health workers looked more kindly on this black woman because, once diagnosed with tuberculosis, she gave up doing laundry work for whites. Her photograph, taken in 1909, differs markedly from that of Sallie Pride. This woman is dressed in her best clothes and is posed in the center of the frame and in front of a decorated wall and a neatly made bed. Courtesy of the Atlanta History Center.

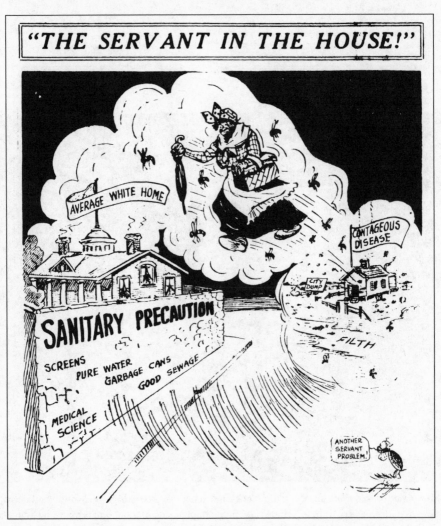

The local press depicted African American domestic workers as the primary agents of contagion to suggest that the city needed to better guard public health. In the minds of many of the city's whites, black women bore the responsibility for carrying tuberculosis from impoverished black neighborhoods into the homes of Atlanta's whites. *Atlanta Constitution,* February 3, 1914.

Appeals for action to stem the spread of tuberculosis remained focused on the desire to protect "clean" white neighborhoods and the city's overall reputation rather than on the desire to provide for the health of Atlanta's African American population. The figures in this drawing are characterized by their relationship to white employers, not as individuals whose health is threatened by sickness. Only "your washerwoman" actually touches the patient. *Atlanta Constitution,* February 4, 1914.

In 1912 a group of evangelical businessmen hoping to restore morality to the city began an unprecedented publicity campaign to challenge the city council to eliminate prostitution. In this classic "white slave" image, which the organization paid the newspaper to run, a naked white woman is being carried away by a beast wearing the hat of protected vice and carrying a weapon of public indifference. The organization's efforts paid off, at least in part, when a zealous police chief took up the challenge and ordered Atlanta's best-known red-light district closed. *Atlanta Constitution,* September 25, 1912.

"The Voice With a Smile" Answers Growing Needs

THE rapid increase in the number of new telephones in Georgia is directly reflected in the greater use and value of the service as a whole.

Approximately 2,920 new telephones were added to the Bell System in Georgia during the first six months of this year.

The telephone operators are handling an average of 996,900 local calls every day, an increase of 6.7 per cent over last year's record.

Long distance calls average 10,100 each day or 6.7 per cent more than in 1923.

To handle such a volume of traffic, twenty-four hours a day, every day in the year, requires a highly trained loyal organization of young women operators.

They are serving you efficiently and cheerfully and they appreciate the considerate co-operation which you extend to them.

C. G. BECK, Georgia Manager

"BELL SYSTEM"

SOUTHERN BELL TELEPHONE AND TELEGRAPH COMPANY

One Policy One System, Universal Service

Like many other Atlanta companies that relied on female labor, Southern Bell liked to promote its workforce as attractive, efficient, and cheerful. This company's workers, however, used at least some of these qualities to launch a well-publicized strike against their employer in 1919. While the women ultimately lost their bid for union recognition, the local press reveled in reporting on the flamboyant pickets and marches of the city's stylish young "hello girls." From *City Builder,* December 1924; photo courtesy of the Metro Atlanta Chamber of Commerce.

During the 1934 general textile strike, women who participated in the union played a decidedly second-tier role. No women held prominent local or national leadership roles, and while photographs clearly show women on the picket lines, the voice given to the strike by both union leaders and the press was that of the male mill hand struggling to support his family. From the *Atlanta Georgian,* September 8, 1934; photo courtesy of the Hearst Corporation.

During the Great Depression, Atlanta's unemployed women found few opportunities for work relief through newly created federal programs such as the Works Progress Administration. The opportunities available to women tended to confine them to indoor, unskilled, and low-paying positions. Courtesy of the National Archives.

While New Deal work relief jobs created during the Great Depression kept most women inside at work on traditional and low-paying tasks such as sewing pillowcases and simple clothes for the state's hospitals and prisons, most men worked to rebuild the city's infrastructure. The common sight of men repairing roads, constructing schools, and laying sewer pipe became a symbol of hope for depression-weary Atlantans. Courtesy of the National Archives.

the structure of a city in the midst of a sustained period of growth. Both boosters and reformers saw mothers and the working-class families they represented as the potential bedrock of Atlanta's reputation as a prosperous but ordered city. Black reformers and social workers also hoped that respectable families, grounded by strong maternal figures, might encourage the white community to soften the harsh edges of segregation and racial discrimination. For working-class Atlantans, however, motherhood embodied a different sort of respectability—having, supporting, or being a good mother was a sign of success in a competitive and difficult urban environment.

In stark contrast to the glowing and heroic terms used to describe women who struggled to keep home and family together by accepting not just assistance but also guidance from middle-class reformers, Atlanta's perceived crisis in public health in the 1910s, the subject of the next chapter, cultivated images of women as the primary carriers of disease and, therefore, the worst danger to the growing population and reputation. Rather than contradict each other, these opposing images of women—respectable mother versus endangered working girl or selfless union wife versus diseased prostitute—served similar ends in a city intent on promoting its economic development through a reputation for a restrained moral and social order. The images communicated expectations for proper behavior for women, their families, their employers, their class, and their race.

CHAPTER FIVE

Physical and Moral Health

DURING THE WINTER OF 1907, the *Atlanta Georgian* published an editorial describing an Atlanta woman, "young, beautiful and of noble character," who suffered from consumption. This white widow worked as a sales clerk in a department store to support her child from "a brief but happy marriage." When she became "too ill to continue working," the article read, she could only sit and look "with despairing eyes toward her baby." In language remarkably similar to that used by welfare agencies to describe the "virtuous mother" of the 1900s, the editorial highlighted a mother of much dignity and respectability, able to maintain her manners, beauty, and "noble character" in the face of death. She was lauded for her commitment to her child and her restraint in not asking for help. And it was precisely through her continued respectability that she became heroic. These qualities, the editors of the *Atlanta Georgian* argued, commanded the men and women of Atlanta to give her "one last chance for life which she cannot seize herself."[1] The story proved to be, as the newspaper had intended, the spark needed to launch an organized campaign against tuberculosis.

The image of respectability embedded in the widow's story portrayed a picture of worthiness—this woman deserved aid as a reward for her upright life. Representing this woman as a mother sacrificing for her only child rewrote her wage work as necessary and reinforced a gendered social structure in which women functioned not as independent persons but in relation to the family members they served and supported. Her race undoubtedly reinforced her worthiness for assistance in the eyes of the *Georgian*'s white readers, and she came to represent the innocent victims struck down by disease in an uncaring city. Notions of protection became central to campaigns to rid the city of tuberculosis and later venereal disease. By the 1910s, however, Atlanta's public health movement relied on a varied set of images and a more complex understanding of who and what needed protecting. At some moments in these later years, working-class women still appeared as the most vulnerable component of society. At others, the imagery tied working-class women of both races to disease as agents of contagion and polluters (or potential polluters) of the civic body—dangerous elements from whom city residents and the city's reputation must be protected.

The timing of public concern over the diseases of the city played a critical role in determining which role women would fulfill—whether they would be pitied or scorned. The poor white women lauded for their noble fight against tuberculosis in the first decade of the 1900s became the prime agents of contagion in the venereal disease epidemic during World War I. The white population largely overlooked the African American women demonized as carriers of tuberculosis in early 1910s when it came to the later concern over the spread of venereal disease. Atlanta's black elite defended the washerwomen accused of spreading TB but quickly condemned working-class black women for infecting black soldiers with venereal disease in 1918. This flexible characterization of women and disease depended not just on race but also on where women fit in the economies of work and leisure, the methods of transmission for the diseases, and the moment when Atlantans declared the diseases to be epidemics.

Private Efforts for Public Health

ATLANTA was often described as healthful, an image boosters coveted and repeatedly used in promoting the city to industrialists, investors, and conventioneers. Located in the Appalachian foothills, Atlanta could and did lay claim to the benefits of mountain air. Observers during the 1881 Cotton Exposition frequently noted "the evident health of the community."[2] Even in the twentieth century, when numerous factories dotted the urban landscape, business leaders touted the "pure condition" of the city's water supply, drawn from the Chattahoochee River, and the "municipally owned sewerage disposal plant" as further evidence of Atlanta's good health.[3] A drawing accompanying this particular proclamation showed a lovely young woman in a flowing white dress, standing on a grassy hilltop while a young girl plays nearby with a butterfly. In the distance, at the bottom of the hill, the outline of Atlanta is just visible, with plenty of sky and few puffy white clouds drifting above it.

Absent from view in this image and most others created by city leaders were the soot and smoke that industries and railroads belched into the sky. "Atlanta was the dirtiest city," resident Durise Hanson recalled, "we would see the trains coming up and spouting out all that smoke and dirt and the chimneys that were left were coal—coal coming up, coal dust and dirt coming out."[4] And while the city did have a ready water supply, a public sewer system, garbage pickup, graded streets, sidewalks, street lamps, and professional fire protection, these services were, as they had been throughout the nineteenth century, restricted to the business district and the wealthiest neighborhoods.[5] The miserable working-class neighborhoods contained inadequate and dilapidated houses on muddy streets with privies and open sewers. African Americans, forced to live on cheap low-lying land in areas such as Beaver's Slide and Buttermilk Bottom suffered worst of all, as the refuse and disease from the rest of the city concentrated in their alleys and yards. Realizing that "hygienic conditions were bad in those areas," many medical professionals, like most of Atlanta's wealthier residents, argued that such circumstances were the fault of poor residents who just "wouldn't keep things clean."[6]

The poor living conditions of many city residents, the lack of resources for protecting public health, and the limited understanding of how diseases spread contributed to a number of epidemics in Atlanta in the early twentieth century, including hookworm, typhoid, malaria, and influenza. Poor residents also suffered from diseases related to vitamin deficiencies, such as pellagra. Reflecting the "harsh discriminatory treatment" of blacks, the African American population's mortality rates consistently exceeded those of whites.[7] By the 1910s, three contagious diseases in particular would grip the city's attention and spur a fledgling public health movement: tuberculosis, gonorrhea, and syphilis. These diseases not only represented a threat to residents' health but more broadly drew on connections the middle class saw between the body and the body politic. Transmitted through close but often casual physical contact, tuberculosis demonstrated the dangers of urban crowding—in streets, neighborhoods, workplaces, theaters, dance halls, shops, and streetcars. The spread of the disease seemed to represent the potential harm that could come from the mixing of races and classes this crowding encouraged, since many whites believed that the disease came from the poor and black populations. When it came to the venereal diseases of gonorrhea and syphilis, the city's middle classes entwined perceptions of moral and physical health: these diseases spread not through casual contact but rather through the intimate relations permitted by the dance halls and dark theaters of the city's seamiest areas.

At one time, Atlanta had a board of health. Starting in the late 1840s, this body patrolled for areas of standing water, poorly maintained privies, and overflowing gutters, although its power was extremely limited and it functioned primarily in an advisory capacity.[8] Only in 1892 did Atlanta complete a public medical facility, Grady Hospital, a racially segregated and woefully inadequate effort in the face of the growing city's needs. According to one historian, the municipal government throughout the nineteenth century "unabashedly adhered to 'business first' in the scope and orientation of municipal services," meaning that little in the way of public resources was put toward projects that did not have immediate and overwhelmingly positive economic rewards. In this respect, Atlanta appears to have been part of a larger trend in which many southern cities "determined expenditures on a simple cost-benefit calculation" that promoted services to the business district while leaving education, poor relief, and public health needs largely unmet.[9]

It fell primarily to the city's middle classes to take up the slack through charity and welfare work and through campaigns to rid the city of disease and the conditions that caused it. White middle-class Atlantans' response to a perceived crisis in public health in the late 1900s and early 1910s represented an attempt both to remedy conditions that might infringe on their families and to save the city's reputation. Black community leaders prodded residents to reclaim their neighborhoods from disease and decay during annual "Clean-Up Campaigns." White organized labor and middle-class club women endorsed similar clean-up campaigns, while the Atlanta Anti-Tuberculosis Association spearheaded the organized public health movement, founding a visiting nurse program, health clinics, and eventually a branch to deal with public health issues among African Americans. The municipal government aided in public health efforts only during World War I, overseeing venereal disease clinics in the city jail.

As the Progressive spirit took hold among the nation's middle classes, Atlanta began to hear calls to control tuberculosis, venereal disease, and, to a lesser degree, other communicable diseases. These efforts found a voice in middle-class reformers and an image in the bodies of working-class women. The moral dangers so readily associated with working-class women by the 1910s translated easily into a connection with fears of epidemic disease during the same years. Many Atlantans thought working-class women of both races to be as polluting as the diseases themselves. In an effort to control the spread of disease as well as to regulate social and moral order, the public health and social hygiene movements of the early twentieth century justified "public interventions" into women's lives.[10] A combination of public and private agencies frequently suspended the civil rights of working-class women detained, tested, and treated. In ways similar to the social welfare network, these policies institutionalized public scrutiny of both women's daily lives and their bodies. The punitive and therapeutic treatments aimed at these women served to reinforce a particular social order while promoting an image of moral and physical health for the city.

Tuberculosis

ALTHOUGH tuberculosis had long been present in Georgia, only with the congestion and poor sanitary conditions of the early twentieth century did a heightened sense of crisis about the disease develop in Atlanta. The movement against TB coincided with, reinforced, and contributed to the increased visibility of working-class women that developed in the late 1900s and culminated in the 1910s.[11] Shortly after the appearance of the *Georgian*'s 1907 story on the white widow, public concern over tuberculosis led to the founding of the Atlanta Anti-Tuberculosis and Visiting Nurse Association. The new organization developed policies and practices similar to those used by the Associated Charities, and much of the treatment relied on the lives and labors of working-class women. A deeply entangled connection between physical surroundings and morality shaped this approach. Health reformers focused on controlling patients' behavior and coercing them to live properly, believing this to be the best means for both preventing and curing the disease.

The Atlanta public health movement that developed in response to the tuberculosis scare of the early 1900s drew on the cultural associations of women with the disease. In public health agencies' day-to-day programs, women functioned as both caregivers and agents of contagion. And it was here that nurses and social workers attempted to impose many of the restrictions that could not be passed by the city council. Atlanta's public health movement approached tuberculosis as a social problem that could most effectively be combated through education programs, therapeutic treatments, and welfare-style assistance.[12] Consistent throughout both Associated Charities and Anti-Tuberculosis Association literature were images of poor white women as mothers and poor black women as domestic workers. These images represented different perceived threats to middle-class urban society. Public health activists feared that working-class white women would raise a diseased generation that would threaten public life. Working-class African American women's bodies evoked fears of disease being brought into white homes, thereby threatening white families. In either case, the foundation of the city's social structure was at risk if the disease continued unchecked.

From the Gould Building in downtown Atlanta, the Anti-Tuberculosis Association ran a free clinic for the poor. A potential patient came to the clinic for examination but would not be accepted for treatment until after his or her home had been investigated by a visiting nurse, even if the patient presented strong evidence of tuberculosis. Once in the house, the nurse would attempt to educate the family on the proper care of the patient and the means for preventing the spread of the disease. Between the home visit and the type of therapies available during this period, much of the burden of treatment and prevention fell on women. Patients had to be well fed, and their bedding, along with the rest of the house, had to be cleaned and aired daily. The primary caregiver also had to keep the patient isolated from the rest of the family and escort the patient to clinic visits, so women tended to bear responsibility for not allowing the disease to spread.

The Atlanta Anti-Tuberculosis Association's policies and practices promoted the public viewing of women's bodies in the course of treating the disease, thereby contributing to working-class and poor women's visibility in the cultural landscape. Policies aimed at controlling the spread of tuberculosis subjected to public scrutiny poor and sick women's lives and even their bodies. The association's medical clinic had only a screen separating general examination areas from waiting areas. The room used for chest examinations also served as the cleaning area for instruments, so health care workers would come and go while patients were being examined. [13] Even one of the most important diagnostic practices, the X ray, rendered the body of the patient transparent. [14] The frequent association of tuberculosis with the lungs and the dicta of modesty attached to the torso of the female body meant that these experiences were probably more traumatic for women than for men.

The strong cultural associations of women with the spread of disease also invited public scrutiny of working-class women's homes and personal lives. The public health movement relied heavily on neighborhood surveys and home visits, casting a civic eye over women. [15] At the behest of the Anti-Tuberculosis Association, individuals were urged "to notify the authorities at the sanitarium whenever they discovered or suspected a case of tuberculosis among the Negroes." [16] The responsibility of social workers and visiting nurses, according to the health workers, was to "get people to see themselves correctly." [17] So, in the name of public health, potential disease carriers forfeited their privacy, especially in their homes, and intervention by health workers was justified as necessary to curb the spread of disease and protect the city's health. Without a full understanding of germ theory, treatments for tuberculosis were often based on the belief that "to be cured, the patient has to be taken out of his or her daily routine." [18] Illness was associated with environment—poor food, bad sanitation, and so forth—so the cure was thought to lay in changing these circumstances. Intervention, then, was justified as both treatment for the disease and protection from it.

Tubercular women generated great fear among the general population and great concern among Anti-Tuberculosis Association workers. Association case studies also reveal that health workers held women largely responsible for the spread of disease through their families, especially when tuberculosis appeared in children. Consequently, the organization often sought to place women in institutions or to remove children from the home. [19] As potential healers as well as carriers of disease, women of both races often walked the fine line between the agency's views of them as either "helpless and pitiable" or "the most dangerous member[s] of society." [20]

The Anti-Tuberculosis Association directed unconcealed contempt at women who were believed to be "a source of infection to [their] family and neighbors," would "not follow medical advice," were "too poor to help themselves," or would "not try to protect others from infection." [21] In addition to placing such women or their children in institutions, the association would coerce them with reduced material aid, cessation of treatment, and community ostracism. "Neighbors are often reached and made familiar with the plan of work," wrote organization secretary Rosa Lowe, "and they may be shown that the patient is not following instructions; then, as the case grows worse, it becomes an object lesson of disobedience in the neighborhood."[22]

While the majority of the Anti-Tuberculosis Association's money funded health care programs for the white community, the organization increasingly emphasized the need to work with the black population as well. More than a third of the city's population was African American, and blacks were two to three times as likely to contract tuberculosis as whites.[23] The organization developed a democratized language of equality that stressed the dire need of blacks as well as whites for health care and relief. Driving these expressions, however, was the fear that unless blacks could be kept healthy, they would remain a threat to whites. The Anti-Tuberculosis Association concluded as early as 1909 that "any movement directed toward the ultimate elimination of the disease in any Southern city must, of necessity, include the negro population."[24] Whatever its motivation, the Anti-Tuberculosis Association provided the majority of relief distributed to black residents by white social workers in Atlanta between 1909 and 1917.[25]

The Anti-Tuberculosis Association hosted a substantial and often punitive set of programs aimed specifically at African Americans. The association's "Negro Committee" represented the city's most significant pre–World War I effort toward interracial work. Rather than a grassroots approach to combating tuberculosis, this cooperation of whites and African Americans functioned more as a middle-class surveillance effort. The African American branch of the association, run by white health workers and black community leaders, promoted health care and sanitation in black neighborhoods. Neighborhood clinics, home visits, home nursing classes, and direct relief sponsored by this organization meant that for a brief time in the 1910s Atlanta's interracial public health work was based on programs that depended on working-class black women.

But in the process of ridding the city of tuberculosis, the Anti-Tuberculosis Association's work contributed to many whites' generalized fears of black women as agents of contagion. A close association developed between the city's domestic servants and the spread of tuberculosis. Case histories kept by Lowe and the visiting nurses reveal a prevalent contempt for washerwomen as dangerous and ignorant. Atlantan Minnie Freeman, for example, suffered from tuberculosis for two years before her death at age twenty-two. Her mother scrubbed Minnie's clothes and bedding and white families' washings in the same tubs. The visiting nurse noted with disgust that Minnie "should have been placed in a hospital, where she would not have been a menace to others."[26]

The washerwoman "menace" represented the confluence of many troubling trends in the early-twentieth-century city. A long historical association of blacks with disease overlapped with contemporary fears of tuberculosis.[27] The troubling relationship between black domestic workers and their white employers became more dramatic in the 1910s as expanding black employment opportunities and improving white economic fortunes translated into a shrinking number of domestic workers just as more families could afford to hire them. At a time when racial lines hardened through transportation and residential segregation ordinances, black women remained the one group that could and did travel between the separate black and white worlds. The combination of these factors led to methods for eliminating tuberculosis that often focused more on controlling black women's behavior than on providing health care.

While problematic race relations existed in many realms of the city, African American female domestics functioned in one of the thorniest sites of racial tension. Whether cooking, washing, nursing, or cleaning, domestic workers' paid labor was characterized by a close though often antagonistic relationship with their employers. Paid domestic labor was particularly tied up with notions of womanhood, the "racial realities of privilege and need," and culturally constructed notions of good and bad.[28] Hiring a domestic worker meant status and leisure for white women, yet the work often meant drudgery and loneliness for black women. Most of Atlanta's black women earned their livelihood in this charged atmosphere.

Work expectations for domestic workers could vary among households, but as many women recalled, black women usually performed a variety of tasks. Alice Adams was hired as a cook, but as she remembers, "I didn't just cook—I kept house, and I kept everything in place and raised them boys."[29] A typical day for household servants started early in the morning and lasted well into the evening, often including cooking meals, cleaning, and watching employers' children.[30] The appeal of domestic work for African American women was almost as varied as the duties the job required. Some wanted to leave school and sought work as an alternative, contributing their wages to the family. One domestic worker recalled, "I wanted to come to Atlanta and work; so that I could help my parents."[31] Mary Morton took her first job to buy schoolbooks. She later remembered that she "kept on til I saved the money, got my books, [and] helped momma."[32] Many domestic workers also found great satisfaction and pride in their work. Willie Mae Jackson declared, "I likes to work alone . . . and I don't like factory work because I don't like to come in contact with so many different people, and cooking, the hours are long, but I love it. It's not hard work, it's enjoyable and I love when they have parties. . . . I just like to serve people and I think that's what I like about it most."[33] Despite the obvious pride many workers took in their labor, Atlanta's black women were quick to point out the negative aspects of domestic work: long hours, unwanted advances from male employers, little respect, isolation. Adams summed up one of domestic workers' most frequent complaints about their jobs when she concluded that employers were "willing to do anything to help me—but the money. Four dollars a week. Just no money."[34]

Although laundry was possibly the most physically demanding form of domestic work, many black women and even a few whites chose this work over other domestic jobs because of the relative autonomy it afforded.[35] While whites carried suspicions about domestic workers in general, the autonomy of the washerwoman meant that she became the physical representation of the tuberculosis threat. Black women who worked as laundresses represented one of the most blatant disruptions of segregation, since their work brought them all the way into white homes but gave employers little control over their time or behavior. Washerwomen also became a prime target for white fears because of their status as independent wage-earning women and their easy identification. Laundresses literally wore their profession on their bodies as they moved through the city streets with bundles of clothes on the their heads or tied to their backs. Their yards were filled with the marks of their trade: washtubs, fires, and laundry lines. Washerwomen often worked cooperatively, building support systems by performing their labors within the black community rather than as isolated workers in white homes. As self-employed workers, black washerwomen subverted traditional work roles in relation to white women as whites became clients instead of bosses.

The press frequently represented generalized anxieties attached to the activities of domestic workers when they were not in white homes. The white middle classes could only imagine the immoral behavior in which their servants engaged when they were away from their employers' protective eyes. With blacks increasingly living in separate districts and more and more washerwomen working out, their white employers had little knowledge of or access to employees' homes or activities. Black women also found a slowly increasing number of opportunities for other types of paid labor in the 1910s. The vigor with which whites demonized domestic workers hints at the transgressive nature of African American women and their work: washerwomen and other servants entered the most private and sacred realm of the city's middle classes and brought with them the dirt and disorder of the city's public spaces and working-class neighborhoods.[36]

Public health workers, city officials, and white employers linked African American domestic workers to both the transmission and the control of tuberculosis. Prescriptions for halting the spread of disease from black workers to white homes employed a language of practicality that underscored black women's place as service workers in the city's economic structure and reinforced the perception that African Americans spread disease into the white community. Columnist Isma Dooley, for example, ordered readers to "stop prattling" about public immorality "and look into health conditions at your home." She challenged white Atlanta to consider that "whether we wish to look after those of the colored race who require it; whether it is our moral obligation to do so or not; whether we think they ought to be segregated or not segregated, has nothing to do with the facts as they are, pertaining to this population, and the conditions surrounding them. They represent a large part of the population; they live within the corporate limits. We meet with them, come in contact with them in our every daily relation."[37] Disguised in these discussions of treatments and preventatives was the reiteration of a labor system in which blacks worked as servants for whites and the fear that black servants brought contagious diseases into white homes. Governmental and press concern with factors that might produce an unfavorable reputation for the city finally prodded Atlanta to take at least rudimentary steps to eliminate the unsanitary conditions that contributed to disease, even in the black community.[38]

The focus on African American female domestics during tuberculosis scares also stemmed from the history of their labor in white homes and the tensions embodied in these intimate work spaces. Work had often served as the site from which black women launched the most threatening attacks on racial hierarchies in Atlanta, including the notable washerwomen's strike of 1881. These incidents challenged city boosters' carefully crafted images of the "Atlanta Spirit."[39] For how could the city be the leader of the New South if it could not control its menial laborers? Through such activism, black women proved themselves inconvenient service workers, socially difficult at best and dangerous at worst. By locating measures to protect public health in the realm of work, policies that received widespread support throughout the city, middle-class whites could also control a workforce on which many in the city depended and that entered the most vulnerable physical spaces of whites' lives, their homes.

The work of the Anti-Tuberculosis Association fed the connection of domestic workers, especially washerwomen, with the spread of disease. Caseworkers revealed their narrow and negative views of African American clients in records that focused as much on black women's attitudes and work, including the number of washings each did for white families, as their health. The case history for Lulu Cartwright, for example, read, "The girl was in the [second] stage of marked tubercular laryngitis and was doing 2 washings but had to give them up. She has since given up treatment and is taking patent medicine." "This girl," reported the case history of Minnie Willis, "when she came to the dispensary was doing washing. She was found to be in the [third] stage of the disease. She at once stopped washing according to the doctors orders and has tried faithfully as far as possible to follow out the direction given by the nurses and doctor." This relatively positive pronouncement, however, was tempered by the description of Willis's living conditions: "six people live in this house of five rooms [and] mother and grandmother take in five washings." Sallie Pride had, according to her case records, "sole care of a dying daughter, who has tuberculosis, and also does washing for seven hospital nurses, two families, and one man! Only two rooms to the house, and her next door neighbor . . . is a far advanced case of TB also. She also did washing as long as she was able."[40] The concern over these patients centered on their role as workers for white families rather than as individuals or members of families.

To solicit funds, the Anti-Tuberculosis Association often played on whites' fears of infection and uneasy relationship with African American domestic workers. In one of the quirks of the Jim Crow era, many black women had access to the intimacy of the white home, so fund-raisers had enormous success. In 1909 the organization included the story of a young black woman in its plea for financial support, releasing her story to the newspapers and emphasizing that "she had up until a week past been in the daily service of a white family, cleaning the house, waiting on the table, nursing the children."[41] Another published meeting report from 1909 bore out the opinion of the association's visiting nurses that if the "environments of many of the servants, washerwomen[,] and a large majority of the negroes were known to their employers they would be aroused to action, and before employing a servant would investigate the location of the home, the inmates, etc."[42]

In the spring of 1910, tuberculosis captured the interest of the city at large when the Atlanta Woman's Club petitioned the city council to pass an ordinance that would require all black washerwomen to register with the city. The particulars of the ordinance included mandatory medical examinations of all washerwomen, inspection of their homes, and prohibitions against either sending out or taking in washing when there was a consumptive in the house.[43] Attempts to license laundry workers had been discussed in Atlanta in 1881, during the washerwomen's strike, and again in 1905, but those measures had focused more explicitly on work conditions—keeping black women's pay low in the first instance and preventing theft in the second.[44] The proposed 1910 measure, however, used an explicit focus on protecting public health (generally meaning white health) to control the labors of African American washerwomen. By requiring the registration of black laundresses, the all-white club might force black women back into live-in employment situations or at least ensure that white women would continue to have inexpensive laundry services since the trouble and expense of registering would tie black women to the profession.

Before the city council could make any decisions concerning the registration of washerwomen, however, Nellie Peters Black of the Anti-Tuberculosis Association stepped into the discussion to ask, "What about protecting negro washerwomen from contagious diseases in the home of white people who send out soiled clothes?"[45] The council took the question to heart and amended the proposed ordinance so that it forbade residents from taking in or sending out washing if tuberculosis was present in the home. Even the *Atlanta Constitution* was quick to adopt the point, writing in an editorial, "The question of health is not one of racial distinction or the dividing lines of caste. It is mutual and inevitably interdependent."[46] White Atlantans blamed African American women for the spread of disease, but the fear of introducing tuberculosis into their homes stopped few white households from sending their out laundry. "Apparently," in the words of historian Margaret Parsons, "the fearful community contained a threshold of practicality which prevented wholesale deference to the [TB] plague."[47] With proposed amendments to the action that might restrict white access to inexpensive laundry services, the city council tabled the proposed ordinance without voting on it.

The entrenched connection between Atlanta's black washerwomen and the spread of tuberculosis resurfaced during the fall 1912 mayoral election. Candidate George Brown, a physician, built his platform on the issue of improved sanitation and public health. Brown promised to create an agency to track domestic workers' histories, habits, character, and health. He promised white voters more than just healthy servants: he pledged "absolute control of the servants in this town."[48] The Atlanta Ministers Union, a group of black clergy, objected to this proposal on the grounds that proper "sanitary appliances installed in the homes and on the premises of the tenant class and a proper enforcement of the sanitary laws of the city would reduce the probability of disease germs to the minimum," more than controlling domestic servants.[49] The ministers found little support for their plea in the white community, but Brown lost his bid for mayor.

Despite another failed registration campaign, the close connection of black women with disease did not disappear from the white community, nor did the issues embedded in this relationship. As cultural symbols, black women continued to serve as potent icons for larger white anxieties about shifting economic and spatial relations between the races, and Atlanta's white press continued to depict washerwomen as agents of contagion. In one 1914 editorial cartoon, a patient with a contagious disease is attended by a group of blacks, all labeled with their service positions—"your cook," "your butler," "your maid," and others. Only "your washerwoman" actually touches the sick individual, however, and "your clothes" hang in a corner of the room. A rejected application for city care lies on the floor, an indictment of the city's lack of effort toward controlling contagious diseases among the African Americans who would then bring these illnesses into white homes.[50] A cartoon run by the *Constitution* the next day proclaimed "another servant problem" as a disease-carrying domestic worker leaves her home of "contagious disease," located on a river of filth next to the city dump; easily bypasses the wall of "sanitary precaution" built on screens, pure water, garbage cans, good sewage, and medical science; and travels into the "average white home."[51] While both drawings point to the lack of adequate sanitation and health care for blacks, the African American domestic worker was pictured as the threat of contagion to whites, the link between the diseased black community and the healthy white population. As in 1909, the call to action in black neighborhoods remained focused on the desire to protect "clean" white neighborhoods and the city's overall reputation.

In large part because of the association of black women with tuberculosis, African American women became the site on which the white public health movement intersected with black reform efforts in 1910s Atlanta. As health care historian Edward Beardsley has noted, "In an era when black people were virtually shut off from participation in white society, promotion of the health and welfare of the race offered one of the few outlets for Black leadership . . . which had sympathy if not support from whites."[52] Indeed, Rosa Lowe, the white secretary of the Anti-Tuberculosis Association, concluded public health workers bore the responsibility for establishing "a friendly relation between these two races living in one community, upon both of whom the responsibility rest for a healthful city."[53]

For African American reformers, whites' concern over black health, even if it stemmed from fears of the menace to white society, offered an opportunity to advance community issues. Public health became an arena in which the African American elite could make political demands, such as better city services, with little fear of retribution. Considering the dearth of overt political organizing in the decade and a half following the 1906 race riot, then, this represented a campaign of significant proportions for a third of the city's population. The Anti-Tuberculosis Association's black-run Negro Committee used its relationship with white public health organizers to successfully petition the city government for better sanitation and recreation facilities in black neighborhoods, for example.[54] Lugenia Burns Hope, a member of the committee, persuaded the association to apply monetary resources to Neighborhood Union health programs, including the annual clean-up campaign, neighborhood surveys, and community education. In the end, antituberculosis programs for African Americans expanded and reinforced the health work of Atlanta's black organizations, including the Urban League, the ministerial association, life insurance companies, and the Young Men's Christian Association.

For black civic organizations, TB provided an unmatched opportunity to deploy the racial uplift philosophy. These groups took white dollars, combined them with substantial monetary support from the black community, and set out to remedy the poor conditions in black neighborhoods. African American organizations hoped that improving physical surroundings would build respectability and that this trend toward cleanliness and morality would challenge the basis of discrimination. A desire to not alienate white benefactors might have shaped this approach. A belief that even if tuberculosis had come from white families and that even if a lack of city sanitation services nurtured it, black domestic workers remained the key figure bringing the disease into African American households might also have been at work. Consequently, the efforts of the Negro Committee, the Neighborhood Union, and the other organizations involved never directly countered the negative portrayals of black women. As long as tuberculosis still seemed out of control, the washerwoman would continue to carry the stigma of pollution.

Despite extensive programs aimed directly at eliminating tuberculosis from Atlanta's white population, blacks' health received the most sustained attention in discussions of the disease. Jim Crow laws and practices functioned fairly effectively to separate the races in this era, but the implications of this policy go a long way toward explaining why white Atlanta saw tuberculosis as the disease of the black washerwomen. Although racial segregation was largely complete in Atlanta in the 1910s, domestic work still brought blacks and whites into close physical proximity and did so in the most intimate spaces of white life. And unlike most other employment situations, whites had few alternative labor sources. Racism of the day and the "business first" philosophy of white elected officials also meant that Atlanta's meager city resources went first to downtown and to elite white residences. Sewers and lighting barely made it into middle-class white neighborhoods, let alone into black areas. The spread of tuberculosis highlighted the folly of that prioritization. Atlantans grappled in the 1910s with the choice of giving up black domestic labor or funneling at least a pittance into the black community. The city chose the latter, but the demonization of black washerwomen in the process reveals that white Atlanta did so reluctantly and only to protect access to domestic workers and claims to being a healthful city.

Venereal Disease

ATLANTA in the early twentieth century demonstrated remarkable persistence in its association of women with the spread of infectious disease. A second public health movement developed in Atlanta just as the tuberculosis scare was losing its grip on the city in the late 1910s, but this time young white women most often played the role of diseased villain. Perceptions of venereal disease tainted its female victims with immorality because of the parts of the body infected and because of transmission through sexual activity. The military and Atlanta's government officials united in their attacks on women, proclaiming prostitutes and single women the source of all disease spread to soldiers and civilians. The culpability of men's sexual liaisons outside of marriage received scant attention during the war in the face of women's growing economic independence and visible presence on the streets.

As a direct result, attempts to stop the spread of the diseases suspended women's individual rights in the interest of public health. By 1917 medical communities understood the transmission of venereal disease and had developed both tests and treatments (prophylactic and therapeutic) for them. While doctors could treat VD, the key to controlling the disease remained preventing its spread. The onset of World War I gave the social hygiene movement a sense of crisis in battling venereal disease. The location of three military bases in and around Atlanta pushed the city to inaugurate one of the most thorough campaigns to restrict single women's activities and again brought the city's working-class women to the center of controversy.

While the association of African American women with tuberculosis had a strong connection to the city's labor structures, the venereal disease crackdown sprang largely from political efforts to promote economic growth. The persecution of known and suspected prostitutes during World War I was born not so much from a sincere effort to rid the city of vice but from an urban booster project designed to attract national war disbursements to the city. With growing American involvement in the European war during late 1917 and early 1918, prostitution came to prominence in Atlanta's politics as most city officials and influential businessmen became united in their opinion that a crackdown on prostitution would be the key to bringing a lucrative military base to the area. Prostitutes, widely blamed for the spread of venereal disease by local reformers and city officials, became the internal enemy to be conquered, and all efforts to this end made the city appear willing to take the measures necessary to ensure a wholesome environment for the country's fighting men.

In preparing troops for the war in the spring of 1917, the federal government developed a bureaucratic and legal structure to battle venereal disease. In April 1917, the War Department created the Commission on Training Camp Activities, which sought to slow the spread of venereal disease through "uplift and distraction," creating a host of in-camp recreational activities for soldiers.[55] The commission also coordinated the efforts of private organizations such as the Young Men's Christian Association in the creation of these types of programs. Also in April, the General Medical Board of the Council of National Defense and its Committee on Hygiene and Sanitation were formed to help control venereal disease in the communities surrounding the military camps. The legal foundation for battling venereal disease was set with the passage of the Selective Service Act of 1917. Sections 12 and 13 of the act forbade liquor and prostitution in areas around the camps. This became the basis on which both local and federal government agencies could attack prostitution during the war. These "moral zones" were protected by the Law Enforcement Division of the Commission on Training Camp Activities, which carried out the provisions of the Draft Act. With federal assistance, local agencies took over responsibility for policing prostitution and liquor in the moral zones in the fall of 1917. Meanwhile, national officials turned their attention to education as a means of prevention with the creation of the Committee on Protective Work for Girls.[56]

Fort McPherson had existed on Atlanta's outskirts since the 1880s. With the onset of the war, however, Atlanta businesses, led by the Chamber of Commerce, sought to bring another training camp to the area. In preparing Atlanta to host a camp, the chamber urged the city to clean up "the 'black cloud' of drunkenness, vice and immorality that threatens" and to "lend your undivided assistance in staying this tidal wave of moral filth and depravity from engulfing us, to the ruin of our young men and women of today." Atlanta's leaders promised the federal government a "healthy moral atmosphere, and a zone free from drunkenness, prostitution and kindred vices" if a camp were to be located near the city.[57] A site in De Kalb County was selected, and Camp Gordon opened to soldiers in September 1917.[58]

Both the federal and local campaigns to eradicate VD understood prostitutes to be the main carriers and transmitters of the disease. In Atlanta and across the country, prostitutes who might have been seen as the victims of male lust in earlier decades drew no such sympathy during the war.[59] The military and the social hygiene movement accepted male lust as a given and represented single and potentially sexually active women as "predatory and diseased."[60] Popular notions reinforced the idea that prostitutes transmitted venereal diseases to soldiers, who would then take the illnesses home to infect "innocent wives and children."[61] As one social hygienist and government official boldly stated, "the human beings who individually expose the most of the rest of humankind to this disease are women."[62] The only women who appear to have been exempt from these generalizations were married and did not work outside the home. Popular notions of women shifted as young women lost their former association with sexual passivity and instead shouldered the burden of being labeled "dangerously lustful" by society.[63]

In Atlanta, this suspicion of any woman who moved around the city streets dovetailed with the persecution (arrest, detention, mandatory testing, and treatment) of prostitutes, further blurring the line between working women and prostitutes, who often occupied some of the same boardinghouses, dance halls, theaters, and streets.[64] While official policies targeted only prostitutes, city and military officials expanded the category's definition to include almost any woman found in a public place. Local aldermen even attempted to create citywide regulation of wage-earning women by proposing that all female workers between the ages of sixteen and fifty-five carry a work card when on the streets, implying that coming and going from work represented the only legitimate time for women to be on the street.[65] The police, supported by military officers, bore the brunt of the responsibility for controlling Atlanta's prostitution and, consequently, Atlanta's women. Police Chief James L. Beavers enlisted the aid of the Recorder's Court and Judge George E. Johnson to crack down on the vice trade and inflict "severe penalties" on prostitutes. In 1917, women brought before Judge Johnson on prostitution charges "received a minimum of thirty days in the Stockade or $25 fine, and a maximum of sixty days, a $100 fine, and [were] ordered to leave the City on the completion of the sentence." Johnson also reportedly promised women in open court to "make it too hot for your kind of woman in Atlanta."[66]

Attempts to control liquor and especially prostitution in the fall of 1917 included arresting suspected streetwalkers and closing hotels and dance halls where soldiers were supposedly being solicited. Military police were assigned to appear as soldiers and induce women to approach. Any who did were then turned over to local police. During these sting operations, officers allegedly found "prostitutes who are registering in the Hotels, staying there permanently, and having their customers brought to them by the bell-boys, and other employees of this type in the Hotels."[67] Military and local police soon realized that news of their undercover operations had spread throughout the venues they patrolled. Women became "much more cautious in soliciting business, and in the majority of cases the soliciting [was] done by pimps or cadets who are driving public automobiles," officials reported to their superiors.[68] The sanitation officer for Camp Gordon came to believe that prostitutes were marrying soldiers to hide "in [the] supposed security of [their] marriage license [while] plying [their] trade."[69] Although married women were not usually associated with prostitution, even they entered the realm of those suspected of immoral behavior and disease when they ventured onto the streets or into commercial amusements. This ultimately became the crux of the crackdown, as word of the stings spread and prostitutes became more difficult to find: all women traveling alone became suspected carriers of venereal disease.

By the winter of 1917 and early 1918, local, state, and national agencies had created laws and practices allowing the police wide latitude in controlling women. Military officers and federal health officials began discussing mandatory examinations, detention, and treatment of Atlanta's "lewd women" under the Draft Act.[70] Officials quickly adopted this policy and set up space for examining women inside the police department. The Georgia legislature passed the Lewd House Law in 1917 to facilitate the closing of red-light districts. And in 1918, legislators finally raised the age at which a female might legally give sexual consent from ten to eighteen. The impetus for this bill's passage was far different than the protection of young women and girls envisioned by the middle-class women who had first brought the issue to the legislature in 1900. The 1918 act, according to its supporters, protected "girls" not so much from men as from themselves.[71] Also in 1918, venereal disease clinics opened in the city jail, commonly referred to as the stockade, where women were detained while being treated and tried. With federal money, the city opened the Pinecrest Detention Home for Girls in Fulton County to house wayward girls, although most women were still held in the stockade.[72] The state also passed the Venereal Disease Control Law, which ensured the police had similar powers to those outlined in the Selective Service Act. This act allowed the Recorder's Court to detain women with a high bail bond requirement while binding them over to the state courts. The process of binding over women suspected of carrying venereal disease ensured that the women would remain in custody, where they could be tested and treated, even if the charge on which they were arrested had no chance of leading to conviction.[73] Even the Georgia Training School for Girls adopted a policy of conducting VD tests on all women remanded to the institution.[74] In essence, women's potential sexuality and their presence in public places was criminalized in an effort to control venereal disease.

To counter the growing ineffectiveness of plainclothes detectives and military officers in entrapping women for sex-related crimes, the police department hired two women police officers in 1918.[75] This move was widely supported by civic organizations, including the Atlanta Woman's Club, the City Federation of Women's Clubs, and the Evangelical Ministers Association, as well as by the federal government. At the urging of the district supervisor for the Committee on Protective Work for Girls, the Chamber of Commerce resolved that "the Police [Committee] of the City of Atlanta be urged to appoint two women protective workers with police power for this work with women and girls, and that the finance committee of the City Council be urged to make the necessary appropriation, not only as an emergency need, but as a patriotic duty."[76] Dance halls, theaters, and hotels fell under the investigative purview of the new policewomen, who also, in conjunction with the Committee on Protective Work for Girls, patrolled the city streets looking for wayward young women.[77]

With the institution of measures to battle venereal disease, the Atlanta police received numerous requests to extend their efforts even further, revealing the new policies' popular support among the middle classes. A group of nurses, represented by the pastor of the Baptist Tabernacle Church, alerted the police committee to "the degrading type of negro prostitutes living in houses in the immediate vicinity of the Grady Hospital" in the hopes that the police would raid the district. Reverend John Ham "insisted on the Board condemning certain zones, in that locality, where vice is being tolerated, in such a manner that it was a disgrace to the City of Atlanta."[78] Fulton County, in which most of Atlanta lies, convened a grand jury on the subject of prostitution and increasing crime, recommending to Atlanta police that "with regard to liquor peddling, gambling, prostitution and other crime of various nature being indulged in . . . the houses of ill repute operating in the city should be broken up."[79] While women were experiencing increasing pressure from both public and private agencies, men were treated with complete leniency by both military and civil police. A prophylactic station and sleeping accommodations were even established in the City Auditorium to facilitate soldiers on leave from the training camps.

The efforts at legal and moral discipline for the city's working-class women served to destabilize images of women as independent or responsible individuals. Many women's mental capacities were challenged, as a number of those arrested and detained were declared "feeble-minded."[80] The emphasis on women as "emotionally unstable" or as having "defective personalities," argues historian Barbara Hobson, supposedly "offered proof that these women needed protection."[81] In other instances, women, "attracted by the lure of the uniforms," were painted as too young to understand that their presence in the city placed them "unconsciously in moral danger."[82] Local and federal officials tended to divide women into two groups, prostitutes and "young girls [who] would come in contact with prostitutes."[83] In response to claims that VD control measures were biased against women, social hygienists argued that "the careful laboratory examination should bring the individual relief and reassurance, if the test is negative; if positive, surely no sane mind could but welcome a scientific treatment of these diseases as soon as he or she is informed of their seriousness."[84] The message in this statement was clear: women who objected to their treatment at the hands of police, venereal disease clinics, and the military were not sane.

The stigmatization of women, particularly young and single women, as criminal or mentally defective crossed racial lines. As in other southern cities with training camps, Atlanta's social hygienists and police showed great interest in controlling the activities of black women as well as white. The least vitriolic descriptions of the threat posed by African American women drew on references to their poor environment and their status as sexual prey. "The colored girl," argued a prominent social hygienist, "has less education, less legal protection. She lives under less sanitary conditions in over-crowded houses in dark streets and alleys. She has less recreational opportunities. Her economic status is lower. She is herself the offspring of a girl with the same or a worse environment, and she is the prey of the men of both races."[85] In other cases and despite copious medical literature that described the mode of transmission for these diseases as sexual contact, some white social hygienists explained the spread of VD between the races as the result of "infection of the white population generally by negroes through contacts other than sex intercourse."[86] Even for those who chose to entertain the possibility of consensual interracial sex, however, blacks still carried the blame for transmitting the disease to whites.

While African American women generally attracted less attention than white women during the World War I venereal disease hysteria, efforts to stop the spread of venereal disease by black women usually resembled the measures directed at white women. Atlanta police frequently raided "disorderly houses in the colored section" looking for prostitutes.[87] At the urging of members of the police committee who felt "it was a disgrace to the city to allow negro women to meet boys and men in the alleys and rooms in this vicinity," African American streetwalkers also received particular police attention.[88] Police arrested, examined, and detained black women much like white women, though prisoners in the jail were segregated by race. In the fall of 1917, military health officers declared off-limits African American sections of the city and white mill districts, where white soldiers might meet young women, and in 1919, Atlanta hired a "colored matron" to process the increasing number of African American women arrested in the wake of the venereal disease crackdown.[89]

As in other locations across the country during this period, Atlanta's fight against venereal disease brought together a variety of agendas and organizations, including medical, legal, and educational authorities. Women were arrested, prosecuted, and detained under a combination of federal legislation (the Selective Service Act), state laws (the Venereal Disease Control Law and the Lewd House Law), and local ordinances. The clinics that tested and treated women were locally run—the Emory University clinic at the Atlanta Medical College, the Grady Hospital dispensary, and the Auburn Avenue clinic for blacks—but were funded with federal money.[90] So it was with full legal and monetary support at every level of government that Atlanta's women were pursued and criminalized as the carriers of venereal disease.

Private agencies also joined in the battle against disease. The Young Women's Christian Association gave lectures to young working-class women on the evils of promiscuity and the moral dangers of the city and sponsored clubs and guilds for young women in hopes of keeping them off the streets. Other organizations, including parent-teacher associations and women's clubs, took advantage of government-sponsored educational programs, especially lectures, to educate young women away from popular amusements. The Travelers' Aid Society intercepted women in the train station and on the street, sending them home again or to an approved boardinghouse, where they could be supervised. Even factory managers ran programs for their industrial workers, particularly women, on sex hygiene.[91] In 1918 groups of Atlanta women first began watching the film *Fit to Fight*, which had previously been directed only at soldiers.[92] All of these educational programs were supported by federal agencies. The Commission on Training Camp Activities and the Committee on Protective Work for Girls distributed literature, posters, and movies used by private organizations in Atlanta in hopes of creating a national movement against vice, and therefore against vp.[93]

Federal and local mobilization against venereal disease represented layers of anxieties attached to the war in Europe and changes on the home front. Key among these, according to Allan Brandt, was the transformation of sexuality as a public issue.[94] At the heart of this transformation was the increasingly common public viewing of working-class women's bodies. On the most basic level, the arrest and involuntary examination and treatment of women gave police and military officials almost unlimited control over women's bodies. Labeled "speculum rape" by contemporary feminists, these inspection and treatment practices were supported by law and institution.[95]

Other, less invasive measures also placed women on display as both physical bodies and cultural symbols. Public amusements became sites for observation of women by police and "soldier detectives." These undercover agents reported private conversations to local officials and national agencies and often repeated these stories during court hearings for women arrested as prostitutes.[96] Even in outdoor public gathering places, young single women were on display. In one instance, "mill authorities placed upon the roof of the building several large flood lights, and this park is now brilliantly illuminated after dark."[97] New police measures required officers to record "the name and address of every girl and woman arrested for any cause, the time and place of arrest, the charge upon which the arrest was made, the name of the arresting officer, and his statement, the statement of the person arrested, their description, name of their parents, family history, age, education, health, employment and such other personal history as may be obtained, and the disposition of the case."[98] The information gathered on arrested women extended far beyond that collected for men.

Beyond these specific measures, the most pervasive effect of the social hygiene movement was the rewriting of women's sexuality through middle-class standards. Indeed, as Brandt argues, the World War I venereal disease crisis enabled reformers to demand a "civilized morality" that meant "sexual continence outside of marriage" for all classes.[99] Middle-class moral codes had previously served to reinforce the distance between social classes. Unmarried working-class women who appeared in the public spaces of the city, as evidenced by crackdown on female dance hall and theater patrons in 1912, were viewed as promiscuous. This characterization acquired a new taint of danger in the context of World War I and the rapid spread of venereal disease. Women suspected of being prostitutes "were considered immodest, and their bodies were consequently viewed as public property."[100] Held responsible for the transmission of venereal disease, both white and black women became "friends of the enemy" and therefore forfeited their right to privacy.[101] The only safe recourse for women lay in the adoption of the older generation's middle-class moral standards, which advocated intraracial sex and sex only within the confines of marriage.

With the end of World War I in November 1918, national support for anti–venereal disease work was discontinued. Local programs, such as the Pinecrest Detention Home for Girls, that had relied on federal funds were also shut down.[102] The Evangelical Ministers Association and other private organizations lobbied the city to maintain examination and detention policies, but the programs withered without financial support. The city council also abandoned the practice of detaining women with venereal disease in the city stockade. As a local paper reported, the council resolved, "This was a war measure, and the war is over. The city prison is not a place for the detention and treatment of such people afflicted with contagious and infectious diseases."[103] Atlanta did not abandon all venereal disease work, however, and small sums of money were contributed to the maintenance of local VD clinics.[104] This now voluntary testing and treatment of both men and women continued through the 1920s, though it never again reached its wartime scale, and the focus on women as the cause of the diseases evaporated.[105]

The persecution of women as carriers of venereal disease developed as a direct response to the wartime conditions that brought young men and women to Atlanta in record numbers. Employment for white women, in particular, jumped with the expanding job market and the need to replace men in the industrial sector. The growing economic independence of wage-earning women threatened established gender roles, as women used their paychecks to live outside of the confines of family and to explore the variety of available amusements. Government officials and businessmen stepped in to restrict women's movement and, with widespread middle-class support for controlling venereal disease, constructed an elaborate system of confinement and treatment that ultimately made city streets dangerous for unescorted women. With the war's end, however, these programs were dismantled under the assumption that stable family structures would return, eliminating the need for external controls of women.

The Language of Protection

THE FLIP SIDE of the persecution of women as potential carriers of VD during World War I was, of course, the issue of protection. The social hygiene movement sought to protect soldiers against "the greatest destroyer of man-power," venereal disease.[106] Some reformers also asked that "women be honored and protected as the sisters, wives, and future mothers of the race we are fighting for."[107] By promoting women identified primarily by their family relationships, which were rooted in the home, the anti-VD campaign labeled as loose women who functioned outside of these roles and tainted such women with the suspicion of a social disease. These constructions helped to counteract women's growing mobility during the war years. Increased industrial opportunities led both urban and rural women into factories and other types of wage work. Other women, labeled camp followers, moved to cities to be near husbands, friends, and family involved in the war effort. For many Atlantans, the spread of venereal disease bore out the chaotic possibilities inherent in the changing lives of women brought on by rapid urbanization and the war. The resulting social hygiene movement struggled to rein in women who ventured too far outside of accepted gender roles and to warn others away before they followed a similar path.

Even as Atlanta cracked down on women in public spaces, local officials and social hygienists sought to control women not yet labeled loose, especially new migrants. The Chamber of Commerce, interested in ensuring the continuance of the military spending that members had worked so hard to bring to Atlanta, were particularly interested in "the welfare and guidance of the girl on the outside," particularly if she was "employed in proper vocations in the city, the mother, wife, sister, or sweetheart."[108] Consequently, the city and private businesses supported the Hostess Houses maintained by the YWCA. Few who came to "temporarily be citizens of Atlanta" were left unobserved. As Mayor Asa Candler noted, "even if they are all intent on doing the right thing and living in harmony with the moral code," this transient population "will need by precept and example to be directed as well as protected."[109] Arguments of protection, then, became as much a justification for public viewing and control of women as suspicion of venereal disease was.

Beyond solidifying gender distinctions, the language of protection also reinforced class and racial hierarchies. Policing public amusements and hotels frequented by the working classes was justified in terms of patriotic duty. Atlanta's civic leaders stressed that controlling the spread of venereal disease was a form of "loyal, patriotic and unselfish service."[110] Those who opposed the city's attempts to control the use of public spaces and to enforce a middle-class moral code were "laggards" or "slackers." By emphasizing the spread of venereal disease through the vices of prostitution and liquor, usually associated with such working-class spaces as black neighborhoods, cheap theaters, and dance halls, the city's white business and political elite created a comfortable distance between their social class and diseased lower classes.

In the hands of African American leaders, arguments for protection took on new meanings. The Atlanta Colored Women's War Committee, a body appointed by the Atlanta Division of the War Department Commission on Training Camp

Activities to represent black organizations' viewpoints, urged "the same rigid measures be adopted for the suppression of the colored prostitute as for the white." Explicit in this request was the class-based fear that the police crackdown on brothels and hotels had driven prostitutes into "the best [black] residential sections of the City, proving thereby a menace to the moral well-being of the entire community."[111] The targeting of women as the carriers of disease and a threat to social order appears secondary, though, to arguments of protection that advocated improved rights and services for the black community as a whole.

African American neighborhoods, struggling under the limits of segregation, received almost no city services. For more than a decade, the Neighborhood Union and other civic organizations had argued for better sanitation, recreation, and other improvements. With the outbreak of World War I, however, black institutions developed new arguments using the language of protection. Realizing that African American communities were blamed for much of the city's vice, the Colored Women's War Work Committee suggested better lighting to counteract the "menace to the welfare of the City." The committee also played on white fears of vice and crime with its proposal to materially improve the lives of wage-earning African American women by advocating that domestics "be relieved from duty so as to return to their homes before dark." Arguing that "such action on the part of employers would be eminently patriotic and conducive to general public safety," the committee remained ambiguous on whether it was advocating protection *from* black women or *for* black women.[112]

The most pervasive argument advanced by the black civic elite during World War I called for increased police protection in African American neighborhoods. In calling for increased law enforcement, black advocates aware of the traditional tensions between white police officers and African American residents requested that officers "be selected with great care, so that only men of reliable and dependable character be chosen, and that such men be chosen for provost guards as are not so pronounced in their racial antipathies and antagonisms."[113] To gain this end, leaders required the cooperation of the city and military officials from local training camps. Some poor and working-class black women were subtly sacrificed to meet this goal when community leaders held them up as a lure for law enforcement officers. The Neighborhood Union, for example, accelerated its practice of pointing out the race's "bad" elements, primarily women suspected of prostitution, to city officials in the hopes of proving the overall respectability of the city's black communities.

By encouraging vice raids to target some women, middle-class African American women could deny the myth of promiscuity so often applied to all black women. In clashes between black community leaders and YWCA officials for control over southern black branches of the organization, Adelle Ruffin, the "colored work" organizer for the South, accused Neighborhood Union founder Lugenia Burns Hope of trying to save "immoral Alley Girls." Hope and her supporters responded that "a good girl [living] in the 'alley' should not be cut off from the opportunities offered by the YWCA."[114] By establishing homes for women working in factories and hostess houses to shelter wives visiting their husbands in the camps, African American war workers promoted most black women as worthy of protection.[115] The Atlanta Colored Women's War Work Council also organized Patriotic Leagues for the "protection of our girls."[116] Similar to the politics of respectability employed by the Neighborhood Union in the preceding decade, African American elites' dealings with women during World War I enforced distinctions and class hierarchies within the black community and used the images of working-class black women as fodder for political wrangling.

After World War I, African American organizations incorporated some arguments for the protection of black women. In these later efforts, the protection of black womanhood became even more clearly linked to the promotion of racial equality. Members of the Southeastern Federation of Negro Women's Clubs allied themselves with white reformers by highlighting similarities in their "visions [that] include the welfare of women of every race and condition." Realizing that most contact between and black and white women took place between employer and domestic worker, the Southeastern Federation and Women's Missionary Council's Committee on Inter-Racial Relations argued for improved "physical, moral and spiritual life of those so employed."[117] These organizations also advocated protection of domestic workers from "exposure to moral temptations" and "undesirable housing conditions." To ensure this "protection in and out of the home," reformers recommended standardized hours, duties, and pay and advised white women to investigate the "character of recreation" in which domestics engaged.[118] In the wake of World War I, however, interracial work became the overarching focus of the black community's race work.

BY ASSOCIATING women with disease in early-twentieth-century Atlanta, the city's middle classes created the "dangerous" counterpart to the hopeful mother image used by welfare and civic agencies. The transgressive nature of women's paid labor—bringing women out of the home, into the street, and even into the homes of elites—and increasing anxiety over women's presence in public spaces resurfaced in the battle to preserve public health in the 1910s. In the minds of many Atlantans, working-class women provided the crucial links among respectability, morality, and the physical environment. Consequently, controlling women's behavior through "social uplift" programs in the name of public health became one way Atlanta's elite and middle classes sought to create a morally and physically safe environment for themselves and, they hoped, the city as a whole.

permanent compensation for loss of the store. Mrs. Christian's actions in this case reveal much of the content and tone of working-class women's direct interaction with the government and legal structures of the city by the 1910s.

Mrs. Christian created an identity for herself outside her role as wife and based on her ability to earn an income. Her story demonstrates some of the opportunities available to women in Atlanta in the 1910s as well as women's willingness to take advantage of them. Mrs. Christian did not completely eschew her wifely identity, but she did see it as distinct from her life as the proprietor of a tiny grocery store. Through her hard labors in a more traditional woman's occupation, running a boardinghouse, she had earned the right to the status and profits created by the store. When she thought she needed to defend her rights, she—and numerous other working-class women like her—took action. But she did not sue her husband for ownership of the store; instead, she sought a divorce. She softened the potentially threatening nature of her independence by taking her claims to a venue, divorce court, in which women were common and by couching her claims in a familiar narrative of domestic strife. If she won (unfortunately there is no record of the outcome of the case), she could regain a source of income and rid herself of a "quarrelsome" spouse. A favorable divorce ruling would protect her independent status—she would again be a single woman, but this time she would have financial assets and business skills.

Despite not be able to vote, working-class women in the 1910s in Atlanta influenced the political milieu and demonstrated a clear conception of themselves as citizens, though, like Mrs. Christian, they often did so in individualistic and indirect ways. Working-class women utilized clubs and organizations, petitions to government agencies, and the court system to effect change for themselves, their families, and their neighborhoods. Black and white working-class women alike participated in these activities, and although they did not work together, their approaches demonstrated remarkably similar strategies for pursuing their goals.

In general, Atlanta's political debates of the 1910s—highly contested mayoral campaigns, bond issues, charter reforms, and moral crusades—recognized little of working-class women's political perspective or claims to citizenship status.[2] Images of working-class women, however, peppered the dialogues surrounding many of these issues. Atlanta's antiprostitution crusade in the fall of 1912, for example, demonstrated how easily working-class women could become voiceless political symbols to be manipulated by others. Prostitutes served as props that reformers, political candidates, the city council, the police committee, the chief of police, and middle-class reformers manipulated in a struggle for power. The campaigns for women's suffrage, particularly those waged in the 1910s on behalf of the municipal vote for women, also relied on the symbolic potency of white working-class women's lives. In the first two decades of the century, middle-class women from a variety of organizations crusaded for the vote in the city and state.

In contrast to the prostitution crackdown, working-class women found at least a limited voice in these suffrage crusades. While their role was small, working-class women provided a valuable constituency for the middle-class suffrage organizations and the middle-class political organizations that emerged after women were granted the vote.

Atlanta's African Americans, especially elite business owners and educators, worked diligently to create a political dialogue on the matter of race relations with white Atlanta. For example, Benjamin Davis Sr., the outspoken editor of the *Atlanta Independent,* regularly challenged his readers to exercise their right to vote whenever possible. But most of the political dialogue created by the city's blacks in the decade or so following the riot of 1906 focused on the politics of respectability and racial uplift—proving blacks a moral, hardworking race, worthy of political inclusion. The language of uplift suffused discussions of public health and welfare, but the approach was indirect and therefore easily ignored by white power holders. When the issues raised by blacks seemed to overlap with concerns for whites' health and welfare, Atlanta's politicians and white middle class would pay it some heed, as was the case during the tuberculosis scare. Essentially, however, blacks could not push their voices into discussions of formal political issues in the 1900s and 1910s. Consequently, black women as political actors are more readily seen in discussions of welfare and public health than in the discussions of suffrage or city services. This invisibility in one realm did not reflect African American inactivity or complacency but rather the racially circumscribed world of segregation-era politics.

By far the most pervasive political activism of Atlanta's black and white working-class women was far less sensational than the closing of the red-light district, the tuberculosis scare, or the suffrage campaigns. Instead, working-class women enacted their political aspirations through city and state courts, the city council, the police committee, and limited club work. While these activities had little impact on the structure of city government or the parties in power, the victories of women in these small battles changed families, neighborhoods, and daily lives in far more significant ways than any election could. While only passing participants in the suffrage movement and campaigns for bond issues and charter reforms, working-class women such as Mrs. Christian interacted as citizens with governing and legal institutions, asserting the right to address these bodies and expressing clear expectations that grievances would be remedied through these channels.

Eliminating the "Houses in Our Midst"

ONE OF Atlanta's most sensational early-twentieth-century political battles erupted during the fall 1912 antiprostitution campaign. Indeed, the conflict over the closing of the city's red-light district was one extreme in the range of political interests invested in the image and control of working-class women. The sense of crisis during these months was built around the potent image of white women forced into prostitution by unscrupulous factory owners and white slavers, yet women themselves had virtually no influence on the unfolding events. Black prostitutes were largely ignored despite the efforts of groups such as the Neighborhood Union to prompt city officials to crack down on black vice as well as white.[3] Not only were individual women notably absent from the antiprostitution campaign, but the events surrounding the closing of the vice district, despite their focus on working-class women, white slavery, and prostitution, did little to alter women's relationship to the formal political structure. As the prostitution crackdown demonstrates, images of working-class women appeared almost overnight, but once the issues they had been created to represent were resolved, the images disappeared almost as quickly. Consequently, the occupants of the closed brothels and the women placed under suspicion were quickly forgotten in the wake of power struggles among city and county officials, police, and reformers.

On September 24, 1912, Atlantans woke to headlines announcing a war against prostitution. The chief of police, James L. Beavers, ordered all brothels in the segregated vice district around Manhattan Street to close their doors immediately and all residents to vacate the houses within two weeks. Beavers threatened to arrest and prosecute any prostitutes, managers, or owners remaining in the brothels after October 7. Reformers and church groups canvassed the neighborhood, seeking to "secure homes and positions for those of the outcasts who are willing to make the attempt toward leading decent lives."[4] By October 7, most of the houses had been vacated. Local papers, which followed the unfolding events with great interest, reported that many prostitutes left the city and that a hundred or more accepted the help of reformers in finding legitimate work and respectable housing.[5] In the weeks following the announcement of the closing of Atlanta's tenderloin district, political factions in the city became increasingly divided over Beavers's actions. The ensuing debates shaped that year's mayoral race as well as the power relations between the police chief and members of the police committee and between reformers and the city council.

Prostitution, of course, was not new to the city, but the process of urbanization increasingly commercialized the trade.[6] The segregation of vice into distinct neighborhoods in the late nineteenth century, however, kept most Atlantans content to let prostitution exist without much incident as long as it did not intrude into their neighborhoods. By the 1880s, Atlanta's most concentrated prostitution district ran along Collins Street, starting one block from the railroad station.[7] The brothels in this area became so infamous that nearby wealthy residents petitioned the city council to change the name of the northern end of the street to Courtland in an effort to disassociate their neighborhood from the red-light district south of Decatur Street.[8] Shortly after the turn of the twentieth century, the red-light district shifted toward Terminal Station as speculators built new brothels in the Manhattan, Hulsey, and Magnolia Street area. At the heart of this new district lay Mechanic Street, "an out-of-the-way little street in the shadow of the gas tanks and city incinerator," where police largely ignored the presence of vice until 1912.[9]

During the first decade of the twentieth century, scattered and sensationalized stories of white slavery appeared in the local papers, along with reports of consistently high numbers of arrests for prostitution-related activities. In 1907, for example, reports of "Chinamen" drugging young women in a Decatur Street chop suey parlor briefly captured the city's attention.[10] While newspapers promised that the case would "develop into one of the most sensational . . . in Atlanta for a long time," a series of arrests quickly dissipated public interest. Each year between one and two hundred people were arrested on charges of "being a lewd woman on the streets at night," "keeping and occupying a house of ill fame," or "being in company with lewd women on streets at night."[11] Vague calls for better opportunities for the city's working-class women usually accompanied newspaper stories, but an organized movement against vice never materialized.

Before the 1910s, the municipal government, police department, and many businessmen openly tolerated prostitution. Complaints from citizens and neighborhoods about the presence of vice resulted in more evictions of individual prostitutes than arrests.[12] Even Atlanta's growing reputation as a convention site was in part based on the notoriety of its red-light district and leniency toward vice.[13] This began to change in the spring of 1911, however, when members of the evangelical Men and Religion Forward Movement (MRFM) initiated a campaign to eliminate Atlanta's segregated vice districts.

The MRFM, part of a national movement to bring men back to the Christian Church, upheld a broad social justice agenda through which members hoped to assist the less fortunate in leading better lives.[14] Holding its first meeting in April 1911, the organization immediately dedicated itself to improving the living standards of the city's poor through better working conditions, education, and, in the words of one historian, "the application of Christian principles to social issues."[15] Reportedly inspired by a speech by Jane Addams, the MRFM chose the elimination of prostitution as its first campaign. After surveying prostitution in the city, the organization concluded that local officials and police openly tolerated segregated vice districts that housed forty-four brothels and 265 prostitutes. In the segregated district alone, the seven rented brothels furnished landlords somewhere in the neighborhood of forty-four thousand dollars a year.[16] The MRFM believed that its members had the right and duty by virtue of business connections and church membership to influence public policy by demanding an end to protected vice.

In the same mode as other preventive societies functioning in cities such as New York, the MRFM attacked the city government and police force for their indifference toward prostitution. [17]

In the spring of 1912, the MRFM approached the city council with the results of the survey and a recommendation that the segregated vice district around Manhattan and Mechanic Streets be closed. The council responded with "the appointment of a Commission to study the subject of the social evil in the City of Atlanta with a view to its suppression." [18] According to MRFM Vice President Marion Jackson, rumors circulating in the city's newspapers that the vice commission's report would favor the segregation of prostitution convinced the reformers to begin a publicity campaign to raise support for closing the city's brothels. The organization ran a series of newspaper advertisements claiming that brothels existed with "the knowledge of the mayor, the City Council, the Police [Committee], and the police force, and carry on their traffic openly as commercial establishments." [19]

The image of prostitutes painted by the Men and Religion Forward campaign against vice portrayed women as victims of speculators, landlords, and even the factory owners who paid female employees less than a living wage. [20] Members believed the inmates of city's brothels were "driven by need and lured by greed into these dens." [21] In September, the MRFM published a symbolic representation of its belief that a white slavery trade that preyed on the underpaid and unprotected women of the city was flourishing in Atlanta. In this image, a naked woman is being carried off by a beast wearing the hat of protected vice and carrying the weapon of public indifference. The MRFM advocated a "fight for proper treatment, particularly of working women in the way of living wages and recreation," to battle the disastrous effects of the city's governmental complicity in prostitution. [22]

More than a battle against vice, however, Beavers's action was a single incident in a larger struggle for power with the police committee, precisely timed to undercut the authority of both the committee and the city council. The high-profile newspaper coverage of the crackdown on prostitution placed these bodies and the candidates running for mayor that fall in an awkward position. Both the candidates and city officials were forced to frame their response to Beavers in a way that would not offend the reformers, churches, and individuals who had responded favorably to the MRFM's educational campaign and now supported a war on vice.

Beavers acted alone on this issue, informing none of his superiors on the police committee of his plans. Animosity between Chief Beavers and the police committee, which was governed by the city council, had been building over the preceding months. Appointed in 1911, the chief battled almost constantly with the committee, though not publicly, over who controlled the policies and practices of Atlanta's police department. By dramatically taking the initiative in the antiprostitution campaign, Beavers publicly demonstrated his unwillingness to subordinate himself to the committee. By choosing such a popular issue on which to stake his claim to autonomy, Beavers left his superiors little room in which to maneuver. Any reprimand of the chief was bound to become public, where it might be interpreted not as a matter of police policy but as evidence of the committee's support of organized prostitution.

The battle lines that emerged during the prostitution crackdown pointed to different understandings of the origin of prostitution, yet all factions seem to have shared the basic assumption that Atlanta's reputation would best be served by the elimination of a distinct red-light district. Perhaps realizing this, Beavers had made a brilliant choice in opting to close the Manhattan Street district. This district was the most notorious red-light area in town, adding drama to Beavers's actions and making it difficult for any politician to argue for the district's continued existence. The area's eleven brothels housed only white women, furthering the image promoted by the MRFM that these prostitutes were victims of unscrupulous capitalists and appealing to white voters.[23] Rather than attempting to stop all prostitution, which would have been an expensive and time-consuming task, Beavers chose to focus on a well-defined space that could easily be patrolled and in which results would be highly visible.

Immediately following Beavers's order to close "the houses in our midst," city officials cautiously offered their support for the crackdown. The chairman of the police committee, Carlos Mason, agreed to back the chief only after making it clear to reporters that Beavers had acted alone and without the committee's prior approval. Recorder's Court Judge Nash Broyles and Mayor Winn Courtland also tendered verbal support for Beavers's campaign. The only vehement opposition to the chief came from county officials who feared that the prostitution trade would move outside of the city limits and into the jurisdiction of the county sheriff.

As Beavers became more and more of a folk hero among local clergy and readers of the *Atlanta Georgian* newspaper, other groups were drawn into the drama. Pressure from the MRFM in the press forced candidates in the mayoral election that fall to choose sides. Aldine Chambers, a local businessman and city alderman, eventually became the pro-Beavers, MRFM-endorsed candidate, while James Woodward sided with the city council. Woodward came into the race as a former printer and longtime ally of the city's white trade union community. His alliance with the city council, however, probably represented more of a politically savvy attempt to win the support of the council, to which he had been elected numerous times, rather than a working-class perspective at odds with middle-class proselytizing about prostitution. Woodward had already served three terms as Atlanta's mayor, so he knew how to work with the council, and the Atlanta Federation of Trades, which would look to Woodward as its representative, did not carry a conception of a respectable working-class that included prostitutes as working-class sisters to pipe fitters and printers.[24] Businessmen involved in Atlanta's sporting trades—gaming houses, saloons, and the like—quickly sided with the city council and police committee, fearing that a maverick police chief might next choose to harass these legal but morally suspect establishments.[25] The call to rid the city of vice had quickly become a struggle for access to political power.

Beavers carefully used his popularity with the *Atlanta Journal* and the *Atlanta Georgian* to force continued support from the city fathers. The *Journal,* for example, reported on September 25, 1912, "The lid is going down tight, it would seem, and it will stay down as long as he, James L. Beavers, is chief of police. It can be lifted only by lifting him from his official position, or by a complete revocation of the law under which he is acting."[26] Almost daily, articles detailed Beavers's story of agonizing over how to be "not only a policeman, but a man; not only an official, but a good citizen, a churchgoer, a man who loves friends and family and right living."[27] This publicity clearly made it difficult for the police committee or city council to rein in the maverick police chief lest they be accused of fostering vice.

City officials ultimately chose unequivocally to support the closing of the Manhattan district, but they warned Beavers not to "go too far" in policing other leisure trades.[28] Atlanta officials realized the symbolic use of prostitutes in public discourse had brought the chief of police momentary fame, so they shied away from openly opposing his actions, waiting for publicity surrounding the vice crackdown to subside. Attempting to capitalize on his man-of-the-hour popularity, Beavers again moved to make policy without the approval of his superiors. Almost immediately after announcing the closing of the brothels, he brought even more working-class women into his power struggle with the city government by launching a campaign against "the woman of the streets." He created a squad of plainclothes detectives to wage a "war" on "loose-living hotels and boarding houses, and the cheap motion picture shows, and the cheap soda water 'joints.'"[29]

At this point, the police committee, city council, and many of Atlanta's businessmen closed ranks to oppose the chief's zealous attacks on legitimate amusements. Atlanta officials did not oppose Beavers on this issue to protect working women's rights on the streets. Instead, businessmen and public officials understood Beavers's latest efforts to control working-class women's mobility as the first step in a crusade to close Atlanta's powerful and profitable gambling and liquor establishments. The entrepreneurs who profited from these businesses represented important constituencies that many councilmen were unwilling to alienate. Displaying the mutability of the narratives and images of working-class

women in the streets during the 1910s, both urban boosters and the city government would come to support reformers' efforts to close cheap amusements
that catered to women later in the decade. In addition, businessmen and political
leaders spearheaded the restriction of working-class women's movement with the
anti–venereal disease campaign during World War I.

In an effort to appease all sides, the city council formed the vice commission
when the MRFM confronted the council with accusations of complicity in the
prostitution trade. Seeking not to offend businessmen who profited from the
city's "sporting life," the council undoubtedly hoped the formation of a commission to study the problem would put off the MRFM and allow enough time to
pass so that public sentiment on the issue would die off. The timing of Chief
Beavers's actions, however, thrust the vice commission and its long-overdue report into the public eye. Once word of the prostitution crackdown reached the
vice commission, members called an emergency meeting to finalize their report
and respond to Beavers's actions. Seeking to counteract the image of the city
council as a supporter of segregated vice, the commission released its report on
October 7, 1912, the date all brothels in the Manhattan Street district were closed.
The commission ultimately chose to endorse Beavers's actions as well as Atlanta's
organized play movement by recommending improved recreational facilities in
the city, sex education for boys and girls, separate parks for blacks and whites,
better treatment of venereal disease, a home for wayward girls, and the complete
suppression of vice. The last point was the most difficult for the commission to
agree on. Members originally planned to advise the city council to first close down
all vice outside the segregated district and then gradually work toward the total
elimination of prostitution. With the popularity of Beavers's actions, however,
the commission feared appearing too tolerant of vice and changed its original
report.[30]

Charles Jones emerged as the spokesman for the businessmen who profited
from Atlanta's leisure trades. He accused Beavers of making no provisions for the
women who would be thrown out of their homes by the closing of the tenderloin
district. He also accused Beavers of grandstanding, wondering "whether this
crusade would have been begun if there had come to the main characters in it no
sensational advertisement." "A good many conservative citizens," he continued,
"have also wondered if any real good has come to the plain, thoughtful citizens
by charging the atmosphere with this delicate sex question about which the
less said the better."[31] In a move designed to upstage the police chief, Jones
then offered rooms in four of his houses located in the Manhattan Street area, all
former brothels, to any prostitute willing to give up her trade. Beavers retaliated by
threatening to arrest any women who accepted Jones's offer.[32] The two eventually
reached a standoff when Jones revealed that he knew the addresses of 286 brothels

still operating that he would turn over to the police only if his businesses and property were left untouched.[33]

For Jones, the offer to help prostitutes reform represented a means to attack an ambitious official whose crusading threatened the profitable gambling and liquor trade. The MRFM, however, saw the reform of prostitutes as part of a larger campaign to uplift the poorer classes in the city. The MRFM and several church groups sent reformers into the vice district, offering women assistance in finding jobs and respectable lodging (not including former brothels owned by Jones). Using money donated by former prostitute Belle Sommers, the MRFM founded the Martha's Home as a temporary shelter for women looking for legitimate work. Some churches offered women places as domestic workers in the homes of congregation members. While the reformers did find a few women willing to accept their assistance (and these cases were well publicized), most prostitutes chose to strike out on their own in other parts of town or other cities.

Only a few reports dealing with prostitutes and other women affected by the crackdown appeared in newspapers during these weeks. These printed accounts clearly map the stance of Atlanta's newspapers in the political battle between Beavers and the city government by painting prostitutes in one of two ways. In the *Atlanta Constitution,* which fully and openly supported the city council, the story of Nellie Busbee received the most attention. Busbee deeply resented the loss of her livelihood and reportedly told the police chief to "go to hell."[34] Busbee undoubtedly said what the city council thought but could not publicly say to Chief Beavers. Other accounts in the *Constitution* highlighted the scorn with which "young women from whose faces the pink tint of youth had not yet faded" calmly planned their future and rejected church organizations' offers to find them domestic positions.[35] The *Atlanta Georgian,* a pro-Beavers paper, regaled its readers with the story of Belle Sommers, a resident of the segregated district who thanked Beavers for freeing her from her wretched life. Both the *Georgian* and the *Atlanta Journal* claimed that many prostitutes contacted police and reformers, thanking them for their actions, but these women remained nameless, faceless "victims."[36] Even Busbee, who committed suicide shortly after Beavers closed the district, was never mentioned by name in the *Georgian,* and the paper reported only one line from her suicide note: "I have nothing left to live for."[37]

The *Atlanta Constitution* subtly defended the city council and police committee by offering space in which prostitutes could air their opinions of the events. One woman claimed, "The reformers and city authorities have made a mistake in their methods. There are men behind that movement who have brains enough to recognize our existence as a necessary evil, and to realize how nearly impossible it is for us to lead anything but a miserable life outside of this business." Echoing the theme of limited opportunities outside the trade, another prostitute complained of low wages offered in traditional jobs: "I tried that before I came here. The people that are offering us these princely wages never knew what it was to want in their lives, and they can't understand." Despite the centrality of prostitutes to the political battle between Beavers and his superiors, prostitutes' appeals for better job opportunities, more pay, and more "time to plan ahead what was best to do" went unheeded by both factions involved in the crackdown.[38]

By the time the houses closed in October, two political camps were clearly visible. The city council, police committee, and businessmen from the city's leisure trade all opposed Beavers. Using the supportive *Atlanta Constitution* as a mouthpiece, this faction painted Beavers as a fanatic more concerned with laws than with people. Opponents pointed to Beavers's disregard for the welfare of reforming prostitutes and innocent working-class women who were only seeking a few diversions in their otherwise miserable lives. Despite the council's commitment to protecting profitable gambling and liquor, public opposition to Beavers was continually couched in the image of the prostitute cast out on the street, only to start up her trade again in a new section of town. To them, guarding fallen young white women from the wrath of an overzealous police chief represented a politically safer stance than did government protection of the vice trade. Consequently, the *Constitution* began to run advertisements accusing Beavers of overzealously attacking white women while allowing criminals to run free.

Chief Beavers found a supportive chorus in the MRFM, among ministers, and in both the *Atlanta Journal* and the *Atlanta Georgian*. Fearing reprisals against Beavers, the MRFM continued to run bulletins heralding the chief as a hero of the people and the guardian of the city's morals. The evangelical men also succeeded in channeling much of the animosity between these two factions into the mayoral runoff scheduled to take place on October 15, 1912.

The MRFM spearheaded the effort to get candidates Woodward and Chambers to state their positions on Beavers's actions during the prostitution crackdown. By this time, women—both the prostitutes of the segregated district and those frequenting the city's commercial amusements—had become faceless pawns in the city's political battles. As relatively powerless workers in illegitimate or low-status trades, women were easily sacrificed. Even MRFM members veered away from their earlier concerns over the exploitation of women in the city's factories to advocate for business and community leaders' right to influence city government policies. Along the way, the organization also made quite a name for itself on the national reform scene. Numerous articles appeared in national publications heralding the MRFM's efforts and particularly its innovative use of newspaper advertisements to lobby for reform.[39] The MRFM's desire for political influence became starkly apparent as the organization badgered the mayoral candidates to move beyond vague statements supporting law and order and offer explicit support of Chief Beavers.

The MRFM took the unprecedented step of endorsing a candidate. Thinking the organization was leaning toward supporting Woodward, Chambers issued the concrete statement for which the MRFM had been lobbying. The organization immediately dropped any pretense of impartiality and proclaimed Chambers the candidate of choice. Horrified by this overtly political move, the city's ministers disassociated themselves from the MRFM in an attempt to maintain the Church's traditional neutrality. At the heart of the factionalization that occurred in the city's formal politics in the wake of Beavers's actions was a struggle to define the balance of power between local government officials and departments as well as the power and influence of Atlanta's wealthy business class. This phenomenon explains the evaporation of public interest in the crackdown immediately after the closing of the brothels. While the public was greatly interested in sensationalized accounts of house closings, people seemed to care little for city officials' fine distinctions over who had the power to authorize such raids. A testament to how far removed from public interest the political maneuvering of the prostitution crackdown had become, voters handed Woodward an easy victory despite his opposition to the actions of Chief Beavers.

With fall turned to winter, publicity about vice died away. Now outside of the public eye, the police committee and city council retaliated against Beavers. The committee disbanded the plainclothes detective squad that had been assigned to shadow women on the streets and in 1915 demoted Beavers to captain on grounds of insubordination and incompetence.[40] The battle for control of Atlanta's police force continued, however. Beavers successfully appealed the demotion in 1917, but the police committee filed new charges in 1923. Beavers beat those charges as well and returned as chief in 1925 and served uninterrupted until his retirement in 1932. The city council adopted many of Beavers's policies starting in 1917, when the city hired female officers to restrict women's behavior in commercial amusements during the venereal disease scare.[41] Beavers's potential to harm prosperous businesses and his flagrant attempt to usurp the power of the council-appointed police committee—not his attacks on women—led to his firing. City officials favored dispersing prostitution and policing women in dance halls and theaters as a compromise between the highly moralistic MRFM position and the profitable business of leisure—a way to foster both a good reputation for the city and a profitable leisure industry.

Likewise, the MRFM's attempts to defend Beavers from police committee attacks, not the organization's stance on prostitution, ultimately cost it much of its influence. The Chamber of Commerce convinced local newspapers to stop accepting MRFM bulletins. The MRFM tried to continue its publicity campaign through an in-house paper called *The Way,* but little market existed and the organ soon ceased publication. With the mayor elected and Beavers and the MRFM effectively silenced, Atlanta officials distanced themselves from discussions of morality. Revealing their malleability, the narratives and images that had brought working-class women and prostitutes into the center of public discourse quickly lost their symbolic importance once the struggle for political positioning had been settled. Working-class women played at best a minor role in the episode, since the issues at its heart did not concern the place of prostitutes in the city but rather the possibilities for political power.

Suffrage

UNLIKE the prostitution crackdown, the battle for woman suffrage in Atlanta in the 1910s blended women as political symbols with the political actions of working-class women themselves. White middle-class women dominated efforts to win the municipal vote for women, but their organizations and their reliance on arguments invoking the plight of Atlanta's "working girl" offered working-class women a space to contribute to the movement as political actors in their own right. Even after the local enfranchisement of women in 1919, working-class women continued to function as an important constituency for middle-class women's voter registration drives and political reform campaigns into the early 1920s.

As Georgia's largest city, Atlanta was home to both the statewide campaign for suffrage and a strong movement for municipal enfranchisement. The bond between the primarily middle-class suffrage organizations and working-class women developed only during agitation for the municipal vote. A similar connection never materialized in national or even state-level campaigns, in large part as a result of Atlanta suffrage leaders' highly specific arguments, goals, and tactics, which drew on local urban conditions and were directed toward improving the city's moral and social environment. Many of the ideas about working-class women's role in the city since the turn of the century, then, could be deployed in this overtly political campaign.

Organized support for women's suffrage began late in Georgia, appearing only in the 1890s. The members of the Georgia Woman's Suffrage Association, the state's first suffrage organization, worked hard during its first five years, successfully hosting in Atlanta the National American Woman Suffrage Association's first national meeting outside of Washington, D.C. Organizer H. Augusta Howard overcame local objections to the enfranchisement of women by appealing to boosters and businessmen to make the convention a success, realizing, "While Atlanta is not in sympathy with the movement, she is always ready to help Atlanta."[42] In the years following the 1894 convention, the Atlanta Equal Rights Club, the Atlanta Civic League, and a Georgia branch of the National Woman's Party joined the ranks of the state's growing suffrage movement. White middle-class women and men opposing suffrage also began to actively lobby against enfranchisement.[43] Based in Macon, Mildred Rutherford and other "antis" focused their fight against arguments for an amendment to the state constitution, leaving virtually unopposed arguments for municipal suffrage in Atlanta.

On the state level, arguments for suffrage paralleled those advanced by national leaders, including taxation without representation and the rights of citizenship.[44] In the South, however, the race issue also played a significant role, as white southerners contemplated the impact woman suffrage might have on race relations. Since southern culture tied together patriarchy and white supremacy, a threat to one could be easily read as a threat to the other.[45] Would women voting prove enough of a challenge to white southern patriarchy to bring down Jim Crow? If women no longer needed to be protected from the corrupt world of politics, might blacks or the federal government also rightly question whether white women still needed to be protected from black men? Challenged by those opposing women's enfranchisement, many southern suffragists argued that black women would be prevented from voting in the same manner as black men and therefore posed no threat to white supremacy. Some suffragists even attempted to convince legislators that suffrage would further solidify the disempowerment of blacks in the South by providing a new, invigorated constituency of white women to the Democratic Party. In the case of Georgia, suffragists advanced these racist arguments only in response to accusations raised by the opposition. Georgia's suffrage organizations usually chose to avoid the race issue whenever possible and instead emphasized the advantages that women's suffrage could offer the state and the protection that the vote would afford the state's taxpaying women.[46]

A different set of arguments and tactics, both of which often relied on working-class women, guided the campaign for municipal suffrage in Atlanta. Arguments opposing suffrage on the grounds that it would allow black women to vote, for example, rarely surfaced since the disfranchisement of African Americans in the city had been well secured through the Democratic Party's exclusionary policies, which allowed only whites to vote in the primary (where political contests really took place in the one-party South) and through African Americans' hesitancy to engage in overt political organizing after the 1906 riot. The Atlanta Civic League, formed early in the twentieth century, led the way for municipal suffrage for women. Every year the organization would petition the city council "asking that the [city] Charter be amended so that the Wom[e]n of Atlanta have a voice in the expenditure of their tax money."[47] The league also succeeded in adding woman suffrage clauses to several of the many charter reform movements that materialized between 1902 and 1915. In the 1910s, the suffrage movement in Atlanta and in Georgia as a whole reached its peak of activity.[48] Several new organizations joined

the Civic League in its fight for municipal suffrage, including the Atlanta Equal
Suffrage Party and the Fulton County Suffrage Association. Emily MacDougald,
longtime president of the Equal Suffrage Party of Georgia, claimed municipal
suffrage in particular as "a long-time dream of mine."[49] Even state leaders from
Atlanta, like Eleonore Raoul, committed themselves to a municipal suffrage campaign distinct from their activism on the state and national levels.

Among these organizations, the Atlanta Civic League was the most conservative and the Atlanta Equal Suffrage Party the most militant, with the Fulton
County organization falling somewhere in the middle. These organizations received widespread support from women's clubs in the city, including the Atlanta
Woman's Club, the Council of Jewish Women, the Home for Old Women Association, the Fulton High School Improvement Club, the Saturday Morning History
Club, the Wednesday Morning Study Group, and local parent-teacher associations as well as from Atlanta's organized labor community. Despite their different
tactics, Atlanta's suffrage groups and supporters united behind their belief that
woman suffrage could remedy the "living problems" of the city "and those of
public welfare and the child of the community."[50] Municipal suffragists generally
agreed that women should be granted the vote so that they might carry out the
social welfare programs they had pioneered. "Take the playgrounds, the kindergartens, and the juvenile courts," suffragists argued, "as examples of women's
initiative, for it was the women who began the agitation for every one of these
things."[51] Through the vote, women hoped to implement many of the progressive
reforms for which women's clubs and civic organizations had been lobbying for
years, including improved sanitation, schools, parks, and markets. These women
reasoned that men were too busy with politics and business to concern themselves
with the social and cultural welfare of the majority of the city's residents. As one
local editorialist argued, women "are going to add morality, benevolence and
kindness to man's governing selfishness, AND NOTHING WILL STOP IT."[52]

All three of the main organizations supporting women's right to vote in city
elections also brought the image of the working girl, forced to compete economically with men, to the forefront of their arguments for municipal suffrage. "It is
easy," suffragists frequently argued, "for the right and prosperous 'lady' to discuss
in a distant, indifferent way her future and her rights. She has comfort, luxury
and ease now," but "the poorer women—women whose husbands or fathers earn
two dollars a day, or five or ten dollars a day perhaps, they are the women that
really pay the cost of government to-day."[53] This stance gained the movement
widespread support within the organized labor community. Jerome Jones, editor
of the *Journal of Labor,* agreed that industrial women needed suffrage "to protect their own welfare, to obtain better conditions, better wage laws, [and] better
working hours."[54]

In all of these arguments trumpeting the necessity of the vote for working-class women, suffragists narrowly defined the interests of wage-earning women. Middle-class suffragists expected wage-earning women to both need and use the vote only to "secure short work hours" or have a say in "the conditions under which they work."[55] Suffragists essentially divided Atlanta's women into three groups. The first group consisted of women working for wages outside the home who needed the vote "for the same reason that men do—to protect themselves" in the workplace. The second group comprised "women who do not work outside the home but contend with conditions outside of the home [that] are vital to the well-being of the race in this day and time." The third group of women were those who stayed at home but were relieved of civic responsibilities by "public opinion," which opposed women suffrage. Referring to the latter, one suffragist complained, "For the good of the race they should not be allowed to live a life of idleness. Men cannot do their own work and women's too, and as long as they attempt it the work will be badly done and women will deteriorate from lack of development."[56] Once granted the vote, suffragists expected middle-class women to deal with wide-ranging social reform and bring an "infusion of purity . . . into politics to make it better."[57] Working-class women, conversely, would use their vote only to improve the "hours of labor and sanitary conditions [that] often injure their health and that of the future generation."[58]

In invoking the image of working-class women, most middle-class suffragists relied on two basic premises. First, working-class women needed protection from exploitative employers and male competitors. Middle-class women clearly felt it their responsibility to use their votes to benefit working-class women by helping to protect them. "We need to be citizens," argued Atlanta's middle-class suffragists, "for with this citizenship we are truly our sister's keeper, her welfare is our own."[59] Members of the Georgia Woman's Suffrage Association acted on this impulse by advocating the construction of special jails, detention centers, and police to deal with female offenders, noting that while "women are admitted on an equal footing with men in jails, the police stations, on the gallows, and the chain gangs . . . they are guarded by men and have no police matrons to stand by them in these places of detention."[60] Suffragists also concerned themselves with the poor living conditions of Atlanta's laborers, especially during campaigns for protective labor legislation and the yearlong strike at Fulton Bag and Cotton Mills.[61] Suffragists' noblesse oblige extended beyond the families of poor white women. The Equal Suffrage Party encouraged its members to visit "districts and see what they could do to help these colored people."[62] The organization also pledged its support to the work of the Neighborhood Union and Gate City Free Kindergarten, surveyed conditions in black schools, and lobbied for improved city resources for African American neighborhoods. If working-class women were to use the vote only to protect their personal interests, middle-class women saw no such restrictions.

The stance adopted by Atlanta's middle-class suffragists served as a modernist critique of southern men's formal and informal politics. In particular, suffragists attacked the white male tradition of lynching, referring to it as the "fury [that] seizes upon our men" when women were the victims of a crime. As one suffrage supporter wrote in response to the lynching of Leo Frank in 1915, "If woman suffrage will do anything to eliminate the tiger element from chivalry, and to prevent such crimes as that which has just shocked the nation, it is certainly an argument for granting women the ballot as soon as possible."[63]

The second premise of Atlanta's suffragists further circumscribed white working-class women's participation in the movement. Middle-class organizers consistently excused working-class women from campaigns and meetings, believing that wage workers were too busy to participate. The assumption that working-class women would not have time to devote to suffrage functioned to exclude these women from the day-to-day work of organizing. Most organizational meetings were held in the afternoon or in the homes of elite families north of town, both of which prohibited working-class women from attending and barred their participation in leadership positions. Indicative of this approach, the Atlanta Civic League worked to improve the welfare of the poorer classes by calling for government regulation of industry and amusements. Rather than canvassing for the signatures of individuals, the organization's petitions usually bore the names of women's clubs that supported the causes. Working women had no direct input in this organization.

Of the three local organizations interested in municipal suffrage, only the Atlanta Equal Suffrage Party did not dismiss working-class women's participation.[64] Formed in 1913, the Equal Suffrage Party encouraged working-class women to attend meetings and parades, sign petitions, and generally have a voice in the movement. And through their participation, working-class women contradicted most suffrage organizations' narrow view of such women only as workers or the mothers of workers, thereby demonstrating a larger vision for the community to be reached through suffrage. At least some of the party's more elite members, aware of how their relatively privileged positions might be perceived, felt awkward when recruiting working women into their ranks. One such member referred to "Shop girls" as the "most eerie of all to approach."[65] Despite such hesitancy, the organization held special meetings at night "to suit [employed women's] convenience."[66] Eugenia Estill also wrote a regular *Journal of Labor* column chronicling suffrage activities for the labor community and emphasizing the Equal Suffrage Party's work. Mary McLendon, a leader in both state and city suffrage campaigns, even convinced the Georgia Woman's Suffrage Association to hold part of its 1913 state convention at the Atlanta Temple of Labor.[67]

Whereas the Atlanta Civic League favored political lobbying, the Equal Suffrage Party's strength lay in its large membership. Accordingly, the party was the first state organization to sponsor street speaking and parades. In 1913 and again in 1915, the organization sponsored "auto floral parades" through downtown. Despite the city's fondness for parades, a certain hostility against these public demonstrations materialized. The 1915 parade, for example, was carefully planned to follow the Harvest Day Parade. Once the last float from the first parade had passed, however, the police (who had been fully informed of the plans for the suffrage parade) released the crowds and allowed traffic to resume creating utter chaos. Incensed by the police actions, Emily MacDougald fired off a telegram to National American Woman Suffrage Association describing the events and asking them to "syndicate if possible."[68] Thinking better of her actions the next day, MacDougald sent another telegram to New York asking that the national organization release only positive stories about the parade. Privately, however, MacDougald continued to reprimand the chief of police, police committee, and city council.[69]

The Atlanta Equal Suffrage Party's activities built a strong and committed constituency among the city's working-class women, including Emma V. Paul, a stenographer in several downtown firms in the 1910s. Paul collected many newspaper articles and suffrage leaflets during her years as a party member. Revealing her particular positioning in the suffrage movement, most of the articles she clipped stress the Equal Suffrage Party's activities, support from organized labor, appeals for the support of working women, and campaigns for protective labor legislation.[70] When municipal suffrage was finally granted in 1919 and middle-class suffragists turned their attention to registering women to vote and to reforming the local political scene, the Equal Suffrage Party relied heavily on this constituency to support the work. Atlanta's working-class women proved themselves committed voters and allies in the campaign for a new city charter in the early 1920s.

Rather than coming through the city government, woman suffrage in Atlanta was obtained through the Democratic Executive Committee. This committee was responsible for the city's white primary elections. Because only one candidate usually advanced to the general election, voting in the primary was where the real campaigning and voting took place. The Atlanta Civic League, Fulton County Suffrage Association, and Atlanta Equal Suffrage Party had lobbied the committee through most of the 1910s to allow women to participate in the primary. In 1916, for example, the Equal Suffrage Party presented to the committee a petition containing ten thousand signatures favoring the enfranchisement of women. Mary McLendon, one of the suffrage organization's representatives, reported, "The Committee treated us with scant courtesy and handed us back the petitions as they did not care for them."[71] With the growing acceptance of women's suffrage on the national level, however, the Democratic Executive Committee abruptly changed its position in the spring of 1919.[72]

While most state suffrage leaders focused on lobbying the Georgia legislature to ratify the federal suffrage amendment that had passed in May 1919, the Equal Suffrage Party regrouped as the Central Committee of Women Citizens under the leadership of Eleonore Raoul.[73] With the opportunity to vote in the city primary at the end of the summer of 1919, the committee (which would soon become the Atlanta League of Women Voters) dedicated itself to registering women to vote. A further incentive to wage a massive registration campaign came in the form of a promise from the Democratic Executive Committee that all money raised from women's registration fees could go to any worthy civic project chosen by the committee if that organization initiated the citywide registration drive for women.

On the first day of registration, crowds of women turned out to pay their fees. Wealthier suffragists used their cars to transport women downtown, and a crush of women from nearby office buildings descended on the city clerk during the lunch hour. The newspapers helped create a festival atmosphere by reporting humorous stories of women refusing to give their age or answering only, "over age." One woman reportedly proclaimed, "This is an expensive registration for me." Her husband had decreed that if she was going to vote, she would have to earn her own money. The *Atlanta Constitution* concluded, "The suffragists were entirely pleased with the first day's work and showed by their beaming faces the satisfaction they found in at last beginning to enjoy a taste of the fruit of their long and faithful labors."[74]

With the excitement of the first day of registration out of the way, the Central Committee of Women Citizens set to work canvassing the city to encourage white women to register. Working from ward to ward, the committee organized rallies in most white neighborhoods, appealing to potential voters to take their "share of responsibility in civic improvement . . . as the woman's vote has always meant improved home conditions."[75] The committee also convinced the tax collector and city clerk to stay open until seven o'clock at night so that wage-earning women would have a chance to register. Drawing on her experience during the suffrage movement, Eleonore Raoul again sought to reach Atlanta's numerous office workers, shoppers, and theatergoers by holding rallies and open-air meetings downtown every night for more than two weeks near the end of the summer.[76] As the organization refined its registration drives, the committee took these types of meetings into each ward over the next few years. Cars would be decorated and driven into crowded intersections, where a city representative would be waiting to take registrations.

The Central Committee of Women Citizens succeeded in registering nearly four thousand women during the summer of 1919. With the promise that they could direct the money generated from women's registration fees toward a cause of their choosing, the committee had worked hard to encourage women of all classes to register early. When the Democratic Executive Committee announced in early August that the committee would not be allowed a say in the expenditure of the funds, the women were furious. Raoul and other leaders wrote angry letters to Democratic Committee members and to the press, accusing the men of "playing petty politics."[77] The women persuaded tax collector Lucien Harris to hold all monies generated from women's registration in trust until the matter could be decided.[78]

While the women ultimately lost their battle in court, the 1919 registration campaign represents two important moments in political organizing for Atlanta's women. First, this was the only campaign that targeted white working-class women as much as white middle-class women. This alliance grew out of cross-class ties built by the Equal Suffrage Party during municipal suffrage campaigns. Second, the women engineering the registration drive had hoped that the disbursement of the registration funds for some "splendid purpose of benefit to the city" would prove the benefits of women's voting. When the women were refused control of these funds, they thought they had found the true nature of the "present conditions of political matters in the city," which allowed the city's most powerful political body to break agreements on a whim. The net result of this controversy was that, however briefly, the battle over women's registration funds convinced some politically active women that women were not yet accepted as equal citizens and needed to continue to work together as women and across class lines to have a say in the voting booth and to enforce "upright and square dealing" in city politics.[79]

The next great test of this political alliance of white women across class lines came with the 1922 campaign to reform the city's charter. Attempts to alter the city's charter were not new—at least five such campaigns had been waged since the turn of the century.[80] In 1922, however, the Atlanta League of Women Voters created a new movement in support of a manager-style charter. Organized a month before its national counterpart and committed almost exclusively to municipal politics, the league sought "to educate women politically so that they may intelligently use the vote so recently acquired" and to reform the divisive style of ward politics that ruled the city.[81] The organization created the "Get out the Vote" campaigns and citizenship schools to educate voters and hoped a charter reform would eliminate ward politics. Both efforts sought women of all classes as potential voters and, in the minds of the league's leaders, as "natural" supporters of reform. Working-class women actively participated in these efforts, attending citizenship classes and lobbying others of their class to register and vote. Despite the apparent success of this organizing among the city's newly enfranchised women, the initiative failed and the cross-class approach disappeared. Successive campaigns for charter reform instead drew their strength from middle class men and women's organizational efforts.

Pragmatic Citizenship

THE PROSTITUTION CRACKDOWN and municipal suffrage organizing represent the two poles of middle-class political interaction with working-class women. Yet in stark contrast to images of the often faceless prostitutes invoked in the political scramble of 1912 and the working woman who would vote only to protect her job, working-class women in 1910s sought to directly influence and benefit from the city's political and legal structures. Many working-class women of both races proficiently expressed their demands and received remedy, although in ways different from those used by the city's middle classes and working-class men. Rather than relying on large-scale organizations, bloc voting, or moral crusades, working-class women turned to individual actions, directly addressing the governing bodies that the women believed could best alleviate their situation. Emphasizing that this was a class-based strategy, black women who were essentially invisible as political images in both the prostitution crackdown of 1912 and the suffrage movement appear almost as frequently as whites in petitioning the courts, city council, and police committee. Court cases, formal complaints, participation in public demonstrations, strikes and other workplace activism, and even negotiations with social workers all represented opportunities through which Atlanta's working-class women expressed visions of family and community and demanded city resources and civic rights for themselves.

Women's historians and scholars who have studied oppressed groups in many cultures suggest that definitions of *politics* need to be expanded to include, in the words of Paula Baker, "any action, formal or informal, taken to affect the course or behavior of government or the community." Politics need not be a singular venue in which only a limited number of groups and methods of participation could act.[82] In Atlanta, political subcultures existed around race, class, gender, and often even neighborhood and family. The dominant role white, middle-class men played in the city's formal political structures, even with the limited franchise given to others, did not completely prevent these subcultures from affecting city development or at least using government structures to protect the groups' interests. Boundaries existed between formal politics, which dealt with officeholding, suffrage, and laws, and informal politics, where individuals and smaller groups might utilize less standardized channels to effect change. While some scholars have used terms such as *infrapolitics* and *protopolitics* to describe these less standardized methods, the implication is that the outcomes of these activities are somehow less potent than "real" politics.[83] When looking at the impact on individuals of personal negotiation, collective action by disempowered groups (however limited), and individual uses of the courts, it is hard to see these actions as less significant than voting in a one-party political system such as that in power in Atlanta in the early twentieth century. A successful petition for a divorce often had a larger and far more direct effect on a working-class woman's life than the granting of women's suffrage.

The most organized efforts by working-class women to effect change came from their participation in various neighborhood, religious, and civic clubs, many of which blended leisure and spirituality with political activism. At the Fulton Bag and Cotton Mills, for example, white mill women organized the Wesley House Woman's Club in 1910 with the help of the Methodist missionary women who ran the settlement house in the mill village. The club, whose members were drawn entirely from the working classes, met monthly for more than seven years. Structured after the meetings of the Ladies Board of City Missions, the Woman's Club elected officers, kept meeting minutes, sang religious songs, and held devotional services. While the two groups' minutes are barely distinguishable from each other at times, the Woman's Club functioned as an essentially autonomous organization of working-class women.

The mill women who belonged to the Woman's Club used the organization as a vehicle for influencing the settlement house's daily operations and initiated community projects, including studies of health and general neighborhood conditions. These women educated themselves and their neighbors about the spread of tuberculosis, measles, and other common diseases and demanded that the city and mill owners improve sanitation in the mill village. In 1910, the club joined the City Federation of Women's Clubs, an umbrella organization that united more than a hundred women's organizations from all socioeconomic classes. Mill women involved in the Woman's Club also participated in parent-teacher organizations and joined the citywide campaign by club women to oppose the removal of "physical culture, music, and drawing from the public schools."[84]

At the turn of the century, the American Federation of Labor discovered the ballot as a tool of labor and initiated a push for working-class men to use their votes wisely. Women of the labor movement began a related political campaign, though they chose as their methods consumerism and lobbying rather than suffrage. Label leagues encouraged all women to exercise "politicized purchasing" by buying only union-made goods. "Ladies Auxiliaries" of local trade unions supported legislation designed to protect married women from nonsupporting husbands, end child labor, educate children, and reform wayward girls. O. Delight Smith, a columnist for the *Journal of Labor*, used her forum to promote political action among the city's union wives. Women, Smith wrote, needed to be active because the capitalist labor market forced them to "bump up against the world."[85] Women involved in the Fulton Bag and Cotton Mills strike in 1914 heeded this call, using the opportunity not to be at work to successfully lobby the state legislature to pass a bill restricting child labor.

Like the Methodist women at the Wesley House, the Neighborhood Union formed several mothers' clubs for working-class women in Atlanta's African American communities. While these clubs seem to have centered on providing "wholesome recreation," working-class women actively influenced the Neighborhood Union's activities.[86] The Neighborhood Union established a top-down organizational structure in which elite women organized poorer women.[87] It is significant, however, that working-class women were part of the organization at all. These women participated in a variety of activities sponsored by the Neighborhood Union, helping to survey their immediate neighborhoods and reporting families that needed assistance and those that refused to cooperate with the organization. Working-class women also formed the backbone of neighborhood events sponsored by the union, including the health fairs, clean-up campaigns, and fund-raising carnivals. Working-class women in the Neighborhood Union joined forces with black middle-class women to remove prostitutes and improve lighting and sanitation in the city's African American communities.

Middle-class club women, both black and white, encouraged working-class women to form similar organizations. While many of these clubs crossed class lines, they did not bridge racial divides. Alliances between working-class and middle-class women proved to be quite fragile, however, and as the 1920s advanced many coalitions broke down. Working-class women rarely had the time or educational or financial resources to engage in extensive organizing. Black and white middle-class and elite women, after all, generally had both the income of white-collar husbands and the domestic labor of black women to support organizational efforts.

More common than those who joined clubs and civic organizations, however, were the black and white working-class women who pursued their individual goals and political rights through institutionalized channels and spontaneous actions. For black working-class women in Atlanta (and in cities generally), early-twentieth-century streetcars functioned as a "moving theater" of racial and gender tensions, where black women challenged Jim Crow segregation and risked clashes with white conductors, passengers, and the police.[88] Black Atlantans had to perform the insulting rituals of segregation on a daily basis to ride the streetcars, and even when they followed the racial etiquette, African Americans often still faced insults and threats from white passengers.[89] On these public conveyances, economic power equalized. Black and white passengers were both consumers when riding streetcars, and blacks who had paid the same fare as whites felt entitled to equal treatment. Black women's resistance to the indignities of segregation could be at least somewhat protected on well-lit, crowded, and public streetcars. Black women, who used the streetcars with great frequency to reach their jobs in the white sections of town, also found some protection from retribution in employers who wanted their maids at work on time. But because the streetcar routes traveled through both white and black neighborhoods, the boundaries of segregation were strained, casting streetcars as sites of frequent friction.[90] Public transportation became one of the few places where black women met whites outside of a structured work environment, often resulting in volatile situations. In describing her frustration with a seating system that forced blacks to stand even if there was an empty seat in a row with white passengers, domestic worker Alice Adams declared, "Look, you going in their house, cooking for them, making their beds, cleaning their house, doing everything and then you couldn't sit by them. But you could go there and cook their food, serve their food, but still you couldn't sit by them."[91] Adams emphasized that racial tensions within domestic work in particular often spilled over into these conflicts on public transportation. "Sometimes we'd have arguments, little specks on the bus or streetcar," she explained, "some peoples would just get determined—'I'm not going to work all day and stand!' "[92]

Women of both races also aired their grievances and sought redress through the city's formal structures in everything from divorce cases to suits against the city. In these cases, women initiated legal proceedings, testified on behalf of, and often won their complaints. For both black and white working-class women seeking to establish their independence, protect themselves and their families, or maintain their property, the legal system often offered the surest opportunities for success. For example, when Ethel McElroy's husband deserted her after two years of marriage, she filed for divorce as soon as the law allowed, receiving a complete divorce, custody of the couple's child, and the right to marry again.[93] Such divorce cases were not unusual in Atlanta after the turn of the century. Some women increasingly found the constraints of married life unbearable and chose to support themselves or otherwise seek a different path. In the United States as a whole, the divorce rate jumped in the early 1900s, and one out of every six marriages ended in court by the 1920s.[94] Fulton County appears to have followed these trends, as women sought to defend themselves against abuse, insure their financial future, or assert their rights to independence. These divorce cases also reveal the rising tensions between working-class men and women, particularly over competing ideals of respectability and women's increasing economic independence.

During the first two decades of the twentieth century, Georgia had only three grounds for an assured divorce: adultery, "willful and continued desertion by either of the parties for the term of three years," and "conviction of either party for any offense involving moral turpitude" that carried at least a two-year prison sentence.[95] Divorces could be granted on discretionary grounds if plaintiffs proved cruel treatment or habitual intoxication on the part of their spouses. Juries hearing divorce cases held the power to place "disabilities" on the parties involved. A jury could refuse to restore a woman's maiden name or forbid one or both parties from remarrying. Individuals so restricted would then have to petition a judge if they wanted to marry again. Despite these potential difficulties, Fulton County residents continued to file for divorce in increasing numbers, fitting complaints against their spouses into the legal categories that allowed divorce.[96]

As 1910s divorce proceedings reveal, however, not all women bothered to explain their stories to a jury and chose instead to flee abusive or otherwise unsatisfactory husbands without the benefit of a court decree. Married twenty years, Josephine Thompson deserted her husband in 1912 and went to Michigan. When she did not return after five years, Freemont Thompson filed for divorce.[97] Also in 1912, Ada Arnold left her husband and son, "disregarding the solemnity of her marriage vow." As was the law for a desertion of at least three years, the court granted the divorce and forbade her from marrying again. It is unlikely she ever knew of this restriction since she had been gone for four years at the time of the ruling.[98] In 1918 Susannah Lake left her husband of one year and headed for California.[99] Mrs. H. C. Petree married her husband just before he went to France to fight in World War I. When he returned to Atlanta in September 1919, she fled to her sister's home in Eastman, Georgia, and after one more failed attempt to live together, she left her husband for good.[100]

Of those women who did choose to take their cases to court or to defend themselves against charges by their spouses, most accused their partners of both physical and mental abuse. Visalia Davis, an African American woman, left her husband in 1912 and filed for divorce after five years of marriage. She accused him of repeatedly beating her and causing her mental anguish by constantly grumbling and quarreling with her. "His treatment became so cruel and inhuman," her complaint told the court, "that her health was impaired and her happiness completely destroyed."[101] Those seeking divorces in Fulton County in the 1910s often filled their petitions with similar cries of "mental suffering" and "impaired health," even though cruel treatment represented discretionary rather than total grounds for divorce. Consequently, petitioners had to argue their cases in front of as many as three juries (at least two juries had to concur) before a divorce could be granted. That they chose this path rather than claiming adultery or some other guaranteed grounds for divorce implies that these women felt completely justified in making their complaints and trusted the court system to grant them relief.

The court was most likely to respond favorably when a divorce petitioner claimed a spouse violated gender norms.[102] Proceedings regularly included descriptions of women refusing to stay home or care for their houses, children, and husbands. Lena McElreath's husband of eight years alleged that she showed "no care as to whether the home was kept properly or not." She had a paying position in Atlanta and preferred to work and stay in town with women her husband found "disreputable" instead of keeping her own home in "proper condition." Men wishing to divorce their wives for failing to meet gender expectations had to fit their complaints into one of the discretionary grounds for legal divorce; most, like A. M. McElreath, chose to frame a woman's failure to meet wifely expectations as cruel treatment causing "great mental worry."[103]

Gender conventions often worked in favor of women as well, especially when it came to financial support. Cases indicate not only that the court firmly believed in a man's role as breadwinner but also that the new economic independence of many women was often born of men's unwillingness or inability to fulfill that role. When Lois Griffin filed for divorce, she claimed that her husband had never provided any money for the couple. She got a job to support herself, her husband, and his mother. Then, according to her court petition, her husband forced her to sign loans against her fifty dollars a month salary. By September 1915, one month shy of their first anniversary, she wanted out of the marriage. Sympathetic to her plight, the court awarded her the divorce, the return of her maiden name, and, in an unusual move for the 1910s, three hundred dollars in alimony.[104] In 1919 Beulah Jones separated from her husband. She asked the judge not for a divorce but instead to order her husband to pay alimony so that the family would not "become without a home and starve." The mother of eleven children, she told that court that she had "no income whatever and is unacquainted with any trade, calling, profession or gainful occupation except keeping house after the fashion of a workingman's wife."[105] Like many of the cases brought before the Fulton County Superior Court, there is no ruling recorded on this case. Perhaps the initiation of legal proceedings gave women the added leverage they needed in their marriages.

Working-class women who filed for divorce in Atlanta after the turn of the century demonstrated a determination to assert their independence, particularly economic independence. In some cases, women sought to protect their property, as Mrs. Christian had. In others, women demonstrated another type of independence. Irmalee Davis, like many of her working-class counterparts, fully enjoyed the variety of activities offered by city life and traveled Atlanta freely by herself at all hours, much to the dismay of her husband. Charles Davis, married only five months, complained in his divorce petition that his wife neglected "indoor sports such as housekeeping but was an artist in outdoor sports." Irmalee Davis regularly stayed "away from home especially at night visiting the dance halls and other places of amusements" despite his pleas that she remain at home.[106]

Through divorce proceedings, Charles Davis and many other husbands expressed dismay and frustration that their wives favored the increasing variety of jobs and leisure activities open to Atlanta's women over traditional caretaking activities. Wilborn O'Connor asserted that his wife, Janie, "soon grew tired of him and would refuse to perform even the little domestic duties, such as darning his socks or mending the small defects in his clothing which the natural wear and tare brought on." Janie May O'Connor reportedly also drank whiskey and "would have men to call on her" when her husband was away. His divorce petition reveals, however, that his greatest frustration came from the public nature of her actions—she would "curse him in public places" and allow embraces with other men to be "seen by his relatives and neighbors," leaving him "humiliated and embarrassed."[107] There must have been another side to this story that is not reflected in the existing records, however. Janie O'Connor countersued, and the court awarded her a complete divorce, including the return of her maiden name, while restricting Wilborn's right to remarry until 1924.[108]

In one of the more publicized Atlanta cases of the decade, Edgar Smith sued his labor activist wife, Ola Delight Smith, for a divorce in 1915. This case's notoriety stemmed from O. Delight Smith's job as an organizer for the 1914–15 textile strike at the Fulton Bag and Cotton Mills. When Edgar filed for divorce shortly after the strike's unsuccessful conclusion, the counsel for Fulton Bag represented him in his petition.[109] Delight was the target of a large industrial employer who wanted to remind recently striking mill workers of the dangers of unionism by humiliating a leader of the union movement. And, as Delight had noted in her column in the *Journal of Labor,* capitalists accomplished such ends by attacking women's character on moral grounds. Edgar withdrew his original petition, but Delight sued him for divorce a year and a half later, and he responded with a countersuit. She accused him of cruel treatment, including failing to provide for her financially. He accused her of being drunk and in a compromising situation with another man. Each followed the gendered scripts for divorce in the 1910s—he was a failure as a breadwinner, and she displayed questionable morality—but the animosities between the Smiths were not unusual in 1910s Atlanta. Neither was the ruling: the court granted the divorce and his liberty to marry again but denied that right to Delight.[110]

Differing expectations of marriage seem to have been at the root of most divorce cases filed in Fulton County after the turn of the century. Many of these discrepancies arose from changes in the city, including unstable male employment and increasing opportunities for women in the job market. Not only did divorce petitioners allude to women's wage work or women's unwillingness to care for the home, but women also filed cases against men who would not support their families or otherwise did not live up to their expectations of the male role in marriage. Women also accused men of not upholding their gender duties in marriage, often claiming that a spouse showed "utter disregard of his duties as a husband."[111]

Atlanta's rising divorce rate was the only instance where working-class women's interactions with the city's government and legal structures captured much in the way of popular attention.[112] Largely overlooking women's demands during divorce proceedings, their reasons for filing petitions, or even their right to initiate such proceedings, press reports of the increasing frequency of divorce invoked familiar fears of moral decay. Contemporary social commentators focused mainly on the changing role of women in society and the friction women created in marriage.[113] The blame for the increasing failure rate of marriages, then, fell squarely on the shoulders of women in the 1910s.

Like the rest of nation, Atlanta demonstrated great concern over the rising divorce rate and its impact on society. The *Atlanta Georgian* ran a special Sunday forum on the causes of divorce in 1919, while memories of the anti-VD campaign were undoubtedly still fresh in the minds of the city's residents.[114] Printing the thoughts of ministers, judges, and social scientists, the forum represented a range of opinions—some hostile to divorce, others more supportive. The theme that united all of the articles, however, was the focus on "independence of women" as a root cause of divorce. "The home is the very foundation of our civilization," wrote Judge George Bell, "and anything that tends to weaken the interest in the home is a stab in the heart of civilization." And in case anyone missed the point, he continued, "The duties of citizenship are incompatible with the duties of wifehood and motherhood. . . . I tremble for the future of little children who grow up under such a regime."[115] Even the more sympathetic views represented in the forum included misogynistic allusions to the doom of society. Seeking to find the good in divorce, Reverend W. W. Memminger wrote, "the wife no longer feels that she must submissively submit to bullying, beatings, infidelity and insults." Yet, like most of his contemporaries, he undercut this sympathy by advocating more restrictive divorce legislation to combat the "dwindling importance and sacredness of the family as a unit."[116]

Fulton County divorce records provide one of the clearest examples of how working-class women of both races took action to improve their lives when opportunities for doing so existed. In fact, African American women may have been more successful than white women in attempts to end unsatisfactory marriages. Prevailing white notions about black moral inferiority often translated into relatively easy divorces. Black petitioners generally filed shorter and less detailed complaints, perhaps implying that they did not have to demonstrate circumstances as dire as those required of whites. Also, proceedings were more commonly initiated among African Americans than among whites after a spouse had deserted. In these cases, the law decreed a total divorce, and no jury verdict was necessary. Even in cases filed only on discretionary grounds, juries often granted African Americans complete divorces without restrictions against marrying again. Since the moral crisis and blame associated with divorce focused on white women, black litigants found less courtroom pressure to maintain their marriages and possibly less social stigma in their communities.

Outside of the divorce court, Atlanta's working-class women used legal and political channels mainly to redress grievances involving property damage, personal injury, and individual rights. Women found fault with everything from the police force to civic improvements and filed complaints with civil courts, the city council, and the police committee. Women of both races also testified in many cases. When standard channels seemed to be moving too slowly or in the wrong direction, some women also attempted to register their grievances in the local press and enlist the assistance of civic organizations. The actions of these women indicate that the "new womanhood" of the 1920s, an ideology of female behavior that stressed female independence and modernity, was already a part of many of Atlanta's working-class women's lives in the 1910s.[117]

Atlanta's working-class women, it seems, had numerous problems with Atlanta's all-white police force, and charges of misconduct against patrolmen appeared regularly in the minutes of the police committee. Mrs. K. L. Culver formally accused officer W. E. Ball of stealing a revolver from her washstand, for example. She claimed to have made "repeated efforts to have him return the pistol," all to no avail.[118] Both Culver and her female neighbor testified against Ball in front of the committee. Ball escaped this incident with his job, but accusations of kidnapping and drunkenness brought by three women a few years later led to his permanent discharge from the force. Like those who pressed charges against Ball, women filed, testified in, or were the victim in virtually every case brought by citizens against local police officers. Atlanta's women policed the police who were thought to have abused their power.

Many of the charges against officers involved sexual or other interpersonal relationships between working-class women and patrolmen. Ida Greer brought charges against her husband, an Atlanta police officer, claiming that he had shot her, infected her with a venereal disease, and fought publicly with her while on his beat. Like many domestic dispute cases, the charges were dropped when Ida Greer did not appear to testify at the hearing.[119] Perhaps alerting Patrolman Greer's bosses to their marital troubles was enough for Ida Greer to let him know she expected a serious change in his behavior. Charged with acting "in a manner unbecoming an officer," P. H. Maddox was accused of having intercourse with Ruth Clayton. His conviction resulted in a fifty-one-dollar fine and a fifteen-day suspension. While it is unclear who filed the initial charge, Maddox's guilty verdict turned on the testimony of Clayton and two other women.[120] If the police committee failed to reign in the unwanted sexual advances of local police, women found other avenues. In 1913, for example, Mrs. N. P. Powell filed charges against the Atlanta police force in Fulton County Superior Court. She won a restraining order against members of the department who were trying to evict her from her home after she reportedly refused "to accede to improper advances."[121]

Cases brought or argued by women against police officers remained consistent through the 1910s and early 1920s. The cases involving sexual conduct, however, illuminate subtle shifts in the city's racial and moral constructions. According to the earliest minutes of the police committee in the 1910s, officers were dismissed or otherwise reprimanded for their sexual relationships with white women, particularly if the women were young and single and especially if their mothers caught wind of the trysts. But even in the 1910s and early 1920s, black women as well as white challenged police authority. Two pairs of African American mothers and daughters filed complaints against officers J. W. Lowe and J. A. Etheridge, who reportedly "tried to get the women to 'go to bed' with them." During the hearing, Willie Williams reported, "He then asked me to sit in his lap, or on his knee, and I refused to do it, and I walked out of the room and Officer Lowe used some cursed words and left the house." All four of the women testified at the hearing, and both officers were discharged from the force after being found guilty of misconduct.[122] Police committee hearings seem to have been one of the few legal arenas in which African Americans could testify in and win cases against whites. Long-standing difficulties between the city's all-white police force and the African American population, white southern males' traditional assumption of sexual prerogative when it came to black women, and cross-class support in the black community for challenging discrimination through legal channels combined to make common black women's attempts to mediate police power.

Working-class women's desire to protect personal and property rights also brought them into contact with other parts of the city government. A highly sensationalized case appeared in the papers in 1922 when Hattie Harper filed slander charges against the city warden, W. H. Johnson. The legal battles of the city's working-class women generally did not receive much press, but this case proved the exception because the Associated Charities learned of it and played it up as a means of discrediting the work of the warden's office. Harper alleged that when she applied to the city warden for assistance, he made sexual advances toward her, claiming there would be no more relief money unless she would be a "good sport."[123] When she repeatedly refused his propositions, Johnson reportedly approached the woman's uncle, telling him Harper was immoral. For the city warden, the case was political. He dismissed Harper's charges as a ploy by his political enemies who "were stealthily striking at his character through the woman who brought the suit."[124]

For Harper, however, the trial embodied a very different set of issues, hinging primarily on her respectability. Harper brought the suit in defense of her character. The charges she filed focused only on the reports of immorality allegedly given to her uncle. Harper's sexual harassment served only as an explanation of Johnson's motivation in approaching her uncle, not an indictment in and of itself. Harper's original aid application claimed that she had become destitute when her husband, a war veteran, fell ill. The city warden countered her stance as a respectable wife, worthy of assistance, by indicating to the press that Harper's husband had actually deserted her so that she would qualify for city funds. Johnson further suggested that the husband was secretly being supported by the relief money Harper had obtained. Harper seems to have won the later battle as the press, particularly the *Atlanta Constitution*, chose to trumpet her as something of an underdog battling the abuses of the system and accepted her story of the honest and persevering wife with an ill husband. [125] Despite this public victory, Harper ultimately dropped the charges, though it is unclear why. Perhaps the city government's pressure and threats were too strong, or she may have felt that her point had been proven once the press sided with her interpretation of events. [126]

While cases involving definitions of respectability and civil rights seem particularly important for understanding working-class women's informal political activism, most cases brought by working-class women against the city actually involved property or personal injury. In 1916 Flossie Nealy, an African American laundress, demanded fifty dollars from the city council "for damages on account of personal injuries." [127] Nellie May Reeder, a white woman who sold lunches on Alabama Street, won a full settlement of twenty-five dollars from the city council for "damages and injuries, past, present and future." [128] These types of petitions appeared before the council so frequently that in 1917 the body voted to set aside nine hundred eighty-five dollars to pay off all the claims that had accumulated in the preceding months. [129] In a subtle way, these cases represent actions on the part of poor and working-class women to declare their rights. By demanding redress for actions of the city, they indirectly defined themselves as citizens of the municipality—worthy of consideration, city resources, and the right to property.

WOMEN'S CONTINUED WILLINGNESS to use legal channels in the face of frequent losses raises questions about what other rewards these cases offered beyond favorable court rulings. Juries, for example, often granted divorces to husbands even when wives filed the original petitions. Even if these decrees carried restrictions, however, women usually attained the legal dissolve of their marriages that they had originally sought. Court cases tried in the press before they ever reached the courtroom, as in the case against the city warden, offered women an arena in which to air their grievances publicly and perhaps more successfully than in a courtroom. Despite little attention in the local press or from the city at large for these activities, Atlanta's working-class women continued to act on a pragmatic model of citizenship that often brought them into the realm of formal politics. Working-class women's interaction with city politics and the courts ultimately demonstrates how removed many of the political images created around these women became from their lives and politics and from the arenas in which working-class women found their greatest successes in asserting their rights. The gap between political symbol and lived experience helps to explain why working-class women continued to exercise their pragmatic citizenship through and beyond the 1920s, even after images of working-class women had lost their potency and usefulness to the city's middle classes.

CHAPTER SEVEN

The Transitional Twenties

Rose Hickey came to Atlanta from Boston in 1919 as a union organizer for International Brotherhood of Electrical Workers (IBEW). During the Atlanta telephone workers' walkout in the summer of that year, Hickey, at the urging of the local operators, became the primary leader and organizer for the strike. Her work as an aggressive and creative organizer, negotiator, and speaker earned her the respect of the strikers, Atlanta's trade union leaders, and the local press, despite the failure of the "hello girls" to achieve union recognition from Southern Bell. After the strike, the IBEW hired Hickey to act as the southern organizer for the newly established Telephone Operators' Department of the national union. Hickey played a pivotal leadership role as the union waged a campaign against company-sponsored and management-run unions in the years following World War I.

Hickey's commitment to Atlanta grew, and she made the city her permanent home. In the fall of 1920 she married Emmett Quinn, a machinist and vice president of the Atlanta Federation of Trades. She resigned her high-level IBEW post and concentrated her efforts on improving the position of working women in Atlanta. An ardent supporter of women's suffrage, Hickey followed her middle-class allies from that campaign into efforts to clean up Atlanta politics through charter reform. Hickey also campaigned for the establishment of an industrial department in Atlanta's YWCA, improved educational opportunities through the passage of school bonds, and a tenure policy for teachers. She became a regular contributor to Atlanta's *Journal of Labor* and wrote numerous articles supporting women's education, advocating racial cooperation, and explaining the history of unionism. Hickey acted as a liaison between the Georgia Federation of Labor and the liberal Southern Council for Women and Children in Industry in the early 1930s and helped to create the Southern Summer School for Women Workers later in the decade.[1]

Hickey's commitment to working-class women and the rights of laborers did not waver between the time of her arrival in Atlanta in the late 1910s and the 1960s, when she died. Yet Hickey virtually disappeared from the political landscape of the city after the unsuccessful 1922 campaign to alter the city's charter.[2] A woman lauded for her commitment to the city's laboring classes in the 1910s and early 1920s, a woman who rose to prominence in the hierarchy of white organized labor during this time, and a woman who continued to expand her political activities in subsequent years essentially found herself increasingly invisible to both Atlantans of her own day and later historians.[3] Like her contemporary O. Delight Smith, also a *Journal of Labor* columnist and a Fulton Bag strike organizer in the 1910s, Hickey became "a woman who almost wasn't there." Both Smith and Hickey espoused a kind of "feminist progressivism" that has traditionally "been marginalized by historians of women, of labor, and of the South alike."[4] More than this, however, Hickey and Smith became invisible, even to their contemporaries, largely because the issues of most concern to them lost their cultural currency of the 1910s.

Hickey's transformation from a prominent figure in Atlanta labor circles to being known only as Mrs. Emmett Quinn, the wife of a vice president of the Atlanta Federation of Trades (when she was noticed at all), parallels the larger story of working-class women's visibility in the early-twentieth-century city. Women, particularly those who worked for wages or who tended to the families of wage earners, moved into a central place in Atlanta's culture during the first decade of the twentieth century. In the 1910s, images of working-class women served as focal points in many of the city's most dramatic moments—contentious strikes, a shocking murder and even more sensationalized trial, sweeping antivice crusades, and campaigns to preserve health and morals. But between the end of World War I and the mid-1920s, the political and cultural dialogues surrounding or using the place, status, and behavior of working-class women in the city evaporated. The shift away from working-class women as symbols of both the progress and pitfalls of urban development did not happen in a single dramatic moment, but once begun, it did happen swiftly and in all realms where images of working-class women had been so common.

The impact of Atlanta's moral and social atmosphere on the city's reputation faded in the face of changing political and economic imperatives in the 1920s. Following the war and especially the postwar recession, Atlanta's business leaders returned to promoting the city almost solely on the basis of its economic attributes, fearful of losing out on the era's prosperity. The city's political landscape narrowed around formal politics during the 1920s, leaving organized labor, club women, and elite blacks, who had renewed their push for political inclusion, struggling to maintain any influence in discussions of Ku Klux Klan officeholders or graft among city officials. Working-class women, like Hickey and those she dedicated so much of her life toward helping, appeared peripheral to the issues facing the city.

The "Voice with a Smile" Says "Union"

ATLANTA'S female telephone operators who struck in the summer of 1919 in many ways represented the pinnacle of women's visibility in the city, but the strike also held elements of the social and economic changes that would help to move Atlanta's focus away from working-class women in the 1920s. The "hello girls" waged a flamboyant strike that riveted Atlanta's attention for a few weeks in June 1919, but interest in the strikers' cause represented little more than amused curiosity and some concern that phone service might be disrupted. For all of the dramatic language surrounding women in the streets used earlier in the decade, women had become relatively accepted figures in the city's public spaces by the end of the 1910s. Efforts by the male-dominated Atlanta Federation of Trades to settle the strike marginalized the telephone operators. In many ways, that move represented the larger marginalized but stable position women occupied in the city's paid labor force by this time. The threats seen in women working for wages in earlier years had not come to fruition and had therefore largely evaporated. The uncertain economic prospects at the conclusion of the war, the continued outmigration of African American laborers, an organized labor movement facing government-backed antiunionism, and an important school bond defeated at the voting booth by repoliticized black voters all drew as much or more press attention than the striking operators, and each topic was emblematic of the kinds of concerns that would dominate public discourse in the 1920s.

Atlanta's telephone operators organized a local under the Commercial Telegraphers' Union of America in the spring of 1919. Undoubtedly inspired by a massive and largely successful strike of telephone workers in New England that same spring, Atlanta operatives enthusiastically began organizing. Conditions relating to World War I had transformed the position of telephone operator from one of the better-paying and more prestigious jobs open to wage-earning women into a stressful job with long hours, little flexibility, tight supervision, and low pay.[5] Telephone companies also often required that operators work split shifts (two shorter shifts in one day with a few hours of downtime in between). This schedule rarely allowed women enough time to travel home, yet it kept them downtown for far longer than the hours for which they were paid. Workers suggestively referred to this practice as the "split trick."[6] To quell labor unrest and maintain communication lines during the war, phone companies, like the railroads, were placed under federal government control. Postmaster General Albert Burleson oversaw the management of phone companies across the country, including Southern Bell. Obviously sympathetic to management and overtly hostile to organized labor, Burleson's policies caused labor relations to deteriorate rapidly during 1918.

Organizing campaigns and strikes among female telephone operatives spread across the country at the close of the war. More than a hundred new local unions formed across the country during 1919. Central to this labor militancy was the postmaster general's refusal to raise workers' wages to keep pace with spiraling inflation and the success of the Boston operatives' April 1919 strike.[7] In Atlanta, low wages certainly contributed to organizing efforts in the spring of 1919, and approximately 400 of Southern Bell's 450 female operators joined the union.[8] Southern Bell's antiunion policies and the firings of local union leaders ultimately forced a walkout. Reports of the number fired or otherwise punished for their union involvement varied widely from a low of eight fired to a high of eighteen fired and one hundred reprimanded with fines or shift changes.[9] On May 31 local union leaders issued an ultimatum to the company, demanding the reinstatement of unionized workers to their previous jobs and shifts and threatening a strike if these demands were not met. When the company allowed the deadline to come and go without taking action, operatives "walked out in an orderly file but with a flutter of excitement and short bursts of cheering."[10]

Southern Bell at first responded coolly to the strike. Company officials claimed that only 300 operatives had left their posts, far lower than the 750 reported by newspapers supporting the strikers' efforts.[11] The company also stalled union leaders' attempts to discuss their demands. Officials even refused to refer to the women as strikers. Calling the women "misguided," the company carefully used the phrase "former employee" in all discussions with the union and the press.[12] Despite company claims that telephone service was not being interrupted by the strike, Southern Bell had to ask Atlantans to limit their calls until the strike could be settled. Mayor James Key dodged the issue of the strike by calling on Congressman William Upshaw to recommend an investigation into the strikers' charges. The postmaster issued an edict in support of Southern Bell, ordering all strikers back to work in twenty-four hours; failure to return in that amount of time, he threatened, would result in permanent dismissal.[13]

Postmaster Burleson's threats and Southern Bell's reluctance to negotiate did not deter the striking operatives. Elaborate demonstrations, mass meetings, and pickets drew crowds of strikers as well as supporters and kept the strike prominent in the press for the next few weeks. Pickets were formed around the main exchange and several others. Strikers confronted any women who tried to report for work and shouted up through the windows at those already on duty, "Come on down, scab."[14] Parades through downtown streets and in front of the Southern Bell offices drew attention to the striking women. During one march, reported to be a thousand strong, the strikers stopped to cheer a contingent of soldiers passing by, who in turn stopped to cheer the striking women. Despite the festive and flirtatious atmosphere of the strikers' public demonstrations, the women planned their parades carefully, marching in front of the various exchanges, through downtown, in front of the offices of local newspapers, and ending in front of the state capitol. The operatives also countered company claims that few women had actually gone on strike by gathering for a group photograph "which will be displayed throughout the city in order that the public may learn their number." [15]

The mass meetings of strikers and their labor allies contained a similar mix of excitement, entertainment, and media and political savvy. At these events, the women of the telephone operators' local mingled freely with the city's male trade unionists. The women undoubtedly had a pleasurable notoriety within the union community during the early and most dramatic days of the strike. In the midst of the Red Scare of 1919, when many Americans easily linked labor actions with anarchy and radicalism, the striking operatives successfully distanced themselves from such associations by opening meetings with the singing of "America" and closing with the "Star Spangled Banner." Strike leaders also filled the gatherings with stirring rhetoric. In fiery speeches responding to the postmaster's antiunion actions, Rose Hickey compared Burleson's threats of massive firings to "the edicts of the Kaiser" and accused Southern Bell of misrepresenting the strength of the strike. [16] Between the cheering and singing, the telephone workers' leaders continued to challenge Southern Bell's policies, oppose the postmaster's actions, and demonstrate patriotism.

The size and strength of the women's fight in Atlanta eventually drew the attention of national unions. The commercial telegraphers and Western Union employees threatened a national sympathy walkout if the fired Atlanta operators were not rehired. The International Brotherhood of Electrical Workers also promised a regional strike if Burleson did not recognize the telephone operatives' right to unionize. None of the national unions, however, followed through on their promised actions. The threats had merely been union attempts to capitalize on the militancy of Atlanta strikers and to further political vendettas against government control of communication lines. When Burleson and Congress refused to change the situation, the unions backed out of their support for the Atlanta telephone operatives. Local support for the union and the strike was just as scarce during the first month of the walkout, leaving the hello girls to fight on largely unassisted. Ironically, the strikers received their best press coverage during this period. Indicative of the fading association between women in public and moral danger, the stylish young women of labor merely intrigued and amused reporters and the public.

By the end of June, with national support dwindling and no progress in local negotiations, the Atlanta Federation of Trades (AFT) decided to step in and resolve the situation. Pushing aside the women of the operatives' union who had been attempting to meet with company officials, the AFT claimed to represent the strikers. The agreement that emerged from these talks did little to end the dispute. It did, however, squelch the militant demonstrations of the strikers. "The young women pickets of the strikers," reported the *Atlanta Georgian* in announcing the results of the talks, "hereafter will confine their efforts to personal persuasion and argument, avoiding the use of the word 'scab' and other opprobrious terms, and the men assigned by the unions to protect the women pickets will be stationed across the street from the picket stations."[17] These new rules required that women abandon the noisy and boisterous pickets that had brought them so much public support and good press early in the strike and that the few men involved in the strike, who may have offered the women at least psychological support and protection, be removed from the sites of protest.

Only after this new policy effectively silenced the women did the AFT finally issue formal support for the strike. "The girls are making a splendid stand in spite of adverse conditions that have presented themselves," praised the *Journal of Labor* in its next issue. "The striking telephone workers are to be commended for the magnificent stand they are making in spite of the fact that they are practically inexperienced in the labor movement, they are adhering strictly to the fundamentals and principles of trade unionism, which fact shows that trade unionism as taught today is of such simple construction that those new in the movement very easily grasp and apply those principles in a way that would do credit to some of our older and more experienced members."[18] The qualifiers contained in this editorial functioned to control the operators in much the same way as the agreement about conduct on the picket line did. The "inexperienced" women needed guidance; unionism for them needed to be "simple." The only appropriate issues for the operators to tackle would be strictly related to trade unionism. And anything the AFT did in relation to the strike would be a generous gift from those "older and more experienced." Now that the strikers had been reined in, silenced, and belittled, the AFT could take them under the wing of established trade unionism, explaining away the confrontational aspects of the operators' behavior as the result of inexperience and youth.

Early in July, the president of the Commercial Telegraphers' Union of America, the national affiliate of the striking operatives, officially called off support of the Atlanta walkout. At a mass meeting, strikers voted to continue the walkout under the auspices of the International Brotherhood of Electrical Workers. Hickey, the veteran IBEW organizer who had been offering guidance to the strikers for weeks, emerged as the leader of the new local when she decided to permanently relocate to Atlanta. After the AFT's intervention, Southern Bell refused to negotiate, claiming the company president was out of town, and press coverage evaporated during this period of stalled talks. The striking telephone operatives, however, continued their pickets and demonstrations for almost a month, trying with little success to regain the momentum of the early days. In late July, the operatives finally gave in and called off the strike.

Southern Bell agreed to deal with reemployment of the former strikers on an individual basis once the walkout collapsed, offering the women "the privilege of making applications for positions, and promising to grant them hearings upon their cases."[19] Rubbing salt in the wounds of the telephone operators, the company also released to the press a statement declaring that Southern Bell had never had an official antiunion stance. To place their involvement in the best possible light, the AFT and the *Journal of Labor* declared the end of the strike a victory for the telephone operators. The paper misleadingly reported that all striking workers would be put back to work within ten days and that those women who had been fired before the strike began (the incident that started the strike) would be allowed to present their cases at a hearing. The editors also chose to interpret the company's statement that union membership would not be a consideration in the hiring process as an affirmation of workers' right to organize rather than as a denial of the efficacy of unions.[20] This was a bitter defeat for organized women in the city. The AFT's actions and the *Journal of Labor*'s editorial policy clearly demonstrated that women would not be a priority for the male-dominated trade union movement, despite language praising the hard labor of the working girl.

The telephone operators' strike was the last major collective uprising of Atlanta's white wage-earning women in the early twentieth century. The walkout may have contained more spectacle than other strikes, but it was no more successful. The strike revealed fissures along gender lines in the solidarity of the city's trade unions. These rifts go far in explaining the dearth of collective activism by working-class women in the 1920s. Unlike those involved in the short and successful Boston strike, Atlanta's female telephone workers found little support from the local women's movement and lacked a long-standing connection to the labor movement through family or experience. In addition, the city's federated trade unions did not provide much of a tradition of radical struggles for worker control.[21] While the AFT officially celebrated women as union wives and blossoming trade unionists in their own right, the actions surrounding the telephone operators' strike reveal that the organization and the community it represented were not willing to support women's independent collective action. As Elizabeth Faue has noted, this hostility stemmed in part from "the highly sexualized character of the telephone workers' protest—with its images of women in carnival . . . and physically assaulting pickets [that were] not . . . compatible with labor's politics of the family wage."[22] These "carnival" strikes also appeared increasingly frivolous to a labor movement facing a nationwide period of retrenchment in the big-business 1920s. Organized labor encouraged women to be community members, supporters of male unions, and aware consumers. Limited support was also offered to young, single women who wanted to join unions. By vociferously leading their own strike and by abandoning a national union in favor of their own goals, the striking telephone operators crossed gender boundaries to which the paternalistic trade unions of the city clung. The AFT responded in ways that silenced the striking women, undercut their effectiveness, and would eventually become a part of a larger silence in relation to working-class women within the city.

War, Women, and Work

THE TELEPHONE operators' strike was a part of a broader process relating to changes in the labor force brought on by World War I and the armistice of 1918. As men were quickly pulled into the military and the demand for Atlanta's manufactured goods increased, new opportunities opened to women workers of both races. Government and business leaders on the national, state, and local levels created campaigns and plans to draw more women into industry. But this growth was carefully managed as these coalitions sought to "investigate the local labor conditions, and determine in what departments women could replace men."[23] Union and employer efforts to control the growth of women's paid labor expanded and in many cases coalesced into a coherent movement. Under this limited and regulated expansion, women received great praise for their war efforts. The *Journal of Labor* lauded the "womanhood of the American working class" for "doing a man's part."[24] The *Atlanta Georgian* went even further and argued that the "capable manner in which they filled the men's jobs" should justify equal wages for women workers.[25]

In reality, working-class women in Atlanta seemed to have needed little inducement to fill jobs in the industrial sector during the war. Chaddie Wertham, an African American, left her work as a laundress and cook for a job at the Union Box Company. Her position stacking boxes had been filled by men in the past, but female replacements were allowed to maintain the jobs after the war "because they like the work and because they have made good."[26] Interestingly, Wertham not only took over a man's job but also adopted a man's style of dress, preferring overalls to skirts. Wertham's case seems to have been unusual, though, since most jobs women gained during this period were not in the economic realms traditionally reserved for males. Instead, women usually filled newly created positions. Expansion also progressed in such a way as to maintain sex-segregated workplaces: rather than using a woman or two to fill vacant positions in the existing labor force, companies tended to recategorize whole categories of jobs, such as box stacking, as appropriate for females. In instances where women did take over men's jobs, as in Wertham's case, companies filled entire departments with women employees rather than inaugurate mixed-sex work spaces.

At the close of World War I, business leaders and organized labor quickly turned their energies to reining in the growth and changes in women's employment precipitated by the war. Newspapers began to regularly run articles calling for the removal of women from the workforce, claiming, "We must not forget in all the excitement of war that these women have a higher mission in life than saving the commercial and industrial interest of the country."[27] Indeed, many women were pushed out of the jobs they had gained during the war. A woman identified only as Miss Hines, for example, worked as an elevator operator, a traditionally male task, during the war. She enjoyed this job because she could sit down for most of the day, but all female operatives lost their positions to men after the war.[28] The war had little long-term impact on women's employment in the city, and women's share of the labor force subsequently dropped to its lowest level since 1890. By 1920, the number of white women in the paid labor force approached that of black women, and that equal distribution would hold throughout the decade.[29] The fantastic growth in the number of employed women and the shifting composition of the female labor force seen in the first two decades of the twentieth century had come to an end along with the war.

The end result of the campaign to return women to home and hearth after the war fortified boundaries that kept women in low-paying, sex-segregated jobs. The contradictions between the need for women's labor and desires to continue to define women primarily by their domestic roles could be muted by limited options for paid labor open to women.[30] Women would not compete directly for wages with men but would continue to exist in roles apart from men, even when women worked outside the home. There was little chance for advancement, a situation employers justified with the myth that women did not need to work for pay, thereby encouraging women to see a life as a homemaker as the most feasible and rewarding avenue open to them. A YWCA member trying to survive as an industrial worker for one summer shortly after the war unknowingly testified to the success of these controls on women's advancement when she wrote of her working sisters, "When I began to realize the trials, hardships and suffering they had, and still had, I could not blame them for being ambitionless or anything else."[31] The changes increasing employment for women threatened in the 1900s and 1910s did not materialize. Atlanta, and much of the nation, came to accept the presence of wage-earning women once it became apparent that women would not encroach on male domains, lower men's wages, or abandon family life altogether.

As the 1920s progressed, even organized labor lost interest in the plight of the working girl. The *Journal of Labor* ran very few articles aimed specifically at the interests of wage-earning women during these years. Only a few reports of auxiliary and label league meetings still appeared, celebrating the work of union wives. The rich dialogue about unionism, individual responsibility, and the role of women in the community that emerged from the paper's regular columnists and editors in earlier decades had all but disappeared. Unlike the newspaper in the 1900s and the 1910s, women appeared more as potential consumers (advertisements for Hoosier cabinets in varying heights to accommodate both short and tall women) or eye-catching subjects for advertisements (sexy drawings of female actresses to plug movies being shown locally) than as active members of broad-based union movement. Even the label leagues faded, removing the political component of consumerism built in the 1900s and 1910s. As growing male unemployment, rising racial tensions, and the tightening of the city budget converged in the late 1920s, the resources of reformers, labor leaders, and other organizations moved away from a focus on wage-earning women. The *Journal of Labor* did briefly run a page "Of Interest to Women" in the early 1930s. The bold headers encouraged women to turn to the page and men to skip over it and implied that women's interests were discrete from the main (male) issues of organized labor.

A similar shift occurred in the various educational programs offered to the city's white working classes during the 1920s. Atlanta's Opportunity School, for example, had offered industrial training to working-class women since 1906. Classes in "beauty culture," home nursing, and millinery provided women with skills that would allow them to work independently or in female-managed occupations. Reports of the popularity of the school insisted that women consistently filled the classes, "ambitious to fit themselves for better positions in the business world."[32] By the time of its tenth anniversary, the Opportunity School had become a completely different institution, focusing more on elevating the "quality of our citizenry" than on alleviating "industrial or educational handicap[s]."[33] With the leveling off of women entering the paid workforce and the firm establishment of women in the clerical trades, the school largely abandoned the "widow suddenly thrust upon the world to earn her own living" and instead focused on the education of working-class men.[34] Of all the education programs directed specifically at women that had appeared in the early decades of the twentieth century, only the industrial department of the YWCA maintained its exclusive commitment to meeting the needs of working-class women beyond the 1920s. Most of the night schools begun to aid young women in the 1910s, such as the Girls' Night School, were canceled by the 1920s or were shifted to coeducational citizenship-training classes.[35] With these shifts, night schools no longer represented the same opportunities for advancement in employment and inexpensive business training as they had in the 1910s, and their popularity among single working-class women dwindled in subsequent decades.

New Political Agendas

WORLD WAR I initiated significant changes in Atlanta's political landscape that would similarly contribute to the declining visibility of working-class women. The war had opened up a new set of opportunities for African Americans in the nation's manufacturing centers, and as demands for goods rose and European immigration fell off, industrial jobs became available to black men, particularly in the urban North. Black women could also increasingly find employment in Detroit, Chicago, and other northern cities but generally filled the same domestic work positions as in the South. Employers paid better in the North, however, and more educational opportunities, fewer voting restrictions, less obvious segregation, and thriving black communities on the south side of Chicago, in Paradise Valley in Detroit, in Harlem, and in virtually every other northern industrial city drew women and men alike out of the South during the war years and throughout the 1920s.[36] Believing that "Negroes [were] acting for themselves, self-consciously, almost for the first time in their histories," journalist Ray Stannard Baker labeled the migration perhaps "the most noteworthy event" in black history.[37]

Measuring the impact of African American migration on Atlanta is no easy task. Atlanta had been a destination for blacks seeking a better life since Reconstruction and remained popular even as some black Atlantans quit the city for urban North in the twentieth century.[38] Because of Atlanta's continued power to draw African Americans (the city's black population increased 43 percent during the 1920s), discussions of the migration northward never reached the fevered pitch experienced in some rural communities where agricultural decline created substantial black outmigration. Unlike Georgia's smaller cities and many of its rural communities, Atlanta never took advantage of the state law allowing individual locales to create stiff restrictions for representatives from northern industries recruiting black workers.[39] Some whites—local employers, real estate agents, and politicians—noticed the migration and showed some concern over its potential to create a shortage of menial laborers, but their responses were largely conciliatory. The *Atlanta Constitution* advocated on several occasions in 1919 and 1920 for the better treatment of African Americans—improved wages and schools, a crackdown on lynching, and so on—as an inducement for blacks to stay in the South.[40]

The black elite, especially Benjamin Davis Sr., the outspoken editor of the African American *Atlanta Independent,* initiated much of the city's dialogue on the northward movement of blacks and applauded sentiments such as those expressed by the editors of the *Constitution.* Davis endeavored "to point out in plain, simple and manly language" that while the South was the "natural home" of blacks, whites could never convince the black to stay in the South "until they are willing to give him the right to the ballot, equal accommodation on railroads and street cars, representation on the jury and a fair and equitable distribution of the school funds."[41] For Davis and other elite black leaders, both in Atlanta and nationally, the migration represented a "great racial awakening" and a way to create "race unity."[42] The threat of black labor abandoning the South became a means to press for political inclusion and economic gains. This local and national dialogue developing around the impact of the migration had an unmistakable though not exclusively male focus despite the significant number of black women who headed North during and after the war. The war and its attendant labor shortage encouraged bold and very masculinist pronouncements from Davis and other leaders: "The Negro is conscious of his racial identity, and is not ashamed of it. He is proud of his race and his color, but he does not like to have the word 'Negro' define his relation as a citizen."[43] The common phrase used to express black demands in these years became "give the Negro *manhood* rights."[44] In a migration driven so heavily by the lure of industrial jobs for men and with a political dialogue developed around the threat of a loss of male menial labor in the South, the women who left Atlanta in the 1920s received scant notice.[45]

A decline in the organized club work of the city's middle-class women also contributed to the marginalization of working-class women from the political discussions of the 1920s. This trend did not happen in the same way or for the same reasons on both sides of the color line, but the net effects on working-class women and the dialogues of city building were remarkably similar. The changing focus and declining power of Atlanta's middle-class women provides one of the most important contributing factors in the shift away from working-class women's visibility. The decline in club work in the 1920s was a national as well as local phenomenon among middle-class women. With suffrage secured, a new individualism taking hold among the younger women of the middle class, and no clear consensus on where to go next, membership dropped precipitously in organizations such as the National Association of Colored Women and the National Woman's Party.[46] Club work for both white and black women became increasingly less important in 1920s Atlanta, and the issues of interest to the city's organized middle-class women also shifted. Middle-class club women had been a source of much of the concern over working-class women, waging struggles to regulate public amusements, create welfare programs, preserve public health, and win suffrage. When their time and resources shifted toward consumerism and new agendas in the 1920s or lost their effectiveness in the face of new political challenges, the working-class women who had been the objects of so many efforts consequently faded from view.[47]

Atlanta's elite black women had held powerful positions in civic organizations after the 1906 riot, helping to cultivate the theory of racial uplift that relied on morality and created groups that depended heavily on the leadership of women as the traditional guardians of morality. With the interracial movement begun during the war and the black elite's increasing focus on economic development and political inclusion in the 1920s, the old moral uplift philosophy, with its attendant focus on women, faded from the agenda. Black soldiers serving in the war provided the opening wedge in a new dialogue on race relations that carried an inherently male bias. Local leaders argued that police should "show the same tolerance to colored and white soldiers alike" and that black soldiers should receive better treatment on streetcars and in public places of recreation.[48] The Great Migration furthered this trend as race leaders used the threat of removing black male labor from the South to argue for improved economic opportunities for African American breadwinners. The new generation of "race men" emerging in the years before 1930—business owners, professionals, and ministers—increasingly viewed segregation as "a denial of dignity and manhood" rather than the result of African American moral failings.[49] This more militant leadership and its focus on restoring manhood through political power and economic inclusion left little maneuvering room for women of any class. Men served as the titular heads of prominent organizations, the fund-raisers, and the agenda setters.

Many elite black women, even those who had played dominant roles in the uplift politics of the 1910s, became increasingly marginalized in their efforts "to represent concerns that centered most consistently, although not exclusively, on their families and communities."[50] The Commission on Interracial Cooperation, founded in 1919, continued this policy. The organization lauded individual African American males' achievements in an attempt to educate blacks and whites on the worthiness of racial cooperation. Members of the Women's Missionary Society and the Southeastern Federation of Colored Women's Clubs, which early in their history had promoted the protection of black women, found themselves absorbed into the ranks of the Commission on Interracial Cooperation and shifted their attention to protecting black men from lynching.[51] As a result of these changes, some women's work went unrecognized in the community, while others adapted their views of racial uplift to mesh with these changes, carving out significant roles for themselves only when they shifted attention away from their traditional areas of concern—mothers, families, and neighborhoods. Lugenia Burns Hope, for example, increasingly distanced herself from the organization she had created in 1908, the Neighborhood Union, and focused her efforts instead on starting citizenship schools for the National Association for the Advancement of Colored People in the early 1930s. As a part of these political and gender transitions, black working-class women lost the prioritization and identification they had received during the era of moral uplift as good race politics.

On the other side of the color line, white middle-class club women increasingly moved away from political and educational activities targeting working-class women. By 1926, for example, the Atlanta League of Women Voters had re-created itself as the "sponsor [of] principles rather than parties or persons," focusing its efforts on researching issues and candidates rather than drawing women into formal politics.[52] During a 1927 campaign to revise the city's charter, the organization cultivated a new relationship with Atlanta businessmen, leaving little room or need for alliances with working-class women. By abandoning organizing tactics that singled out women voters, the league received more support, especially money, from this partnership with the city's male business elite. League women still provided most of the leadership and even the office space for the charter campaign, but they willingly downplayed their role to appeal to local politicians. While the 1927 initiative failed to win approval, the political alliances the league built during this campaign proved more enduring than the brief cross-class coalition of women formed in 1922.[53]

Having reached the pinnacle of their influence in Atlanta through their war work in the late 1910s, middle-class club women's authority diminished.[54] With support from white trade unions and the alliance with local businessmen, organized white women voters and white women's civic groups continued to work for political reform in the 1920s, but none of their efforts resulted in the new city charter they desired. By the 1930s, white women's role in Atlanta's formal politics was even further marginalized by the growing national economic crisis. Middle-class women, who like labor also faced a period of retrenchment, struggled to maintain their political relationships to the city's business elite, further distancing themselves from working-class women. In 1932 the Atlanta League of Women Voters considered changing its name to something that would invite the participation of both women and men.[55]

Even former supporters of women's suffrage and the work of the Atlanta League of Women Voters began to dismiss women's influence on government. Historian Nancy Cott's work emphasizes similar trends on the national level, where the strength of many women's organizations dissipated once the woman suffrage amendment passed.[56] Mildred Seydell, a columnist for the *Atlanta Georgian,* threatened politicians with the wrath of women voters if the leaders continued to relegate women to "secondary places in the political field." The editors of the *Journal of Labor,* advocates for women in politics in earlier decades, countered that "the politician is measuring [the woman voter's] strength and up to now has found it to be much weaker than at first anticipated. Speaking locally as well as nationally, the women, by their vote, have not cut a very big figure." Then, in a passage emblematic of larger changes in city politics, the editors dismissed Seydell's argument by constructing her and all women as sexual objects: "Dear Mildred, we have no doubt that the politicians are looking at the women. It has ever been characteristic of man to do so, whether he be a politician or something else."[57] Despite the league's success in promoting voter education and keeping political reform on the table during the 1920s, women of all classes found little discreet space in which to act on their political agendas as Atlanta entered the Great Depression of the 1930s.

The political issues that captured the city's attention during the 1920s also reinforced the marginalization of women through the masculinization of politics. The revival of the Ku Klux Klan, headquartered in Atlanta between 1916 and 1925, contributed to this process. The Klan prospered locally only after 1920, when membership rose and the organization began regular public demonstrations. By 1921, forty thousand Atlantans belonged to the Klan, and a congressional investigation revealed that the organization could claim at least three members in the upper levels of city government and substantial influence in the city's police force. In 1922, Walter A. Sims, an acknowledged Klan member, won the mayoral race against the old Progressive incumbent James Woodward (who had banned masked parades). Sims's platform, endemic of the political tenor the Klan brought to Atlanta in the 1920s, supported white supremacy, Protestantism, and "the inviolate protection of Southern Womanhood."[58] The political culture emerging from the Klan's prominent role in the city's infrastructure resurrected the rallying cry from the 1906 gubernatorial election (which had contributed to the race riot of that year), defended the patriarchal family, and resisted or obscured the challenges presented by modern women.

The Klan built its brand of white supremacy around the dependency of wo-men. This construction allowed urban white Protestants of the middling sort to respond to both the growing political unrest among African Americans, evident in the discussions of the Great Migration, and the power feminism seemed to have achieved during the war years.[59] But in Atlanta, where Jim Crow held strong throughout the 1920s, the local Klan assumed white supremacy and focused more of its efforts on routing Catholics and Jews and restoring masculine rights and presence.[60] The Klan's language bears a striking resemblance to that used by elite African American men, with references to the "souls of manly men" and to "bringing untold thousands of big, manly men into the fellowship."[61] The two groups' politics certainly differed in dramatic ways, but their emphasis on reasserting masculinity in pursuance of their political goals did not.

By the late 1920s, an internally divided Klan had largely devoured itself, middle-class women relied on their male allies to speak for them, and the immediacy of the Great Migration had evaporated. The working-class had been thoroughly removed from Atlanta's political culture. Formal politics and corruption of city government dominated the second half of the decade. The charter reform cam-paigns spearheaded by the Atlanta League of Women Voters were only one piece of a larger movement to reform a government based on what historian Cliff Kuhn calls "a structure that lent itself to ward politics, political patronage and corrup-tion."[62] Like Progressive movements across the country, Atlanta reformers were continually frustrated by special interests' control of city politics. "It made it very hard," according to suffragist and League of Women Voters organizer Emily MacDougald, "to get any kind of ordinances passed [for] the good of the whole.

The people elected from each ward wouldn't have an interest in the city as a whole, they'd only have an interest in their own ward."[63] Only a vehement campaign by the *Atlanta Constitution* and the clean government platforms of several post-1925 mayors would break the stranglehold of ward politics just as the city was beginning to feel the worst effects of the depression. In 1929 a grand jury finally investigated charges of widespread government impropriety that had been circulating for several years.[64] The *Atlanta Constitution* won a Pulitzer Prize for its series of articles that exposed graft and bribery in City Hall. In the wake of this political scandal, anti-incumbent sentiments ran high among voters in the 1930 primary. James L. Key, a former mayor and favorite of the city's white working classes, captured the mayoral race largely because of his distance from city government at the time of the scandal. Coincidentally, Atlanta's municipal government moved from its old location on Marietta Street into a new, million-dollar building in 1930, symbolizing a new political era.

Public Space

SIMILAR TO shifting ideas about political control and agendas were changing conceptions of public space. A 1924 controversy that developed around Washington Park, the only public park for the city's blacks, suggests the subtle ways in which this shift played out. Generational and class conflicts took center stage this time. And perhaps more telling than if they had not appeared at all, working-class women played a minor and remarkably uncontroversial and unemotional role, even though much of the discussion of the park's problems turned on perceptions of morality. The concern over the evils of the park was also suggestive of the new political relationship elite blacks sought to build with the city's white politicians.

Washington Park opened in 1920 and almost instantly became enormously popular with young African Americans. Both black civic leaders and the city government raised familiar charges of impropriety against the facility, echoing middle-class perspectives honed in debates over the city's dance halls and cheap theaters in the 1910s. Concerns were expressed over the availability of liquor in the park, the moral atmosphere of the dance pavilion, and conditions of the swimming pool. In Washington Park the morals of wealthier and older blacks clashed with those of working-class youth. Many nearby residents complained that the dance pavilion was "just terrible, especially for the girls," a "notorious joint," and a "meeting place for girls and boys." Those who enjoyed the park, however, defended it as giving "the neighbors someplace to go" and a "good thing." They appreciated the skating and swimming despite the park's generally poor conditions.[65]

The Neighborhood Union directed E. Franklin Frazier and the Atlanta School of Social Work to survey the park and its surrounding homes to determine the veracity of the allegations and offer remedies to the problems. The final report supported the opinions of most of the middle-class blacks who lived around the park. Frazier and his associates found the park to be filthy, both physically and morally. They concluded that the "amusements are unwholesome," dismissing the opinions of "those who take pleasure in the park." Considering the "vulgar dancing" at the dance pavilion, the committee urged that it be closed. Justifying its objections, the committee reported, "Lights are poor; conduct bad; crowd in streets is awful rough; conduct terrible on edge of park grounds; both night and day; the disorder is terrible, cursing and throwing rocks." The investigative committee's overall recommendation to the Neighborhood Union and the city was that "people do need some place for recreation, but seems like the present condition of the park is worse than none."[66] Many whites agreed that "Washington Park must be reformed or closed. . . . it will be far better for the race at large and the public morals to shut it up in short order."[67] While the park remained open, fears of intimate interaction between the sexes similar to those raised in the debates over commercial amusements in the 1910s won out, and the city council closed many of the park concessions and the dance hall.

The park that remained after the 1924 closings was a part of a larger trend in organized and commercial leisure emerging after World War I. The Washington Park controversy is worthy of mention in part because it comes as one of the last in which women functioned as the important symbols in debates over the shape and meaning of protection. Their inclusion with the list of ills facing the park, however, lacks the focused, excited energy attached to women's presence and behavior in public spaces during the 1910s, when debates focused on dance halls and theaters. The excitement caused by women flocking to inexpensive amusements waned after the war, and the patterns followed by discussions of public space were echoed in the other arenas in which working-class women had seemed so central only a decade earlier.

Saving the Poor and Policing the Streets

JUST AS the city's political terrain shifted in the 1920s, welfare and public health movements underwent their own transformations. In these realms, social workers and public health advocates created new policies centered primarily on the city's children. Between the cultural associations of tuberculosis and the social practices of treatment, working-class women had served as apt symbols of Atlanta's fledgling public health movement in the early twentieth century. Perceptions of disease and programs to combat it pushed working-class women, particularly blacks, to the cultural forefront most often in the despised role of infector.

As tuberculosis became better understood and more successfully treated in the 1920s and 1930s, however, public health work with tuberculosis took a decided turn away from issues involving women. Anxieties over the disease melted into a sense of hope that was better represented by the relative tractability of children. No longer did the Anti-Tuberculosis Association help children by helping their parents; instead, the organization directly sought out children. The Anti-Tuberculosis Association jettisoned its visiting nurse corps and forced the city to take over the responsibility of administering screening clinics. The association then focused its attention on its education programs in both black and white schools. These programs attempted to interest children in "finer citizenship, city cleanliness, and city health."[68] Children were called on to participate in annual spring "Clean-Up Campaigns" and to contribute pennies to the milk fund for tubercular patients. The association even started its own "open-air schools" to help stop the spread of tuberculosis among high risk—that is, poor—children. In these schools public health workers hoped that children would stay healthy so as to be "of the greatest use to their city and society."[69] The end of World War I also heralded the end of the public health movement targeting working-class women in Atlanta. Efforts on the part of the federal government to battle venereal disease halted abruptly after the armistice, and local programs dwindled shortly thereafter. In the end, these changes resulted in the general disassociation of women with epidemic disease.

With the coming of the 1920s, social welfare organizations joined the public health movement in shifting their focus to the plight of poor and sick children. Sweeping histories of social welfare, like those by Michael Katz and William Trattner, point to the child saving of the Progressive Era, but a narrower focus on this period reveals that concern for children was interwoven with other concerns for the poorer classes. In Atlanta, a child-centered movement reached ascendancy only in the mid-to-late 1920s.[70] Attendant to this shift was a move toward centralization of Atlanta's private social welfare network and the development of new county and state agencies. The net result of these changes was a dearth of support for the poor women of the city where there once had been an abundance. Most female welfare recipients' reluctance to conform to social workers' mandates undoubtedly encouraged them to focus their efforts elsewhere. As welfare agencies sought to prove themselves efficient and successful entities, children represented more pliable subjects who could be easily accessed through schools instead of costly and time-consuming home visits.

Leading the way among Atlanta's social welfare organizations, the Associated Charities also changed its name and policies in the 1920s to reflect its new emphasis on children. Renamed the Family Welfare Society (FWS) in 1924, the organization turned over all basic relief cases to the city warden and took on as clients only families in which children were at risk. The organization's policy meant that social workers would only accept families "where the problem arises out of difficulties in social relationships rather than out of pressing economic need."[71] Even the agency's case studies changed: women were no longer referred to by name but instead were described as "Elizabeth's mother," "little Sallie's mother," or, even more generically, "the mother of the family."[72] The FWS also forged a new working relationship with the school system. Teachers and administrators, rather than mothers, took on the role of bringing troubled children to the organization's attention. The Associated Charities was not alone in making these changes. The Home for the Friendless stopped admitting women in the 1920s, changed its name to Hillside Cottages, and accepted only children under the age of fifteen. The Wesley Settlement House closed in 1920, as missionary women concentrated their efforts on evangelizing and child welfare and opened a kindergarten for black children in 1928.[73]

In the mid-1920s, men begin to appear in welfare agencies' case histories as the originators of families' requests for aid.[74] This phenomenon may result in part from the decline of home visits. Increasingly, cases were dealt with from the FWS offices, located downtown, an area in which men still predominated. The office interview was explained by social workers as the natural outgrowth of professionalization as "case work becomes more scientific in character." Further explanation of this policy, however, reveals that home visits were abandoned because "a private interview can never be held with the man—the head of the family—except in the office."[75] As a consequence of the new orientation toward aiding children and reconstructing or saving their families, social workers restored men to discussions of the fate of poor families.

Atlanta's network of social welfare agencies underwent a concurrent reorganization that further institutionalized welfare work with children. In 1923, a group of Atlanta businessmen organized the Community Chest in an effort to centralize fund-raising and, consequently, relief efforts. This agency, which for a time shared offices with the FWS, influenced the work of other organizations by controlling their budgets. The most money by far was allocated to the FWS, endorsing the shift toward a focus on children and their dysfunctional families.[76] When the Neighborhood Union refused to join the newly created Atlanta Urban League in 1924, the union found itself cut off from Community Chest funds and could only be restored to the budget by agreeing to restrict its efforts to programs for African American children.[77] The Community Chest also reduced support to day nurseries, despite the lip service paid to "saving families," while increasing support to orphanages and other institutions that removed children from the home. The Gate City Free Kindergarten, which for nineteen years had operated five child care centers, was reduced to only two nurseries.

Changes were afoot in public agencies in the 1920s as well. The police department increasingly curtailed its efforts at intervention and welfare activity. Standard procedure for dealing with women became arrest, detention, trial, and sentencing as welfare intervention work declined. Arrest rates for both white and black women jumped as women were incorporated into the legal system in a way similar to men. Arrest rates start to climb for white women after 1917, and rates for black women increased significantly starting in 1920. The police committee raised female officers' pay to match the levels of the men of their races but then replaced the women with male officers. The matron's ward, which had been an independent department, became part of the police bureau, under direct control of the chief of police. This is not to say that all protective work ceased, but it did decline significantly following World War I. [78]

The aid supplied by the city warden's office, with its long-established policy of minimal investigation, became the single largest source of direct relief. And as periodic depressions became more severe and regular in the 1920s, Atlanta opened an employment bureau to deal exclusively with male unemployment problems. The policy reinforced the notion—held by much of white Atlanta—that women's wage work was secondary in all cases to that of men. Rising unemployment also fed the relief rolls of the city warden; consequently, most available aid was channeled through working-class and poor men.

Founded in 1920, the Georgia Department of Public Welfare represented public efforts beyond those of the city to fight "dependency and delinquency." [79] By creating new agencies and taking over the few existing ones, the department demonstrated a strong commitment to the issues of poor children outside the private welfare network. The department's main objectives were to oversee children's institutions, adoption, and juvenile courts as well as supervise county relief. In its first year, the department operated seventy-seven juvenile courts, a dramatic jump from the eight that had existed the year before. [80] Even the Georgia Training School for Girls, founded in 1914 and overseen by the Department of Public Welfare after 1920, shifted its focus from housing women under the age of eighteen who had been accused of everything from vagrancy to insufficient guardianship to accepting only girls "too young to be held responsible for their conduct in the past as they have been unrestrained and unprotected by proper home influence." [81] This shift became evident in 1919, when the school began to separate the "smaller and younger girls . . . committed because of dangerous environments at home" from the older girls. When the state slashed the school's budget in 1921, only those who fell into the former category received "the protection of the school to prevent them from becoming a menace to society." [82]

As Georgia created public welfare agencies in the 1920s, a split developed between public and private organizations. Private agencies leapt to the defense and reformation of children of pathological families, altogether abandoning direct relief except in extreme cases. Public agencies adopted both a focus on children and a developing interest in temporary material relief for out-of-work men. As private and public organizations negotiated distinct territories, working and poor women, who had been so crucial to the development of Atlanta's social welfare network, fell through the cracks, with virtually all relief channeled to children and unemployed men.

Social welfare organizations' changing focus had somewhat contradictory meanings for women. Women still outnumbered men in the city, and while the trend had slowed, women were still increasing their numbers in the paid workforce. But as the 1920s progressed, women's experiences in the city became less sensationalized and more regularized. As with the police department, women's experiences were incorporated into city structures in ways similar to those of working-class men. Women's poverty became more normalized as the lives of at-risk children were invested with anxieties about moral decay and individual pathologies. Poor women could seek out local government agencies such as the city warden's office and receive direct relief without intrusive home visits from social workers. Yet through these home visits, social welfare agencies had often developed their pro-woman policies that aided families, maintained homes, and alleviated abusive relationships. The network of social welfare organizations that had developed in relation to these women still existed, though, and in some cases still helped working-class women, even if its focus had changed. What is most different about Atlanta's welfare system and public health campaigns in the 1920s, then, is that the sense of urgency that had previously been invested in poor women was now invested primarily in their children.

Pragmatic Citizenship

MANY of the sources—organizational papers, newspapers, police reports, and the like—that pointed to the pervasiveness of working-class women's visibility in the 1900s and 1910s also illustrate the shift away from the symbolic importance of women by the 1920s. These sources can also tell us, however, that working-class women themselves probably did very little to create this shift. Indeed, women demonstrated a remarkable consistency in their actions as they negotiated the complex intersections of family and work, getting by and having fun, and the liabilities and advantages of city life. Women of both races continued to seek employment and pleasure in Atlanta's public spaces and demanded rights, protection, and even retribution in front of Atlanta's commissions and courts much as they had in the decades previous.

Through the 1920s and into the 1930s, for example, little change is evident in the divorce cases brought to Fulton County Superior Court. Lennie Belle Aaron sued her husband, A. E. Aaron, for divorce in 1925. She claimed that her husband beat her, causing her to miscarry, and infected her with a venereal disease. A. E. Aaron filed a cross-bill claiming that his wife had sought abortions, used "the most vile and degrading language," and "was always nagging at the defendant and in every way possible [making] life unpleasant for the defendant." He also repeated her opinion "that she was not 'cut out' for a married woman, that she was a business woman." Lennie Aaron preferred to move through the city unaccompanied by her husband. As he explained to the court, "she told him that she did not have any pleasure with him along and that she could have a good time by herself." The two juries and a judge who heard the tales of this deeply troubled marriage sided with the husband, awarding him the divorce and ordering Lennie Aaron "not at liberty to marry again."[83] Working-class women may have functioned less as symbols of moral order in the 1920s, but gendered expectations for spouses apparently had not undergone any major revisions. Women such as Aaron continued to risk the condemnation of the court and the social stigma attached to divorce, and by 1928, the number of divorce cases filed by women nationwide climbed to 71 percent.[84] Determined to regain her independence, Lennie Aaron appeared in front of the court again a year later. This time she prevailed in her petition to have the "disabilities" imposed on her by the court removed so that she could live her life "as if said marriage with . . . A. E. Aaron had never been solemnized."[85]

In essence, most divorce suits of the 1920s and the 1930s remained remarkably consistent with those filed in the 1910s. After two years of marriage, Louise Talley Griffith left her husband in the fall of 1925. Alexander Griffith then started following her to her job as a typist and threatening "to throw carbolic acid in her face and disfigure her for life." Louise Griffith won a restraining order against her husband while she petitioned for and received a full divorce in superior court.[86] In divorce proceedings, women not only claimed the right to work and travel the city as they pleased but also sought court recognition of the economic contributions they had made to their families, such as using their wages to buy a house, furnishings, or other possessions.[87] Divorce provided an avenue for women of both races to re-establish independence and assert property rights. The proceedings indicate the extent to which women expected the assistance of the state and the lengths to which they were willing to go to assert their autonomy.

For African American women, the Great Migration represented another venue for and continuation of the pragmatic citizenship they had demonstrated in earlier decades. Unlike nineteenth-century black migrations, the 1920s carried more men than women out of the South and drew families, not just individuals, into the migration stream.[88] The ratio of African American women to men in Atlanta dropped substantially in the 1920s, suggesting that a significant number of women participated in the move northward. Women still outnumbered men 116.6 to 100, but this was down from a ratio of 141.3 to 100 in 1900. And, at the same time that the urban South experienced a drop in sex ratio disparity, the disparity increased in northern cities, as black women began to outnumber men.[89] The war and subsequent economic prosperity created significant pulls for many of the South's black women and men, but it is important to remember that many left as "self-propelled actors seeking respect, space in which to live, and a means to earn an adequate living."[90] Sometimes leaving husbands and children behind, black women from across the South abandoned the region. Unable to attain all they felt entitled to in Atlanta, some sought to have their demands and desires met elsewhere.[91] One woman leaving Atlanta in 1917 asked the editors of a black newspaper for help finding a job and "some place to stop with some good quiet people," but she also noted that her letter was "personal" and should not be printed in the paper. Female migrants prized their respectability and independence even when they did have to ask for help and expected to maintain and enhance these qualities in the urban North.[92]

In the 1920s, working-class women, both black and white, who chose to stay in Atlanta continued to petition the city council for redress of grievances and to file complaints with the police committee. In 1923, for example, Mrs. E. Y. Rainier convinced the police committee to reprimand patrolman Thomas Smith for entering her home and beating her.[93] Mrs. M. L. Calhoun, Mrs. Fuller, Nellie Watkins, and Mamie Billings successfully pressed charges against W. E. Ball. According to testimony before the police committee, Ball forced three of the women into his car, claiming that he would raid their houses and lock them up if they refused him. He proceeded to drive them around town under these threats until he fell asleep, drunk, in an alley. The committee took the women's complaints seriously, finding Ball guilty and discharging him from the force.[94] Pearl Drake came home one day in 1923 to find Officer W. K. Bailey "taking off his coat, cap and pistol and laying on the bed with his arms around" her daughter. Seeking to protect or perhaps control her daughter (the records are unclear as to whether the relationship between the officer and Belle Drake might have been consensual), the elder Drake filed charges with the police committee and testified at the hearing at which Bailey was dismissed from the force.[95]

The ability of women to use venues such as the police committee to advance their interests did contract as the city's concerns shifted. As the moral and social environment drew less attention from local officials and the middle classes, for example, white women would find it increasingly difficult to find protection from the sexual advances of police officers. Modern sexual mores had taken hold in Atlanta by the mid-1920s, and relationships between white police officers and white women rarely drew the intervention of members of the police committee, as they had in the 1910s. When the committee did level misconduct charges against patrolmen, the issue was not that an officer had been found "in bed with a woman" but that he had been found there while on duty.[96]

Contact between black women and white police officers, however, remained taboo throughout the 1920s. In 1925, for example, the police committee charged W. G. Baldwin with "conduct unbecoming officers and neglect of duty" for attempting to have intercourse with Julia Gholston, who was described as "a young negro girl."[97] The testimony of three black women, including Gholston, provided the only evidence against the officer. The police committee remained a venue in which black women could seek retribution against the unwanted sexual advances of white policemen even after the committee had ceased to serve such a function for white women. In a similar case, the committee suspended William Goodwin from the police force for "having sexual intercourse with negro women."[98] That cases such as these continued to appear in the city records suggests that the white police force harassed black women who too freely or confidently used the public spaces of the city, even after policemen had given up such practices with white women. Sexual advances toward African American women can be read as part of the larger system of racial discrimination. By expecting black women to acquiesce to requests/demands for sex, white policemen could potentially erase all black assertions of respectability. But each time a woman complained to the police committee, she reestablished a claim to respectability, citizenship, and the right to travel the city unmolested.[99]

That sexual relationships between white men and black women would raise any concern in the pre–civil rights movement South or continue to raise concern even after penalties for sex between officers and white women disappeared does run counter to much of what we think we know about the South.[100] But cases such as these offer reminders of why we need to historicize race and of how useful other categories of identity can be, even in learning something new about race. Punishing white police for having sex with black women had little to do with the all-male, all-white police committee protecting the virtue of black women or responding to the concerns of a politically marginal population but rather centered on preserving an orderly image. The committee may have tolerated its officers sleeping with black women, but when women filed complaints against officers, the matter became (or had the potential to become) public, and that violated white southern customs allowing only discreet sexual relationships between white men and black women.[101] Flagrant and unpunished interracial sex had the potential to draw attention to the miscegenation of the past and call into question the city's racial purity. Atlanta's carefully crafted image of respectability relied on firm divisions between and hierarchies of race and class. Physically responsible for preserving order in the city, police officers who violated these hierarchies through sexual contact with black women threatened the moral and social order and, consequently, Atlanta's prized reputation. The police committee valued the respectability of the city over traditional racial power structures that would have reinforced white male sexual prerogative with black women. This last lingering vestige of Atlanta's obsession with its moral image passed with the 1920s; thereafter, charges against officers for sexual misconduct with women of any race disappear altogether. The only remaining cases against officers involving sex involved alleged homosexual encounters. [102]

THE 1920s were, as Sarah Deutsch notes for Boston, a period of "mixed messages" and trade-offs for urban women. [103] Women had been accepted as public persons, yet they were, as divorce cases reveal, still supposed to fulfill all the private roles of wife and homemaker. That women worked outside the home raised few eyebrows, but then neither did women's poor work conditions or lack of advancement opportunities. And their collective attempts to alter these conditions four.d little support, even from their organized brethren. Atlantans had grown more comfortable with modern sexual standards, freeing women from middle-class moralizing and police harassment, but that acceptance in turn closed some of the avenues women had used to demand protection from the city. Local newspapers filled their pages with advertisements encouraging women to partake in the rising consumer culture and to enjoy the city's many amusements, but wages for women remained dismal, and better-paid men might offer the only avenue through which women could participate in these pleasures. The moment when working-class women's lives, both real and imagined, had fostered the city's fascination with its moral atmosphere and social respectability had passed. With this passing, at least some of the groups that had been most involved in creating working-class women's visibility, particularly the middle-class women of both races, also lost at least some of their political standing in the contested process of urban growth.

The shift away from working-class women as frequent symbols in the urban discourse occurred gradually in the years following World War I. For Atlanta, the decade of the 1920s was a time of transition. Concerns over moral and social order received increasingly less attention. The arenas in which the working girl or the "wandering cook" had represented the highly contested nature of urban growth did not disappear from the city, but the issues—decency, respectability, and protection—that had pushed women to the forefront disappeared over the course of the decade. Atlanta's public health movement and social welfare network grew stronger during the 1920s, but their focus, like that of the city at large, shifted away from the women who had held such symbolic import in the early decades of the century. Formal politics held the attention of whites, who vied with each other for power, and of blacks, who fought to be included at all. The city struggled to define and meet the needs of its still expanding population, but those needs were now more often couched in the language of efficiency and less focused on morality. No single issue or group immediately appeared to replace working-class women in the 1920s. Not until the 1930s and the Great Depression would the concerns, fears, and hopes of the city again coalesce around a coherent set of images. In place of women rose the figure of the working-class man, thrown into unemployment by the growing depression. He became the symbol of the decade as well as the site for the city's racial and class tensions.

CHAPTER EIGHT

The Forgotten Man Remembered

IN THE SUMMER of 1932, Atlanta police arrested Angelo Herndon as he picked up his mail from a local post office.[1] Police targeted Herndon, an African American and a known Communist, because he had led a peaceful, integrated demonstration by the city's unemployed only days earlier. They waited to bring him into custody, however, until they could capture him with physical evidence of his radicalism. In Herndon's mailbox police found that evidence, confiscating Communist literature, including copies of the *Daily Worker*. Using a state law from the 1830s, prosecutors charged him with attempting to incite insurrection and overthrow the government of Georgia.[2] Herndon's subsequent trials and appeals became one of the most sensationalized legal battles in the city's history, surpassing even that of Leo Frank two decades earlier. Herndon realized the symbolic role he played: describing the interest in his trial in a 1937 autobiography, he concluded, "At [that] moment I was not only an entertainer in a legal burlesque show to divert them from their boredom, but, even more, I became the outlet for all their hatred, all their fear of the rising power of a working class becoming fully aware of its rights and its ability to enforce the granting of those rights."[3]

Two years later, a wave of textile strikes swept across New England and the South. Worker walkouts at ten of the eleven Atlanta area mills caused shutdowns in early September 1934. On a picket line outside the city's Exposition Mills, police arrested Nannie Leah Young and Annie Mae Leathers, both white native Georgians, and later charged them under the state's insurrection statute.[4] The women, in their words, were "grabbed by the law [and] carried to the police station as two red agents, we was two red agents and they got us for insurrection, same thing they did Angelo Herndon. . . . We didn't ever have a gun, just had a *Daily Worker*."[5] The women, sisters and longtime textile workers, had been passing out radical literature and freely admitted to being Communists. The police even reported that the sisters sang the "Internationale" all the way to the police station. Despite being such vocal radicals, the women's case received relatively little notice even in Atlanta. That Herndon's trial became a cause célèbre and a flash point for Atlanta's fear of interracialism, radicalism, and revolution while most of the city overlooked Young and Leathers highlights Atlanta's changing atmosphere in the late 1920s and 1930s.

Working-class female symbols dominated Atlanta's public debates and crises during the first two decades of the twentieth century; radical and unemployed men gradually took over center stage by the early 1930s. The ascendancy of men to this position represented a confluence of trends, some of which started as early as World War I. The economic downturn of the late 1920s and early 1930s further escalated the process. In essence, concerns over political and economic order replaced the focus on moral order that had characterized earlier decades. In the process, unemployed men replaced working-class women as the most visible cultural images, representing fears of radicalism, revolution, and the breakdown of the city's racial and class hierarchies.

The meanings invested in unemployed men point to the dangers that these new symbols of public order represented. Fear of radicalism on both ends of the political spectrum and racial violence repeatedly surfaced in images of men cut loose by the Great Depression from the restraining effects of hard labor. During this period of economic distress, the fears attached to unemployed men help bring into focus the sense of danger and hope working-class women had represented in the earlier era of urban development. Following the theme of visibility into this later period also allows a further examination of the relationship between public culture and daily life for Atlanta's working-class women. Heightened visibility had helped working-class women create social and cultural spaces to advance their own visions for neighborhoods, employment, leisure, and city services. When their visibility declined in the 1920s, women did not cease their activism, and much of the texture of their day-to-day lives remained the same, but there existed fewer venues in which these women might be heard.

The Economic Downturn

GROWING working-class unemployment increasingly captured Atlanta's attention during the depression. Starting in the late 1920s, seasonal unemployment during the winter months worsened with every year. Black men and women of both races experienced the effects of the depression first, but by the early 1930s the economic downturn was taking its toll on whites as well. The *Journal of Labor* responded early to the growing crisis as seasonal unemployment spread to a general depression. The paper warned "people living elsewhere not to come to Atlanta with the hope of getting a job" and called on Mayor James L. Key to initiate a work relief program to revive "the chain of prosperity."[6]

Most of the business elite, however, maintained an optimistic tone in discussing Atlanta's economic health and denying the growing permanency of the Great Depression. In what historian Douglas Smith refers to as the "sunshine syndrome," the daily newspapers and the Chamber of Commerce hung their hopes of recovery on the coming of spring.[7] With warming weather but no return to prosperity in 1931, it became apparent that the city needed more than hopeful editorials and civic pageants to offset the industrial decline. Federal agencies estimated that nearly half of the city's employables could find no work between 1930 and 1933.[8] Crime and growing racial tensions accompanied rising unemployment as the city's poorest residents and newest migrants vied for jobs and survival. Within this tense atmosphere, debates over the city's moral order disappeared, and the threat that the depression posed to civic and national politics came to dominate public debate.

For most of Atlanta's working classes, the coming of the 1930s meant a hard life getting worse. As domestic worker Willie Mae Cartwright described it, "jobs was hard to find, and I sure went to catching the devil every way. Everybody else was having a hard time too; there just wasn't no work to be found."[9] Nellie Bryant, a child during the depression, remembered years later, "building just halted. As of the crash it halted. Mama saw that it was necessary to go out and go to work, she got out and she was able to find a job, even though it was paying only five dollars a week. But with Daddy, he couldn't find anything to do."[10] Many families depended on the income of only one worker or found themselves "borrowing and living on the hands of other folks" to get by.[11] Nannie Young and her family migrated to Atlanta to live with her parents when her husband lost his job in a textile mill. "My mother was living in a little three room house," she later recalled, and it "just broke my heart. I hated to pile up on my poor mother. It was like sticking a knife in me to bring my children back on my parents, and they [so] old. My mother had nine. There were seven of us. I didn't think these three rooms were large enough with sixteen in the family."[12]

Suffering in the city's black communities was particularly acute during the early depression years. Surveys commissioned by the Neighborhood Union and carried out by students at the Atlanta School of Social Work revealed widespread unemployment and underemployment. Many African Americans suffered from "insufficient food, bad housing, over-crowding, sickness, lack of medical care, insufficient clothing, resulting in the case of the children in non-attendance and retardation in school." The social workers also attributed "complete breakdowns in family income, and other ills threatening the morals, health and morale of these people" to long periods of unemployment. Echoing the sentiments of many of the city's black residents, the social workers concluded that "white persons were suffering primarily from an emergency situation, but the Negroes were the victims of long existing economic evils, which were only intensified by the depression."[13]

Rising unemployment created tensions between workers, races, and classes; the competition for jobs threatened established social relationships and hierarchies. Radicalism erupted on both the right and the left as desperate members of the working classes mobilized for economic relief. While women participated in several of these movements, the organizations that emerged during the early depression promoted the visibility of the city's male unemployed through parades and public meetings. Men also occupied the most powerful and visible leadership positions as liaisons to the press and public speakers for these radical groups. The police and city government, fearing this rising tide of radicalism, reinforced the emergence of the unemployed male as the dominant symbol of the era through strategic arrests, parade permits, and highly sensationalized trials.

Although Communists started organizing poor whites and blacks in the South in the late 1920s, the reactionary Black Shirts emerged as Atlanta's first depression-era mass radical organization. Officially called the American Fascisti Association, this extremist group claimed a membership of forty thousand at its height during the summer of 1930. The group was formed both to counteract the organizing efforts of Communists, who promised social equality to the city's African Americans, and to promote white supremacy by forcing employers to replace black workers with whites. Offering themselves up as a kind of employment agency, the Black Shirts drew large numbers of white men, desperate for work, to its meetings and demonstrations. The group was short-lived, however, and when the press finally turned against it in the fall of 1930, several of the leaders moved to Florida to form a new organization. [14]

Replacing black workers with whites offered many of Atlanta's white unemployed men an appealing answer to their economic problems. The language, leadership, and activities of the organization also carried an unmistakable male focus. "We believe in protecting our home and the chastity of American womanhood," defenders of the Black Shirts explained, linking the ability to obtain a job with racial and gender order in language frighteningly reminiscent of that immediately preceding Atlanta's 1906 race riot. [15] The Black Shirts encouraged jobless whites to blame competition between the races for the city's economic downturn and offered white racial supremacy as answer to white Atlanta's financial woes. Such arguments fingered African Americans as the cause of white joblessness rather than pinning the blame on an ailing economy or some other large and hard-to-define phenomenon over which white workers had little control. In pursuing their goals, the Black Shirts confronted employers by offering them the pick of the organization's white men if black employees were fired. The hotel industry was a particular target of the Black Shirts, who hoped to reracialize bellhops and similar positions as jobs for whites. Members even set up African American workers in hotel rooms with white prostitutes in hopes of getting the blacks fired. Working within the established southern labor system, in which jobs were consistently race typed, the Black Shirts hoped to convert whole areas of employment into "white" jobs rather than to integrate workplaces or job categories. Most employers ignored pressure from the Black Shirts altogether or promised only not to hire any more blacks in the future. A certain loyalty to employees and the lower pay usually given to African Americans kept hotel owners and others from giving in to the organization's demands. [16]

The Black Shirts initially found little resistance from the press or the city government, which consistently granted parade permits to the group, and the organization thrived during the late summer of 1930. Black Shirts conducted all-male public demonstrations in downtown Atlanta and Piedmont Park with the approval of the mayor and a full police escort. A witness recalled one parade with "four or five thousand of these people in black shirts marching four abreast, right through Five Points, with the streets on both sides just packed and jammed with their supporters." [17] The appeal of the Black Shirts reflected the growing intensity of the depression and not only the city's failure to act to alleviate the situation but also its reluctance to even admit the extent of the crisis. [18] When the Black Shirts were implicated in the murder of an African American student late in the summer of 1930, however, government compliance and press indifference ended. The Fulton County Superior Court refused the organization's application for a twenty-year charter, while the *Atlanta Constitution* and the *Atlanta Journal* finally began to question the group's dedication to eliminating dependable and skilled blacks in favor of unskilled whites. [19]

With the initiation of violence, public interpretation of the Black Shirts' mission changed. Fears of widespread racial violence on par with the race riot of 1906 surfaced, giving rise to concerns over the city's reputation during a time of economic difficulty. The crowds of unemployed men roaming the streets in black shirts lost their benign status. Instead, they became a symbol of the depression's potential threat to a racial structure that had, in the minds of most of Atlanta's white leaders, been functioning smoothly for more than two decades. Even the Ku Klux Klan, which preferred to work secretly or through government offices to maintain white Protestant privilege, found the Black Shirts' aggressive and public tactics distasteful. When newspaper editors from outside Atlanta began ridiculing the city for tolerating the organization, the local white press and public officials grew increasingly critical of the Black Shirts. An African American newspaper, the *Pittsburgh Courier,* noted that the Black Shirts' success might mean an "increased payroll" for employers and an "end to the slavish docility of Southern white labor caused by fear of Negro competition and replacement." [20] The negative attention brought to Atlanta, a city obsessed with its reputation and the potential for racial violence, threatened the highly racialized labor structure that guided the city's economic order.

Angelo Herndon became the symbol for the next great burst of radicalism—and fears of radicalism—in Atlanta. Herndon was one of many organizers for the city's small but growing number of communists.[21] Atlanta's Communist Party served as the local center of radical political and racial ideas, advocating black membership in trade unions and admitting both blacks and women to leadership positions. Despite these radical goals, police and city officials most feared the idea of a black revolution that threatened political order. Since the late 1920s, Atlanta's Communists had been quietly organizing by holding small meetings and distributing literature. Between the time of the 1930 arrests of an interracial group of communists dubbed the "Atlanta Six" and Herndon's arrest in 1932, local officials had become increasingly convinced that communism would encourage blacks to aggressively attempt to dismantle Jim Crow and achieve equality.[22] Editors of the Communist *Daily Worker* realized this, noting that Georgia's "slave rule" was threatened by Communist success in "uniting the oppressed Negroes and whites for joint struggle."[23] The police continued to raid Communist meetings through the mid-1930s, charging attendees with everything from disorderly conduct to attempting to incite insurrection. A series of raids on private homes and even the offices of the Atlanta Urban League occurred in October 1934, for example, just after the arrests of Nannie Young and Annie Leathers. The county solicitor general's claim to have discovered a secret "Communist Operation" in the city prompted a grand jury investigation of local radical organizing.[24]

Although the police and city government despised the Communists, their consistent support of all the city's unemployed made the organization popular with many of Atlanta's working-class people. As the depression took a firm hold, the Communists formed an unemployment committee to promote the mutual interest of black and white workers who "both were being exploited, starved and abandoned by the same white oppressors."[25] The committee also investigated and documented thousands of families that were denied relief. When a Fulton County commissioner announced in June 1932 that the county intended to halt all relief work for lack of funds, ceasing assistance to thousands more families, the unemployment council quickly mobilized. On June 30, Herndon and his associates led a mass demonstration of Atlanta's unemployed at the county courthouse. Their intent was to demonstrate the extent of Atlanta's poverty, giving the lie to the commissioner's statement that the city had no hungry people. The rally was quiet and peaceful; whole families, both black and white, occupied the courthouse steps for most of the morning, representing the Communists' commitment to interracialism and familialism.[26]

This demonstration represented the city's largest interracial rally since Reconstruction, and the rapidity with which it had been organized concerned county and city officials. Fanned by the *Atlanta Georgian,* fears that Communists might organize a revolution spread through the police department, resulting in Herndon's arrest as he retrieved his mail a few days later. His brutal treatment while in the legal system was clearly meant to serve as an example for the city's blacks of the dire consequences attached to radical activities. Herndon and many of his supporters realized, "It was not me alone whom they wished to crucify; it was the entire downtrodden Negro people they aimed to strike at through me, so that we might all continue as slaves in Egypt." Herndon functioned as a symbol for segments of the black community, but not as police and prosecutors had hoped. Poor African Americans saw in Herndon's case the racial hatred they had felt for years and celebrated him as a hero for standing up to it. Whites and blacks alike sent him money, presents, and "testimonials" while he was in jail, and liberal organizations such as the NAACP joined forces with the more radical International Labor Defense to defend him.[27]

Although it supported Herndon's legal defense, Atlanta's NAACP opposed communism and used that opposition to gain a wider black membership. The group's moderate leaders wanted all of Atlanta's blacks to see it as having "a sane but militant program."[28] Arguing that "sensible Negroes in Georgia cannot afford to line up with the Communists as communism will never succeed in Georgia and Negroes who do . . . will find themselves frozen out in the business world and will stand to lose everything," the NAACP used the Herndon case to strengthen its membership among middle-class blacks. Leaders also hoped that advertisements in the *Atlanta Constitution* would dissipate some of the "racial discord" stirred up by the Herndon case and encourage the city's whites to favor the "saner program of the NAACP."[29]

Like the black elite, the white press, businessmen, and workers were well aware of the power accusations of communism could have in 1930s America. In the midst of the General Textile strike of 1934, for example, the *Atlanta Constitution* happily repeated employers' explanations for the factory closings. Rather than blaming the closing on a lack of workers, which might inspire workers to continue their militancy, the press informed the general public that mill owners wanted to "protect" their workers from "outside agitators." Answering a suit filed on behalf of children injured by police tear gas used against picketers, Atlanta's police chief declared, "much of the trouble incident to the strike has been fomented by communists."[30] The few newspaper reports of the arrests of Nannie Leah Young and Annie Mae Leathers claimed that striking workers had called the police to complain about the communists' presence, thereby prompting the women's arrest.[31] If this assertion were true, the strikers could defend their walkout and claim to be free of outside influences and radical ideas.

Communist organizing in Atlanta, which had diminished little in the face of Herndon's arrest or the growing hysteria over radical politics, regularly brought together workers across race and gender lines. Yet nothing in the sensationalized accounts of Herndon's case intimated that part of the danger he posed to the city was as an African American male in an organization that openly condoned meetings between black men and white women. Herndon's opponents never trotted out this central trope of southern racial order. This also was not made an issue in the case of Young and Leathers. An African American man, John Greer, even defended the sisters through part of their legal battles, making them the first white women to be so represented.[32] In 1936, when Young and others again faced charges resulting from arrests made during a Communist meeting in a private home, the judge dismissed charges of insurrection but levied convictions for disorderly conduct based on the "mixed races" assembled at the meeting.[33] Even the Ku Klux Klan did not directly connect communism with miscegenation or rape, instead focusing its objections on Communist "preaching to these Negroes the doctrine of social and political equality and at the same time telling them to accompany their demands for this with violence."[34] The notable absence of fears of sexual transgressions across racial lines indicates just how much the cultural terrain of the city had changed by the 1930s. The ideological sway of taboos against interracial relationships and fears of black aggression through sexual violence toward white women lessened as threats of racial alliances and racial tensions between men of the two races came to the fore.

Wage Work

IN EARLIER DECADES, when the city's economy was expanding and interracial competition for jobs was less acute, Atlanta allowed itself to debate the merits of women working for wages. The growth of the economy during these years created new jobs and new types of employment, and through a process of negotiation, women were incorporated into a relatively stable labor structure in which jobs were typed by both race and gender. With the shrinking economy of the 1930s, however, views of women's wage work appeared superfluous or unworthy of discussion, almost completely negating the developments of the 1900s and 1910s. Atlantans sidestepped the effect of the depression on women in general and as workers in particular. In the place of dialogues on the merits of women's work surfaced a renewed focus on a conception of masculinity that centered on wage labor and men's ability to provide financially for their families. Organizations such as the Black Shirts also promoted definitions of manhood that encouraged men to aggressively guard their economic territory through intimidation and violence. The bodies of women seemed to disappear from the streets, as parades and demonstrations of unemployed men riveted the city's attention during the depression.

During the 1930s, even the local organized labor community no longer paid much attention to the causes or the presence of women in the workforce. Women still appeared in the discourse of a few union locals, but the *Journal of Labor* dealt with women almost exclusively as wives, consumers, and housekeepers. During a 1937 protest against a chain store tax, men at the demonstration were defined by their money-producing occupations (as laborers or farmers) that would be negatively impacted by the tax. Reports of the women present referred to them as housewives, thereby defining women's interest in the tax as strictly that of consumers.[35] When reports in the paper did note women's unionism, the stories were drawn from locations outside Atlanta and generally outside the South.

When Atlanta's white trade union leaders ruminated on working women, these men echoed a national backlash against women's previous gains in paid employment. Local labor leaders questioned "whether or not the entrance of women in such a large scale has added anything to the wealth or welfare of this country." The potential threat that women had represented to men's jobs in the first decade of the twentieth century, a threat organized labor thought had disappeared in the 1920s, seemed now to have come to fruition. Union officials concluded "that conditions in the industrial field, in the social realm as well as in the home would be better if the latter place received a major instead of a minor portion of [women's] interest." Women who argued in the face of this heavy criticism that their work was necessary for family survival were answered with the pronouncement that "as a whole, those who feel that they are helping their husbands are really not helping them at all."[36] In essence, the depression created what labor historian Alice Kessler-Harris has called a "curious double message" for women. Economic pressures pushed more women to seek paid labor, yet the public at large and organized labor in particular told women to focus on family and stay out of the workforce so that more men might be able to fulfill their roles as breadwinners.[37]

The initial reaction of the Atlanta Federation of Trades (AFT) and the American Federation of Labor to the depression was to use the threat of growing unemployment as a tool for a massive organizational drive among skilled white workers. As mechanization of industry reduced the skill levels workers needed and lower pay standards for women increased their appeal to employers, some women found new jobs in industry. These women benefited from the American Federation of Labor's organizing drive not because trade unions had changed their ideas about women's primary role being in the home but rather because male unionists felt threatened by women's gains. The male-dominated leadership reinforced job classifications based on gender and continued to bargain for fewer benefits for their female members.[38] Reflecting organized labor's nationwide renewed hostility toward wage-earning women, each of the six new AFT locals established in 1930 proudly proclaimed an all-male membership.

With the deepening economic crisis of 1931 and 1932, the AFT entered a period of retrenchment, struggling to maintain its membership. In Chicago, the Great Depression served as a catalyst for the most successful organizing campaigns in the city's history, but this was not the case for Atlanta where economic setbacks pushed the already conservative AFT to close ranks around male skilled workers, and no organization emerged to support a mass movement of unskilled workers.[39] Not surprisingly, organized labor fought hardest to maintain jobs for its mostly male members. The AFT, for example, praised mill owners for eliminating women's night work, arguing that those positions could go to men.[40] Even as the AFT lobbied for better assistance for the city's unemployed, the organization promoted the plight of the male breadwinner as the key to a stable family and social order. This revaluing of the husband's position in the family stood in marked contrast to the policies of Atlanta's social workers in earlier decades, which equated the mother's status with family stability. "The idea of a whole community being interested in a man out of work," argued the editors of the *Journal of Labor,* "and the picture of a great nation enjoining itself to take care of the man out of work is a recognition of a degree of responsibility not known in this country until recently."[41] Organized labor's efforts to ensure male employment represented a decidedly different definition of family than had been used in the 1900s and 1910s. Instead of the family being the cornerstone of urban morality, the family of the 1930s was an economic construct built around the existence of a male breadwinner. Women working for wages threatened to topple this structure.

The extent of this development is visible in the arguments and strike practices followed during the 1934 General Textile strike, which differed vastly from the 1914–15 Fulton Bag and Cotton Mills strike. In the 1910s, women had played central roles at all levels, with key organizers including O. Delight Smith and Sara Conboy. Women walked the picket lines, harassed replacement workers and those who kept working, fed the strikers, and led the parades. Women testified to government investigators and provided the physical images of worker exploitation and working-class respectability to the media and the wider Atlanta community. In 1934, however, the women who joined the textile strike played a decidedly second-tier role. No women held prominent leadership roles locally or nationally.[42] Instead of the stories of women, union leaders used children teargassed by police outside one of the local mills to draw sympathetic attention.[43] Photographs printed in local newspapers clearly show women on the picket lines, but the voice given to the strike by both union leaders and the press was that of the male mill hand struggling to support his family. When criticizing the "flying squadrons" of strikers that moved from mill to mill bringing workers out of the factory and onto the picket line, for example, the promanagement *Atlanta Constitution* quoted reluctant male workers as saying, "we believe if we continue at work our lives and the lives of our women and children will be jeopardized and that many people will be killed."[44] Issues related directly to women's work in the mill or their existence as the caretakers of mill families were wholly absent from all sides of the strike dialogue, as if the women on the picket lines' only interest was in supporting the ideal of the male breadwinner.

In the wake of this emphasis on family and masculinity defined by male wage work, the Young Women's Christian Association (YWCA) stood alone among Atlanta's civic, labor, and welfare organizations in its dedication to wage-earning women.[45] While most of the YWCA's resources went to white women, the Phyllis Wheatley branch served many young African American women.[46] The organization's first response to the growing number of unemployed women was to subsidize meals for working-class women. Free meals, however, did little to remedy the root of unemployed women's problems. YWCA officials reinvigorated the organization's industrial department in the early 1930s to "bring into play forces which supply work, play and love to hundreds of lonely girls and discouraged women." "We are now," declared organizational secretary Flora Hatcher, "as concerned about what is happening to a girl's personality in a time of unemployment as we are about what is going into her stomach."[47] Consequently, the YWCA organized a rash of new educational and recreational activities, including classes in crafts, dancing, and sports, to fill the empty hours of the city's unemployed women.

As the resources of the YWCA were increasingly channeled into the industrial department and its white membership, the organization expanded its goals beyond simply amusing unemployed women while they idled their hours away waiting for the depression to end. Longtime labor activists Mary Barker, who organized the city's schoolteachers, and Rose Hickey Quinn, leader of the 1919 telephone operators' strike, stepped in to educate Atlanta's working-class women in the ways of unionism. The two women hoped to create a cadre of prounion wage-earning women who would then spread the ideals of organizing to other women. In the meantime, the YWCA's industrial department continued to offer what material support it could to women while using the media to defend women's right to wage work. In the face of work relief programs and AFT policies that catered to the needs of working-class men, YWCA secretaries appeared as the lone voice asking, "Who knows what becomes of the department store clerk here in Atlanta who loses her job? What becomes of the many other girls dependent upon their own income for a living, who have been thrown out of work during the past two years?"[48]

The evolution of worker education in the Atlanta YWCA's industrial department was part of both a regional and national movement to train white women workers as leaders.[49] Barker was instrumental in establishing the Southern Summer School for Women Workers, a six-week institute that taught English, economics, and the basics of unionism to women from a variety of industries across the South. Workers from Atlanta's overall, box, candy, and textile factories attended these schools, meeting workers who shared many of the same problems. The organizers of these institutes focused on teaching a new generation of wage-earning women to give voice to their problems and to view their experiences as part of a larger economic system that treated workers in much the same way. According to one Atlanta participant, the school "offered to the worker something she could not get elsewhere, something that is very vital to her well-being. This is an understanding of the very important part she plays in our great industrial world." [50]

Many of the school's students adopted the organizers' philosophies. Some participants "realize[d] that we have not only personal difficulties but that we are part of the working class who has its own problems that we must help to solve. We realized how powerful the workers would be if united in class organizations. We decided that we would take our share in the [struggle] for a larger control of the factors of production by those who produced the goods of the world." [51] In developing students' class consciousness, teachers also encouraged participants to develop a regional identity and to privilege their class interests over race differences. In clear contrast to the attitudes overtaking most of white Atlanta at the time, speakers repeatedly reminded students that "the South will [n]ever progress unless racial and class prejudices are overthrown and the two races become willing to work out problems together." [52]

In teaching students to look beyond their day-to-day existences, organizers hoped that the women would return to their homes and workplaces and share what they had learned. Once trained, however, there was little room for these women in Atlanta's organized labor community in the 1930s. The economic and social crisis strengthened unions' focus on men, reemphasizing the view that men needed to work, whereas women did not. Interviews with students after they had left the summer school revealed a host of problems that interfered with their ability to establish worker education courses in their home communities. Many were afraid of losing their jobs or had had the jobs of other family members threatened. One woman concluded that she could not hold classes because of "the worry of not knowing whether you will be out of a job tomorrow and if you are, where to get another job. [It] gets on your nerves and you can't do any good work." Even in a factory where workers were organized, another woman found "union members not interested, and since no one shared any feeling, my enthusiasm went down a few degrees." [53]

The Atlanta YWCA's industrial department offered some of the few opportunities for women from the summer schools to pursue worker education. The offices also existed as unique physical spaces where organized women could gather without the dominating presence of male unionists. Many students became secretaries for the department, helping to promote class consciousness, a regional identity, and racial cooperation among the workers who sought assistance and recreation from the organization. Federal support materialized in 1934 when the Federal Emergency Relief Administration and national educators joined workers from Atlanta's YWCA to create six-week institutes on worker education for both blacks and whites. Messages about the importance of interracial alliances, however, were undoubtedly weak because all courses were racially segregated. Better support for these activities targeting all workers, not just women, emerged from the city's black communities, where organizations such as the Urban League merged their adult education classes with the worker education program.

Ultimately, it seems that few of the divisions between workers were dissolved by these programs. The organized workers, overwhelmingly male and white, fought to protect their unions. African American organizations continued to train black adult workers and offer assistance to unemployed black men when they could.[54] And women of both races were left to the segregated YWCA. While radical critiques of the southern economy and divisions between workers continued to emerge from the industrial department of the Atlanta YWCA, these ideas found little resonance among a wider audience.[55] Most of the city's laboring people, facing the worst of the Great Depression, focused on fighting for jobs and relief for their own.

African American Political Organizing

IN THE MIDST of these shifting economic tides, political organizing among Atlanta's blacks began in earnest. The emerging focus on formal politics initiated by the black elite during the 1920s solidified during the depression, and a new class of African American business and professional men rose to prominence. These new leaders included individuals such as John Wesley Dobbs, a federal postal employee who headed Georgia's Prince Hall masons; L. D. Milton, president of Citizen's Trust Bank; and the publisher of the new *Atlanta Daily World,* C. A. Scott.[56] Dobbs and his cohort responded to the Great Depression by committing themselves to improving the lot of blacks in the city, state, and nation. But instead of emphasizing the morality-based visions of respectability and race progress promoted by the black elite in the 1910s and 1920s, these new leaders used overtly political language and goals. Admission to formal politics increasingly became the flagship cause of Atlanta's African American leaders. "The ballot in Georgia," according to these leaders, would "mean better race relations" and more political power for the black elite.[57] Elaborating on this point, Morehouse College President Benjamin Mays concluded, "if you don't have the ballot you aren't anybody. If you can't elect the officials who govern you, that's tantamount to being a slave. I think the ballot is the most precious thing in the hands of a man in democracy."[58]

The state Democratic Party restricted voting in primaries to whites, but disenfranchisement laws left runoff, bond, and special elections open to black voters, and the rising black leadership moved to exploit the power these elections might carry.[59] Dobbs created the Atlanta Civic and Political League, one of the first associations designed to promote black political ascendancy through voter registration.[60] Other efforts to rally Atlanta's black voters included the NAACP's citizenship schools, which focused on the rudiments of voting, politics, and American government.[61] Pastors Martin Luther King Sr. and William Borders joined the campaign by promoting political participation from the pulpit. The final power in the leaders' arsenal was the *Atlanta Daily World:* Scott openly sought through his paper to "educate and inspire people, to make better citizens out of them . . . to over[come] injustice and segregation."[62] The "better citizens" Scott and other black elites envisioned would not be the respectable working-class mothers of earlier days but rather an aware and active electorate that used the power of the bloc vote so that, in the tellingly masculinist language of these leaders, segregation's "denial of dignity and manhood" could not continue.[63] The shifting political dialogue downplayed issues related to racial uplift in favor of a language of equality, a language that pushed the rights of black men—to work and to vote—to the fore.

Providing Relief

NOT SURPRISINGLY, the issues dominating Atlanta's politics during the depression centered on the city's economic difficulties, particularly how and when the city would offer relief to its indigent population. The city government's initial response to the growing economic crisis developed only slowly. Reluctant to initiate new programs or send the city into debt, a particularly important issue in the wake of recent political scandals, Atlanta's city council increased support for private welfare agencies in the hope that these sources could provide relief until the economy recovered. The city did create a relief committee to channel limited public funds into established private organizations, but in the early depression the city warden remained the only public agency directly providing relief to the destitute. Maintaining earlier policy, this office consistently turned away families and blacks, choosing to deal only with white individuals.[64] Applicants requesting relief for their families were handed over to the Family Welfare Society (formerly the Associated Charities) and other private organizations until well into 1932. The Community Chest created the Emergency Relief Committee in 1931 to provide unemployment relief and to help lighten the Family Welfare Society's overwhelming caseload. The Neighborhood Union also again took up the task of giving direct relief as well as trying to coordinate private relief efforts for the black community.[65] The Urban League joined in the effort by establishing the Emergency Relief Committee, which operated a free soup kitchen. The crisis of the early depression forced private organizations to abandon the interest in children and dysfunctional families that had guided their efforts in the 1920s and return to the business of giving direct relief in the form of grocery orders, fuel, clothing, and rent.

When the city and county finally took up the task of providing relief, their efforts were focused only on unemployed men. Programs established in mid-1932 provided work relief for unemployed men and housing for the ever-increasing number of male transients migrating to Atlanta in hopes of finding work. These public programs put men to work repairing roads, paying the workers with federal funds from the Reconstruction Finance Corporation. Reflecting the growing masculinist sentiments of the organized labor community and private relief organizations, no public agency provided any work relief jobs for women until after 1934.[66] Both the Neighborhood Union and the Family Welfare Society, increasingly swamped with applicants for relief, tried to push the city and county to expand public services beyond simple work relief. This lobbying was to no avail, and the Fulton County Relief Administration and the Unemployment Relief Council maintained their limited assistance policies until federal programs took their place.

This chaotic relief system proved wholly inadequate. Public and private agencies overlooked many families who applied for relief or supplied them with only minimal assistance. This was especially true for African Americans, since the Family Welfare Society prohibited blacks from coming directly to the agency's offices after they had made their initial requests for relief. Social workers enacted this policy out of fear that growing racial tensions in the long lines at the relief office might turn into violence. The city's African Americans had to wait for a visitor from the agency to come to their homes, a process that could take weeks. An informal economy of bartering and resale of relief goods developed in poor people's attempt to survive despite the limited assistance available.[67] To stretch inadequate budgets, Atlanta's destitute would often sell the sacks of flour and other supplies provided by relief agencies or trade them for items not available through direct relief. Social workers constructed elaborate restrictions and punishments, including fines and imprisonment, to counter these developments, further contributing to the humiliation and frustration the city's indigent felt as they sought relief. Many of those hit hardest by the depression undoubtedly would have agreed with one black resident's assessment of the situation: "it don't do a body too much good to be warm in the winter and such as that if your very heart and soul gets stomped on twenty-odd times a day."[68]

Relief organizations' policies and practices encouraged the city's attention to fall on the plight—and threat—of the unemployed man. Work relief programs reinforced prevailing beliefs that male employment ensured family welfare. Even community kitchens distributing food to the needy from the City Auditorium became a male domain. "The soup line," recalled Nellie Bryant, "stretched down Edgewood Avenue almost to Five Points. . . . You could see black and white folks in that line, some of them with buckets, pails and things like that, just to get something to eat."[69] But, as Sanders Ivey, a policeman at the time, added, "All the men would come around. I don't recall any women, but men would come around and eat soup."[70] Without steady work, many of Atlanta's men gathered on street corners and roamed the city. Those who did find work through city and county programs tended to work outdoors in public settings, repairing streets and buildings. Numerous reports of assaults on women filtered through the Neighborhood Union as the organization unsuccessfully sought to improve police protection for domestics traveling to and from work.[71] As working-class men took to roaming and working in the most public of city spaces, the streets became a more dangerous place for women. But the attention that arose from these incidents tended to focus on the economic forces that had placed men on the streets. The Neighborhood Union, for example, concentrated its efforts in the First Ward on eliminating the "Street Corner Gang" by offering more programs for boys in the neighborhood center.[72]

In the realm of private relief as well, the situation of unemployed men garnered the most attention. The West Side Unemployment Relief Committee, created by the Neighborhood Union in 1931, carefully recorded the plight of jobless men, but space for information on women's employment was left blank.[73] Men filled the offices of the Family Welfare Society seeking aid for their families, and grocery orders and other supplies were now issued to these men, in marked contrast to policies for direct relief established in the 1900s and 1910s. By giving men control of direct assistance for their families, men's role as economic provider for the family was reinforced in the face of an economy that made it difficult for many men to fill this role through wage work. The practice of visiting the homes of applicants had been abandoned in the 1920s and, in the face of ever-increasing relief rolls, could not be fully reinstated when the society returned to providing direct relief. Even for African Americans, who received their assistance from social workers who visited the city's black neighborhoods, relief was now placed in the hands of male heads of households whenever possible. Nellie Blackshear, a social worker, recalled that the path for a family through the relief system depended on the husband's status: "If they had no money, that they could prove, coming in, and if the father had deserted them," she recounted, "we knew then that the mother had to be looked after and the children. We had to determine if there was a man in the family, if there was a man in the family we tried to put him to work and allow the mother to remain in the home with the children. That was the way we determined it. [74]

Emphasizing the shift in policy, caseworkers cajoled and threatened men into supporting their families. In earlier decades the Family Welfare Society might have encouraged women to take in sewing or washing to free themselves from dependency on unreliable husbands or helped wives take legal action in cases of continued nonsupport. With the increasing instability of family structures in the face of widespread unemployment, however, social workers instead chose to shore up traditional relationships, often feeling that only their efforts "kept laboring families together." [75] As a result, the husband—the parent most likely to desert—became caseworkers' primary concern. Mr. Davis, for example, had been living apart from his family and had contributed only five dollars of his recent earnings toward their support. To force Mr. Davis to return home, the Family Welfare Society threatened that "it would be necessary for us to aid Mrs. Davis in taking out non-support actions unless he assumed responsibility for the care of his family [and] his wife." [76] Similarly, in a 1934 staff meeting, the disposal of the Sanders family case was held up as an example of model social work. After a frank meeting with a social worker, "Mr. Sanders rose to the occasion and showed that he was capable of looking after the family affairs and was not dominated by his mother." [77] The success of this case turned not on the family's removal from the relief rolls but on the caseworker's ability to convince Mr. Sanders to take on a dominant—that is, "manly"—role in his family.

African American relief agencies pursued parallel relief efforts centering on the husband's position. The West Side Unemployment Relief Committee helped place black men in neighborhood jobs, repairing houses and yards. Families in need of assistance were given temporary relief until the husband could be placed in a job. If the husband refused to work or did not keep the job secured for him, the agency would stop all relief and report the family to other area agencies to ensure that no more assistance was provided until the man returned to work. The unemployment committee also campaigned in black neighborhoods for residents to report all beggars and vagrants to the organization without providing any handouts. [78]

When federal programs finally pushed Atlanta and Fulton County directly into the business of relief, little changed. [79] Unemployed men remained at the center of assistance efforts, both in direct relief and work programs. Indeed, New Deal programs solidified the practices implemented by private agencies in the early years of the Great Depression. By focusing relief efforts on unemployed men, New Dealers believed that they were aiding families in need while maintaining order. Augusta Dunbar, an Atlanta social worker in the 1930s, proclaimed unequivocally,

"I think Roosevelt prevented a revolution. I'm not sure it would have been a Communist revolution, but there would have been some sort of revolution because you cannot let that many people go hungry very long without a good deal of violence."[80] Beyond highlighting the plight of unemployed men and privileging their needs over those of other depression victims, these federally sponsored programs also helped turn the city's attention away from the debates over moral order that had promoted working-class women's visibility in earlier decades. What replaced these older debates, in part, were both opportunities for organized city planning offered by government funds and political wars among local, state, and federal officials over the administration of New Deal programs.

The New Deal

THE NEW DEAL quickly came to overwhelm and reshape political debates in and around Atlanta in the 1930s. Storms brewed in Georgia from the moment of Franklin Roosevelt's election in 1932. The most vocal New Deal critic in the state, conservative Democratic Governor Eugene Talmadge, resented the introduction of federal officials into state politics, where the significant federal financial resources might lure away his constituencies. Talmadge twice stymied attempts to establish New Deal programs in Georgia, forcing government administrators to create or extend federal agencies in the state beyond his powerful reach.[81] Other political attacks emerged from the state legislature, where Democrats called the New Deal a "new era of carpetbag days," complaining that too many administrative, professional, and white-collar jobs went to non-Georgians.[82] Most of Atlanta's government officials and business elite, however, had long cultivated a vision of the New South that promoted cooperation with the North and welcomed the influx of new capital the New Deal brought to the city. While many in the state dragged their heels, Atlanta and Fulton County rushed to develop an infrastructure for distributing federal dollars, and local leaders willingly squared off against anti–New Deal elements. Cooperation between Atlanta officials and federal New Dealers further secured the city's existing power structure and its booster policies, allowing, in the words of historian Douglas Smith, local leaders to work toward efficiency in government while "holding steadfast to the established social and political order."[83]

The infusion of federal money for work relief programs pushed Atlanta's government and civic leaders into the business of city planning. Little in the way of organized planning had ever been done: although a few parks and suburbs had previously appeared, they were, for the most part, carefully planned private ventures created without concern for the larger development of the city.[84] The New Deal offered a new means for tackling the problems of Atlanta's inadequately developed infrastructure and working on issues now deemed crucial to public health. The city's slums, most in areas close to downtown, became the focus of much of this attention. The neighborhoods themselves, rather than the residents who lived there, became the threat to the city's physical and economic well-being. Atlanta leaders quickly became interested in the opportunities offered by the wealth of federal funds that New Deal programs offered for building projects, not just to aid the unemployed but to rebuild elements of the city itself.

With the rapid growth of the early twentieth century, Atlanta's sanitary services and city facilities had never been able to keep pace with the burgeoning population. Efforts to channel New Deal funds into city projects were so successful that the city garnered half of Georgia's entire building budget under the Works Progress Administration (WPA). New Dealers designed programs like the WPA to supply work relief to unemployed men, but with careful planning and minimal investment from the city, the projects on which these men worked could allow the city's physical infrastructure to catch up with decades of population growth. The city council created a subcommittee to prioritize projects and to request funds from national programs. By 1938, the metropolitan Atlanta areas of Decatur, De Kalb County, and Fulton County all had planning boards as well. In the end, a national focus on the problem of unemployed men created work programs that allowed Atlanta to revamp parks and schools, build a hospital and police station, and finally complete the city's sewer system. Not only did working-class men reconfigure the cityscape with their labor, but the place of the male breadwinner at the head of a nuclear family was literally built into one of the decade's most significant planning projects when city slums were replaced with single-family housing projects.

Public housing was one of the most ambitious and focused building projects undertaken in Atlanta and was the first of its kind in the country. Charles A. Palmer, a businessman and property owner, organized a coalition of interested parties to take advantage of federal funds and clear a slum area north of downtown at Techwood Drive. Palmer later joined forces with John Hope, the president of Atlanta University, to remove dilapidated housing in Beaver Slide, a notorious black slum west of the central business district. The campaign to build the Techwood and University Homes housing projects was, more than anything else, a business project undertaken by entrepreneurs and civic leaders who squared off against the landlords of these districts. [85] In this scramble for control, the residents of the neighborhoods being cleared and even the slums themselves became a political battlefield for the various interested parties. These negotiations ultimately resulted in the building of groups of single-family apartments, thereby reinforcing a family structure in which women cared for the home and children while men provided economically for the family.

At the core of the slum clearance project, two issues predominated: public health and the image of the city. For downtown property owners such as Palmer, the Techwood Flats district represented both an eyesore detracting from the city's major business center and a threat to property values in the area. In the minds of Hope and other civic reformers, the city's slum districts bred physical and social disease. Emphasizing this connection, Hope declared in a speech to the Atlanta University community, "Beaver Slide is a health condition, Beaver Slide is an educational condition, Beaver Slide is an economic condition, Beaver Slide is a condition of character, Beaver Slide is a state of mind."[86] Foregrounded in all of these discussions of the city's slums, however, was the issue of crime. Residents of the slums, concluded Palmer, "were past caring, licked by their surroundings."[87] With a mass of out-of-work men left in the depressing and unhealthy atmospheres of run-down neighborhoods, few of the proponents of slum clearance questioned the inevitability of residents' deterioration into "bootleggers and thieves."[88] "Hard times and criminality," reflected Police Chief Herbert Jenkins, "seem to go together."[89] "Crime was hand in hand with want," repeated a Neighborhood Union social worker who found numerous cases of coal being stolen, vacant houses being torn down for fuel, and muggings.[90] The crime associated with Atlanta's slums centered on the activities of unemployed or non-wage-earning men. Arrests for drunkenness and disorderly conduct soared. Police patrolled these areas, which Palmer called "human garbage dump[s]," in pairs for safety.[91] Resident Clara Render recalled Beaver Slide, in particular, as "a kind of rough neighborhood. . . . People doing anything they wanted to. I'd visit over here occasionally, but we was always careful to go home before night."[92]

Despite the bad reputation of these neighborhoods, opposition to clearing the areas and building public housing did emerge. Landlords objected to being forced into selling their moneymaking property and claimed that the city already had a surplus of housing. Governor Talmadge again opposed federal intervention and refused to introduce a housing bill in the state legislature that would have facilitated the project. Some in the city viewed the housing as "communistic" and feared that "those projects were going to crop up every six inches all over the city."[93] The city council ultimately approved the plan, and the Atlanta-based board of trustees won federal support for the projects. Techwood Homes, an apartment complex for whites, opened in 1936, followed by University Homes, for African American residents, in 1937.

The housing projects built in Atlanta during the depression were a far cry from the conditions that generally prevailed in the city's poorer neighborhoods. As late as the 1930s, many Atlanta residents still lacked indoor plumbing. As Blackshear recalled, "[Poor] families lived in cubby holes. The families lived in one room [and] in this room was everything. They cooked on charcoal buckets . . . and this was very dangerous because you know that if you didn't open the door you might get sick from this gas from the charcoal bucket. They would cook in there and sometimes seven or eight people would live in one room. They had a communal toilet outside. They brought water in for the tin tubs to bathe in. It was a deplorable sort of thing."[94] For many of the residents used to the conditions Blackshear described, Atlanta's public housing projects seemed almost luxurious. Each unit had heat, indoor bathrooms, and hot and cold running water.

In re-creating these Atlanta neighborhoods, the local board of trustees and federal officials worked hard to ensure that the housing projects would have better reputations than the slums they replaced. Housing officials carefully screened applicants before assigning apartments, focusing on women's housekeeping skills and men's earning ability and work history. According to one resident, Lula Daugherty, officials from the housing projects "found out your reputation, how you paid your rent, and what kind of neighbor you had been, and all such as that. And then they sent somebody out to interview you and see what kind of housekeeper you are. Even you had to tell them what church you belonged to. And when they done that, then if you had a good reference, you moved in."[95] Through the process of approving residents for the new housing, the administrators could ensure a particular vision of domesticity and respectability. This process reinforced gender ideologies in which women were primarily responsible for the physical and moral atmosphere of the home while masculinity depended on providing economic security for the family. Once given an apartment, residents found a myriad of rules governing life in the housing projects: "You wasn't supposed to be too noisy at night, you know, disturb your neighbor," recalled Render.[96] Parties and loud music were forbidden, and lights were to be out at midnight. Housing officials enforced rules forbidding residents from taking in boarders or from having messy yards.[97]

The coalescing African American elite of the 1930s embraced Atlanta's efforts at housing reform and worked hard to ensure that local projects would include housing for blacks. Black members of the public housing project boards, such as Hope and businessman L. D. Milton, understood public housing as both a "powerful factor . . . in building up the loyalty of Negroes to the federal government" and a way to "advance steps that the federal government took on the whole problem of housing and education" for blacks.[98] Reviving at least some elements of racial uplift, the elite hoped to strengthen ties between the city's blacks and the federal government by filling new public housing developments with "Negroes with their minds uplifted and wanting to advance themselves and the race generally."[99] Managers and strict rules ensured that public housing would be a suitable "laboratory" for sociological study and political organizing.[100] The housing projects allowed the black elite to finally attain the political inclusion they had sought for so long, but at the same time the projects drew a clear dividing

line in the community between "respectable" blacks and those who did not fit
the behavioral code outlined by black leaders and reinforced with federal dollars.[101] Unlike the earlier morality-focused respectability that had highlighted the
presence of working-class African American women, the 1930s version centered
on behaviors and outward appearances and prized a family model in which men
worked for wages and women cared for homes and families.

Despite black and white housing officials' efforts to keep many elements commonly associated with working-class neighborhoods out of the housing projects,
the new apartments thrilled most residents. Women in particular benefited from
the apartments' modern conveniences, even though their voices and interests
had largely been overlooked in the political discussions that shaped the projects'
development. Daugherty proclaimed, "Now, I was in heaven and still living, because I hadn't lived in a house like that before in my life."[102] Willie Mae Cartwright
moved into public housing in Atlanta in the late 1930s, and it became her "world
with a fence around it" for more than ten years.[103] Between the new housing
projects and the improvements to city services provided by work relief programs,
perhaps the biggest change the lives of the working classes during this period
came in the realm of living conditions.

While most Atlantans gratefully accepted the New Deal, the infusion of money
into the city invited contests over who would benefit from the distribution of the
new funds. Substantial New Deal funds dedicated to providing relief to the city's
indigent and unemployed exacerbated class and racial tensions. Skilled workers,
for example, complained vehemently, and ultimately successfully, against hiring
procedures and pay structures that did not maintain organized labor's relatively
privileged status among the city's working class. The AFT even secured the ability
to have its president oversee the placement of AFT members in all skilled jobs
opened under federal work relief programs. Organized labor also experienced
a boom locally and nationally as a result of the National Industrial Recovery
Act (NIRA), which promised to create more jobs for the country's industries
by suspending antitrust regulations, overseeing the creation of industry-wide
fair-competition codes, and guaranteeing workers' right to unionize. Under the
protection of the NIRA, skilled white male workers at Atlanta's Fisher body plant
struck to preserve their union, and workers at Georgia Power finally settled long-
standing disputes with their employer. The workers at local mills who joined the
national textile strike in the fall of 1934 also hoped to use the protection of the new
law to protest mill owners' violation of the codes established under the NIRA.[104]

While workers generally celebrated Roosevelt and the New Deal, the potential
of color-blind federal programs to undermine the racial hierarchy of the labor
market threatened many Atlanta whites. The policies of National Recovery Administration (NRA), the oversight body created by the NIRA, exacerbated the racial

tensions between black and white men that had been building since 1930. White employers and workers objected to the requirement that blacks be paid the same as whites. Opponents of the agency's regulations began joking that NRA stood for "Negro Relief Act" or "No Roosevelt Again." In reality, neither work relief nor programs designed to stimulate federal growth had the impact whites feared. The NRA's equal pay policies actually meant that blacks were more likely to be removed from jobs they already had and not hired in others.[105] According to Atlanta sociologist Arthur Raper, white business owners "tended to just not hire any more Negroes and hire a white man when the time came, under the Southern ethic that if you're going to pay a white man's wage you'd just as well have a white man." Many blacks felt that since employers could easily ignore the federal codes, the NRA might better be called the "Negro Removal Act" or "Negro Rarely Allowed."[106]

While debates raged over the act's racial implications, working-class women found that many of the occupations in which they were employed, like domestic work and other service jobs, were not covered at all by the NRA working condition and wage codes or by the Fair Labor Standards Act provisions that would follow later in the decade. Work relief programs turned a similarly blind eye to the plight of the nation's indigent and unemployed women. As Harry Hopkins, the head of the major New Deal work relief programs, explained prevailing attitudes, "Without work, men actually go to pieces. They lose the respect of their wives, sons and daughters because they lose respect for themselves."[107] Priorities attached to providing jobs to men first received virtually no attention in Atlanta or the nation and, even when challenged, were rarely reconsidered.[108]

The Public Works Administration, Civil Works Administration, Federal Emergency Relief Administration, and WPA projects primarily employed men, particularly those who "could be designated as unskilled in the extreme."[109] The bulk of assistance provided by these agencies in Atlanta went to white men who performed such tasks as cleaning parks, building schools, and laying sewer lines. At the behest of Eleanor Roosevelt and with the support of other women active in the national Democratic Party, federal programs also included divisions for "women's work." However, these programs provided only a handful of jobs. In the WPA, the largest government employment program, for example, women never held more than 17.5 percent of the jobs even though women made up more than 24 percent of the nation's unemployed.[110] Beauticians and manicurists were sent to work on inmates in public institutions. Sewing rooms were established for women to learn "homey and practical" arts and crafts.[111] Unlike work projects designed to distribute relief while maintaining male workers' dignity, programs for women tried to "re-establish the morals of the individual woman and to encourage rehabilitation of the home and community life."[112] New Deal work relief also channeled women into service positions, most of which centered on the "womanly" pursuits of home, beauty, and community. Women were paid to make clothes for their families and redecorate their homes while men were given the work of physically rebuilding the city. Consequently, the majority of Atlanta's unemployed women, particularly those looking for industrial work, found little support through federal work relief.

Most of Atlanta's poor who sought relief cared little for the political debates that raged over where the money came from or who controlled its distribution. Asking for relief at all was a new and traumatic experience for many in the city's working class. Having to seek aid provoked feelings of shame among many applicants, while others feared the judgments of social workers and the complicated steps involved in securing relief. Nannie Leah Young's first experience with a relief office proved disastrous. Acting on the advice of a caseworker and the Legal Aid Society, Young took out a warrant on her husband for nonsupport, thinking that doing so was only way she could receive support. She later recalled, "I thought I had to do what this visitor and lawyer told me, although it was killing me to have my husband arrested."[113] The city's poor devised a variety of ways to deal with the uncomfortable situation of being forced to ask for assistance. Social workers from some districts reported that communist groups were comparing grocery orders and "generally trying to make trouble" to increase their relief allotments.[114] Other groups of men threatened that the "community would hear from them" if they did not quickly receive relief for their families.[115]

By far the easiest way for most of the city's poor, black and white, male and female, to ask for assistance was by offering to work in exchange for support. The city, county, and private work relief programs run in 1931 and 1932 were wholly inadequate for the number of unemployed in the city. Consequently, very few applicants found support in these programs. The competition for work relief positions grew intense. The local press soundly rebuked women asking for government jobs for participating in "a mad scramble for political jobs made all the madder with the women adding their bit of madness."[116] With federal intervention, several work relief programs were introduced, but like earlier organizations, New Deal agencies focused their efforts on promoting social stability and supporting indigent families by offering jobs almost exclusively to unemployed men.

In addition to the programs run by the Civil Works Administration and Federal Emergency Relief Administration, Atlanta's unemployed benefited from the work relief efforts of the Public Works Administration, the wpa, and the National Youth Administration. These programs included some employment for the city's jobless women, though these jobs favored pink-collar and skilled workers and left the bulk of Atlanta's unemployed women with few new options.[117] Opportunities for women's programs to place unemployed women as librarians, seamstresses,

social workers, and secretaries existed largely because Americans so readily associated these professions with women. Whether skilled or not, women, like men,
preferred to work in exchange for any assistance they received. For example, Willie
Mae Cartwright jumped at the chance of a work relief job after being on direct
assistance for more than a year. Like most women in WPA jobs, she was placed in
a sewing room, making pillowcases.[118] In Georgia, sewing rooms provided the
great bulk of women's work relief, totaling nearly 80 percent of all women's WPA
work.[119] By the end of the 1930s, women working in Atlanta-area sewing rooms
had produced more than four million garments for distribution to the needy.[120]

The sex typing of work relief jobs in all of these programs and in the preceding
local efforts reinforced Atlanta's shifting cultural terrain in the 1930s. Work relief
programs put women in back rooms doing traditional tasks. Attempts to treat
women as wage laborers and industrial workers met with vehement disapproval.
When the National Youth Administration, for example, started running a retreat
for unemployed women at Camp Highland, charges of communism surfaced.
These accusations of radicalism leveled by the *Atlanta Georgian* hindered the
program for jobless women from its inception, and shortly after these stories ran in
the city's newspapers, an arsonist burned much of the camp.[121] Job programs for
men sent them out into the streets, and the sight of work groups cleaning parks
and repairing buildings quickly came to symbolize the potential for economic
recovery embodied in the New Deal programs. While blacks and whites worked
on segregated projects, this sex typing of jobs held across racial lines.[122] Just
as the parades of Black Shirts or communist demonstrations led by black men
represented the potential danger of the Great Depression, racially segregated
groups of men with shovels and pickaxes building up Atlanta's infrastructure
represented the hope of recovery.

THE GREAT DEPRESSION took political changes already under way in Atlanta
during the 1920s and gave them an economic imperative. In the face of substantial
unemployment, rising radicalism, and aggressive black political organizing, especially in the early 1930s, Atlantans seemed far less certain that the class and racial
hierarchies established in preceding decades would continue to hold. Debating
the moral implications of family became a luxury when the economic underpin-
nings of the institution seemed so imperiled. Unemployment for women was a
matter to discuss, an opportunity to assess the merits of paid labor for women.
Unemployment for men, however, revealed weaknesses in the city's economy and
threatened, in a way far different than prostitutes or dance hall girls did, the city's
sense of order in the 1930s. Where would men vent their frustration at not fulfilling
their assigned roles? If jobs that identified men as black or white, working class
or middle class, no longer existed, what would define the lines between classes

and races? No longer did the city fear that an inattentive wife with a fondness for the theater would disrupt the family and harm the city's reputation; Atlantans now feared that the depression might lead to a collapse in family structure and race and class hierarchies.

The new municipal-federal partnership of the 1930s designed, in many ways, to deal precisely with this crisis further anchored unemployed men at the center of public discourse. With new money to be spent, the nation and the city had to define their priorities. In the face of economic crisis, Atlanta's moral atmosphere and reputation, so important in the 1900s and 1910s, hardly appeared at all. Women, so heavily associated with the order of these earlier years, likewise became virtually invisible in civic debates. Men without work and, therefore, purpose became the icon of the imperiled economic order. Men without work, not the financial structures that had put them there, might be the symbol of what could destroy the city, but they could also be the actors in that destruction—through a race war, radical revolution, or wholesale desertion of their responsibilities of family and society. But if leaving men without work or purpose might devastate the city, then providing employment and restoring the male breadwinner could save it. The 1920s had provided no clear symbol of order to replace the fading importance of working-class women in civic debates. But the pressures of the Great Depression did.

Conclusion

FROM THE FAILED ATTEMPT in the 1850s to locate the state capital in the city to the successful bid to host the Centennial Olympics in 1996, Atlanta has consistently manifested what residents referred to as the "Atlanta spirit."[1] It is this brash self-confidence that makes the city fascinating to study. Atlanta's nineteenth-century boosterism focused almost exclusively on economic development. During this era, Henry Grady and other New South advocates proclaimed Atlanta the "Gate City," inviting commerce, finance, and industry to enter the South following the Civil War. While most Atlantans remained faithful to this earlier booster creed as the city entered the twentieth century, residents rarely agreed on what path Atlanta's expansion should follow. In the wake of phenomenal growth came significant power struggles among residents. The crises and debates of this era reveal a struggle to define moral and social order in the midst of economic growth. As Atlantans wrestled with these issues, they often invoked images of working-class women, both black and white, as one of the dominant symbols of public order and the potential for urban disorder.

During the first two decades of the twentieth century, public culture and politics focused to a striking extent on incidents of moral panic, violence, and debate concerning the actions and bodies of working-class women. On a national level, working-class women received enormous attention during the Progressive era—as prostitutes, workers in factories and offices, immigrant mothers, and the objects of middle-class reform. In Atlanta, the seemingly sudden visibility of working-class women illuminated a social and cultural terrain in which gender ideals often stood for competing notions of moral and social order. The common association of black and white women in the South with opposing images of defenselessness and danger made them particularly suitable to represent arguments over order. Women consequently appeared as both the linchpin of social order and its biggest threat. Far from being passive subjects of cultural debates, working-class women and their real-life activities also helped to shape these gender images. Black and white working-class women refused to be silent partners in the debates over the city's future.

The bodies of working-class women mirrored the political landscape and provided both a literal and figurative focus for dialogues over new uses of urban space, the changing social order, class and race relations, and developing political structures. In part, this was because working-class women flocked to many of the city's newest institutions and social niches. For example, 113 percent more white women worked for wages in 1910 then had in 1900. Black women's increased participation in the paid labor force was a more modest 55 percent, but that was because so many had already been working for wages in 1900.[2] Women of both races also proved themselves remarkably willing to brave the city streets, streetcars, theaters, and dance halls. The social mores governing new industries, new uses of the city's streets, and commercial amusements had yet to be established, and debates over the limits of social interaction took place in light of women's overwhelming presence at these sites. Much of the sense of urgency and concern that pervaded public discourse during this period represented more than an attempt to maintain women's traditional social roles or to resurrect rural values.[3] Rather, these crises, debates, and battles were used to create and control the city's developing structures. Women were the symbolic vehicles for these processes because of their rapidly changing positions in the urban economy and spatial order as well as their cultural association with motherhood, morality, vulnerability, disease, and vice.

Women's role as wage workers, the moral atmosphere of dance halls, the physical conditions of theaters, the health of the city's poorest residents, the "servant" problem, and the need for women to vote represent key themes in Atlanta's urban development during the first two decades of the twentieth century. Atlantans of all classes and both races and genders prized respectability for themselves and for the city, yet they disagreed over how to best define and act on it. Did respectability mean that women did not work for pay outside their homes or that they did not work after they were married? Could Atlanta maintain both a viable commercial leisure economy and a reputation as a moral and orderly city? How could both races use and serve the city without a recurrence of the violence of 1906? What did epidemics in tuberculosis and venereal disease project about the city, and how might that be controlled? As a relatively young city, Atlanta had borne witness to the rapid and seemingly chaotic growth of the country's older, more established cities, and as a result the city's business community, public officials, and club women were determined to prevent Atlanta from following the same path. Agreeing on the goal was considerably easier than reaching a consensus on a course of action.

Working-class women emerged as useful cultural symbols in dialogues about respectability and economic expansion. Such women generally lacked the organized voice of other groups and represented ideals—most notably, motherhood and respectability—that, at least on the surface, seemed widely agreeable. Issuing pronouncements on the behaviors and lifestyles of the city's working-class mothers or female dance hall patrons also allowed the city's still young and expanding middle class to feel safe, distant from the changes taking hold and above the struggles of the city's laboring classes. The middle class offered pronouncements on how to solve the problems of those lower in class standing but did so in ways that left middle-class status, as well as access to cheap black domestic labor, firmly in place.

The visibility of working-class women also provided a useful and well-utilized avenue for middle-class blacks and whites to indirectly approach questions of race and race relations. For whites, the presence of working-class women who traveled the city's streets out of economic necessity provided a justification for segregation. Whites equated the separation of the races and the disempowering practices of the Jim Crow system with protection for the city's white women. The black middle class developed its own theories of protection, arguing that working-class black women also needed protection from the rough atmosphere of Decatur Street, the unhealthy atmosphere of underserved poor neighborhoods, and abusive whites. Even at the height of segregation and discrimination, race was not a "settled" or totalizing category for Atlantans on either side of the color line. The visibility of working-class women, through both images that circulated in the public discourse and the actions of the women themselves, provided moments of striking similarities across the color line and run counter to much of what we think we know about this period. These similarities remind us not to assume that a separation of races meant that other identities might not, at times, matter more or matter in a way that could cross the racial divide. Striking parallels existed in the relationships of working-class women to the middle-classes of their respective races, the continual linking of women to urban respectability, the women's survival strategies, and the demonization of women as polluters of the body politic and as competition for male breadwinners. Women's experiences most certainly remained racialized, but the racial distinctions between women sometimes mattered less than the similarities they shared as women.

Atlanta's cultural terrain changed enormously during the early twentieth century as the process of city building shifted from debates over moral and social order to battles over political and economic structures. Working-class people were central to this process as workers, citizens, neighbors, and cultural icons. In the early decades of the century, working-class women were pushed to the fore, but with the shifting politics and economy of the 1920s and 1930s, these women no longer represented the most pressing issues. Racial tensions and fears of radicalism encouraged urban residents to invest perceptions of hope and danger that had formerly been focused on working-class women in the images of working-class men. The cultural images produced throughout these periods crossed racial lines: images of women and men of both races, still racialized but now configured through the lens of gender, represented key elements of Atlanta's social order. As a consequence of their growing invisibility on the urban landscape, Atlanta's working-class women lost some of the social and cultural spaces that had helped their efforts to improve their lives. Neither black nor white women entirely abandoned their activism or changed significantly their sense of themselves as citizens, but many of the organizations and structures that had previously offered them support evaporated in the 1930s.

THE TWO QUESTIONS that often arise in relation to the story of working-class women's visibility are "Why Atlanta?" and "Why this moment?" Atlanta has so often marketed itself as a unique city—at the forefront of or at least distinct from its region—that we can hardly be blamed for believing that its story of development must somehow also be unique. It is a city of the South—indeed, it is very often the symbol of the region's rise from the destruction of the Civil War. We have been well taught, often by historians of the region, to think of the South as an exception in American history. Working from that perspective, Atlanta's story should be Atlanta's and not a piece of a larger pattern of urban growth to be found throughout the nation. Urban historians, for their part, have also done little to dissuade us from looking at Atlanta's story in isolation. The classic form of urban history, the urban biography, certainly cultivates the widely held notion that cities have individual personalities from the beginning. For all this, and for all of the individualistic tics Atlanta demonstrates, I have come to believe that the basic elements of the story told in this book—contested visions of order, creating symbols to represent these contests, ambiguous views of growth—are part and parcel of urban development in general.

Why it happens when it does seems to me to be the more compelling question because it forces us to assess the general yet pivotal forces at work in a particular stage of urban growth. Atlanta women's critical role in creating and using new spaces and new institutions in the early twentieth century created a situation where gender order became synonymous with moral and social order. This story represents the moment when a city has begun to ride the crest of economic growth. The trick for Atlantans, however, was figuring out how to stay on top of the wave without being sucked under by vice, corruption, and moral decay. Two decades of substantial population, geographic, and economic growth allowed Atlanta to turn its attention to matters beyond the realm of economic growth. Concern over the city's reputation became a key component in urban development, something that has generally been overlooked in assessments of urban growth, even by historians who proclaimed cities "processes" rather than "sites" of political, demographic, organizational, and economic interactions.[4]

While social history has become firmly rooted in urban history, cultural history is just beginning to make a significant impact on the field.[5] The decades following the turn of the century represented Atlanta's first serious attempt to rewrite the rules of social order around the contours of a new, big, and competitive environment, and cultural factors defined much of the public discourse of this period. The city's politicians and business leaders would have said that they were focusing on building the city's culture along with its size and wealth. But much of what was happening was a contest for who would control the growth in this new era and a reaction against that power struggle on the part of many of the city's least powerful residents—blacks, women, and the poor. The iconography of working-class women served as an important vehicle through which a variety of Atlantans, including working-class women, played out these power struggles.

American culture constantly produces symbols and crises in an effort to re-create itself. Understanding the historical process of creating and debating cultural icons and moral panics is the first step to understanding our society and its fears. A heightened visibility of working-class women during the early twentieth century is only one instance of this sort of crisis production. It is a particularly telling example, however, because it turns on both gender and race, two of the most persistent categories that appear at the center of many American crises throughout the twentieth century. The process through which working-class women became symbols for their era helps to illuminate why arguments surrounding the "underclass" during the last three decades or gang violence in cities today often dominate the American political and cultural dialogue. An examination of these symbols and debates opens the door to discovering a variety of competing voices and contrasting visions in American society.

The two decades following the turn of the century represented a time of rapid change for urban America. The multifaceted focus on women so prevalent in Atlanta and other cities during this period reveals the boundaries of debate and differing conceptions of the urban environment. Both vastly and subtly different understandings of women's place in the urban economy, commercialization, public health, and the privileges of class, gender, and race all surface in the context of the attention heaped on working-class women. Today, we locate many of our societal fears in different, though certainly no less meaningful, images—football stars accused of murdering their ex-wives, teenagers shooting their classmates, working families living without health insurance, and so on. Each of these images can be picked apart for its connections to particular anxieties gripping the society that sensationalizes them at that particular historical moment. The message of this book is powerful in that it suggests that these crises are products of human thought and action and therefore not beyond our control.

NOTES

Introduction

1. Stansell, *City*.

2. Spain, *How Women Saved the City*.

3. Gilmore, *Gender and Jim Crow*; Freedman, *Maternal Justice*; Ethington, "Recasting"; Ryan, *Women in Public*; Matthews, *Public Woman*; Salem, *To Better Our World*; Turner, *Women, Culture, and Community*; Crocker, *Social Work*; Higginbotham, *Righteous Discontent*; McCarthy, *Lady Bountiful Revisited*; Flanagan, "Urban Political Reform"; Flanagan, "Women in the City"; Lasch-Quinn, *Black Neighbors*; Giddings, *When and Where*.

4. Rosenzweig and Blackmar, *Park and Its People*; Hayden, *Grand Domestic Revolution*; Flanagan, "City Profitable"; Benson, *Counter Cultures*; Wright, *Building*; Stimpson, *American City*; Wirka, "City Planning for Girls."

5. Deutsch, *Women*; Gordon, *Heroes*; Kunzel, *Fallen Women*; Pascoe, *Relations*.

6. Ewen, *Immigrant Women*; Glenn, *Daughters*; Peiss, *Cheap Amusements*; Meyerowitz, *Women Adrift*; Cameron, *Radicals*; Gabaccia, *From the Other Side*; S. Kennedy, *Weep at Home*; Tax, *Rising*; Tentler, *Wage Earning Women*; Harzig, *Peasant Maids*; Diner, *Erin's Daughters*; E. Kennedy and Davis, *Boots*.

7. Stansell, *City*; Deutsch, *Women*; Hunter, *To 'Joy My Freedom*; Lemke-Santangelo, *Abiding Courage*; Murolo, *Common Ground*; Rabinovitz, *Love*; Peiss, *Cheap Amusements*; Meyerowitz, *Women Adrift*; Meyerowitz, "Sexual Geography"; Orleck, *Common Sense*; Enstad, *Ladies*; Frank, *Purchasing Power*.

8. Gordon, *Heroes*; E. DuBois, "Working Women"; Wertheimer, *We Were There*; Payne, *Reform, Labor, and Feminism*; R. Rosen, *Lost Sisterhood*.

9. Monkkonen, *America Becomes Urban*; Zunz, *Making America Corporate*; Warner, *Private City*; Doyle, *New Men*.

10. C. Smith, *Urban Disorder*; Wilson, *Sphinx*. Other useful examinations of watershed "moments" that assess the long- and short-term impacts of crises on cities and the ways in which these incidents laid bare the relationships and hierarchies of cities include Stowell, *Great Strike*; Sawislak, *Smoldering City*; Horne, *Fire This Time*; Tuttle, *Race Riot*.

11. Grossman, *Land of Hope*; Trotter, *Black Milwaukee*; Ethington, *Public City*; Wilentz, *Chants Democratic*; Goings and Mohl, *African-American Urban History*; H. Taylor, *Race and the City*; Pacuyga, "Chicago's 1919 Race Riot"; P. Jones and Holli, *Ethnic Chicago*; Bodnar, Simon, and Weber, *Lives*; Zunz, *Changing Face of Inequality*.

221

12. With the work of Christine Stansell, Kathy Peiss, and Joanne Meyerowitz, we seemed to be on the verge of this kind of analysis in the 1980s, but all three stopped short, providing tantalizing conclusions about the impact of cities on women and the adaptability of the lives urban women created but failing to consider women's impact on the cities in which they lived. No one immediately picked up where these scholars left off. Recent publications by Sarah Deutsch and Daphne Spain suggest that the tide is turning and that the history of women will become a coherent subfield of the study of cities. A flourish of studies of the relationship between African Americans and cities appeared in the latter half of the 1990s (see Goings and Mohl, *African-American Urban History*). It now seems like a similar outpouring of scholarship blending women's and urban history is about to appear.

13. *City Builder,* November 1922.

14. Jacqueline Jones proposes a similar understanding of the shared experiences of poor blacks and whites across the color line that kept them segregated (see *The Dispossessed*). In contrast, the work of Dolores Janiewski emphasizes the factors that prohibited the development of a biracial alliance of women textile workers (see *Sisterhood Denied*).

15. Odem, *Delinquent Daughters;* Ullman, *Sex Seen;* Enstam, *Creation;* Hanchett, *New South City;* Faue, *Suffering and Struggle;* H. Taylor, *Race and the City;* Murphy, *Mining Cultures.*

ONE. *Rising, Ever Rising*

1. Blaine Brownell suggests that this high early-twentieth-century growth rate was one of the most crucial characteristics marking a "modern urban framework" in southern cities ("Urban South," 123).

2. Writers' Program, Georgia, *Atlanta,* 14.

3. J. Russell, *Atlanta,* 32–37.

4. On boosterism in the South, see Doyle, *New Men.*

5. J. Russell, *Atlanta,* 112.

6. Clarke, *History,* 129–30.

7. J. Russell, *Atlanta,* 164–68, 256–58.

8. Junius G. Oglesby, quoted in ibid., 252.

9. Ibid., 115

10. Garrett, *Atlanta,* 2:1.

11. T. Martin, *Atlanta,* 2:87.

12. Garrett, *Atlanta,* 2:202

13. A. King, "International Cotton Exposition"; Newman, "Atlanta's Hospitality Business."

14. Doyle, *New Men,* 152.

15. W. Cooper, *Cotton States,* 13.

16. Walter G. Cooper, quoted in M. Davis, "Industrial Expositions," 16.

17. An exhaustive list of Atlanta goods can be found in T. Martin, *Atlanta,* 97.

18. J. Russell, *Atlanta,* 271.

19. Rabinowitz, *Race Relations,* 64–65.

20. Maclachlan, "Women's Work," vi. Elizabeth York Enstam explores women's role in home production, community building, and market economies in great depth in the first part of *Creation.*

21. Kimball, *International Cotton Exposition,* 584–85, quoted in Hunter, *To 'Joy My Freedom,* 96.

22. *Daily Atlanta Intelligencer,* August 11, 1862.

23. Such bread riots were an almost common experience in 1863 (Thomas, *Confederate Nation,* 203–5). On the strikes, see J. Russell, *Atlanta,* 106; Garrett, *Atlanta,* 2:573.

24. A. K. McClure, quoted in T. Martin, *Atlanta,* 2:114. On the increasing class cleavage in politics, see Watts, "Characteristics," 245–50.

25. J. Russell, *Atlanta,* 187.

26. *Atlanta Constitution,* November 26, 1887.

27. J. Russell, *Atlanta,* 152, 267.

28. For a fuller discussion of the push and pull of black urban migration, see Rabinowitz, *Race Relations,* 18–24.

29. Reiff, Dahlin, and Smith, "Rural Push." See also Harley, "Black Women," 60.

30. Maclachlan, "Women's Work," 2. In 1890, for example, there were almost 127 African American women for every 100 black men. In 1900 the imbalance peaked at 141.3 women for every 100 men. Starting in 1900, a similar trend appeared among the white population, although the imbalance peaked in 1930 at 108.3 women for every 100 men.

31. Rabinowitz, *Race Relations,* 17.

32. T. Martin, *Atlanta,* 2:102.

33. J. Russell, *Atlanta,* 151.

34. Rabinowitz, *Race Relations,* 48.

35. Looking at Charlotte, North Carolina, Thomas Hanchett refers to this residential pattern as a "patchwork quilt" (*New South City,* 3).

36. Rabinowitz, *Race Relations,* 108; Hunter, *To 'Joy My Freedom,* 45. This pattern may not have been the case for all southern cities. See Greenwood, *Bittersweet Legacy,* for a discussion of how elites in Charlotte, North Carolina, seriously considered alternatives to racial segregation between the end of Reconstruction and the 1890s.

37. Bethel Congregation, quoted in Rydell, *All the World's a Fair,* 85.

38. Rabinowitz, *Race Relations,* 339.

39. *Atlanta Constitution,* August 3, 1881.

40. Ibid.; Hunter, *To 'Joy My Freedom,* 94.

41. For a variety of conclusions on the outcome and meaning of the strike, see Hunter, *To 'Joy My Freedom,* 88–97; Rabinowitz, *Race Relations,* 73–76; Thornbery, "Development," 215–20.

42. Hunter, *To 'Joy My Freedom,* 95.

43. *Atlanta Constitution,* September 10, December 12, 1881.

44. Tera Hunter, for example, reads this strike as white workers' effort to "preserve racial purity." "The strike," Hunter continues, "had opened the floodgates of the race issue and exposed the unstable quality of the color line in Southern industry" (*To 'Joy My Freedom,* 115, 116).

45. "The Strikers Still Hold Out," *Atlanta Journal,* August 6, 1897.

46. "One Thousand Men, Women and Children Strike at Fulton Bag and Cotton Mills," *Atlanta Journal,* August 4, 1897.

47. Kasson, *Rudeness and Civility,* esp. 34–47.

48. Maclachlan, "Women's Work," 290–94.

49. *Atlanta Journal,* August 4, 1897.

50. "One Thousand Men."

51. Ibid.

52. Ibid.

53. Kuhn, *New South Order,* 27.

54. See LeeAnn Whites's discussion of the role "protection" played in white southern ideology during this period ("Rebecca Latimer Felton," 41–61).

55. "Manifesto of the Strikers Issued by Textile Union," *Atlanta Journal,* August 5, 1897.

56. Ibid.

57. "Strike Settled at Noon Yesterday," *Atlanta Constitution,* August 6, 1897.

58. One of the best discussions of the wealth of fears and anxieties bound up in notions of white womanhood and African Americans can be found in Hall, *Revolt,* esp. xxxii–xxxiii, 154–55.

TWO. *Laboring Women, Real and Imagined*

1. "The Auxiliary to the Printers," *Journal of Labor,* October 23, 1903.

2. "Mrs. Wm. Strauss," *Journal of Labor,* October 16, 1903.

3. "Personal and Otherwise: Miss Lizzie Wright," *Journal of Labor,* October 16, 1903.

4. *Journal of Labor,* October 16, 1903.

5. "Factories Crippled by Marriages," *Journal of Labor,* November 8, 1907.

6. In 1900, 92 percent of the jobs held by black women were in domestic work. The proportion of domestic jobs in the African American female labor force did decline somewhat after the turn of the century, dropping to 84 percent in 1910 and 75 percent in 1920 (Hunter, "Household Workers," 75–76).

7. Maclachlan, "Women's Work," 16.

8. Only 0.7 percent of black women were clerical workers (Maclachlan, "Women's Work," 17).

9. Those interested more detailed characteristics of women workers, including growth rates, sex ratios, and industry breakdowns, should consult Maclachlan, "Women's Work," 376–77, which offers the fruits of her samplings of manuscript censuses.

10. Goldin, "Female Labor Force Participation," 87. By 1920, 36.7 percent of Atlanta's female workforce worked in stores, 49.6 percent in factories, and 13.7 percent in laundries (which primarily served the city's hotels, restaurants, and transportation companies) (U.S. Department of Labor, Women's Bureau, *Women,* 61; Blackwelder, "Mop and Typewriter," 24). These changes in both the types of jobs open to women and the number of women

working for wages led historian Julia Kirk Blackwelder to conclude that during this period, "Atlanta surpassed other southern cities in the degree to which women's roles changed" ("Mop and Typewriter," 21).

11. Hunter, *To 'Joy My Freedom*, 241.

12. All calculations for Atlanta's female workforce were taken from Maclachlan, "Women's Work," 11, 378, 382, 385.

13. Ibid., 378, 382, 385.

14. In 1890, black women made up 74.2 percent of the female labor force. By 1920, however, they represented only 51.9 percent (Maclachlan, "Women's Work," 378).

15. On the alliance of business and white organized labor behind economic booster-ism, see Deaton, "James G. Woodward," 22.

16. Carrie W. Allen, "Neglected Factor Is Woman," *Journal of Labor*, April 12, 1912.

17. Advertisement for Stone's Cakes, *City Builder*, June 1918.

18. This trend in the insurance industry is discussed at length in Kwolek-Folland, *Engendering Business*, 42.

19. Strom, *Beyond the Typewriter*, 7.

20. James Montgomery Flagg, "The Adventures of Kitty Cobb," *Atlanta Constitution*, September 1, 1912. These messages seemed to have been aimed at women, as the stories appeared on a page dedicated to women's interests.

21. "Improvements Have Come to Atlanta," *Journal of Labor*, November 11, 1927. In this interview conducted twenty years later, the woman who conducted this study implied that the findings were indeed dismal and a disgrace to the city. The city council appears to have gone to great lengths to prevent the study's findings from becoming public: the results were reported to council members but kept out of the minute books (Atlanta City Council Minutes, June 2, 1908, Atlanta History Center).

22. *City Builder*, January 10, 1918.

23. "Women out of Work," *Journal of Labor*, July 17, 1908.

24. "Girl Wanted: Opportunity for Profitable Employment," *Journal of Labor*, March 5, 1909.

25. Katherine D. Tillman, "The Paying Professions for Colored Girls," *Voice of the Negro* 4 (January–February 1907): 56; Fannie Barrier Williams, "The Colored Girl," *Voice of the Negro* 2 (June 1906): 400–403.

26. See the sampling of sex ratios in Maclachlan, "Women's Work," 2. In 1880, for example, there were 94.8 white women for every 100 white men. Starting in 1900, white women began to outnumber white men: in 1900 the ratio was 103.9 to 100, and in 1930 it reached 108.3 to 100. However, black women, consistently outnumbered black men and did so by a much greater margin. In 1900, for example, there were 141.3 black women for every 100 black men.

27. Minutes of the Evangelical Ministers Association, February 2, 1913, Christian Council of Atlanta Collection, Atlanta History Center (CCC).

28. "Protection for Girls," *Journal of Labor*, May 20, 1910.

29. Marion Jackson, quoted in "$3.50 a Week for Women Workers," *Journal of Labor*, February 7, 1913.

30. Summer Students in Industry Report, 1922, Industrial Bureau, YWCA National Board Archives.

31. "A Plea for Our Young Women," *Atlanta Georgian,* January 15, 1907.

32. "Real Respect for Women Urged by City's Pastors," *Atlanta Journal,* September 30, 1912.

33. "Stop This at Once," *Journal of Labor,* January 30, 1919.

34. The most persuasive and thorough discussion of these points appears in Dinnerstein, *Leo Frank Case.*

35. For a full discussion of the details of the murder, investigation, trial, and probable guilt of Jim Conley, see Frey and Thompson-Frey, *Silent and the Damned;* Dinnerstein, *Leo Frank Case;* Golden, *Little Girl Is Dead.*

36. Slaton based his decision on supposedly new evidence that had not been available to the original jury during the trial. He also objected to the mob spirit that had prevailed during the trial and had forced the jury to its decision with the threat of violence. While Slaton was never specific, the new evidence to which he was referring was probably letters written by Conley in which he admitted to having murdered Phagan. Copies of the letters can be found in the John M. Slaton Collection, Georgia Department of History and Archives. The commutation order is reprinted in Golden, *Little Girl Is Dead,* 320–53.

37. Williamson, *Rage,* 240.

38. Nancy MacLean, "Frank Case Reconsidered," views the denial of Phagan's (potential) sexuality as the result of sexual conservatism. Jacquelyn Hall, however, argues in "Private Eyes, Public Women" (264) that the preoccupation with sex during the Frank trial was actually a growth pang of modern sexuality. I tend to fall in the middle of these two views, believing that while working women often displayed more modern sexual behavior, their actions certainly were not uniformly accepted in the larger society. Because Phagan could not say or do otherwise, conservatives could mold her image to fit their agenda. The pervasive image of Phagan as an innocent child was, I believe, a testament to just how much mores were changing among her contemporaries.

39. "The Case of Mary Phagan," *Atlanta Constitution,* May 4, 1913.

40. MacLean, "Frank Case Reconsidered," 924–25.

41. *Jeffersonian,* November 19, 1914, reprinted in Woodward, *Tom Watson,* 439.

42. Wiggins, *Fiddlin' Georgia Crazy.* See also Wiggins, "Socio-Political Works."

43. This particular version of "The Ballad of Mary Phagan" (also referred to as "Leo Frank and Mary Phagan") appeared in Snyder, "Leo Frank and Mary Phagan." The last line of the first stanza appears in other versions of the song as "To get her little pay." Both variations relay important information about why Phagan's death generated such widespread publicity. On the one hand, she was going downtown unescorted to join in the crowds at the Confederate Memorial Day parade. On the other, she was a woman working for wages that left her susceptible to both economic and sexual exploitation. For variations on this song, see, Wiggins, *Fiddlin' Georgia Crazy,* 35–37.

44. Wiggins, *Fiddlin' Georgia Crazy,* 40–41.

45. Ibid., 42–43.

46. Petition for Commutation, Atlanta, Georgia, 1915, Slaton Collection. Interestingly,

only the petition from Atlanta contains the signatures of women. Half the names on this document are those of women.

47. MacLean, "Frank Case Reconsidered," 928.

48. "Women of Every Class and Age," *Atlanta Constitution,* August 5, 1913.

49. Dinnerstein argues that "the crime [of killing Phagan] channeled the fears and frustrations of the people in Atlanta, themselves the victims of the Southern industrial transformation" (*Leo Frank Case,* xiii). In this way, Frank, a northern Jew, represented the quintessential capitalist and exploiter. MacLean complicates Dinnerstein's conclusions by arguing that the opposition to Frank stemmed from "hostility toward both big capital and working-class radicalism; extreme racism, nationalism, and religion; [and] militant sexual conservatism" ("Frank Case Reconsidered," 920).

50. See, for example, "Frank Innocent, Said Conley, According to a Girl Operator," *Atlanta Constitution,* August 16, 1913.

51. "Girl Says Frank Often Looked in Dressing Room," *Atlanta Constitution,* August 17, 1913.

52. "Girl Called by Defense," *Atlanta Constitution,* August 17, 1913.

53. "Girls Testify to Seeing Frank," *Atlanta Constitution,* August 21, 1913.

54. "Mother-in-Law of Frank Denies Charges," *Atlanta Constitution,* August 15, 1913; "Starnes Tells How Affidavit from Negro Cook Was Secured," *Atlanta Constitution,* August 21, 1913.

55. "Hopkins Woman Denies Charges," *Atlanta Constitution,* August 9, 1913.

56. "Grilled Five Hours by Luther Rosser," *Atlanta Constitution,* August 5, 1913.

57. "Women of Every Class and Age" and "Handsome Woman," *Atlanta Constitution,* August 5, 1913.

58. "Frank's Fate Is Now in the Hands of the Jury," *Atlanta Journal,* August 25, 1913.

59. Hall, *Revolt,* xx.

60. "Case of Mary Phagan."

61. MacLean, "Frank Case Reconsidered," 938.

62. *Atlanta Constitution,* July 27, August 5, 25, 1913.

63. For many of the incidents described in this chapter, working women left no written record of their intentions. The conclusions drawn here and elsewhere consequently are based on the premise that actions often reflect the way people think. For another historian's treatment of this idea, see Brown, "Womanist Consciousness."

64. "Frank Waits with Wife in Tower for News from the Courthouse," *Atlanta Constitution,* August 26, 1913. The *Constitution* noted on this day that "few will live to see another such demonstration."

65. "Frank Starts Prison Work: Noisy Crowd at Governor's Home Dispersed by Militia," *Atlanta Constitution,* June 22, 1915.

66. "Mob's Own Story in Detail," *Atlanta Constitution,* August 18, 1915.

67. Maclachlan, "Atlanta's Industrial Women," 23.

68. Dunlap, "Reform." For another discussion of "age of consent" campaigns, see Sims, *Power,* 72.

69. "What Are We Going to Do?" *Journal of Labor,* October 19, 1923; "The Removal of Chief Beavers," *Journal of Labor,* February 26, 1915.

70. Maclachlan, "Women's Work," 117.

71. O. Delight Smith, "Office Holding and Politicians," *Journal of Labor,* October 4, 1907; Hall, "Smith's Progressive Era."

72. O. Delight Smith, "Keep Cool—Keep Cool," *Journal of Labor,* November 8, 1907.

73. Kessler-Harris, *Out to Work,* 153–56.

74. Allen, "Neglected Factor."

75. "Chivalry Forgotten," *Journal of Labor,* June 19, 1908.

76. "The Working Girl Problem," *Journal of Labor,* March 1, 1912 (reprinted from *Kansas City Labor Herald*).

77. "Married Working Woman Is Menace to Unionism," *Journal of Labor,* January 13, 1911.

78. "Chivalry Forgotten."

79. In her analysis of O. Delight Smith, Jacquelyn Hall mistakenly claims that Smith and her counterparts in organized labor were the only ones in Atlanta to relate moral "depravity" to long hours and poor working conditions. Severely oversimplifying their reactions, Hall writes, "Middle-class observers in Atlanta responded to the surge of white women into wage labor with pity, puzzlement, and disapproval" ("Smith's Progressive Era," 178).

80. Kessler-Harris, *Woman's Wage,* 84.

81. "Working Girl Problem."

82. "Women Should Organize," *Journal of Labor,* December 17, 1909; "Working Girls," *Journal of Labor,* October 19, 1906.

83. "Low Wages and Sin," *Journal of Labor,* March 30, 1917.

84. Gordon Nye, "Real Betrayer of Working Girls," *Journal of Labor,* April 28, 1911.

85. "Keep the Girls at Home," *Journal of Labor,* June 20, 1913.

86. "Our Working Girls," *Journal of Labor,* February 22, 1924.

87. "Women in Industry," *Journal of Labor,* November 27, 1908.

88. "A Prayer for Working Women," *Journal of Labor,* November 18, 1910 (reprinted from *American Magazine*).

89. Skill level often had little to with the worker's actual abilities and education and more to do with gender, race, and ethnicity. See Baron, "Questions."

90. Dill, " 'Making the Job Good,' " 35–36; J. Jones, "Political Implications," 109.

91. Robin Kelley draws on James Scott's "infrapolitics" to discuss these kinds of "oppositional practices that constitute the foundational politics for all organized mass movements" (Kelley, "Black Poor," 295).

92. Kytle, *Willie Mae,* 118–20.

93. Interview with Mary Morton, WRFG/Living Atlanta Collection, Atlanta History Center (LAC). Clifford Kuhn and Bernard West collected the Living Atlanta oral histories in the 1970s for a radio series produced by WRFG-FM. In interviews with a wide range of Atlantans, both black and white, subjects were asked for their recollections of the city

around the time of World War I. Rarely did interviewers ask for specific dates, but the scope of the project as well as evidence from other sources, such as the *Journal of Labor* and Fulton Bag and Cotton Mills records, suggest that these recollections of work in Atlanta fairly represent conditions in the city in the 1910s and early 1920s. They are one of the few sources for working-class women's voices unmediated by the press, reformers, or government officials of that period, and, therefore, I have relied on them heavily to communicate women's perspectives.

94. Kytle, *Willie Mae,* 119, 120, 138.

95. Interview with Annie Alexander, LAC.

96. Kuhn, "History," 48–49.

97. Bond hearing for Annie Mae Leathers and [Nannie] Leah Young, Fulton County Superior Court, 1934, International Labor Defense Papers, Schomburg Center, New York Public Library (ILD).

98. Life history written by Leola Young, American Labor Education Service, Southern Summer School for Women Workers, Cornell University, Labor-Management Documentation Center, M. P. Catherwood Library (ALES). In the early 1930s, young women attending the Summer Schools for Women Workers wrote their autobiographies. These documents often contained work histories that began when the women were children in the late 1910s and early 1920s. See Fredrickson, "Southern Summer School."

99. Interview with Mrs. Campbell, support for bulletin 22, Records of the U.S. Department of Labor, Women's Bureau, RG 86, National Archives II. The bureau's personnel conducted the research for *Women in Georgia Industries* in early 1920 and 1921. Surveys of industries employing women were conducted, and researchers interviewed female employees, recording information on both their current positions and their previous work experiences.

100. Interview with Mrs. Smith, support for bulletin 22, U.S. Department of Labor, Women's Bureau.

101. Life history written by Leola Young, ALES. Young recalled shortly after World War I that she "went to work and in three years . . . had saved a thousand dollars." While she wanted to use the money to move to Florida, her family convinced her to buy a house in Atlanta.

102. Home interview with Mrs. Campbell, support for bulletin 22, U.S. Department of Labor, Women's Bureau.

103. Life history written by Lucile Reynolds, ALES.

104. Hine, "Inner Lives."

105. Kessler-Harris, *Woman's Wage,* 84.

106. Scholars have recently begun to shift questions away from why women were excluded from unions to more nuanced studies of when the interests of women and unions intersected. For an overview of this literature, see Milkman, "Gender and Trade Unionism."

107. For an analysis of the contested images of working-class women embedded in this strike, see Hickey, "Visibility, Politics, and Urban Development," 60–69, 222–32; Hall, "Private Eyes, Public Women." Elizabeth Faue addresses the existence of these

temporary alignments between union politics and the lives of working women (*Suffering and Struggle,* 4).

108. For a full account of the events leading up to the strike, see Fink, *Strike of 1914–1915;* Fink, "Labor Espionage"; Kuhn, *New South Order,* chap. 4.

109. Report of Operatives J.W.W. and A.E.W. 10, Fulton Bag and Cotton Mills, Records of the Federal Mediation Conciliation Service, RG 280, Washington National Records Center (FMCS).

110. Kuhn, *New South Order,* 160–61.

111. Hall, "Private Eyes, Public Women," 257.

112. Both Kuhn (*New South Order,* 199–201) and Hall ("Smith's Progressive Era," 183) note that this practice also served to reinforce class consciousness among the strikers.

113. Report of Operative 115, July 7, 1914, Fulton Bag and Cotton Mills Company Collection, Institute Archives, Georgia Institute of Technology (FBCM).

114. Kuhn, *New South Order,* 167–74; Hall, "Private Eyes, Public Women," 267.

115. *Atlanta Constitution,* June 13, 1914, quoted in Hall, "Private Eyes, Public Women," 269.

116. Men and Religion Forward Bulletin 119, Disputed Case File, 1913–48, FBCM.

117. Hall, "Private Eyes, Public Women," 269.

118. Men and Religion Forward Bulletin 124, Disputed Case File, 1913–48, FBCM.

119. Report of Operative, December 23, 1914, FBCM.

120. Ibid.

121. Ibid.

122. Hall, "Private Eyes, Public Women," 256.

123. Ibid., 254; Kuhn, *New South Order,* 157.

124. "Rules of the Camp," Disputed Case File, 1913–48, box 3, Fulton Bag and Cotton Mills, FMCS.

125. Report of Operative #115, July 7, 1914, FBCM.

126. One of the now-common critiques leveled against many social movement theories and, in particular, the resource-mobilization theory involved the undervaluing of women's activities. Leadership roles have been commonly understood to include public speaking, publicity, fund-raising, and tactical planning. This definition ignores the crucial day-to-day organizing and recruiting often done by women. The Fulton Bag and Cotton Mills strike was unusual in that women participated in all levels of local leadership. For an overview of resource-mobilization theory, see Morris, *Origins.* Lipsitz, *Life,* addresses the critical relationship of community organizing to the success of social movements. For a critique of the ways women's activism has been rendered invisible by traditional definitions of leadership, see Robinson, *Montgomery Bus Boycott;* Kingsolver, *Holding the Line.*

127. Hall, "Disorderly Women," found that women in other southern textile mills used similar tactics during strikes.

128. Report of Operative, December 23, 1914, FBCM.

129. Deposition of Alice Carlton, Atlanta, Fulton County, State of Georgia, Disputed Case File, FMCS.

130. James I. Brush, quoted in Kuhn, "History," 247.

131. Deposition of Mrs. Margaret Dempsey given to Inis Weed, July 28, 1914, Records of the U.S. Commission on Industrial Relations, Washington National Records Center (CIR).

132. Deposition of Mrs. Blanche Prince given to Inis Weed, July 28, 1914, CIR.

133. Deposition of Addie Camp, FMCS.

134. Deposition of Mrs. Josie Sisk, July 28, 1914, CIR.

THREE. *Public Space and Leisure Time*

1. Kimmel, quoted in Bauerlein, *Negrophobia,* 125.

2. Researchers examining these rape claims shortly after the riot concluded that three of these attacks were committed by white men and that four of the allegations were completely fabricated (R. Baker, "Following the Color Line").

3. On the riot, see Bauerlein, *Negrophobia;* Godshalk, "In the Wake"; Mixon, "Atlanta Riot"; Mixon, " 'Good Negro—Bad Negro,' " 593–621; Williamson, *Crucible,* 209–23; Tagger, "Atlanta Race Riot"; Dittmer, *Black Georgia,* 123–31; Crowe, "Racial Massacre"; Crowe, "Racial Violence"; Rainey, "Race Riot."

4. White rioters moving through downtown frequently targeted economically independent African Americans, such as Adams, for attack. Revealing the larger tensions at work in the riot, few Atlantans, black or white, would have placed these entrepreneurs in the same class with the black criminals supposedly responsible for the recent series of rapes (Godshalk, "In the Wake," 67).

5. Godshalk, "In the Wake," 15; Bauerlein, *Negrophobia,* 165.

6. Bauerlein, *Negrophobia,* 168.

7. "It Is Time to Act, Men," *Atlanta Evening News,* September 21, 1906, as quoted in Bauerlein, *Negrophobia,* 129.

8. Crowe, "Racial Massacre," 151; Godshalk, "In the Wake."

9. *Atlanta Evening News,* September 18, 1906, quoted in Dittmer, *Black Georgia,* 130.

10. In the boomtown of Atlanta, unemployed men were considered lazy. Due to the racial climate of the period, however, limited opportunities existed for regular employment for black men (Crowe, "Racial Violence," 235–37). Addressing the success of Prohibitionists' arguments, Williamson explains, "whites generally thought that black men were especially excited by alcohol, and that their excitement was most especially erotic" (*Rage,* 142).

11. *Atlanta Journal,* quoted in Bauerlein, *Negrophobia,* 138.

12. "Let the Women Arm Themselves" and "Protect Our Women," both in *Atlanta Journal,* August 25, 1906.

13. For the now-classic description of this ideology of southern womanhood, see A. Scott, *Southern Lady,* 3–21. See also Whites, "Rebecca Latimer Felton," for a discussion of how ideals of protection were transformed in the late nineteenth and early twentieth centuries.

14. W. White, *Man Called White,* 11.

15. *Atlanta Journal,* August 1, 1906, quoted in Woodward, *Tom Watson,* 379.

16. Interview with Ethel Meyers, LAC. Meyers recalled that her family purchased a gun to protect itself from blacks "because it had been reported the negroes had raped white women, and had assaulted white women." Revealing her relatively safe racial and class positioning in Atlanta, Meyers also noted, "I don't remember hearing anybody being killed. I think it may have been more of a scare than anything else."

17. *Atlanta Georgian,* September 23, 1906, quoted in Bauerlein, *Negrophobia,* 183.

18. Bauerlein, *Negrophobia,* 147.

19. "In a Time Like This," *Atlanta Georgian,* September 24, 1906.

20. H. Y. McCord, quoted in Bauerlein, *Negrophobia,* 207.

21. Quoted in ibid., 211, 212.

22. Quoted in ibid., 217.

23. On segregation as Progressivism, see, Crowe, "Racial Violence," 234; Hunter, *To 'Joy My Freedom,* 126–27. Not surprisingly, some blacks believed that the riot represented the failure of segregation practices implemented in the late nineteenth century to protect African Americans from violence. The two most vocal adherents to this position, Atlanta University Professor W. E. B. DuBois and Jesse Max Barber, the outspoken editor of the *Voice of the Negro,* found their views too radical for Atlanta's postriot climate and left the city to continue their work in northern cities (Capecie and Knight, "Reckoning with Violence"; Mixon, "Atlanta Riot"; Bauerlein, *Negrophobia,* 223–36, 269–80; Hale, *Making Whiteness,* 26).

24. Bauerlein, *Negrophobia,* 225.

25. Lewis, *In Their Own Interests.* See also J. Jones, "Political Implications," 111–12. Beyond bloc voting in a few bond elections during the 1920s, direct mass political activism from the black community did not form until the issue of police violence against blacks and the lack of African American police officers came to the fore in the 1940s (Ferguson, "Politics of Inclusion"; Hickey, "Auburn Avenue").

26. This pattern of spatial development was by no means unique. These trends evolved in northern cities in the nineteenth century (Ford, *Cities and Buildings,* 144–46). For a study of this process in a southern city with many characteristics similar to Atlanta, see Hanchett, *New South City,* 188–90.

27. Bayor, *Twentieth-Century Atlanta,* 54–55.

28. Atlanta City Council Minutes, September 20, October 4, 1909; November 21, 1910; January 2, 1911; April 6, 1914.

29. Hickey, " 'Meet Me.' "

30. Citizens' Committee advertisement, reprinted in Garrett, *Atlanta,* 2:537–38.

31. On the way in which organized labor used Labor Day parades to build unionism and court wide public support, see Kazin and Ross, "America's Labor Day."

32. Interview with Alice Adams, LAC.

33. Partial transcript of interview with Dan Stephens, LAC.

34. Interview with Horace Sinclair, Sweet Auburn Neighborhood Project, Auburn Avenue Research Library.

35. *Journal Magazine,* May 18, 1913, reprinted in Garrett, *Atlanta,* 2:607–9.

36. M. Harris, *Rise,* 43–44.

37. Anzaldúa, *Borderlands/La Frontera,* ii.

38. *Atlanta, Georgia, City Directory* (Richmond, Va.: R. L. Polk, 1910).

39. "Chinamen Are Accused of Doping Little Girls in Center of Gate City," *Atlanta Constitution,* January 21, 1907.

40. Minutes of Police Committee of the City Council, December 9, 1919, Atlanta History Center.

41. *Wilborn M. O'Connor vs. Janie May O'Connor,* no. 40290, June 1918, Fulton County Superior Court, Civil Division (FCCD).

42. Hall, "Smith's Progressive Era," 183.

43. Interview with Alice Adams, LAC.

44. L. May, *Screening out the Past,* chap. 1.

45. "Mrs. W. B. Lowe Will Take up the Case of Dolly Pritchard," n.d. (probably 1900), Atlanta Woman's Club Scrapbook 2, Atlanta Woman's Club Collection, Atlanta History Center.

46. Ibid.

47. Carby, "Black Woman's Body."

48. Jackson McHenry, 1904, quoted in Hunter, *To 'Joy My Freedom,* 165.

49. Report of Operative 457, January 15, 1915, FBCM.

50. Goodson, *Highbrows,* 63–76.

51. Summer Students in Industry Report, 1922, YWCA.

52. Peiss, *Cheap Amusements,* 62.

53. Kytle, *Willie Mae,* 144.

54. Interview with Lizzie Lou Hanford, support for bulletin 22, U.S. Department of Labor, Women's Bureau.

55. See, for example, Hebdige, *Subculture.*

56. "Vice Commission Urges General City Clean-Up," *Atlanta Georgian,* October 7, 1912.

57. Kytle, *Willie Mae,* 140–41.

58. Peiss, *Cheap Amusements;* L. Cohen, *Making a New Deal;* Enstad, *Ladies.*

59. Dan Stephens, quoted in Kuhn, Joye, and West, *Living Atlanta,* 260.

60. B. Bailey, *Front Porch.* Cars often served such purposes for some middle-class youth, although with a bit more privacy. For those who could afford them, automobiles caught on quickly in the city and provided yet another release from the confines of wage work or the watchful eyes of parents and neighbors. See Preston, *Automobile Age Atlanta.*

61. *Atlanta Georgian,* February 2, 1907, quoted in Goodson, *Highbrows,* 197 n. 44.

62. Peiss, " 'Charity Girls,' " 159.

63. Report of Operative 457, December 26, 27, 1914, FBCM.

64. Report of Operative 810, November 18, 1912, FBCM.

65. Report of Operative 429, September 12, 17, 1916, FBCM.

66. Peiss and Simmons, *Passion and Power,* 5–6.

67. "Atlanta's Vice Crusade an Inspiration to Nation," *Golden Age,* August 7, 1913.

68. Ibid.

69. "Vice Commission Urges General City Clean-Up."

70. "Less Prudery, Fewer Wayward Girls," *Atlanta Constitution*, September 25, 1912.

71. Interview with Alice Adams, LAC.

72. "The Negro and the Opera House," *Atlanta Independent*, September 30, 1905.

73. "Oh Where Is My Wandering Cook Tonight?" *Atlanta Georgian*, July 6, 1919.

74. *Atlanta Constitution*, July 3, 1903.

75. Atlanta City Council Minutes, June 20, 1910, September 2, 1918, July 21, 1919.

76. "Civic Centers Should Displace Cheap Shows," *Atlanta Journal*, September 24, 1912.

77. "Mrs. W. B. Lowe Will Take up the Case."

78. Ibid.

79. "Civic Centers Should Displace Cheap Shows." Jane Addams provides a classic Progressive-era treatment of working-class amusements and the need for constructive alternatives in *Spirit of Youth*.

80. "The Working Girl," *Atlanta Constitution*, June 4, 1913.

81. "High School Girls Not Allowed to Practice 'Zoo' Dances at Recess," *Atlanta Georgian*, September 21, 1912.

82. Goodson, *Highbrows*, 43–44.

83. Kasson, *Amusing the Millions*, 6.

84. *Atlanta Journal*, May 13, 1906, reprinted in Garrett, *Atlanta*, 2:497–98.

85. Ibid.

86. Ponce de Leon Amusement Park, Vanishing Georgia Collection, Georgia Department of History and Archives.

87. "Chief Must Not Go Too Far, Says Mason," *Atlanta Constitution*, September 29, 1912.

88. Goodson, *Highbrows*, 99–100. According to Goodson, national movie distributors found Atlanta's censorship board to be one of the most reasonable in the country.

89. "Business Men Score Results of Vice War," *Atlanta Georgian*, December 29, 1913. Maclachlan's research on working women in Atlanta reveals that prostitution and vice districts, like opera houses, theaters, and other "highbrow" amusements, lured tourist and convention dollars to Atlanta in the early part of the twentieth century ("Women's Work," 211–12).

90. *Atlanta Constitution*, March 13, 1913, quoted in Goodson, *Highbrows*, 91.

91. "286 Places Outside 'District' Defy Law," *Atlanta Georgian*, September 26, 1912.

92. "Crusade Begins Now on Atlanta's Street Evil," *Atlanta Journal*, September 28, 1912.

93. Wilson, *Sphinx*, 46.

94. "Where Is Bertie? Didn't Stay Long in Country Home," *Atlanta Georgian*, 15 January 1907; "Dance Interrupted, Policemen Arrest Bertie Owens Again," *Atlanta Georgian*, 9 January 1907.

95. For secondary literature dealing with dichotomous perceptions of women's sex-

uality and sexual activity around the turn of the century, see Kunzel, *Fallen Women;* E. DuBois and Gordon, "Seeking Ecstasy."

96. "Moral Clean-up Urged for the City," *Atlanta Constitution,* October 8, 1912; "Crusade Begins Now."

97. "Moral Clean-up Urged for the City."

98. "Report of the Martha Home," April 4–11, 1914, Men and Religion Forward Ledger, ccc.

99. "Civic Centers Should Displace Cheap Shows."

100. "Report of the Martha Home," January 9–15, February 6–12, February 13–19, March 1–12, 1914, Men and Religion Forward Ledger, ccc.

101. The annual reports of Atlanta's police department do not break down arrests by gender, and the bulk of arrests in the city fell into the ambiguous category of "disorderly conduct." Work of historians on other locations as well as qualitative evidence for Atlanta, however, suggests that before 1920, women were far more likely to be arrested for crimes against the public order. Atlanta did not arrest women for prostitution per se, and the category of "streetwalker" for reason of arrest appears only in 1928. Interestingly, records kept by the department in the first two decades of the twentieth century, however, used "prostitute" as an occupational category. In 1911, for example, eighty-eight women arrested gave prostitution as their occupation, yet there were only seventy-seven arrests that year for "being lewd woman on the streets at night," and no women were arrested in that year for "occupying house of ill fame." On women's arrests, see Freedman, *Their Sisters' Keepers,* 11; Brenzel, *Daughters of the State,* 81; Hickey, "Rescuing the Working Girl," 3–4.

102. On the introduction of women into policing across the country during this period, see Schulz, *Social Worker,* esp. 9–61; Segrave, *Policewomen,* esp. 5–29, 44–65; Myers, *Municipal Mother;* Feinman, *Criminal Justice System.*

103. "Sleuths to Keep Tab," *Atlanta Georgian,* September 28, 1912.

104. Ibid. Maclachlan ("Women's Work," 203–25) concludes that during the early twentieth century, prostitution was rarely plied in Atlanta through streetwalking. On the whole, prostitution was confined to brothels in well-defined areas. Gilfoyle's work (*City of Eros,* esp. chap. 12) reveals the forces at work in shaping the geography of commercialized sex in New York City. It appears that at least some of these trends, particularly the influence of real estate owners, also influenced Atlanta's spatial arrangement.

105. "Crusade Begins Now."

106. "Lights Are out in Vice District," *Atlanta Constitution,* September 30, 1912.

107. Annual reports of the chief of police, 1893–1932, Herbert T. Jenkins Collection, Atlanta History Center.

108. "Moral Clean-up Urged for the City."

109. Ibid; "Vice Commission Urges General City Clean-Up."

110. Kasson, *Amusing the Millions,* 112.

111. Writing in the early twentieth century, Jesse Frederick Steiner concluded that the commercialization of baseball marked a shift for most leisure seekers from participant to observer (*Americans at Play*).

112. For a discussion of initial fears across the nation of the mixing of classes and genders in movie theaters, see L. May, *Screening out the Past,* chap. 2.

113. As historian Shirley Ardener has noted in *Women and Space,* much of social life is given a physical space, linking the physical world to social reality.

114. E. May, *Homeward Bound,* 47. For an analysis of popular movies in the 1930s and their messages to viewers, see chap. 2.

115. Newman, "Vision of Order," 153.

FOUR. *Class, Community, and Welfare*

1. Garrett, *Atlanta,* 2:473-74.

2. Joseph Logan, "The Ten Years, 1905-1915: The Pioneering Years of Charity Organization in Atlanta, Georgia," unpublished paper, 1915, Joseph C. Logan Papers, Atlanta History Center.

3. Katz, *Poorhouse,* 58.

4. Weisiger, quoted in Garrett, *Atlanta,* 2:484. Not surprisingly, most of this aid went to the city's whites. Aid for impoverished blacks was left almost entirely to organizations created and funded by the African American community before U.S. entry into World War I.

5. Hickey, "Auburn Avenue," 109-44; Meier and Lewis, "Negro Upper Class."

6. Women who were widowed, deserted, or divorced also fell into this category.

7. This was true outside of Atlanta as well. See Harley, "Not Who You Are."

8. Garrett, *Atlanta,* 2:389; *Annual Reports, City of Atlanta, 1899* (Atlanta: n.p., 1899), 19-45.

9. Hertzberg, *Strangers,* 134-38; Branch, "American Settlement House Movement," 71-83.

10. Branch, "American Settlement House Movement," 40-57.

11. Dittmer, *Black Georgia,* 50-64.

12. Joseph Logan to J. H. Lewis, June 25, 1915, Child Services and Family Counseling Collection, Atlanta History Center (CSFC).

13. Annual Report of the City Warden, 1914, CSFC.

14. Unfortunately, the records of the Recorder's Court are regularly destroyed every twenty years, so the case files from this period no longer exist. After sentencing W. A. Summers to the stockade for wife beating, Broyles turned to the wife and told her to get a lawyer and divorce Summers (" 'Get a Divorce,' Advises Judge Broyles to Woman," *Atlanta Georgian,* January 14, 1907).

15. The police records for this period are largely inaccessible. Some hints about how the police department functioned in relation to women can be found in the annual reports of the police chiefs and the minutes of the police committee, both of which are housed at the Atlanta History Center. In 1913, for example, police arrested 636 women, but only 452 of them went to court. Of the women not sent to court, the police matron directed 25 back their parents and placed 36 with private welfare agencies and 3 in public institutions. She sent 17 to other cities, found jobs and homes for 3, held 1 as a witness, and released

another 67 ("Annual Report of the Chief of Police of the City of Atlanta, Georgia, for the Year Ending December 31, 1913," Herbert T. Jenkins Collection).

16. "Is Country Too Dull? Two Girls Flee to City," *Atlanta Georgian,* January 15, 1907.

17. Minutes of the Men and Religion Forward Movement, January 26, 1914, CCC.

18. "Report to the 8th Ward Committee, Case #877, Mrs. Jennie Lewis, 40 Tumlin St., 16 February 1907," CSFC.

19. "Sociology 13, Observations from Study of Family as Treated by Family Welfare Society and Social Result Accomplished," student paper, Comer McDonald Woodward Collection, Special Collections, Robert W. Woodruff Library, Emory University.

20. Evans, *Living for Jesus,* 55.

21. Gordon, "Feminist Scholarship," 13. See also Weinbaum and Bridges, "Paycheck," 190–205.

22. Fraser, *Unruly Practices,* 145–46, 152.

23. *Wesley House Bulletin,* 25.

24. "Eight Outstanding Facts about the Sheltering Arms," promotional flyer; "The Sheltering Arms, Atlanta, Georgia, Annual Report for 1909," Sheltering Arms Day Nursery Collection, Atlanta History Center.

25. Louie D. Shivery, "The History of the Gate City Free Kindergarten Association," reprinted in part in Ross, *Black Heritage,* 260–64.

26. Evans, *Living for Jesus,* 34.

27. Dittmer, *Black Georgia,* 63. See also D. Russell, "Institutional Church," reprinted in part in Ross, *Black Heritage,* 254–57.

28. Rouse, *Lugenia Burns Hope,* esp. chap. 4.

29. *Wesley House Bulletin.*

30. Annual Report of the Associated Charities, 1910, CSFC.

31. "Annual Report—1906, Associated Charities of Atlanta," CSFC.

32. R. C. Dexter to J. M. B. Hoxsey, June 12, 1920, CSFC.

33. "Annual Report—1906, Associated Charities of Atlanta," CSFC.

34. A woman the Associated Charities referred to as "Mrs. L" refused to work at a job the agency had secured for her. Her children were remanded to a local orphanage. The caseworker then reported, "Work again secured for woman, who was given to understand she must make good in three months or the Orphanage would be given legal control of the children." At the time of this report, the woman was working steadily and well on her way to "earning" her children back (Annual Report of the Associated Charities, 1915, CSFC).

35. Willard C. Hay, "Report in Sociology 10 on Desertion Case from Case no. 11432, Family Welfare Society," Comer McDonald Woodward Collection. In her study of Boston welfare agencies, *Heroes of Their Own Lives,* Gordon also found that women cajoled, negotiated, and even tricked social workers into meeting demands. See also Stadum, *Poor Women,* on finding negotiations between social workers and clients in case records.

36. "Vancott Family," Comer McDonald Woodward Collection.

37. "Georgia Moore, #5," July 12, 1907, CSFC. Joseph Logan, one of the founders, attached a note to Moore's case history, writing, "Our longest and most difficult case."

38. "Fourth Annual Report, Associated Charities of Atlanta, January 1, 1909–January 1, 1910," Atlanta Lung Association Collection, Atlanta History Center (ALA).

39. Rosa Lowe to Mrs. E. M. Chapman, November 9, 1911, ALA.

40. "Mrs. Lewis, #877," October 1, 1906, CSFC.

41. Evans, *Living for Jesus,* 34.

42. Associated Charities to Edward Alfriend, October 26, 1910, CSFC.

43. Rosa Lowe to Mrs. E. M. Chapman, November 9, 1911.

44. Abramovitz, *Lives,* 182.

45. Boris, "Reconstructing," 73.

46. Sapiro, "Gender Basis," 42.

47. Executive Committee Minutes, September 30, 1920, Board of City Mission Papers, Wesley Community Center.

48. Gordon, "Visions of Welfare," 586.

49. Untitled typed report of the Associated Charities, 1909, ALA.

50. Annual Report of the Associated Charities, 1910, 16, 10, CSFC.

51. Evans, *Living for Jesus,* 69.

52. Annual Report of the Associated Charities, 1915, CSFC.

53. Annual Report of the Associated Charities, 1911, CSFC.

54. "Anti-Tuberculosis Association 1909 Photographs," Patient Scrapbook, 7, ALA.

55. Report of the City Warden, 1916, CSFC.

56. Abramovitz, *Lives,* 3, 4.

57. *Muller vs. Oregon,* 208 U.S. 412 (1908), quoted in Boris, "Reconstructing," 77. See also Ladd-Taylor, *Mother-Work.*

58. See, for example, the editorial page, *Journal of Labor,* October 21, 1927.

59. Untitled report, 1918–30, CSFC.

60. Evans, *Living for Jesus,* 24.

61. Annual Report of the Associated Charities, 1906, CSFC.

62. Annual Report of the Associated Charities, 1910, CSFC.

63. "A Brief Sketch of the Relations between the Associated Charities of Atlanta and the Warden of the City of Atlanta," 1914, CSFC.

64. Evans, *Living for Jesus,* 58; "Relief vs. Service," 1916, CSFC.

65. *Wesley House Bulletin,* 20.

66. The literature on racial uplift and respectability discourses among early-twentieth-century blacks has grown enormously in recent years. For a specific and uncommon assessment of key roles working-class women played in this political strategy, see Carby, "Black Woman's Body."

67. "The History of the Neighborhood Union," Neighborhood Union Collection, Woodruff Library, Atlanta University Center (NU); "The Neighborhood Union: An Experiment in Community Cooperation," NU. In some versions of this story, the woman did not have children but was still a caretaker for a brother and father. See, for example, Shivery, "Organized Social Work"; Rouse, *Lugenia Burns Hope,* 65; Neverdon-Morton, *Advancement of the Race,* 145.

68. Rouse, *Lugenia Burns Hope,* 90.

69. Draft of the Annual Report of the Neighborhood Union, 1912, NU.

70. In her master's thesis, the longtime Neighborhood Union secretary Louie Shivery concluded, "It is remarkable how uneducated Negroes attacked social problems, single-handed, in religion, education, and civic life, and made noteworthy beginnings in solving these social problems of their racial group as well as relieving the proper authorities of their responsibility in the early history of Atlanta" ("Organized Social Work," 23). This thesis provides a useful and detailed account of many of the Neighborhood Union's activities from 1908 to 1935. While researching and writing, however, Shivery was an active NU member. The organization's stated goals in the 1930s color her conclusions about its focus in the early years. I believe she overemphasizes the focus on children and ignores the importance of programs directed at promoting African American women as mothers. Consequently, subsequent researchers who have relied more heavily on her work than the actual organizational papers reflect a similar view. See, in particular, Rouse, *Lugenia Burns Hope,* 65; Dittmer, *Black Georgia,* 64.

71. *Atlanta Journal* clipping, n.d., NU.

72. Neighborhood Union, quoted in *Atlanta Constitution* clipping, 1911, NU.

73. Draft of speech by Lugenia Burns Hope on poor housing, 1909, NU.

74. In 1911 a special committee was formed to distribute unemployment relief. Union records concluded, "It has worked effectively and has been a vital factor in helping many West-Side families to maintain their morals" ("Neighborhood Union: An Experiment").

75. "Work of the Neighborhood Union," *Spelman Messenger,* November 1916.

76. Deborah White, "Cost of Club Work," 259.

77. "Work of the Neighborhood Union."

78. Gaines, *Uplifting the Race,* xiv.

79. Stallybras and White, *Politics and Poetics.*

80. Shivery, "Organized Social Work," 177.

81. For ties between morality and the physical environment, see Gaines, *Uplifting the Race,* 11.

82. Ibid, 138.

83. Shivery, "Organized Social Work," appendix 2, "Professor Watson, Survey by the Sociological Department of Morehouse College," 432.

84. Rouse, *Lugenia Burns Hope,* 81–82.

85. "Work of the Neighborhood Union."

86. Selena Sloan Butler, "Need of Day Nurseries," in *Social and Physical Condition,* 63.

87. Deborah White, "Cost of Club Work," 257. On middle-class women "mothering" the working-class, see also Carby, "Black Woman's Body," 744.

88. On social housekeeping, see Hewitt, "Beyond the Search."

89. For the politics of respectability, see Higginbotham, *Righteous Discontent,* chap. 7; Rouse, "Attack," 10–23.

90. Rouse, *Lugenia Burns Hope,* 7.

91. Morton, *Disfigured Images.* See also Collins, *Black Feminist Thought,* 170–73.

92. Lugenia Burns Hope, handwritten untitled speech, NU.

93. Lugenia Burns Hope, "What Woman Can Do with the Ballot," NU.

94. Higginbotham, *Righteous Discontent,* 187.

95. Ibid, 191.

96. Ibid, 205.

97. While a complementary process of professionalization was occurring in the black reformer community, including, most notably, the founding of the Atlanta School of Social Work, its proponents do not seem to have defined themselves and their field through dealings with female clients in the way that white social workers did. Instead, blacks focused on their identity as community leaders.

98. Ehrenreich, *Altruistic Imagination;* Leiby, *Social Welfare;* Kirschner, *Paradox;* Leighninger, *Social Work;* Walkowitz, "Feminine Professional Identity."

99. The Board of City Missions, for example, voted in 1919 to close the Wesley House night schools, believing that this type of program should fall under the responsibilities of the Public Board of Education. In 1920, the Board of City Missions voted to abandon all "welfare work," closed the settlement house entirely, and instead focused outreach efforts on Christian missionary work ("A Story of Wesley Community House and of Some of the Peoples It Has Served," unpublished manuscript, Board of City Missions, Wesley Community House).

100. Evelyn Alexander, "Vancott Family," Comer McDonald Woodward Collection.

101. Kunzel, *Fallen Women,* 64.

102. Untitled report, 1918–30, CSFC.

103. Minutes of the General Staff Conference, December 31, 1931, CSFC.

104. Walkowitz, "Feminine Professional Identity," 1067.

105. "Column for the Needy," *Atlanta Journal,* 1915, clipping file, CSFC.

106. *Atlanta Constitution,* May 25, 1920, clipping file, CSFC.

107. R. C. Dexter to editor of *Atlanta Constitution,* May 25, 1920, CSFC.

108. Agnew, "Touch of Class," 70.

FIVE. *Physical and Moral Health*

1. "A Saturday Evening," *Atlanta Georgian,* January 21, 1907.

2. A. King, "International Cotton Exposition," 187.

3. "Atlanta: A Healthful City," *City Builder,* June 1919.

4. Interview with Durise Hanson, LAC.

5. J. Russell, *Atlanta,* 64.

6. Dr. James Anderson, quoted in Kuhn, Joye, and West, *Living Atlanta,* 233.

7. In 1900, black mortality exceeded white death rates by 69 percent. Half of the city's mortality could be attributed to blacks, even though they constituted only 40 percent of the population (Galishoff, "Germs," 23).

8. Hopkins, "Public Health in Atlanta."

9. Goldfield, "Business of Health and Planning."

10. Brandt, *No Magic Bullet,* 4.

11. Bates, *Bargaining for Life,* 6.

12. Parsons, "White Plague," 105.

13. Rosa Lowe to Captain Raoul, January 13, 1909, ALA.

14. Sontag, *Illness as Metaphor,* 12.

15. The association of women with the home is a common ideal in American society. For discussions of women as the foundation of neighborhoods, see Stansell, *City;* Lewis, *In Their Own Interests;* Kuhn, "History," 99–101 (for Atlanta).

16. Rosa Lowe, "Tuberculosis Work among Negroes," 1917, ALA.

17. Dr. R. R. Daly, untitled report, 1916, ALA.

18. Sontag, *Illness as Metaphor,* 36.

19. Johnnie Weeks, who had been living with another woman and a baby, was removed to the Alms House. "She fled from her shelter and wandered in the houses of any who would lodge her for one night at a time" (Anti-Tuberculosis Association, 1909 photographs, Patient Scrapbook, 2, ALA). Mrs. Grogan was thought to be a threat to her small children. When she complained about the lack of attention from the association doctor and continued to take patent medicines, Rosa Lowe reported, "the case has been again reported as a menace to her children and the suggestion made that they be taken away from her" (Lowe to Dr. Barnard Wolf, June 10, 1909, ALA).

20. Rosa Lowe to unknown, n.d. ALA.

21. Rosa Lowe to Dr. Barnard Wolf, June 10, 1909, ALA.

22. Rosa Lowe to Captain Raoul, January 13, 1909, ALA.

23. Parsons, "White Plague," 66–67.

24. "A Tuberculosis Clinic for Negroes," *Atlanta Georgian,* July 13, 1909.

25. The Anti-Tuberculosis Association worked closely with the Associated Charities in formulating relief policy, but only the Anti-Tuberculosis Association had a branch that dealt specifically with blacks. Most of the direct relief distributed to black tuberculosis patients and their families was secured by the association through the city warden's office. Money raised in the black community also supported work with black tubercular patients (Parsons, "White Plague"; Judson, " 'New South' City").

26. Anti-Tuberculosis Association, 1909 Photographs, Patient Scrapbook, 17, ALA.

27. David McBride calls "the collective sociomedical imperative that blacks were one with the causative agents of infectious diseases" the "epidemic paradigm" of the early twentieth century (*From* TB *to* AIDS, 19). On the nineteenth century, see Hunter, *To 'Joy my Freedom,* 188–91.

28. P. Palmer, *Domesticity and Dirt,* 151.

29. Interview with Alice Adams, LAC.

30. Alice Adams, quoted in Kuhn, Joye, and West, *Living Atlanta,* 113.

31. Ibid., 116.

32. Interview with Mary Morton, LAC.

33. Interview with Willie Mae Jackson, LAC.

34. Alice Adams, quoted in Kuhn, Joye, and West, *Living Atlanta,* 118.

35. On the hierarchy of domestic work, see Sutherland, *Americans and Their Servants,* 83–87.

36. Paradoxically, African American domestic workers drew similarly negative con-

clusions about the cleanliness and behavior of their white employers. "She wasn't dirty in her ways at all," concluded household worker Willie Mae Cartwright, "but the way she kept the house was a caution." Similar to the way whites attacked both the morals and environment of black workers, domestics blended notions of dirt to include both the social and the physical. Accordingly, Cartwright proclaimed, "I never worked for nobody went on this nasty kind of talk. I never heard talk like this till I come here, and nobody talks like that but folks what's cheap as gulley dirt" (Kytle, *Willie Mae*, 118, 127).

37. Isma Dooley, "Stop Prattling about Dancing and Stage Evils and Look into Health Conditions at Your Home," *Atlanta Constitution*, 1914, ALA.

38. Galishoff, "Germs," 32.

39. For a more complete discussion of this strike, see Hunter, *To 'Joy My Freedom*, 88–97.

40. Ibid, 36, 5, 44.

41. "Free Dispensary Opened to Treat Tuberculosis," *Atlanta Journal*, March 18, 1909.

42. "Negroes Rally to Science in Campaign That Is Made to Stamp out Tuberculosis," *Atlanta Journal*, November 30, 1909.

43. "Washerwomen Spread Disease through the City," *Atlanta Constitution*, March 11, 1910. The city promised to provide a hospital to treat tubercular blacks, but the institution was not slated to be built for another seventeen years (Hunter, *To 'Joy My Freedom*, 207).

44. Hunter, *To 'Joy My Freedom*, 88–97, 200–201.

45. "Washerwomen Spread Disease."

46. "The Washerwoman a Friend to Contagion," *Atlanta Constitution*, March 12, 1910.

47. Parsons, "White Plague," 197.

48. Brown, quoted in Hunter, *To 'Joy My Freedom*, 210. Hunter, "Household Workers," 221–26, contains a more complete description of Brown's platform and its relationship to the move to register domestics.

49. "Negroes Object to Servant Tags," *Atlanta Georgian*, October 5, 1912.

50. "Contagious Disease," *Atlanta Constitution*, February 4, 1914.

51. "The Servant in the House," *Atlanta Constitution*, February 3, 1914.

52. Beardsley, *History*, 102.

53. Rosa Lowe, "City Tuberculosis Program for Negroes," 1914, ALA.

54. Neverdon-Morton, *Advancement of the Race*, 160–61.

55. Brandt, *No Magic Bullet*, 59.

56. Ibid., 71–73, 77, 81.

57. V. H. Kriegshaber, "What the Community Owes to the Soldiers in the Training Camps," *City Builder*, August 1917.

58. Camp Jesup, an army mechanical repair camp, opened near Fort McPherson early in 1918. The Aviation School was located within the city limits, on the campus of Georgia Tech. The area surrounding these facilities and Fort McPherson was never as heavily patrolled as the moral zone surrounding Camp Gordon. Both Camp Jesup and the Aviation School were small, and Fort McPherson trained officers. The bulk of enlisted

men in the area, who were thought to be at the greatest risk of venereal disease, were routed through Camp Gordon.

59. Ruth Rosen reflects, "Gone were earlier concerns for the prostitute, her exploiters, and the causes of her 'downfall.' Gone was the belief in the potential transformation of sexual morality into a single standard for men and women" (*Lost Sisterhood*, 35).

60. Hobson, *Uneasy Virtue*, 165.

61. Seymour, "Summary," 390.

62. French, "Need," 11.

63. Brandt, *No Magic Bullet*, 81.

64. Deutsch, "Reconceiving the City," 207.

65. Atlanta City Council Minutes, October 21, November 18, 1918.

66. Lieutenant John W. Hart, weekly report, December 1, 1917, Records of the Public Health Service, RG 90, National Archives II (PHS).

67. Ibid.

68. Hart, weekly report, December 15, 1917, PHS.

69. Hart, weekly report, December 8, 1917, PHS.

70. Ibid.

71. Dunlap, "Reform," 364. As Mary Odem concludes, female sex reformers' original intent for these laws ultimately did not matter. These women did not control the institutions of the state and therefore could not ensure that women would be treated as "victims" once in the court system. She writes that "the law was used to humiliate and punish young women who did not conform to dominant standards of female respectability" (*Delinquent Daughters*, 185).

72. "Board to Act on Girls' Home," *Atlanta Georgian*, June 1, 1919.

73. Lieutenant John Hart reported, "The plan adopted last week in the handling of lewd women has been put into effect with the result that all women brought into the City court for sex crimes have been bound over under heavy bond to the State court, no fines being given" (weekly report, January 12, 1918, PHS). While there are no official numbers, Allan Brandt suggests that the federal government alone detained some thirty thousand women during World War I (*No Magic Bullet*, 234).

74. Physicians Report, Georgia Training School for Girls, September 1, 1918, Department of Public Welfare Collection, Georgia Department of Archives and History.

75. According to information supplied to the Chamber of Commerce by the Committee on Protective Work for Girls, six male police officers from the Atlanta force were working full time with women and girls at the time the policewomen were hired (Resolution, submitted by Virginia M. Murray, April 14, 1918, Chamber of Commerce Minutes, Atlanta Chamber of Commerce).

76. Ibid.

77. Besides providing educational programs in the city, the Committee on Protective Work for Girls assigned 150 agents to work directly with women on the streets in major cities around the country. According to Brandt, these women were "trained to survey a town's social conditions, locate runaways and camp-followers and return them to their homes" (*No Magic Bullet*, 83).

78. Minutes of Police Committee, August 12, 1919.

79. Ibid., April 26, 1920.

80. Lieutenant Hart reported to the Public Health Service, "The passage of a bill creating Home for the Feeble Minded for our state will go a long way towards eliminating the problem of prostitution." According to Hart, the law gave precedence to women of childbearing age for admission to the institution (monthly report, 1919, PHS).

81. Hobson, *Uneasy Virtue*, 78.

82. Resolution, submitted by Virginia M. Murray.

83. "Annual Report of the Chief of Police for the Year Ending December 31, 1920," Herbert T. Jenkins Collection.

84. Seymour, "Summary," 391–92.

85. Ibid., 335.

86. Spingarn, "War and Venereal Diseases," 334.

87. Hart, weekly report, December 30, 1917, PHS.

88. Minutes of Police Committee, August 9, 1921.

89. Hart, weekly report, December 15, 1917, PHS.

90. In February 1918 the Red Cross, which had chosen Atlanta as its southeastern headquarters, undertook the responsibilities of the Emory clinic, turning it into Government Clinic IX. By 1918, this clinic saw between fifteen hundred and two thousand patients a month (monthly report, July 31, 1918, PHS). Monthly reports unfortunately do not provide a breakdown of patients by gender.

91. One such factory, the Fulton Bag and Cotton Mills, seems to have consistently supplied female employees with these types of pamphlets, judging from the mills' repeated requests to the surgeon general for more material (C. C. Pierce to Fulton Bag and Cotton Mills, June 19, 1919, PHS).

92. Abercrombie, *Public Health in Georgia*, 95.

93. Brandt, *No Magic Bullet*, 79.

94. Ibid., 92.

95. Hobson, *Uneasy Virtue*, 169. Only in 1920 was the issue of hiring a female doctor for these examinations raised. The Evangelical Ministers Association of Atlanta voted in April of that year to recommend that "a trained nurse and a woman doctor should be jointly employed by the City and County to serve at the City Police Headquarters and Stockade, County Jail, and Detention Home herein after recommended, the Juvenile Detention Home and all other places where there is the possibility of venereal disease among women and girls." The city council denied this request (Evangelical Ministers Association Minutes, April 5, 1920, CCC; Atlanta City Council Minutes, April 19, 1920).

96. Hart, weekly report, December 8, 1917, PHS.

97. Ibid.

98. Minutes of Police Committee, March 29, 1923.

99. Brandt, *No Magic Bullet*, 94–95.

100. Hobson, *Uneasy Virtue*, 168.

101. American Social Hygiene Association, *Keeping Fit*, 4.

102. "Board to Act on Girls' Home," *Atlanta Georgian*, June 1, 1919.

103. "Plan to Probe City Stockade," *Atlanta Georgian*, June 3, 1919. The city council

also noted that the policy had created "a great deal of disorder and confusion" in the prison system and had led to a number of lawsuits against the city.

104. Atlanta City Council Minutes, July 10, 1919.

105. Statistics on statewide work for 1929–33 show that 41.3 percent of white patients and 52.4 percent of black patients were women (E. L. Webb, "Classification of Wassermann Reactions by Race, Sex, Age and Occupation of Patients," Georgia State Board of Health, 1929–33, PHS).

106. French, "Need," 11.

107. American Social Hygiene Association, *Keeping Fit,* 14.

108. Kriegshaber, "What the Community Owes," 7.

109. Asa G. Candler, "Atlanta's Opportunity," *City Builder,* August 1917.

110. Kriegshaber, "What the Community Owes," 8.

111. Atlanta Colored Women's War Council Minutes, 1918, NU. The "measures" to which this quotation refers were policies of driving white prostitutes out of the city.

112. Ibid.

113. Ibid.

114. Ruffin and Hope quoted in Rouse, *Lugenia Burns Hope,* 100.

115. Ibid., 94. Deborah Gray White argues that by advocating protection for all African American women, middle-class black club women were asserting themselves as race leaders and assuming the "traditional male protectionist role" ("Cost of Club Work," 257).

116. The council wanted "to inject into every girls' club the spirit of the Patriotic League" (Atlanta Colored Women's War Work Council, "Plan of Work," 1918, NU).

117. Southeastern Federation of Negro Women's Clubs, "Southern Negro Women and Race Cooperation," June 28–30, 1920, Commission on Interracial Cooperation Papers, Atlanta University Center (CIC).

118. Committee on Inter-Racial Relations, Women's Missionary Council, "The Colored Woman's Statement," May 21, 1921, CIC. This organization was the antecedent of the Women's Committee of the Commission on Interracial Cooperation.

119. Similarly, Mark Caldwell wrote that campaigns against tuberculosis "may have distorted tuberculosis and may even at times have spread misinformation about it, [but] they revealed other truths. They told us what we thought about our cities and our social relations with each other" (*Last Crusade,* 287).

SIX. *Political Alignments and Citizenship Rights*

1. *Mrs. S. A. Christian vs. S. A. Christian,* no. 40911, August 1918.

2. Deaton, "Progressive Era."

3. For reformers such as Lugenia Burns Hope, campaigns against prostitution were part of a larger social justice agenda to rid black neighborhoods of vice and generally improve conditions for blacks (Rouse, *Lugenia Burns Hope,* 130).

4. "Broyles Backs Beavers in Resort War," *Atlanta Georgian,* September 25, 1912.

5. The reports of women leaving or reforming varied widely depending on the source.

See *Atlanta Constitution,* September 27, October 7, 1912; *Atlanta Journal,* September 29, October 4, 1912; *Atlanta Georgian,* September 25, October 4, 1912.

6. Maclachlan, "Women's Work," 204.

7. According to Maclachlan, the Collins Street district was home to ten madams, sixty-five prostitutes, nine servants, and one child ("Women's Work," 208).

8. Neil, "Old Manhattan Street."

9. Garrett, *Atlanta,* 2:574.

10. "Chinamen Are Accused of Doping Little Girls."

11. See the annual reports of the Atlanta chief of police, many of which are to be found in the Herbert T. Jenkins Collection.

12. See, for example, Atlanta City Council Minutes, November 23, 1908.

13. In a campaign to bring the 1910 typographical convention to Atlanta, for example, advertisements picturing a young boy being beckoned to bed by a prostitute bearing the name *Atlanta* were passed out to attendees at the 1909 meeting (Maclachlan, "Women's Work," 211–12).

14. Bederman, " 'Church Work,' " 432–65.

15. Lefever, "Prostitution, Politics, and Religion." This article also contains a list of MRFM members, all of whom were intimately connected to elite social and business circles. This, in part, explains group members' ability to capture the ear of the municipal government in many of their campaigns.

16. M. Jackson, "Atlanta Campaign," 177–78.

17. For a description of these societies in New York, see Gilfoyle, *City of Eros,* 185–96. For another account of Progressive-era campaigns against prostitution, see R. Rosen, *Lost Sisterhood,* chap. 2.

18. Atlanta City Council Minutes, March 18, 1912.

19. Men and Religion Forward Bulletin 6, reprinted in M. Jackson, "Atlanta Campaign," 179.

20. According to Barbara Meil Hobson, despite earlier historians' focus on antiprostitution campaigns as the "last gasp of a dying moral and social order," the critique of local government and big business were common themes in the rhetoric of Progressive-era reformers (*Uneasy Virtue,* 140).

21. Men and Religion Forward to ministers of the city, May 1912, reprinted in Steeper, *John J. Eagan,* 57.

22. Letter from Marion Jackson, *American City* 9 (July 1913): 4.

23. Members of the Atlanta's African American community had been lobbying for better policing of black neighborhoods to prevent vice trades from establishing themselves there, but these efforts garnered only limited results. For a description of one organization's efforts, see Rouse, *Lugenia Burns Hope,* chap. 4.

24. Deaton, "James G. Woodward."

25. "Owner of Resorts Will Ask No Rent," *Atlanta Constitution,* September 27, 1912.

26. "Evil District to Move Across City Line into County?" *Atlanta Journal,* September 25, 1912.

27. "The Remarkable Story of How Atlanta's Police Head Determined to Wipe Out 'System' Tolerated for Years," *Atlanta Georgian,* September 25, 1912.

28. "Chief Must Not Go Too Far, Says Mason," *Atlanta Constitution,* September 29, 1912.

29. "Crusade Begins Now."

30. "Vice Commission Urges General City Clean-Up."

31. "Women Cannot Live in Houses," *Atlanta Constitution,* September 28, 1912.

32. "Owner of Resorts."

33. "286 Places Outside 'District' Defy Law."

34. "Resort Keeper Takes Her Life," *Atlanta Constitution,* September 26, 1912.

35. "Charity Workers Visit Women of Tenderloin," *Atlanta Constitution,* September 27, 1912.

36. "50 Women Hit by Vice Ban Want to Reform," *Atlanta Georgian,* October 4, 1912; "I Am Warring on Vice, Not Business, Says Chief Beavers," *Atlanta Journal,* September 29, 1912.

37. "Broyles Backs Beavers."

38. "Passing of Vice District; Don't Believe They Had Square Deal as Women Occupants See It," *Atlanta Constitution,* September 28, 1912.

39. See M. Jackson, "Atlanta Campaign," 177–78; "An Advertising Campaign against Segregated Vice," *American City* 9 (July 1913): 3–4; William T. Ellis, "Advertising a City Free from Its Vice," *The Continent,* April 3, 1913; "Atlanta's Vice Crusade"; "How Atlanta Cleaned Up."

40. On disbanding the vice squad, see Atlanta City Council Minutes, February 2, 1914. On Beavers's demotion, see M. Jackson, "Atlanta Campaign," 183.

41. Lefever, "Prostitution, Politics, and Religion," 26.

42. *Proceedings of the Twenty-sixth Annual Convention of the National American Woman Suffrage Association, 1894,* reprinted in A. Taylor, "Last Phase," 69.

43. McRae, "Caretakers of Southern Civilization"; F. Bailey, "Mildred Lewis Rutherford."

44. There are numerous accounts of the national movement: see, for example, Kraditor, *Ideas;* Flexnor, *Century of Struggle;* O'Neill, *Everyone Was Brave;* A. Scott and Scott, *One Half the People;* Cott, *Grounding.*

45. Historians differ on whether the race issue came first from southern suffragists or was raised by antisuffragists and then countered by supporters of woman suffrage. See, for example, Wheeler, *New Women,* esp. chap. 4; Lebsock, "Woman Suffrage"; Green, *Southern Strategies.*

46. For a complete discussion of these arguments, see A. Taylor, "Origin"; A. Taylor, "Last Phase"; A. Taylor, "Revival and Development."

47. Atlanta City Council Minutes, January 1, 1912.

48. Only during this decade did local newspapers begin to consistently run reports concerning city and state suffrage campaigns.

49. Emily MacDougald to Georgia presidents, January 1916, Women's Suffrage, Georgia Collection, Georgia Department of Archives and History (WSGC).

50. "Miss Eleanor [*sic*] Raoul Explains the Purpose of the Central Committee of Women's Citizens," undated newspaper clipping, WSGC.

51. "Equal Suffrage," *Journal of Labor,* October 16, 1914.

52. "Why Women Should Vote," *Atlanta Georgian,* n.d., Emma V. Paul Scrapbook, Atlanta History Center.

53. Ibid.

54. "Chivalry Is Dead without Vote, Says Jones," undated clipping, Emma V. Paul Scrapbook.

55. Fulton County Branch of the Equal Suffrage Party of Georgia, promotional leaflet, "Isn't It True," reprinted in A. Taylor, "Origin," 13; promotional leaflet, "Twelve Reasons Why Women Should Vote," wsgc.

56. "Equal Suffrage," *Journal of Labor,* October 23, 1914.

57. J. L. Rodier, quoted in Eugenia Estill, "Atlanta Equal Suffrage," *Journal of Labor,* March 27, 1914.

58. "Equal Suffrage," *Journal of Labor,* October 23, 1914.

59. Mrs. Paul Romare, "What Will We Do with the Ballot?" *Atlanta Georgian,* July 6, 1919.

60. *Minutes of the Georgia Woman Suffrage Association, 1899,* reprinted in A. Taylor, "Revival and Development," 341.

61. "Suffrage for Women," *Journal of Labor,* March 6, April 17, 1914.

62. E. Estill, "Suffrage for Women," *Journal of Labor,* March 6, 1914.

63. A.S.B., "Leo Frank's Murder," *Atlanta Georgian,* August 28, 1915.

64. During this time, Harriot Stanton Blatch headed a similarly militant suffrage organization in New York that focused much of its efforts toward organizing working women. See E. DuBois, "Working Women."

65. Grace Mary Keefer to Eleonore Raoul, June 18, 1915, Raoul Family Papers, Special Collections, Robert W. Woodruff Library, Emory University.

66. "Equal Suffrage," *Journal of Labor,* January 22, 1914.

67. Mary L. McLendon to Mary Ware Dennett, July 14, 1913, wsgc.

68. Emily MacDougald to National American Woman Suffrage Association, November 16, 1915, wsgc.

69. Emily MacDougald to National American Woman Suffrage Association, November 17, 1915, wsgc.

70. Emma V. Paul Scrapbook.

71. Mary McLendon to Mary Sumner Boyd, August 12, 1916, wsgc.

72. While Atlantans generally favored ratification, the rest of Georgia vehemently opposed the imposition of a federal amendment on what many felt was a state issue. Consequently, the state legislature, in which rural districts held an inordinate amount of power, scrambled to be the first state to officially refuse to ratify the national amendment. For more on state's-rights issues and women's suffrage, see Wheeler, *New Women,* chap. 5.

73. There was something of a battle over this name, because several members objected to calling themselves citizens before the Nineteenth Amendment had passed.

74. "400 Atlanta Women Qualify to Cast Ballots," *Atlanta Constitution,* May 27, 1919.

75. Mrs. J. T. Akridge, First Ward chairman, to potential voters, July 18, 1919, wsgc.

A few of the canvasing forms remain in the records of the organization. While they do not show a great amount of success in finding women at home or willing to register, they reveal the characteristic good spirits in which organizers approached their task. One member, after a long day of "not interested" and "violently opposed" responses, recorded for one address, "No one home but a flea, and he bit me!" (League of Women Voters, Atlanta Collection, Georgia Department of Archives and History).

76. Mayor James L. Key to Chief of Police J. L. Beaver, July 24, 1919, wsgc.

77. Central Committee of Woman Citizens to the Democratic Executive Committee, August 7, 1919, wsgc.

78. Eleonore Raoul, untitled manuscript, Eleonore Raoul Suffrage Papers, 1915–20, Raoul Family Papers.

79. Resolution of the Central Committee of Women Citizens, August 5, 1919, wsgc. During the summer, numerous mass meetings were held across the city to generate suggestions on how to spend the funds. While no final conclusion was ever reached, educational and recreational causes garnered the most support.

80. Despite all these attempts, the 1874 city charter still governed Atlanta. See Bolden, "Political Structure."

81. Mrs. Standford Gay, "Every Citizen an Intelligent Voter," *Journal of Labor,* April 11, 1924.

82. P. Baker, "Domestication of Politics."

83. Kelley, "Black Poor," 295; J. Scott, *Domination,* 183–84; Gurin and Tilly, *Women, Politics, and Change,* 4–7; Ginzberg, *Work of Benevolence.*

84. Minutes of the Wesley House Woman's Club, November 18, 1910–April 5, 1917.

85. Hall, "Smith's Progressive Era," 177–79, 181.

86. "Work of the Neighborhood Union," *Spelman Messenger,* November 1916.

87. Draft of the Annual Report, 1912, nu.

88. Robin Kelley, " 'Not What We Seem,' " 83.

89. A local ordinance passed in 1900 required racial segregation on streetcars and dictated that whites would fill cars from front to back and blacks would fill cars from back to front. As more whites boarded a car, however, blacks would be forced to relinquish their seats and stand at the rear.

90. Philip Ethington mapped this phenomenon for Chicago in "Race and Space."

91. Interview with Alice Adams, lac.

92. Ibid.

93. *Mrs. Ethel W. McElroy vs. E. W. McElroy,* no. 39198, December 1917.

94. Riley, *Divorce,* 133.

95. Third Title of Domestic Relations, chap. 1, art. 1, sec. 2, *Code of the State of Georgia,* 788. Total divorces were also granted in cases where mental incapacity; prohibited degrees of consanguinity and affinity; impotency; pregnancy of the wife unknown to the husband; or force, fraud, or duress existed at the time of marriage.

96. The cases cited in this chapter were gathered from the Fulton County Superior Court, Civil Division (fccd). I reviewed a random sampling of fifty cases from 1915–38, the earliest years for which dockets exist. Superior Court records are not currently stored

or processed for access by researchers, which makes gathering any larger sample of cases nearly impossible at this time.

97. *Freemont Thompson vs. Josephine Thompson,* no. 39261, December 1917, FCCD.

98. *C. V. Arnold vs. Mrs. Ada G. Arnold,* no. 35497, April 1916, FCCD.

99. *Herbert G. Lake vs. Susannah Lake,* no. 57995, September 1923, FCCD.

100. *H. C. Petree vs. Mrs. H. C. Petree,* no. 60333, May 1924, FCCD.

101. *Visalia Davis vs. Herbert Davis,* no. 36845, June 1912, FCCD.

102. On this trend nationally, see Cott, *Public Vows,* 169.

103. *A. M. McElreath vs. Lena McElreath,* no. 48188, May 1921, FCCD.

104. *Mrs. Lois M. Griffin vs. Ralph P. Griffin,* no. 34301, September 1915, FCCD.

105. *Mrs. Beulah Jones vs. William Jones,* no. 43172, November 1924, FCCD.

106. *Charles S. Davis vs. Irmalee Davis,* no. 55313, November 1922, FCCD. It appears from the record that both of the Davises were African American. This is one of many cases in which no final decree was ever issued on the petition for divorce. The records remain unclear as to why the case was never completed.

107. *Wilborn M. O'Connor vs. Janie May O'Connor,* no. 40290, June 1918, FCCD.

108. *Wilborn M. O'Connor vs. Mrs. Janie O'Connor,* no. 606236, May 1924, FCCD.

109. Hall, "Smith's Progressive Era," 184.

110. O. Delight Smith, "The Rank and File," *Journal of Labor,* September 15, 1911; Hall, "Smith's Progressive Era," 182; Hall, "Private Eyes, Public Women," 257–58.

111. *Dorothy Dean O'Brien vs. John L. O'Brien,* no. 47905, March 1921, FCCD.

112. In my random sample of fifty cases, only four contained any evidence of property ownership or other indicators of middle- or upper-class status.

113. Riley, *Divorce,* 145.

114. "The American Forum: Why Have Divorces Increased?" *Atlanta Georgian,* June 29, 1919.

115. "Judge Bell Sees Laxity of Laws as the Leading Cause," *Atlanta Georgian,* June 29, 1919.

116. "Dr. Memminger Outlines Many Causes Briefly," *Atlanta Georgian,* June 29, 1919.

117. For a similar conclusion about Chicago, see Meyerowitz, *Women Adrift,* esp. chap. 6.

118. Minutes of Police Committee, March 2, 1920. When Ball claimed he had returned the revolver, the committee dropped the charges. Both Culver and her neighbor were African American.

119. Minutes of Police Committee, November 11, 1919.

120. Minutes of Police Committee, July 13, 1920.

121. "Charges Officer Made Approaches," *Atlanta Constitution,* May 8, 1913. In arguing the unconstitutionality of the order to vacate, Attorneys Gober and Jackson emphasized that forcing Mrs. Powell to leave would "also break up her home."

122. Minutes of Police Committee, November 28, 1923.

123. Quoted in "Slander Charges Made by Woman, Denied by Warden," *Atlanta Journal,* January 1922, clipping file, CSFC.

124. Ibid. The main opponent of the city warden's office had long been the Associated Charities. The charities followed this case closely, clipping newspaper articles chronicling the suit and accepting Harper as a client (no. 10429). The political enemies to which Johnson was referring were not part of the Associated Charities, however. In March 1922 Johnson told the press that he had been framed by an unnamed "city officer" after foiling a real estate deal with the board of education ("Slander Charges," *Atlanta Journal,* January 1922, clipping file, CSFC).

125. "$10,000 Slander Suit Is Filed against Warden," *Atlanta Constitution,* January 1922, clipping file, CSFC.

126. Only after the suit was dropped did Johnson call on the city council to impeach local officials whom he suspected of masterminding the lawsuit ("$10,000 Damage Suit a Frame-up, City Warden Says," *Atlanta Journal,* March 3, 1922).

127. Atlanta City Council Minutes, November 20, December 18, 1916, January 1, 1917.

128. Atlanta City Council Minutes, December 20, 1915.

129. Atlanta City Council Minutes, February 5, 1917.

SEVEN. *The Transitional Twenties*

1. Norwood, *Labor's Flaming Youth,* 201, 221, 259; Rose Hickey Quinn to Kate Lumpkin, February 16, 1921, Kate Richardson Lumpkin Papers, Atlanta History Center; "Hickey-Quinn Wedding," *Journal of Labor,* November 12, 1920; Mrs. E. L. Quinn, "History of the Industrial Department," *Journal of Labor,* May 5, 1932.

2. A legislative effort to provide more work hours for men by restricting the number of hours women could legally work only momentarily revived her prominence in January 1931.

3. For an example of how this process has fooled even some historians, see Storrs, *Civilizing Capitalism,* 82–83. Storrs explains Rose Hickey Quinn's prominent place at a 1931 statewide labor meeting as being "enhanced by the fact that Quinn's husband was a prominent local labor leader." Storrs seems completely unaware of the strong labor credentials Rose Hickey Quinn had brought to the marriage.

4. Hall, "Smith's Progressive Era," 167. Smith left Atlanta sometime after 1915, returning only to divorce her husband and reclaim her right to marry again. She appeared in Portland, Oregon, in 1920 and continued her activism there, much as Hickey did in Atlanta.

5. Greenwald, *Women, War, and Work,* 196–202.

6. Ibid., 198.

7. For a lengthier description of the reasons for national labor unrest in the telephone industry, see Norwood, *Labor's Flaming Youth,* 162–69.

8. Norwood, *Labor's Flaming Youth,* 200.

9. "Demands of Atlanta Telephone Workers May Tie up Whole Nation," *Atlanta Georgian,* June 2, 1919.

10. "Phones Tied Up; 750 Girls Leave Switchboards," *Atlanta Georgian,* June 2, 1919.

11. Ibid.

12. "Another Conference May Be Asked by Strikers," *Atlanta Georgian,* June 28, 1919.

13. "Telephone Strike Situation" (Southern Bell advertisement), *Atlanta Georgian,* June 3, 1919; "Phones Tied Up"; "No Right to Strike, Burleson Says; It's a Fight to Finish, Say Telephone Workers," *Atlanta Georgian,* June 3, 1919.

14. "Phones Tied Up."

15. "No Right to Strike."

16. "Many Operators Coming to Atlanta," *Atlanta Constitution,* June 5, 1919.

17. "A. F. of T. Takes Hand in Strike," *Atlanta Georgian,* June 30, 1919.

18. "Telephone Girls Stand Firm and Loyally to Course," *Journal of Labor,* July 5, 1919.

19. "Phone Operators Return to Work," *Atlanta Constitution,* July 30, 1919. All unionized operatives who were rehired were to be on twelve months of probation, virtually assuring that organizing efforts would cease for the next year.

20. "Phone Strike Over," *Journal of Labor,* August 1, 1919.

21. Norwood, *Labor's Flaming Youth,* 7; Deutsch, *Women,* 206.

22. Faue, *Suffering and Struggle,* 53.

23. "Preparedness in Georgia," *City Builder,* May 1916.

24. "Women and the War," *Journal of Labor,* September 13, 1916.

25. "Equal Pay for Women Vital Industrial Problem," *Atlanta Georgian,* July 1, 1919.

26. Interview with Chaddie Wertham, support for bulletin 22, U.S. Department of Labor, Women's Bureau.

27. "What of the Woman Who Has Taken the Man's Place?" *Journal of Labor,* October 4, 1918.

28. Interview with Miss Hines, support for bulletin 22, U.S. Department of Labor, Women's Bureau.

29. Maclachlan, "Women's Work," 377, 378. In 1920, 32.6 percent of the city's labor force was female, compared to 36.6 percent in 1900 and 33.8 percent in 1910. The number of women working declined, and jobs for men expanded faster. In 1920, 51.9 percent of the female workforce was black, and 47.8 percent was white. In 1930, 51.5 percent of female workers were black, and 48.5 percent were white. Alice Kessler-Harris concludes that changes in workforce compositions and job typing were, "from a structural perspective . . . insignificant" (*Out to Work,* 219).

30. Weiner, *Working Girl,* 27.

31. Summer Students in Industry, 1922, Industrial Department Records, YWCA National Board Archives.

32. Ada Virginia Colvin, "The Atlanta Opportunity School," *City Builder,* August 1916.

33. Emma Harris, "A Day of Opportunity," *Journal of Labor,* February 27, 1925.

34. "Atlanta's Opportunity School," *Journal of Labor,* March 21, 1931.

35. Maude Thornton, cochair of the Citizenship Committee of the Atlanta Woman's Club, started teaching an "Americanization" course in 1925 (Edna V. Farmer, "Atlanta Opportunity School Spring Activities," *Journal of Labor,* May 1, 1925).

36. Marks, *Farewell;* L. Rosen, *South Side;* Lemann, *Promised Land;* Henri, *Black Migration,* chap. 2; and Phillips, *AlabamaNorth.*

37. R. Baker, "Negro Goes North," 319.

38. Contemporary observers and historians alike have too often viewed the migration as a rural South to urban North phenomenon, but southern cities such as Norfolk and Atlanta served as stopping points in a migration chain as well as destinations for many rural blacks. On this point, see Lewis, "Expectations," 22–45; Marks, *Farewell.*

39. Macon, for example, used the state law to require labor agents to pay a twenty-five thousand dollar fee and produce recommendations from ten local ministers, ten local manufacturers, and twenty-five local businessmen before they could recruit in the city (Dittmer, *Black Georgia,* 188).

40. James Grossman, "Black Labor," 61; Henri, *Black Migration,* 54; Ottley, *Lonely Warrior,* 164. See reprints of Richard D. Stinson's letters to the *Constitution* in the *Atlanta Independent,* January 25, February 1, 1919. A similar sentiment appeared in national dialogues and scholarly studies of the migration. See, for example, Woofter, "Migration of Negroes," 89.

41. *Atlanta Independent,* May 26, 1917, September 27, 1919.

42. *Atlanta Independent,* October 16, 1920, May 26, 1921.

43. *Atlanta Independent,* May 26, 1917.

44. *Atlanta Independent,* September 27, 1919 (emphasis added).

45. For an intriguing suggestion that the moral panic associated with black women in Atlanta in early decades may have moved North in the 1920s with the migration, see Carby, "Black Woman's Body."

46. For a northern-focused and more positive assessment of the changes the black club woman movement underwent in the 1920s, see Higginbotham, "In Politics to Stay." On white women, see Deutsch, "From Ballots to Breadlines"; Cott, *Grounding.*

47. Hickey, " 'Meet Me' "; Roth, *Matronage;* Judson, " 'New South' City," 171.

48. Atlanta Colored Women's War Council Minutes, 1918, NU.

49. Mays, *Born to Rebel,* 98. For assessments of this shift in black leadership, see Hickey, "Auburn Avenue," 109–43; Ferguson, "Politics of Inclusion."

50. Moderate black leaders of the 1940s tended to marginalize these women because of the challenges their activism raised (Nasstrom, "Women," 2, 33).

51. This branch of the Commission on Interracial Cooperation eventually spawned the Association of Southern Women for the Prevention of Lynching. For a complete analysis of the association's work as well as background on the commission, see Hall, *Revolt,* 60–65, 86–106, 159–221. On a shift toward interracialism among other black club women, see Gilmore, *Gender and Jim Crow.*

52. "Women as Citizens," *Journal of Labor,* October 2, 1925.

53. Sarah Deutsch argues that elite women in Boston "disappeared in party offices or behind the endorsements of male-dominated reform organizations" in the 1920s. Club women thought they no longer needed working-class women, "but without them, those elite women also lost visibility" (*Women,* 282).

54. Judson, " 'New South' City," 171.

55. Editors of the *Journal of Labor* cautioned the organization to "recognize [the]

distinct differences in points of view between men and women" and keep its focus on women ("Why Change the Name of the League of Women Voters?" *Journal of Labor,* July 29, 1932).

56. Cott, "Across the Great Divide," 153–76.

57. "Note of Warning from Mildred Seydell," *Journal of Labor,* January 31, 1936; "Where Do the Women Go?" *Journal of Labor,* August 25, 1932.

58. Quoted in K. Jackson, *Ku Klux Klan,* 38. On the Klan in Atlanta politics, see Moseley, "Invisible Empire," 45–50.

59. MacLean, *Behind the Mask,* 27–33.

60. For a description of the unofficial policing pursued by the Klan in Atlanta in the 1920s, see Kuhn, Joye, and West, *Living Atlanta,* 313–20; Jenkins, *Forty Years,* 15–16.

61. Quoted in Blee, *Women of the Klan,* 23.

62. Kuhn, Joye, and West, *Living Atlanta,* 311.

63. Quoted in Kuhn, Joye, and West, *Living Atlanta,* 311.

64. Fifteen city officials ultimately were convicted, including Walter C. Taylor, the city clerk with whom the Atlanta League of Women Voters had battled during the debate of the dispersal of women's registration fees in 1919. For a complete list of guilty officials and their sentences, see Garrett, *Atlanta,* 2:868.

65. "A Survey of the Opinions of a Hundred Heads of Families Respecting Washington Park," E. Franklin Frazier, director, December 1924, NU.

66. Ibid.

67. "Some Facts That the Public Does Not Know about Washington Park," John J. Eagan Collection, Atlanta History Center.

68. Radio speech on WSB to grades 5 and 6, October 18, 1926, 1926 Scrapbook, ALA.

69. "Suggestions for Residential Open Air School," 1922, ALA.

70. In their studies of U.S. social welfare history, Michael Katz and William Trattner found evidence of this "child-saving" movement beginning in the 1880s, at least in the Northeast. See Katz, *Poorhouse,* chap. 5; Trattner, *Poor Law,* 114–20.

71. "Field of the Family Welfare Society," 1934, CSFC.

72. "Stories Illustrating the Effect of Inadequate Relief," 1932, CSFC.

73. "A Story of Wesley Community House and of Some of the Peoples It Has Served," unpublished manuscript, Ladies Board of City Missions, Wesley Community Center.

74. The most complete case studies for this period appear in the papers of Comer Woodward's social work students, who studied FWS cases from the 1920s. See, for example, John W. Vann, "Case Read and Visited Under the Supervision of the Family Welfare Society of Atlanta, GA.," and Willard C. Hay, "Report in Sociology 10 on Desertion Case from Case no. 11423, Family Welfare Society," Comer McDonald Woodward Collection.

75. "The Estimate of Field Work of Family Welfare Society for 1924," CSFC.

76. In 1926 the Community Chest allocated $8,968.52 to the FWS, $2,500 more than to any other city organization (Atlanta Community Chest, General Financial Statement, March 1, 1927, CSFC).

77. The Community Chest refused to fund the Neighborhood Union for two reasons. First, the Urban League, frustrated that the Neighborhood Union would not join

the league, blackballed the union with the Community Chest between 1924 and 1925. Second, the Neighborhood Union began fund-raising in black communities to support the programs formerly funded by the Community Chest. Chest organizers felt that this practice seriously undermined the contributions African Americans usually gave to the chest. The Neighborhood Union had to agree to turn over all funds raised to the Community Chest. Unfortunately, the records of the Community Chest (part of the CSFC collection) and the Atlanta branch of the Urban League are silent on this incident. A fairly one-sided account of these events appears in Shivery, "Organized Social Work," 264–66, 288.

78. See Annual Reports of the Chief of Police, Herbert T. Jenkins Collection; Hickey, "Waging War."

79. "Georgia's Fight against Dependency and Delinquency: Report to the Legislature of the Work of the Department of Public Welfare," March 1, 1921, Department of Public Welfare Collection.

80. Ibid.

81. Report of the Superintendent, June 1, 1919, Georgia Training School for Girls Collection, Department of Public Welfare Collection, Georgia Department of Archives and History.

82. Annual Report of the Board of Managers of the Georgia Training School for Girls, January 1, 1927, Department of Public Welfare Collection.

83. *Mrs. Lennie Belle Aaron vs. A. E. Aaron,* no. 60521, 1925, FCCD.

84. Riley, *Divorce,* 133.

85. *Mrs. Lennie Belle Aaron vs. A. E. Aaron,* no. 60521, 1925, FCCD.

86. *Louise Talley Griffith vs. Alexander Griffith,* no. 66214, December 1925, FCCD.

87. *Annie Lou Duncan vs. H. C. Duncan,* no. 76634, May 1928; *Lizzie Aaron vs. Charlie Aaron,* no. 105344, December 1934; *Bernice Treadway Jones vs. Winston K. Jones,* no. 85909, March 1935, FCCD.

88. Woofter, "Migration of Negroes," 75.

89. Maclachlan, "Women's Work," 5.

90. Hine, "Black Migration," 131.

91. Hunter, *To 'Joy My Freedom,* 233–37.

92. Letter from unnamed female migrant, April 11, 1917, quoted in Adero, *Up South,* 114.

93. Minutes of Police Committee, May 16, 1923.

94. Minutes of Police Committee, August 15, 1923.

95. Minutes of Police Committee, October 10, 1923. This is one of the few cases in which the woman named in the incident did not testify.

96. Minutes of Police Committee, April 30, 1931.

97. Minutes of Police Committee, June 12, 1925.

98. Minutes of Police Committee, August 12, 1925.

99. H. Rosen, " 'Not That Sort of Women,' " 272–74, 277.

100. Histories of black and white southern women in particular point to white men's sexual access to black women during slavery (Hine, "Inner Lives"; J. Jones, *Labor of Love;*

Deborah White, *Ar'n't I a Woman?* 164; A. Scott, *Southern Lady;* Fox-Genovese, *Within the Plantation Household*).

101. Bardaglio, " 'Shameful Matches,' " 113, 122; McLaurin, *Celia;* Williamson, *Rage,* 28.

102. W. D. McMichen was dismissed from the force after being accused of having "carnal knowledge and connections against the order of nature with Roscoe Cagle" and several other men (Minutes of Police Committee, December 15, 1932).

103. Deutsch, *Women,* 237.

EIGHT. *The Forgotten Man Remembered*

1. There are numerous accounts of Herndon's arrest and trial. The most complete are A. Herndon, *Let Me Live;* C. Martin, *Herndon Case.* See also Martin's condensed "Herndon Case."

2. Legislators passed the original law in the 1830s to counter slave rebellions and the growing northern abolitionist movement. The law was revised in 1866 and 1871 to provide specific punishment for insurrection and "an attempt to incite insurrection" (C. Martin, *Herndon Case,* 20–21).

3. A. Herndon, *Let Me Live,* 221–22.

4. "Striking Worker Is Killed by Auto," *Atlanta Constitution,* September 12, 1934; see also C. Martin, *Herndon Case,* 124, 129, 212.

5. Young later changed her last name to Washburn (interview with Nannie Washburn, LAC).

6. "Atlanta's Unemployed," *Journal of Labor,* January 16, 1931.

7. D. Smith, *New Deal,* 15–16.

8. Harry Hopkins, quoted in Garrett, *Atlanta,* 2:916–18.

9. Kytle, *Willie Mae,* 170.

10. Interview with Nellie Bryant, LAC.

11. Kytle, *Willie Mae,* 171–72.

12. Bond hearing for Annie Mae Leathers and Nannie Leah Young, Fulton County Superior Court, 1934, ILD.

13. "Summary of Research Projects of the Research Department of the Atlanta School of Social Work, 1931–1933," NU.

14. Moore, "Communists and Fascists," 443–56. Actual dues-paying members numbered only twelve hundred during this period. One enterprising businessman even began marketing black shirts to organization members ("Black Shirts" [advertisement], *Atlanta Journal,* August 3, 1930).

15. Black Shirt editorial, reprinted in *Pittsburgh Courier,* September 6, 1930, quoted in C. Martin, "White Supremacy," 370.

16. Kuhn, Joye, and West, *Living Atlanta,* 202–5.

17. Interview with Glenn Rainy, LAC.

18. Here I differ significantly with Douglas Smith's conclusion that in 1930 "unemployment was affecting few in Atlanta and was not seen as threatening" (*New Deal,* 28).

19. For a more complete description of the demise of the Black Shirts, including the role of newspapers outside of Atlanta, see Moore, "Communists and Fascists"; C. Martin, "White Supremacy," 366–81.

20. *Pittsburgh Courier,* September 13, 27, 1930, quoted in C. Martin, "White Supremacy," 381.

21. Before coming to Atlanta, Herndon had been an organizer in Alabama, where he was also arrested. See Kelley, *Hammer and Hoe,* 15, 18, 38.

22. C. Martin, *Herndon Case,* 29, 129.

23. *Daily Worker,* March 22, 1932, quoted in ibid., 26.

24. Ibid., 128–29.

25. A. Herndon, *Let Me Live,* 167. Communists formed similar unemployment councils in other cities; see, for example, L. Cohen, *Making a New Deal,* 261–65.

26. Martin, *Herndon Case,* 6; "20,000 Atlantans to Be without Aid from Relief Body," *Atlanta Constitution,* June 17, 1932. The *Atlanta Constitution* estimated that only four thousand families (or twenty thousand individuals) would be affected by the closing of the relief office). Herndon claimed the incredibly high figure of twenty-three thousand families left without aid when he recorded the event in his autobiography (*Let Me Live,* 188).

27. A. Herndon, *Let Me Live,* 242, 219.

28. Daisy E. Lampkin to Roy Wilkins, n.d. [1933], National Association for the Advancement of Colored People, Atlanta Branch Papers, Manuscript Division, Library of Congress (NAACP).

29. Daisy E. Lampkin to Roy Wilkins, February 4, 1933, NAACP.

30. "Four More Mills Cease Operation in Atlanta Area," *Atlanta Constitution,* September 11, 1934.

31. "Mediator Goes to Capitol," *Atlanta Georgian,* September 6, 1934.

32. Greer withdrew from the case before the women went to trial, but there is no evidence that any sexual overtones had been attached to his representation through the indictment and bond hearings. The state eventually dropped the insurrection charges against Young and Leathers and the "Atlanta Six" in 1939, two years after the Supreme Court had ruled Georgia's insurrection law unconstitutional.

33. Recorder A. W. Calloway, quoted in C. Martin, *Herndon Case,* 70.

34. Imperial Klaliff, "Georgia's Dangers," *Kourier* 6 (September 1930): 8–12, quoted in C. Martin, "White Supremacy," 373.

35. "Farmers, Housewives, Employees Protest Chain Store Tax," *Journal of Labor,* March 19, 1937.

36. "Women in the Field of Labor," *Journal of Labor,* March 16, 1928. The backlash against women working was part of a national trend in the 1930s. See Kessler-Harris, *Out to Work,* 250–72; Ware, *Beyond Suffrage;* Scharf, *To Work.*

37. Kessler-Harris, *Out to Work,* 201–5, 251; Kessler-Harris, *Woman's Wage;* Faue, *Suffering and Struggle,* esp. chap. 3; Wandersee, *Women's Work;* Weiner, *Working Girl;* S. Kennedy, *Weep at Home.*

38. Kessler-Harris, *Out to Work,* 268–69.

39. L. Cohen, *Making a New Deal,* esp. chaps. 7, 8.

40. "Night Shifts for Women and Children," *Journal of Labor,* August 20, 1931.

41. "The Idea of Community Responsibility," *Journal of Labor,* February 4, 1932.

42. Hall et al., *Like a Family.*

43. "Four More Mills Cease Operations."

44. Ibid.

45. Even though organized labor in Atlanta abandoned the interests of working women, the *Journal of Labor* still allowed YWCA officials to publish short articles and notices of activities. This may indicate union support for the YWCA's classes and meals, which helped keep unemployed women out of relief offices.

46. The Phyllis Wheatley branch of Atlanta's YWCA began after World War I and grew steadily through the 1920s and 1930s. By 1936, work in the city's African American communities had grown enough to merit a move to a much larger building. See Cohron, "Study," 5–7.

47. "Camp Highland Will Be Scene of YWCA Meet," *Journal of Labor,* September 8, 1932.

48. "The Jobless Business Girl," *Journal of Labor,* August 20, 1931. Typical of the editorial board during the Great Depression, the paper supported this line of questioning but reminded readers that the YWCA existed to deal with these women.

49. For an account of these other worker-education programs, see Fredrickson, " 'Place to Speak Our Minds' "; Fredrickson, "Recognizing Regional Differences"; Fredrickson, "Southern Summer School."

50. Georgia Mae Marchbanks, "Purpose," 1935, ALES.

51. "The Southern Summer School for Women Workers in Industry, 1928," ALES.

52. Ira Reid, quoted in "Findings of the Workers' Education Conference Held in Atlanta," February 9–10, 1935, ALES.

53. Dorothy Gardner, "An Investigation into Student Activities, 1927–1937," ALES.

54. Hickey, "Auburn Avenue."

55. Marion Roydhouse has argued that these ideas often found little support among middle-class leaders in the YWCA itself, outside of the industrial department, because of the massive changes to the economic and social system advocated by the workers' education platforms. Roydhouse concludes that "the Southern YWCA would never be as active in labor issues as the most 'advanced' working women or staff wanted it to be" ("Bridging Chasms," 278).

56. Hickey, "Auburn Avenue," 121.

57. Benjamin Mays, "Is the South Better?" *Pittsburgh Courier,* June 15, 1946.

58. Partial transcript of interview with Benjamin Mays, LAC.

59. Led by the educational elite, Atlanta's blacks used bond elections to their advantage in gaining desperately needed school improvements in the late 1910s and 1920s. See Kuhn, Joye, and West, *Living Atlanta,* 138; Dittmer, *Black Georgia,* 147–48.

60. Pomerantz, *Peachtree,* 125–27. The formation of this organization created a rift between Dobbs and A. T. Walden, and the fallout from this conflict contributed to Walden's removal from the leadership of the local NAACP branch.

61. These citizenship programs drew high praise from the national NAACP (May–November 1932 folder, branch files, series I, NAACP).

62. Partial transcript of interview with C. A. Scott, LAC.

63. Mays, *Born to Rebel*, 98.

64. In 1931, the Family Welfare Society (FWS) again confronted the city warden on this discriminatory policy. The society appears to have held enough power to force the warden's office to interview all applicants and expand its caseload (Minutes of the Family Welfare Society, December 9, 1931, CSFC).

65. During these years, the FWS functioned as the clearinghouse for all direct assistance in the city. The FWS asked the Neighborhood Union to direct all applicants for aid to the FWS, which would record the case, make sure that the family was not already being assisted, and then turn the family back over to the Neighborhood Union for relief.

66. Before this time, a handful of teachers were given to public and private agencies running adult education classes, and most of these jobs were filled by women.

67. District Secretaries Meeting, May 18, 1932, CSFC.

68. Kytle, *Willie Mae*, 7.

69. Interview with Nellie Bryant, LAC.

70. Interview with Sanders Ivey, LAC.

71. Minutes of the Neighborhood Union, May 9, 1934, NU.

72. Shivery, "Organized Social Work," 320, 354.

73. "Report Blank for 1931," West Side Unemployment Relief Committee, NU.

74. Interview with Nellie Blackshear, LAC.

75. District Secretaries Meeting, February 3, 1932, CSFC.

76. Rhoda Kaufman to Kendall Wisiger, April 15, 1932, CSFC.

77. Minutes of Staff Meeting, August 15, 1934, CSFC.

78. Shivery, "Organized Social Work," 336–37.

79. For a more complete account, see Fleming, "New Deal in Atlanta."

80. Augusta Dunbar, quoted in Kuhn, Joye, and West, *Living Atlanta*, 207.

81. Talmadge feared losing the power of patronage in crucial rural counties once federal money arrived. He also resented the control a woman, Gay B. Shepperson, had over federal money in the state, federal interference and spending in a time of depression, race-blind aid programs, and what he felt was excessive aid for urban areas (Fleming, "Atlanta, the Depression, and the New Deal," 25; Anderson, *Wild Man*, 92–93, 129–31, 164; Logue, *Eugene Talmadge*, 111, 125, 129, 151; J. Herndon, "Georgia's 'Little New Deal' "; Patterson, *New Deal*, 138–39).

82. Speaker Pro Tem Ellis Arnall, quoted in "Relief in Georgia," *Atlanta Georgian*, February 11, 1935.

83. D. Smith, "Continuity and Change," 7–8. See also Biles, *South*.

84. For more on these projects, see Lyon, "Planning for Atlanta"; Beard, "Hurt's Deserted Village"; Preston, " 'New South' Progressivism"; Crimmins, "Bungalow Suburbs"; Dana White, "Landscaped Atlanta"; Beard, "Defended Neighborhood."

85. Radford, *Modern Housing*, 178.

86. Speech quoted in Torrence, *John Hope*, 356.

87. C. Palmer, *Slum Fighter,* 9.

88. Ibid., 12.

89. Jenkins, *Forty Years,* 15. Total arrest rates increased from 31,000 in 1928 to 41,500 in 1931. Arrests for disorderly conduct and drunkenness in particular soared during the depression (Annual Reports of the Chief of Police, Herbert T. Jenkins Collection).

90. Shivery, "Organized Social Work," 324.

91. C. Palmer, *Slum Fighter,* 7.

92. Quoted in Kuhn, Joye, and West, *Living Atlanta,* 46.

93. Preston Stevens and Edith Henderson, quoted in ibid., 47.

94. Interview with Nellie Blackshear, LAC.

95. Quoted in Kuhn, Joye, and West, *Living Atlanta,* 50. On the class implications of the public housing projects among blacks, see Hickey, "Auburn Avenue"; Ferguson, "Politics of Inclusion."

96. Quoted in Kuhn, Joye, and West, *Living Atlanta,* 51.

97. Ibid., 50–53.

98. Partial transcript of interview with L. D. Milton, LAC.

99. Ibid. Karen Ferguson argues at length that the needs of the black working class were sacrificed for federal housing reform. She also concludes that the residents of John Hope Homes and University Homes fulfilled the political aspirations the black elite had for them by providing crucial votes in a 1946 election ("Politics of Inclusion," chap. 8).

100. Partial transcript of interview with Clarence Bacote, LAC.

101. Ferguson, "Politics of Inclusion," 1–7

102. Quoted in Kuhn, Joye, and West, *Living Atlanta,* 51.

103. Kytle, *Willie Mae,* 6.

104. See Hall et al., *Like a Family,* 328–40.

105. Holmes, " 'Jim Crow Bird' "; Arthur Raper quoted in Kuhn, Joye, and West, *Living Atlanta,* 214. On these issues nationally, see Kirby, *Black Americans,* esp. chap. 6.

106. Quoted in Kuhn, Joye, and West, *Living Atlanta,* 214.

107. Quoted in Kurzman, *Harry Hopkins,* 122.

108. On the New Deal's general masculinist focus, see Mettler, *Dividing Citizens;* Allen, "Fallen Women"; Melosh, *Engendering Culture.*

109. "A History of the Georgia Civil Works Administration, 1933–1934," Gay Bolling Shepperson Papers, 1920–48, Atlanta History Center. On New Deal work relief generally, see Singleton, *American Dole,* esp. chap. 5.

110. Wandersee, *Women's Work,* 97.

111. "Women's Work in Georgia under the Civil Works Administration," Jane Van De Vrede, Works Projects Administration Records and Other Papers, Georgia Department of Archives and History.

112. Ibid.

113. Bond Hearing for Annie Mae Leathers and Nannie Leah Young, Fulton County Superior Court, 1934, ILD.

114. Minutes of the District Secretaries Meeting, February 3, 1932, CSFC.

115. "Stories Illustrating the Effects of Inadequate Relief," June 28, 1932, CSFC.

116. "Women after the Plums," *Journal of Labor*, August 24, 1934.

117. For a description of how the biases of these New Deal programs affected women of another city, see Blackwelder, *Women of the Depression*, esp. chap. 7.

118. Kytle, *Willie Mae*, 174.

119. Holmes, *New Deal in Georgia*, 132.

120. Swain, "New Deal," 249.

121. Corley, "National Youth Administration," 750–51.

122. Blacks faired relatively well in the New Deal programs in Atlanta compared to rural areas of the South. African Americans received jobs in rough proportion to their percentage of the city's unemployed. Of course, they tended to be placed more often than not in unskilled and poorly paid jobs (D. Smith, *New Deal*, 98).

Conclusion

1. T. Martin, *Atlanta*, 2:115.

2. Maclachlan, "Women's Work," 379.

3. Boyer, *Urban Masses*.

4. Hershberg, *Philadelphia*.

5. See Mohl, "American Urban History." On the promising intersection of cultural and urban history, see Gilfoyle, "White Cities."

Manuscript Sources

Atlanta Chamber of Commerce. Records of the Atlanta Chamber of Commerce.

Atlanta History Center. Atlanta City Council Minutes. Atlanta City Directory (1897–1916, 1918–40). Atlanta Lung Association Papers (ALA). Atlanta Woman's Club Collection. Jennie Meta Barker Collection. Child Service and Family Counseling Papers (CSFC). Christian Council of Atlanta Collection (CCC). John J. Eagan Collection, 1870–1924. Hillside Cottages Collection. Herbert T. Jenkins Collection. Joseph C. Logan Papers. Kate Richardson Lumpkin Collection. Minutes of Police Commission of Council, Atlanta. Emma V. Paul Scrapbook. Sheltering Arms Day Nursery Collection. Gay Bolling Shepperson Papers. WRFG/Living Atlanta Collection (LAC).

Atlanta University Center, Woodruff Library, Special Collections. Commission on Interracial Cooperation Papers (microfilm) (CIC). Papers of John and Lugenia Burns Hope (microfilm). Neighborhood Union Collection (NU).

Auburn Avenue Research Library, Atlanta. Sweet Auburn Neighborhood: An Oral History Project.

Cornell University, Labor-Management Documentation Center, M. P. Catherwood Library, Ithaca, New York. American Labor Education Service, Southern Summer School for Women Workers (ALES).

Emory University, Robert W. Woodruff Library, Special Collections Department, Atlanta. Mary Cornelia Barker Collection. Raoul Family Collection. Women's Christian Temperance Union Collection. Comer McDonald Woodward Collection. Young Women's Christian Association Collection, Atlanta Branch.

Fulton County Superior Court, Atlanta. Records of the Fulton County Civil Division, 1915–38 (FCCD).

Georgia Department of Archives and History, Atlanta. Department of Public Welfare Collection. Grady Hospital Auxiliary Collection. League of Women Voters of Atlanta Records, 1920–63. Jane Van De Vrede, Works Projects Administration Records and Other Papers, 1913–73. Vanishing Georgia Collection. Women's Suffrage Records, Georgia (1894, 1911–19) (WSGC).

Institute Archives, Georgia Institute of Technology, Price Gilbert Memorial Library, Atlanta. Fulton Bag and Cotton Mills Company Collection (FBCM).

Manuscript Division, Library of Congress, Washington, D.C. National Association for the Advancement of Colored People, Atlanta Branch Papers (NAACP). National Urban League, Atlanta Branch Papers.

National Archives II, College Park, Maryland. Records of the Public Health Service, RG 90 (PHS). Records of the U.S. Department of Labor, Women's Bureau, RG 86.

Schomburg Center for Research in Black Culture, New York Public Library. International Labor Defense Papers (microfilm) (ILD).

Social Welfare History Archives, University of Minnesota, Minneapolis. National Florence Crittenton Mission Collection.

United Methodist Center, Wesley Community Centers, Atlanta. Board of City Missions Papers.

Washington National Records Center, Suitland, Maryland. Records of the U.S. Commission on Industrial Relations, 1912–15 (microfilm) (CIR). Records of the Federal Mediation Conciliation Service, RG 280 (FMCS).

YWCA National Board Archives, New York. Industrial Department Records.

Periodicals

Atlanta Constitution
Atlanta Daily Intelligencer
Atlanta Daily World
Atlanta Georgian
Atlanta Independent
Atlanta Journal
City Builder
Journal of Labor
Jeffersonian
Pittsburgh Courier
Spelman Messenger
Voice of the Negro

Published Sources

Abercrombie, T. F. *History of Public Health in Georgia, 1733–1950.* Atlanta: Georgia Department of Public Welfare, 1950.

Abramovitz, Mimi. *Regulating the Lives of Women: Social Welfare Policy from Colonial Times to the Present.* Boston: South End Press, 1988.

Addams, Jane. *The Spirit of Youth and the City Streets.* 1909. Reprint, New York: Macmillan, 1923.

Adero, Malaika, ed. *Up South: Stories, Studies, and Letters of this Century's African-American Migrations.* New York: New Press, 1993.

"An Advertising Campaign against Segregated Vice." *American City* 9 (July 1913): 3–4.

Agnew, Jean-Christopher. "A Touch of Class." *Democracy* 3 (spring 1983): 59–72.

American Social Hygiene Association. *Keeping Fit to Fight.* Washington, D.C.: Commission on Training Camp Activities, 1918.

Anderson, William. *The Wild Man from Sugar Creek: The Political Career of Eugene Talmadge.* Baton Rouge: Louisiana State University Press, 1975.

Anzaldúa, Gloria. *Borderlands/La Frontera: The New Mestiza.* San Francisco: Aunt Lute Books, 1987.

Ardener, Shirley. *Women and Space: Ground Rules and Social Maps.* New York: St. Martin's Press, 1981.

Argersinger, Peter H. "The Southern Search for Order." *Reviews in American History* 3 (June 1975): 36–41.

"Atlanta's Vice Crusade an Inspiration to Nation." *Golden Age,* August 7, 1913, 7.

Ayers, Edward. *The Promise of the New South: Life after Reconstruction.* New York: Oxford University Press, 1992.

Bailey, Beth. *From Front Porch to Back Seat: Courtship in Twentieth-Century America.* Baltimore: Johns Hopkins University Press, 1988.

Bailey, Fred Arthur. "Mildred Lewis Rutherford and the Patrician Cult of the Old South." *Georgia Historical Quarterly* 78 (fall 1994): 509–35.

Baker, Paula. "The Domestication of Politics: Women and American Political Society, 1780–1920." *American Historical Review* 89 (fall 1984): 620–47.

Baker, Ray Stannard. "Following the Color Line." *American Magazine* 63 (April 1907): 564–66.

———. "The Negro Goes North." *World's Work* 34 (July 1917): 314–19.

Banta, Martha. *Imaging American Women: Idea and Ideals in Cultural History.* New York: Columbia University Press, 1987.

Bardaglio, Peter W. " 'Shameful Matches': The Regulation of Interracial Sex and Marriage in the South before 1900." In *Sex, Love, Race: Crossing Boundaries in North American History,* edited by Martha Hodes, 112–40. New York: New York University Press, 1999.

Baron, Ava. "Questions of Gender: Deskilling and Demasculinization in the U.S. Printing Industry, 1830–1915." *Gender and History* 1 (spring 1989): 178–99.

Bates, Barbara. *Bargaining for Life: A Social History of Tuberculosis, 1876–1938.* Philadelphia: University of Pennsylvania Press, 1992.

Bauerlein, Mark. *Negrophobia: A Race Riot in Atlanta, 1906.* San Francisco: Encounter Books, 2001.

Bayor, Ronald. *Race and the Shaping of Twentieth-Century Atlanta.* Chapel Hill: University of North Carolina Press, 1996.

———. "Roads to Racial Segregation: Atlanta in the Twentieth Century." *Journal of Urban History* 15 (November 1988): 3–21.

Beard, Rick. "From Suburb to Defended Neighborhood: The Evolution of Inman Park and Ansley Park, 1890–1980." *Atlanta Historical Journal* 26 (summer–fall 1982): 113–40.

———. "Hurt's Deserted Village: Atlanta's Inman Park, 1885–1911." In *Olmsted South: Old South Critic/New South Planner,* edited by Dana F. White and Victor A. Kramer, 195–222. Westport, Conn.: Greenwood Press, 1979.

Beardsley, Edward H. *A History of Neglect: Health Care for Blacks and Mill Workers in the Twentieth-Century South.* Knoxville: University of Tennessee Press, 1987.

Bederman, Gail. " 'The Women Have Had Charge of the Church Work Long Enough':

The Men and Religion Forward Movement of 1911–1912 and the Masculinazation of Middle-Class Protestantism." *American Quarterly* 41 (September 1989): 432–65.

Benson, Susan Porter. *Counter Cultures: Saleswomen, Managers, and Customers in American Department Stores, 1890–1940.* Urbana: University of Illinois Press, 1988.

Biles, Roger. *The South and the New Deal.* Lexington: University Press of Kentucky, 1994.

Blackwelder, Julia Kirk. "Mop and Typewriter: Women's Work in Early Twentieth-Century Atlanta." *Atlanta Historical Journal* 27 (fall 1983): 21–29.

———. "Quiet Suffering: Atlanta Women in the 1930s." *Georgia Historical Quarterly* 61 (spring 1977): 112–24.

———. *Women of the Depression: Caste and Culture in San Antonio, 1929–1939.* College Station: Texas A&M University Press, 1984.

Blee, Kathleen M. *Women of the Klan: Racism and Gender in the 1920s.* Berkeley: University of California Press, 1991.

Bodnar, John, Roger Simon, and Michael P. Weber. *Lives of Their Own: Blacks, Italians, and Poles in Pittsburgh, 1900–1960.* Urbana: University of Illinois Press, 1982.

Boris, Eileen. "Black Women and Paid Labor in the Home." In *Homework: Historical and Contemporary Perspectives on Paid Labor at Home,* edited by Eileen Boris and Cynthia R. Daniels, 33–52. Urbana: University of Illinois Press, 1989.

———. "From Parlor to Politics: Women and Reform in America, 1890–1925." *Radical History Review* 50 (spring 1991): 191–203.

———. "Reconstructing the 'Family': Women, Progressive Reform, and the Problem of Social Control." In *Gender, Class, Race, and Reform in the Progressive Era,* edited by Noralee Frankel and Nancy S. Dye, 73–86. Lexington: University Press of Kentucky, 1991.

Bose, Christine E. "Devaluing Women's Work: The Undercount of Women's Employment in 1900 and 1980." In *Hidden Aspects of Women's Work,* edited by Christine E. Bose, Roslyn Feldberg, and Natalie Sokoloff, 95–115. New York: Praeger, 1987.

Boskin, Joseph. *Urban Racial Violence in the Twentieth Century.* Beverly Hills, Calif.: Glencoe Press, 1969.

Boyer, Paul. *Urban Masses and Moral Order in America, 1820–1920.* Cambridge: Harvard University Press, 1978.

Brandt, Allan M. *No Magic Bullet: A Social History of Venereal Disease in the United States since 1880.* New York: Oxford University Press, 1985.

Brenzel, Barbara. *Daughters of the State: A Social Portrait of the First Reform Schools for Girls in North America, 1856–1905.* Cambridge: MIT Press, 1983.

Brown, Elsa Barkley. "Open Letter about Issues Raised by 1988 Southern Conference." *Southern Association for Women Historians Newsletter* 19 (May 1989): 3–7.

———. "What Has Happened Here: The Politics of Difference in Women's History and Feminist Politics." *Feminist Studies* 18 (summer 1992): 295–312.

———. "Womanist Consciousness: Maggie Lena Walker and the Independent Order of Saint Luke." *Signs: Journal of Women in Culture and Society* 14 (summer 1989): 610–33.

Brownell, Blaine. *The Urban Ethos in the South, 1920–1930.* Baton Rouge: Louisiana State University Press, 1975.

Supremacy in North Carolina, 1896–1920. Chapel Hill: University of North Carolina Press, 1996.

Ginzberg, Lori. *Women and the Work of Benevolence: Morality, Politics, and Class in the Nineteenth-Century United States.* New Haven: Yale University Press, 1990.

Glenn, Susan. *Daughters of the Shtetl: Life and Labor in the Immigrant Generation.* Ithaca: Cornell University Press, 1990.

Goings, Kenneth W., and Raymond A. Mohl. *The New African-American Urban History.* Thousand Oaks, Calif.: Sage Publications, 1996.

Golden, Harry. *A Little Girl Is Dead.* Cleveland: World Publishing, 1965.

Goldfield, David. "The Business of Health and Planning: Disease Prevention in the Old South." *Journal of Southern History* 42 (November 1978): 557–70.

———. *Cotton Fields and Skyscrapers: Southern City and Region, 1607–1980.* Baton Rouge: Louisiana State University Press, 1982.

Goldin, Claudia. "Female Labor Force Participation: The Origins of Black and White Difference, 1870 and 1880." *Journal of Economic History* 37 (March 1977): 87–108.

Goodson, Steve. *Highbrows, Hillbillies, and Hellfire: Public Entertainment in Atlanta, 1880–1930.* Athens: University of Georgia Press, 2002.

Gordon, Linda. "Black and White Visions of Welfare: Women's Welfare Activism, 1890–1945." *Journal of American History* 78 (September 1991): 559–90.

———. *Heroes of Their Own Lives: The Politics and History of Family Violence, Boston, 1880–1960.* New York: Viking Press, 1988.

———. "The New Feminist Scholarship on the Welfare State." In *Women, the State, and Welfare,* edited by Linda Gordon, 9–35. Madison: University of Wisconsin Press, 1990.

———. *Pitied but Not Entitled: Single Mothers and the History of Welfare, 1890–1935.* New York: Free Press, 1994.

Green, Elna, *Southern Strategies: Southern Women and the Woman Suffrage Question.* Chapel Hill: University of North Carolina Press, 1997.

Greenwald, Maurine. *Women, War, and Work: The Impact of World War I on Women Workers in the United States.* Westport, Conn.: Greenwood Press, 1980.

Greenwood, Janette. *Bittersweet Legacy: The Black and White "Better Classes" in Charlotte, 1850–1910.* Chapel Hill: University of North Carolina Press, 1994.

Grossman, James R. "Black Labor Is the Best Labor: Southern White Reactions to the Great Migration." In *Black Exodus: The Great Migration and the American South,* edited by Alferdteen Harrison, 51–71. Jackson: University Press of Mississippi, 1991.

———. *Land of Hope: Chicago, Black Southerners, and the Great Migration.* Chicago: University of Chicago Press, 1989.

Gurin, Patricia, and Louise Tilly, eds. *Women, Politics, and Change.* New York: Russell Sage Foundation, 1990.

Habermas, Jurgen. *The Structural Transformation of the Public Sphere: An Inquiry into a Category of Bourgeois Society.* Cambridge: MIT Press, 1962.

Hale, Grace Elizabeth. *Making Whiteness: The Culture of Segregation in the South, 1890–1940.* New York: Vintage Books, 1999.

Hall, Jacquelyn Dowd. "Disorderly Women: Gender and Labor Militancy in the Appalachian South." In *Unequal Sisters: A Multicultural Reader,* edited by Ellen Carol DuBois and Vicki L. Ruiz, 298–321. New York: Routledge, 1990.

———. "O. Delight Smith's Progressive Era: Labor, Feminism, and Reform in the Urban South." In *Visible Women: New Essays on American Activism,* edited by Nancy A. Hewitt and Suzanne Lebsock, 166–98. Urbana: University of Illinois Press, 1993.

———. "Private Eyes, Public Women: Images of Class and Sex in the Urban South, Atlanta, Georgia, 1913–1915." In *Work Engendered: Toward a New History of American Labor,* edited by Ava Baron, 243–72. Ithaca: Cornell University Press, 1991.

———. *Revolt against Chivalry: Jessie Daniel Ames and the Women's Campaign against Lynching.* Rev. ed. New York: Columbia University Press, 1993.

Hall, Jacquelyn Dowd, James Leloudis, Robert Korstad, Mary Murphy, Lu Ann Jones, and Christopher B. Daly. *Like a Family: The Making of a Southern Cotton Mill World.* Chapel Hill: University of North Carolina Press, 1987.

Hanchett, Thomas. *Sorting out the New South City: Race, Class, and Urban Development in Charlotte, 1875–1975.* Chapel Hill: University of North Carolina Press, 1998.

Harley, Sharon. "Black Women in a Southern City: Washington, D.C., 1890–1920." In *Black Women in American History: The Twentieth Century,* edited by Darlene Clark Hine, 2:487–506. Brooklyn, N.Y.: Carlson, 1990.

———. "When Your Work Is Not Who You Are: The Development of a Working-Class Consciousness among Afro-American Women." In *Gender, Class, Race, and Reform in the Progressive Era,* edited by Noralee Frankel and Nancy S. Dye, 42–55. Lexington: University Press of Kentucky, 1991.

Harris, Michael. *The Rise of Gospel Blues: The Music of Thomas Andrew Dorsey in the Urban Church.* New York: Oxford University Press, 1992.

Harris, William. "Work and the Family in Black Atlanta, 1880." *Journal of Social History* 9 (spring 1976): 319–30.

Harzig, Christiane, ed. *Peasant Maids, City Women: From the European Countryside to Urban America.* Ithaca: Cornell University Press, 1997.

Hawks, Joanne, and Sheila Skemp, eds. *Sex, Race, and the Role of Women in the South: Essays.* Jackson: University Press of Mississippi, 1983.

Hayden, Dolores. *The Grand Domestic Revolution: A History of Feminist Designs for American Homes, Neighborhoods, and Cities.* Cambridge: MIT Press, 1981.

Hebdige, Dick. *Subculture: The Meaning of Style.* New York: Routledge, 1991.

Henderson, Alexa Benson. *Atlanta Life Insurance Company: Guardian of Black Economic Dignity.* Tuscaloosa: University of Alabama Press, 1990.

Henri, Florette. *Black Migration: Movement North, 1900–1920.* Garden City, N.Y.: Anchor Press/Doubleday, 1975.

Herndon, Angelo. *Let Me Live.* New York: Random House, 1937.

Herndon, Jane Walker. "Ed Rivers and Georgia's 'Little New Deal.'" *Atlanta Historical Journal* 30 (spring 1986): 97–105.

Hershberg, Theodore, ed. *Philadelphia: Work, Space, Family, and Group Experience in the Nineteenth Century.* New York: Oxford University Press, 1981.

Hertzberg, Steven. *Strangers within the Gate City: The Jews of Atlanta, 1845–1915.* Philadelphia: Jewish Publication Society of America, 1978.

Hewitt, Nancy A. "Beyond the Search for Sisterhood: American Women's History in the 1980s." *Social History* 10 (October 1985): 299–321.

———. "In Pursuit of Power: The Political Economy of Women's Activism in Twentieth-Century Tampa." In *Visible Women: New Essays on American Activism,* edited by Nancy A. Hewitt and Suzanne Lebsock, 199–222. Urbana: University of Illinois Press, 1993.

Hickey, Georgina. "Disease, Disorder, and Motherhood: Working-Class Women, Social Welfare, and the Process of Urban Development in Atlanta." In *Before the New Deal: Southern Welfare History, 1830–1930,* edited by Elna Green, 181–207. Athens: University of Georgia Press, 1999.

———. "From Auburn Avenue to Buttermilk Bottom: Class and Community Dynamics among Atlanta's Blacks." In *Historical Roots of the Urban Crisis: Blacks in the Industrial City, 1900–1950,* edited by Henry Louis Taylor Jr. and Walter Hill, 109–43. New York: Garland Publishing, 2000.

———. " 'The Lowest Form of Work Relief': Authority, Gender, and the State in Atlanta's WPA Sewing Rooms." In *The New Deal and Beyond: Social Welfare in the South since 1930,* edited by Elna Green. Athens: University of Georgia Press, forthcoming.

———. " 'Meet Me at the Arcade': Women, Business, and Consumerism in Downtown Atlanta, 1917–1964." *Atlanta History* 40 (fall–winter 1996–97): 5–15.

———. "Rescuing the Working Girl: Agency and Conflict in the Michigan Reform School for Girls, 1879–1893." *Michigan Historical Review* 20 (spring 1994): 1–28.

———. "Waging War on 'Loose Living Hotels . . . and Cheap Soda Water Joints': The Criminalization of Working-Class Women in Atlanta's Public Spaces." *Georgia Historical Quarterly* 82 (winter 1999): 775–800.

Higginbotham, Evelyn Brooks. "In Politics to Stay: Black Women Leaders and Party Politics in the 1920s." In *Unequal Sisters: A Multicultural Reader in U.S. Women's History,* 3d ed., edited by Vicki Ruiz and Ellen Carol DuBois, 292–306. New York: Routledge, 2000.

———. *Righteous Discontent: The Women's Movement in the Black Baptist Church, 1880–1920.* Cambridge: Harvard University Press, 1993.

Hine, Darlene Clark. "Black Migration to the Urban Midwest: The Gender Dimension, 1915–1945." In *The Great Migration in Historical Perspective,* edited by Joe Trotter, 127–46. Bloomington: Indiana University Press, 1991.

———. "Rape and the Inner Lives of Black Women in the Middle West: Preliminary Thoughts on the Culture of Dissemblance." *Signs: Journal of Women in Culture and Society* 14 (summer 1989): 912–20.

Hobson, Barbara Meil. *Uneasy Virtue: The Politics of Prostitution and the American Reform Tradition.* New York: Basic Books, 1987.

Holmes, Michael. "The Blue Eagle as 'Jim Crow Bird': The NRA and Georgia's Black Workers." *Journal of Negro History* 57 (1972): 276–83.

————. *The New Deal in Georgia: An Administrative History*. Westport, Conn.: Greenwood Press, 1975.

hooks, bell. *Talking Back: Thinking Feminist, Thinking Black*. Boston: South End Press, 1988.

Hopkins, Richard J. "Occupational and Geographical Mobility in Atlanta, 1870–1896." *Journal of Southern History* 34 (May 1968): 200–213.

————. "Public Health in Atlanta: The Formative Years, 1865–1879." *Georgia Historical Quarterly* 53 (September 1969): 287–304.

Horne, Gerald. *The Fire This Time: The Watts Uprising and the 1960s*. Charlottesville: University Press of Virginia, 1995.

"How Atlanta Cleaned Up." *Literary Digest* 24 (May 3, 1913): 1012–13.

Hunter, Tera. "Domination and Resistance: The Politics of Wage Household Labor in New South Atlanta." *Labor History* 34 (spring–summer 1993): 205–20.

————. *To 'Joy My Freedom: Southern Black Women's Lives and Labors after the Civil War*. Cambridge: Harvard University Press, 1997.

Jackson, Kenneth T. *The Ku Klux Klan in the City, 1915–1930*. New York: Oxford University Press, 1967.

Jackson, Marion M. "The Atlanta Campaign against Commercialized Vice." *Social Hygiene* 3 (1917): 177–84.

Janiewski, Dolores. *Sisterhood Denied: Race, Gender, and Class in a New South Community*. Philadelphia: Temple University Press, 1985.

Jenkins, Herbert T. *Forty Years on the Force, 1932–1972*. Atlanta: Center for Research in Social Change, Emory University, 1973.

Jennings, M. Kent. *Community Influentials: The Elites of Atlanta*. New York: Free Press of Glencoe, 1964.

Jones, Jacqueline. *The Dispossessed: America's Underclasses from the Civil War to the Present*. New York: Basic Books, 1992.

————. *Labor of Love, Labor of Sorrow: Black Women, Work, and the Family, from Slavery to the Present*. New York: Vintage Books, 1986.

————. "Political Implications of Black and White Women's Work in the South, 1890–1965." In *Women, Politics, and Change,* edited by Patricia Gurin and Louise A. Tilly, 108–29. New York: Russell Sage Foundation, 1990.

Jones, Peter d'A., and Melvin G. Holli, eds. *Ethnic Chicago*. Grand Rapids, Mich.: Eerdmans, 1981.

Kasson, John F. *Amusing the Millions: Coney Island at the Turn of the Century*. New York: Hill and Wang, 1978.

————. *Rudeness and Civility: Manners in Nineteenth-Century Urban America*. New York: Hill and Wang, 1990.

Katz, Michael. *In the Shadow of the Poorhouse: A Social History of Welfare in America*. New York: Basic Books, 1986.

————, ed. *The "Underclass" Debate: Views from History*. Princeton: Princeton University Press, 1993.

Katzman, David. *Seven Days a Week: Women and Domestic Service in Industrializing America*. New York: Oxford University Press, 1978.

Katznelson, Ira. *City Trenches: Urban Politics and the Patterning of Class in the United States.* Chicago: University of Chicago Press, 1981.

Kazin, Michael, and Steven J. Ross. "America's Labor Day: The Dilemma of a Workers' Celebration." *Journal of American History* 78 (March 1992): 1294–1323.

Kelley, Robin D. G. "The Black Poor and the Politics of Opposition in a New South City, 1929–1970." In *The "Underclass" Debate: Views from History,* edited by Michael Katz, 293–333. Princeton: Princeton University Press, 1993.

———. *Hammer and Hoe: Alabama Communists during the Great Depression.* Chapel Hill: University of North Carolina Press, 1990.

———. *Race Rebels: Culture, Politics, and the Black Working Class.* New York: Free Press, 1994.

———. " 'We Are Not What We Seem': Rethinking Black Working-Class Opposition in the Jim Crow South." *Journal of American History* 80 (June 1993): 75–112.

Kemp, Kathryn W., and Elaine Kirkland. "The Gay Bolling Shepperson Papers and Photographs." *Atlanta Historical Journal* 30 (spring 1986): 117–19.

Kennedy, Elizabeth Lapovsky, and Madeline D. Davis. *Boots of Leather, Slippers of Gold: The History of a Lesbian Community.* New York: Penguin Books, 1994.

Kennedy, Susan Eastbrook. *If All We Did Was to Weep at Home: A History of White Working-Class Women in America.* Bloomington: Indiana University Press, 1979.

Kessler-Harris, Alice. *Out to Work: A History of Wage-Earning Women in the United States.* New York: Oxford University Press, 1982.

———. *A Woman's Wage: Historical Meanings and Social Consequences.* Lexington: University Press of Kentucky, 1990.

Kimball, Hannibal I. *International Cotton Exposition (Atlanta, Georgia 1881): Report of the Director-General.* New York: D. Appleton, 1882.

King, Augusta Wylie. "International Cotton Exposition: October 5th to December 31, 1881, Atlanta, Georgia." *Atlanta Historical Bulletin* 4 (July 1939): 181–98.

King, Deborah. "Multiple Jeopardy, Multiple Consciousness: The Context of a Black Feminist Ideology." *Signs: Journal of Women in Culture and Society* 14 (1988): 42–72.

King, Martin Luther. *Daddy King: An Autobiography.* New York: Morrow, 1980.

Kingsolver, Barbara. *Holding the Line: Women in the Great Arizona Mine Strike of 1983.* Ithaca, N.Y.: ILR Press, 1989.

Kirby, John B. *Black Americans in the Roosevelt Era: Liberalism and Race.* Knoxville: University of Tennessee Press, 1980.

Kirschner, Don S. *The Paradox of Professionalism: Reform and Public Service in Urban America, 1900–1940.* New York: Greenwood Press, 1986.

Klienberg, Susan J. "The Systematic Study of Urban Women." *Historical Methods Newsletter* 9 (December 1975): 14–25.

Kornbluh, Joyce L., and Mary Fredrickson, eds. *Sisterhood and Solidarity: Workers' Education for Women, 1914–1984.* Philadelphia: Temple University Press, 1984.

Kousser, J. Morgan. *The Shaping of Southern Politics: Suffrage Restriction and the Establishment of the One-Party South, 1880–1910.* New Haven: Yale University Press, 1974.

Kraditor, Aileen. *The Ideas of the Woman Suffrage Movement, 1890–1920.* 1965. Reprint, Garden City, N.Y.: Anchor, 1971.

Kuhn, Clifford. *Contesting the New South Order: The 1914–1915 Strike at Atlanta's Fulton Mills*. Chapel Hill: University of North Carolina Press, 2001.

———. "Reminiscences: Interviews with Atlanta New Deal Social Workers." *Atlanta Historical Journal* 30 (spring 1986): 107–16.

Kuhn, Clifford, Harlon E. Joye, and E. Bernard West. *Living Atlanta: An Oral History of the City, 1914–1948*. Atlanta: Atlanta Historical Society and University of Georgia Press, 1990.

Kunzel, Regina G. *Fallen Women, Problem Girls: Unmarried Mothers and the Professionalization of Social Work, 1890–1945*. New Haven: Yale University Press, 1993.

Kurzman, Paul A. *Harry Hopkins and the New Deal*. Fair Lawn, N.J.: R. E. Burdick, 1974.

Kwolek-Folland, Angel. *Engendering Business: Men and Women in the Corporate Office, 1870–1930*. Baltimore: Johns Hopkins University Press, 1994.

Kytle, Elizabeth. *Willie Mae*. 1958. Reprint, Athens: University of Georgia Press, 1993.

Ladd-Taylor, Molly. *Mother-Work: Women, Child Welfare, and the State, 1890–1930*. Urbana: University of Illinois Press, 1994.

Larsen, Lawrence. *The Rise of the Urban South*. Lexington: University Press of Kentucky, 1985.

———. *The Urban South: A History*. Lexington: University Press of Kentucky, 1990.

Lasch-Quinn, Elisabeth. *Black Neighbors: Race and the Limits of Reform in the American Settlement House Movement, 1890–1945*. Chapel Hill: University of North Carolina Press, 1993.

Lebsock, Suzanne. "Woman Suffrage and White Supremacy: A Virginia Case Study." In *Visible Women: New Essays on American Activism*, edited by Nancy A. Hewitt and Suzanne Lebsock, 62–100. Chicago: University of Illinois Press, 1993.

Lefever, Harry G. "Prostitution, Politics, and Religion: The Crusade against Vice in Atlanta in 1912." *Atlanta Historical Journal* 24 (spring 1980): 7–29.

Leiby, James. *A History of Social Welfare and Social Work in the United States*. New York: Columbia University Press, 1978.

Leighninger, Leslie. *Social Work: Search for Identity*. New York: Greenwood Press, 1987.

Lemann, Nicholas. *The Promised Land: The Great Black Migration and How It Changed America*. New York: Knopf, 1991.

Lemke-Santangelo, Gretchen. *Abiding Courage: African-American Migrant Women and the East Bay Community*. Chapel Hill: University of North Carolina Press, 1996.

Lewis, Earl. "Expectations, Economic Opportunities, and Life in the Industrial Age: Black Migration to Norfolk, Virginia, 1910–1945." In *The Great Migration in Historical Perspective: New Dimensions of Race, Class, and Gender*, edited by Joe Trotter, 22–45. Bloomington: Indiana University Press, 1991.

———. *In Their Own Interests: Race, Class, and Power in Twentieth-Century Norfolk, Virginia*. Berkeley: University of California Press, 1991.

Lipsitz, George. *A Life in the Struggle: Ivory Perry and the Culture of Opposition*. Philadelphia: Temple University Press, 1988.

Litwack, Leon. *Trouble in Mind: Black Southerners in the Age of Jim Crow*. New York: Vintage, 1999.

Logue, Calvin McLeod. *Eugene Talmadge: Rhetoric and Response.* New York: Greenwood Press, 1989.

Lyon, Elizabeth. "Frederick Law Olmsted and Joel Hurt: Planning for Atlanta." In *Olmsted South: Old South Critic/New South Planner,* edited by Dana F. White and Victor A. Kramer, 165–94. Westport, Conn.: Greenwood Press, 1979.

Maclachlan, Gretchen. "Atlanta's Industrial Women, 1879–1920." *Atlanta History* 36 (winter 1993): 16–23.

MacLean, Nancy. *Behind the Mask of Chivalry: The Making of the Second Ku Klux Klan.* New York: Oxford University Press, 1994.

———. "The Leo Frank Case Reconsidered: Gender and Sexual Politics in the Making of Reactionary Populism." *Journal of American History* 78 (December 1991): 917–48.

Marks, Carole. *Farewell—We're Good and Gone: The Great Black Migration.* Bloomington: Indiana University Press, 1989.

Martin, Charles H. *The Angelo Herndon Case and Southern Justice.* Baton Rouge: Louisiana State University Press, 1976.

———. "The Angelo Herndon Case and Southern Justice." In *American Political Trials,* edited by Michal R. Belknap, 159–78. Rev. and exp. ed. Westport, Conn.: Greenwood Press, 1994.

———. "White Supremacy and Black Workers: Georgia's 'Black Shirts' Combat the Great Depression." *Labor History* 18 (1977): 366–81.

Martin, Thomas H. *Atlanta and Its Builders: A Comprehensive History of the Gate City of the South.* Vol. 2. Atlanta: Century Memorial Publishing, 1902.

Matthews, Glenna. *The Rise of Public Woman: Woman's Power and Women's Place in the United States, 1630–1970.* New York: Oxford University Press, 1992.

May, Elaine Tyler. *Homeward Bound: American Families in the Cold War Era.* New York: Basic Books, 1988.

May, Lary. *Screening Out the Past: The Birth of Mass Culture and the Motion Picture Industry.* New York: Oxford University Press, 1980.

Mays, Benjamin. *Born to Rebel: An Autobiography.* Athens: Brown Thrasher Books, University of Georgia Press, 1971.

McBride, David. *From TB to AIDS: Epidemics among Urban Blacks since 1900.* Albany: State University of New York Press, 1991.

McCarthy, Kathleen D. *Lady Bountiful Revisited: Women, Philanthropy, and Power.* New Brunswick, N.J.: Rutgers University Press, 1990.

McLaurin, Melton. *Celia, a Slave: A True Story.* New York: Avon Books, 1991.

McRae, Elizabeth Gillespie. "Caretakers of Southern Civilization: Georgia Women and the Anti-Suffrage Campaign, 1914–1920." *Georgia Historical Quarterly* 82 (winter 1998): 801–28.

Meier, August, and David Lewis. "History of the Negro Upper Class in Atlanta, Georgia, 1890–1958." *Journal of Negro Education* 28 (spring 1959): 128–39.

Melosh, Barbara. *Engendering Culture: Manhood and Womanhood in New Deal Public Art and Theater.* Washington, D.C.: Smithsonian Institution Press, 1991.

Mettler, Suzanne. *Dividing Citizens: Gender and Federalism in New Deal Public Policy.* Ithaca: Cornell University Press, 1998.

Meyerowitz, Joanne J. "Sexual Geography and Gender Economy: The Furnished-Room Districts of Chicago." *Gender and History* 2 (autumn 1990): 274–96.

———. *Women Adrift: Independent Wage Earners in Chicago, 1880–1930.* Chicago: University of Chicago Press, 1988.

Milkman, Ruth. "Gender and Trade Unionism in Historical Perspective." In *Women, Politics, and Change,* edited by Louise A. Tilly and Patricia Gurin, 87–107. New York: Russell Sage Foundation, 1990.

Mixon, Gregory. " 'Good Negro—Bad Negro': The Dynamics of Race and Class in Atlanta during the Era of the 1906 Riot." *Georgia Historical Quarterly* 81 (fall 1997): 593–621.

Mohl, Raymond. "New Perspectives on American Urban History." In *The Making of Urban America,* edited by Raymond Mohl, 335–74. 2d ed. Wilmington, Del.: Scholarly Resources, 1997.

Monkkonen, Eric H. *America Becomes Urban: The Development of U.S. Cities and Towns, 1780–1980.* Berkeley: University of California Press, 1988.

Moore, John Hammond. "Communists and Fascists in a Southern City: Atlanta, 1930." *South Atlantic Quarterly* 67 (summer 1968): 437–54.

Morris, Aldon. *The Origins of the Civil Rights Movement.* New York: Free Press, 1984.

Morton, Patricia. *Disfigured Images: The Historical Assault on Afro-American Women.* New York: Praeger, 1991.

Murolo, Priscilla. *The Common Ground of Womanhood: Class, Gender, and Working Girls' Clubs, 1884–1928.* Urbana: University of Illinois Press, 1997.

Murphy, Mary. *Mining Cultures: Men, Women, and Leisure in Butte, 1914–1941.* Urbana: University of Illinois Press, 1997.

Myers, Gloria E. *A Municipal Mother: Portland's Lola Greene Baldwin, American's First Policewoman.* Corvallis: Oregon State University Press, 1995.

Neil, Nancy. "The Week They Tore Old Manhattan Street Down." *Business Atlanta* (June 1984): 84–90.

Neuman, Shirley. "ReImagining Women: An Introduction." In *ReImagining Women: Representations of Women in Culture,* edited by Shirley Neuman and Glennis Stephenson, 3–18. Toronto: University of Toronto Press, 1993.

Neverdon-Morton, Cynthia. *Afro-American Women of the South and the Advancement of the Race, 1895–1925.* Knoxville: University of Tennessee Press, 1989.

Newman, Harvey K. "Atlanta's Hospitality Business in the New South Era, 1880–1900." *Georgia Historical Quarterly* 80 (spring 1996): 53–76.

Norwood, Stephen H. *Labor's Flaming Youth: Telephone Operators and Worker Militancy, 1878–1923.* Urbana: University of Illinois Press, 1990.

Odem, Mary. *Delinquent Daughters: Protecting and Policing Adolescent Female Sexuality in the United States, 1885–1920.* Chapel Hill: University of North Carolina Press, 1995.

O'Neill, William. *Divorce in the Progressive Era.* New Haven: Yale University Press, 1967.

———. *Everyone Was Brave: A History of Feminism in America.* Chicago: Quadrangle, 1969.

Orleck, Annelise. *Common Sense and a Little Fire: Women and Working-Class Politics in the United States, 1900–1965.* Chapel Hill: University of North Carolina Press, 1995.

Ottley, Roi. *Lonely Warrior.* Chicago: Henry Regnery, 1955.

Pacuyga, Dominic A. "Chicago's 1919 Race Riot: Ethnicity, Class, and Urban Violence." In *The Making of Urban America,* edited by Raymond A. Mohl, 3–18. 2d ed. Wilmington, Del.: Scholarly Resources, 1997.

Palmer, Charles F. *Adventures of a Slum Fighter.* Atlanta: Tupper and Love, 1955.

Palmer, Phyllis. *Domesticity and Dirt: Housewives and Domestic Servants in the United States, 1920–1945.* Philadelphia: Temple University Press, 1989.

Pascoe, Peggy. *Relations of Rescue: The Search for Female Moral Authority in the American West, 1874–1939.* Chicago: University of Chicago Press, 1990.

Patterson, James T. *The New Deal and the States: Federalism in Transition.* Princeton: Princeton University Press, 1969.

Payne, Elizabeth Anne. *Reform, Labor, and Feminism: Margaret Dreier Robins and the Women's Trade Union League.* Urbana: University of Illinois Press, 1988.

Peiss, Kathy. " 'Charity Girls' and City Pleasures: Historical Notes on Working-Class Sexuality, 1880–1920." In *Unequal Sisters: A Multicultural Reader in U.S. Women's History,* edited by Ellen Carol DuBois and Vicki L. Ruiz, 157–66. New York: Routledge, 1990.

———. *Cheap Amusements: Working Women and Leisure in Turn-of-the-Century New York.* Philadelphia: Temple University Press, 1986.

Peiss, Kathy, and Christina Simmons, eds. "Passion and Power: An Introduction." In *Passion and Power: Sexuality in History,* 3–31. Philadelphia: Temple University Press, 1989.

Phillips, Kimberley. *AlabamaNorth: African-American Migrants, Community, and Working-Class Activism in Cleveland, 1915–1945.* Urbana: University of Illinois Press, 1999.

Pomerantz, Gary. *Where Peachtree Meets Sweet Auburn: The Saga of Two Families and the Making of Atlanta.* New York: Scribner, 1996.

Preston, Howard L. *Automobile Age Atlanta: The Making of a Southern Metropolis, 1900–1935.* Athens: University of Georgia Press, 1979.

———. "Parkways, Parks, and 'New South' Progressivism: Planning Practice in Atlanta, 1880–1917." In *Olmsted South: Old South Critic/New South Planner,* edited by Dana F. White and Victor A. Kramer, 223–38. Westport, Conn.: Greenwood Press, 1979.

Rabinovitz, Lauren. *For the Love of Pleasure: Women, Movies, and Culture in Turn-of-the-Century Chicago.* New Brunswick, N.J.: Rutgers University Press, 1998.

Rabinowitz, Howard N. *Race Relations in the Urban South, 1865–1890.* New York: Oxford University Press, 1978.

Radford, Gail. *Modern Housing for America: Policy Struggles in the New Deal Era.* Chicago: University of Chicago Press, 1996.

Reiff, Janice L., Michel R. Dahlin, and Daniel Scott Smith. "Rural Push and Urban Pull: Work and Family Experiences of Older Black Women in Southern Cities, 1880–1900." *Journal of Social History* 16 (summer 1983): 39–48.

Rice, Bradley R. "Urbanization, 'Atlanta-ization' and Suburbanization: Three Themes for the Urban History of Twentieth-Century Georgia." *Georgia Historical Quarterly* 68 (winter 1984): 40–59.

Riley, Glenda. *Divorce: An American Tradition*. New York: Oxford University Press, 1991.

Robinson, Jo Ann. *The Montgomery Bus Boycott and the Women Who Started It: The Memoir of Jo Ann Gibson Robinson*. Knoxville: University of Tennessee Press, 1987.

Rosen, Hannah. " 'Not That Sort of Women': Race, Gender, and Sexual Violence during the Memphis Riot of 1866." In *Sex, Love, Race: Crossing Boundaries in North American History,* edited by Martha Hodes, 267–93. New York: New York University Press, 1999.

Rosen, Louis. *The South Side: The Racial Transformation of an American Neighborhood*. New York: Ivan R. Dee, 1998.

Rosen, Ruth. *The Lost Sisterhood: Prostitution in America, 1900–1918*. Baltimore: Johns Hopkins University Press, 1982.

Rosenzweig, Roy. *Eight Hours for What We Will: Workers and Leisure in an Industrial City, 1870–1920*. New York: Cambridge University Press, 1983.

Rosenzweig, Roy, and Elizabeth Blackmar. *The Park and Its People: A History of Central Park*. Ithaca: Cornell University Press, 1992.

Ross, Edyth L., ed. *Black Heritage in Social Welfare, 1860–1930*. Metuchen, N.J.: Scarecrow Press, 1978.

———. "Black Heritage in Social Welfare: A Case Study of Atlanta." *Phylon* 37 (1976): 297–307.

Roth, Darlene. *Matronage: Patterns in Women's Organizations, Atlanta, Georgia, 1890–1940*. Brooklyn, N.Y.: Carlson, 1994.

Rouse, Jacqueline Anne. "Atlanta's African-American Women's Attack on Segregation, 1900–1920." In *Gender, Class, Race, and Reform in the Progressive Era,* edited by Noralee Frankel and Nancy S. Dye, 10–23. Lexington: University Press of Kentucky, 1991.

———. *Lugenia Burns Hope: Black Southern Reformer*. Athens: University of Georgia Press, 1989.

Roydhouse, Marion W. "Bridging Chasms: Community and the Southern YWCA." In *Visible Women: New Essays on American Activism,* edited by Nancy A. Hewitt and Suzanne Lebsock, 270–95. Urbana: University of Illinois Press, 1993.

Russell, James Michael. *Atlanta, 1847–1890: City Building in the Old South and the New*. Baton Rouge: Louisiana State University Press, 1988.

Ryan, Mary P. *Women in Public: Between Banners and Ballots, 1825–1880*. Baltimore: Johns Hopkins University Press, 1990.

Rydell, Robert W. *All the World's a Fair: Visions of Empire at America's International Expositions, 1876–1916*. Chicago: University of Chicago Press, 1984.

Salem, Dorothy C. *To Better Our World: Black Women in Organized Reform, 1890–1920.* Brooklyn, N.Y.: Carlson, 1990.

Sapiro, Virginia. "The Gender Basis of American Social Policy." In *Women, the State, and Welfare,* edited by Linda Gordon, 36–54. Madison: University of Wisconsin, 1990.

Sawislak, Karen. *Smoldering City: Chicagoans and the Great Fire, 1871–1874.* Chicago: University of Chicago Press, 1995.

Scharf, Lois. *To Work and to Wed: Female Employment, Feminism, and the Great Depression.* Westport, Conn.: Greenwood Press, 1980.

Schofield, Ann. "Rebel Girls and Union Maids: The Woman Question in the Journals of the AFL and IWW, 1905–1920." *Feminist Studies* 9 (summer 1983): 335–58.

Schulz, Dorothy Moses. *From Social Worker to Crimefighter: Women in United States Municipal Policing.* Westport, Conn.: Praeger, 1995.

Scott, Anne Firor. *The Southern Lady: From Pedestal to Politics, 1830–1930.* Chicago: University of Chicago Press, 1970.

Scott, Anne Firor, and Andrew M. Scott. *One Half the People: The Fight for Woman Suffrage.* Philadelphia: J. B. Lippincott, 1975.

Scott, James C. *Domination and the Arts of Resistance: Hidden Transcripts.* New Haven: Yale University Press, 1990.

Segrave, Kerry. *Policewomen: A History.* Jefferson, N.C.: McFarland, 1995.

Seymour, Gertrude. "A Summary of New Public Health Measures for Combating Venereal Disease." *Social Hygiene* 4 (July 1918): 389–94.

Sims, Anastatia. *The Power of Femininity in the New South: Women's Organizations and Politics in North Carolina, 1880–1930.* Columbia: University of South Carolina Press, 1997.

Singleton, Jeff. *The American Dole: Unemployment Relief and the Welfare State in the Great Depression.* Westport, Conn.: Greenwood Press, 2000.

Smith, Carl. *Urban Disorder and the Shape of Belief: The Great Chicago Fire, the Haymarket Bomb, and the Model Town of Pullman.* Chicago: University of Chicago Press, 1995.

Smith, Douglas L. "Continuity and Change in the Urban South: The New Deal Experience." *Atlanta Historical Journal* 30 (spring 1986): 7–22.

———. *The New Deal in the Urban South.* Baton Rouge: Louisiana State University Press, 1988.

Snyder, Franklyn Bliss. "Leo Frank and Mary Phagan." *Journal of American Folklore* 31 (June–April 1918): 264–66.

Social and Physical Condition of Negroes in Cities: Report of an Investigation under the Direction of Atlanta University and Proceedings of the Second Conference for the Study of Problems Concerning Negro City Life, Held at Atlanta University, May 25–26, 1897. Atlanta: Atlanta University Press, 1897.

Sontag, Susan. *Illness as Metaphor.* New York: Anchor Books, 1978.

Spain, Daphne. *How Women Saved the City.* Minneapolis: University of Minnesota Press, 2001.

Spingarn, Arthur B. "The War and Venereal Diseases among Negroes." *Social Hygiene* 4 (July 1918): 333–46.

Stadum, Beverly Ann. *Poor Women and Their Families: Hard Working Charity Cases, 1900–1930*. Albany: State University of New York Press, 1992.

Stallybras, Peter, and Allon White. *The Politics and Poetics of Transgression*. Ithaca: Cornell University Press, 1986.

Stansell, Christine. *City of Women: Sex and Class in New York, 1789–1860*. Urbana: University of Illinois Press, 1986.

Steeper, R. *John J. Eagan—A Memoir*. Birmingham: ACPIPC, 1939.

Steiner, Jesse Frederick. *Americans at Play: Recent Trends in Recreation and Leisure Time Activities*. New York: McGraw-Hill, 1933.

Stimpson, Catherine R., ed. *Women and the American City*. Chicago: University of Chicago Press, 1980.

Storrs, Landon R. Y. *Civilizing Capitalism: The National Consumer's League, Women's Activism, and Labor Standards in the New Deal Era*. Chapel Hill: University of North Carolina Press, 2000.

Stowell, David O. *Street, Railroads, and the Great Strike of 1877*. Chicago: University of Chicago Press, 1999.

Strom, Sharon Hartman. *Beyond the Typewriter: Gender, Class, and the Origins of Modern American Office Work, 1900–1930*. Urbana: University of Illinois Press, 1992.

Sutherland, Daniel E. *Americans and Their Servants: Domestic Service in the United States from 1800 to 1920*. Baton Rouge: Louisiana State University Press, 1981.

Swain, Martha. "A New Deal for Southern Women: Gender and Race in Women's Work." In *Women of the American South*, edited by Christie Ann Farnham, 241–57. New York: New York University Press, 1997.

Tax, Meredith. *The Rising of the Women: Feminist Solidarity and Class Conflict, 1880–1917*. New York: Monthly Review Press, 1980.

Taylor, A. Elizabeth. "The Last Phase of the Woman Suffrage Movement in Georgia." *Georgia Historical Quarterly* 43 (March 1959): 11–28.

———. "The Origin of the Woman Suffrage Movement in Georgia." *Georgia Historical Quarterly* 48 (June 1944): 63–79.

———. "Revival and Development of the Woman Suffrage Movement in Georgia." *Georgia Historical Quarterly* 42 (December 1958): 339–54.

Taylor, Henry Louis, Jr. *Race and the City: Work, Community, and Protest in Cincinnati, 1820–1970*. Urbana: University of Illinois Press, 1993.

Tentler, Leslie Woodcock. *Wage Earning Women: Industrial Work and Family Life in the United States, 1900–1930*. New York: Oxford University Press, 1979.

Thomas, Emory M. *The Confederate Nation, 1861–1865*. New York: Harper and Row, 1979.

Tiffin, Susan. *In Whose Best Interest? Child Welfare Reform in the Progressive Era*. Westport, Conn.: Greenwood Press, 1982.

Torrence, Ridgely. *The Story of John Hope*. New York: Macmillan, 1948.

Trattner, William. *From Poor Law to Welfare State: A History of Social Welfare in America*. 4th ed. New York: Free Press, 1989.

Trotter, Joe William. *Black Milwaukee: The Making of an Industrial Proletariat, 1915–1945.* Urbana: University of Illinois Press, 1985.

Turner, Elizabeth Hayes. *Women, Culture, and Community: Religion and Reform in Galveston, 1880–1920.* New York: Oxford University Press, 1997.

Tuttle, William. *Race Riot: Chicago and the Red Summer of 1919.* New York: Atheneum, 1972.

Ullman, Sharon. *Sex Seen: The Emergence of Modern Sexuality in America.* Berkeley: University of California Press, 1997.

U.S. Department of Labor, Women's Bureau. *Preliminary Report of a Survey of Wages, Hours, and Conditions of Work of the Women in Industry of Georgia, 1920–21.* Washington, D.C.: Government Printing Office, 1921.

————. *Women in Georgia Industries: A Study of Hours, Wages, and Working Conditions.* Bulletin no. 22. Washington, D.C.: Government Printing Office, 1922.

Walkowitz, Daniel J. "The Making of a Feminine Professional Identity: Social Workers in the 1920s." *American Historical Review* 95 (October 1990): 1051–75.

Wandersee, Winifred D. *Women's Work and Family Values, 1920–1940.* Cambridge: Harvard University Press, 1981.

Ware, Susan. *Beyond Suffrage: Women in the New Deal.* Cambridge: Harvard University Press, 1981.

Warner, Sam Bass, Jr. *The Private City: Philadelphia in Three Periods of Its Growth.* Philadelphia: University of Pennsylvania Press, 1968.

Watts, Eugene. *The Social Bases of City Politics: Atlanta, 1865–1903.* Westport, Conn.: Greenwood Press, 1978.

Weinbaum, Batya, and Amy Bridges. "The Other Side of the Paycheck: Monopoly Capital and the Structure of Consumption." In *Capitalist Patriarchy and the Case for Socialist Feminism,* edited by Zillah Eisenstein, 190–205. New York: Monthly Review Press, 1979.

Weiner, Lynn. *From Working Girl to Working Mother: The Female Labor Force in the United States, 1820–1980.* Chapel Hill: University of North Carolina, 1985.

Wertheimer, Barbara Mayer. *We Were There: The Story of Working Women in America.* New York: Pantheon, 1977.

Wesley House Bulletin, 1903–1907. Atlanta: Foote and Davies, 1908.

Wheeler, Marjorie Spruill. *New Women of the New South: The Leaders of the Woman Suffrage Movement in the Southern States.* New York: Oxford University Press, 1993.

White, Dana. "Landscaped Atlanta: The Romantic Tradition in Cemetery, Park, and Suburban Development." *Atlanta Historical Journal* 26 (summer–fall 1982): 95–112.

White, Dana, and Timothy J. Crimmins. "Urban Structure, Atlanta." *Journal of Urban History* 2 (February 1976): 231–52.

White, Deborah Gray. *Ar'n't I a Woman?: Female Slaves in the Plantation South.* New York: W. W. Norton, 1985.

————. "The Cost of Club Work, the Price of Black Feminism." In *Visible Women: New Essays on American Activism,* edited by Nancy A. Hewitt and Suzanne Lebsock, 247–69. Urbana: University of Illinois Press, 1993.

White, Walter. *A Man Called White.* New York: Viking Press, 1948.

Whites, LeeAnn. "Rebecca Latimer Felton and the Problem of 'Protection' in the New South." In *Visible Women: New Essays on American Activism,* edited by Nancy A. Hewitt and Suzanne Lebsock, 41–61. Urbana: University of Illinois Press, 1993.

Wiggins, Gene. *Fiddlin' Georgia Crazy: Fiddlin' John Carson, His Real World, and the World of His Songs.* Urbana: University of Illinois Press, 1987.

———. "The Socio-Political Works of Fiddlin' John and Moonshine Kate." *Southern Folklore Quarterly* 41 (1977): 97–118.

Wilentz, Sean. *Chants Democratic: New York City and the Rise of the American Working Class, 1788–1850.* New York: Oxford University Press, 1984.

Williamson, Joel. *The Crucible of Race: Black/White Relations in the American South since Emancipation.* New York: Oxford University Press, 1984.

———. *A Rage for Order: Black/White Relations in the American South since Emancipation.* New York: Oxford University Press, 1986.

Willis, Paul. *Learning to Labor: How Working Class Kids Get Working Class Jobs.* New York: Columbia University Press, 1977.

Wilson, Elizabeth. *The Sphinx in the City: Urban Life, the Control of Disorder, and Women.* Berkeley: University of California Press, 1991.

Wirka, Susan Marie. "City Planning for Girls: Exploring the Ambiguous Nature of Women's Planning History." In *Making the Invisible Visible: A Multicultural Planning History,* edited by Leonie Sandercock, 150–62. Berkeley: University of California Press, 1998.

Wolcott, Victoria. "The Culture of the Informal Economy: Numbers Runners in Inter-War Black Detroit." *Radical History Review* 69 (fall 1997): 46–75.

———. *Remaking Respectability: African-American Women in Interwar Detroit.* Chapel Hill: University of North Carolina Press, 2001.

Woodward, C. Vann. *Tom Watson: Agrarian Rebel.* New York: Oxford University Press, 1938.

Woofter, T. J. "Migration of Negroes from Georgia, 1916–1917." In *Negro Migration in 1916–1917,* 75–91. New York: Negro Universities Press, 1969.

Wright, Gwendolyn. *Building the American Dream: A Social History of Housing in America.* Cambridge: MIT Press, 1981.

Writers' Program, Georgia. *Atlanta, a City of the Modern South.* New York: Smith and Durrell, 1942.

Zunz, Olivier. *The Changing Face of Inequality: Urbanization, Industrial Development, and Immigrants in Detroit, 1880–1920.* Chicago: University of Chicago Press, 1982.

———. *Making America Corporate, 1870–1920.* Chicago: University of Chicago Press, 1990.

Theses, Dissertations, and Unpublished Papers

Allen, Holly. "Fallen Women and Forgotten Men: Gendered Concepts of Community, Home, and Nation, 1932–1945." Ph.D. diss., Yale University, 1996.

Bolden, Willie Miller. "The Political Structure of Charter Revision Movements in Atlanta during the Progressive Era." Ph.D. diss., Emory University, 1978.

Branch, Anne Lavinia. "Atlanta and the American Settlement House Movement." Master's thesis, Emory University, 1966.

Cohron, Ruby Myra. "A Study of Fifty Volunteers in the Phyllis Wheatley Young Women's Christian Association, Atlanta, Georgia." Master's thesis, Atlanta University, 1942.

Crimmins, Timothy. "The Crystal Stair: A Study of the Effects of Class, Race, and Ethnicity on Secondary Education in Atlanta, 1872–1925." Ph.D. diss., Emory University, 1972.

Davis, Mary Roberts. "The Atlanta Industrial Expositions of 1881 and 1895: Expressions of the Philosophy of the New South." Master's thesis, Emory University, 1952.

Deaton, Thomas. "Atlanta during the Progressive Era." Ph.D. diss., University of Georgia, 1969.

Ethington, Phillip. "Race and Space: The Political Production of Space in the Social Construction of Race in Chicago." Paper presented at the Social Science History Association Annual Meeting, Atlanta, October 1994.

Evans, Mercer Griffin. "The History of Organized Labor in Georgia." Ph.D. diss., University of Chicago, 1929.

Ferguson, Karen. "The Politics of Inclusion: Black Activism in Atlanta during the Roosevelt Era, 1932–1945." Ph.D. diss., Duke University, 1996.

Fleming, Douglas. "Atlanta, the Depression, and the New Deal." Ph.D. diss., Emory University, 1984.

Fredrickson, Mary. " 'A Place to Speak Our Minds': The Southern Summer School for Women Workers." Ph.D. diss., University of North Carolina at Chapel Hill, 1981.

Gilmore, Glenda. "Militant Manhood in a New South City: The Men and Religion Forward Movement and Atlanta's Anti-Prostitution Crusade." Paper presented at American Historical Association Annual Meeting, Atlanta January 1995.

Godshalk, David. "In the Wake of Riot: Atlanta's Struggle for Order, 1899–1919." Ph.D. diss., Yale University, 1992.

Hagglund, Carol L. "Irish Immigrants in Atlanta, 1850–1896." Master's thesis, Emory University, 1968.

Henderson, Alexa B. "A Twentieth Century Black Enterprise: The Atlanta Life Insurance Company, 1905–1975." Ph.D. diss., Georgia State University, 1975.

Hickey, Georgina. "Visibility, Politics, and Urban Development: Working-Class Women in Early Twentieth Century Atlanta." Ph.D. diss., University of Michigan, 1995.

Hunter, Tera. "Household Workers in the Making: Afro-American Women in Atlanta and the New South, 1861–1920." Ph.D. diss., Yale University, 1990.

Judson, Sarah. "Building the 'New South' City: African-American and White Clubwomen in Atlanta, 1900–1930." Ph.D. diss., New York University, 1997.

Klopper, Ruth. "The Family's Use of Urban Space: Elements of Family Structure and Function among Economic Elites, Atlanta, Georgia, 1880–1920." Ph.D. diss., Emory University, 1977.

Kuhn, Clifford M. " 'A Full History of the Strike as I Saw It': Atlanta's Fulton Bag and Cotton Mills Workers and Their Representations through the 1914–1915 Strike." Ph.D. diss., University of North Carolina at Chapel Hill, 1993.

Maclachlan, Gretchen Ehrmann. " 'A Decent Place to Live': The Politics of Working Women's Housing in Atlanta." Paper presented at the Social Science History Association Annual Meeting, Atlanta, October 1994.

———. "Race, Gender and Space in Atlanta, 1880–1920." Paper presented at the American Studies Association Annual Meeting, Boston, November 1993.

———. "Women's Work: Atlanta's Industrialization and Urbanization, 1879–1929." Ph.D. diss., Emory University, 1992.

MacLean, Nancy. "Behind the Mask of Chivalry: Gender, Race, and Class in the Making of the Ku Klux Klan of the 1920s in Georgia." Ph.D. diss., University of Wisconsin at Madison, 1989.

Mebane, Ann Fonvielle. "Immigrant Patterns in Atlanta, 1880–1896." Master's thesis, Emory University, 1967.

Mixon, Gregory Lamont. "The Atlanta Riot of 1906." Ph.D. diss., University of Cincinnati, 1989.

Moseley, Clement Charlton. "Invisible Empire: A History of the Ku Klux Klan in Twentieth Century Georgia, 1915–1965." Ph.D. diss., University of Georgia, 1968.

Nasstrom, Kathy L. "Women, the Civil Rights Movement, and the Politics of Historical Memory in Atlanta, 1946–1973." Ph.D. diss., University of North Carolina at Chapel Hill, 1993.

Newman, Harvey Knupp. "The Vision of Order: White Protestant Christianity in Atlanta, 1865–1906." Ph.D. diss., Emory University, 1977.

Parsons, Ellen Kidd. "White Plague and Double-Barred Cross in Atlanta, 1895–1945." Ph.D. diss., Emory University, 1985.

Porter, Michael. "Black Atlanta: An Interdisciplinary Study of Blacks on the East Side of Atlanta, 1890–1910." Ph.D. diss., Emory University, 1974.

Rainey, Glenn. "The Race Riot of 1906 in Atlanta." Master's thesis, Emory University, 1929.

Rosen, Hannah. "Struggles over 'Freedom': Sexual Violence during the Memphis Riot of 1866." Paper presented at the Berkshire Conference on the History of Women, Vassar College, June 1993.

Roth, Darlene. "Matronage: Patterns in Women's Organizations, Atlanta, 1890–1940." Ph.D. diss., George Washington University, 1978.

Russell, David A., Jr. "The Institutional Church in Transition: A Study of the First Congregational Church of Atlanta, Georgia." Master's thesis, Atlanta University, 1971.

Shivery, Louie D. "The History of Organized Social Work among Atlanta Negroes." Master's thesis, Atlanta University, 1936.

Stokes, Allen Heath, Jr. "Black and White Labor and the Development of the Southern Textile Industry, 1800–1920." Ph.D. diss., University of South Carolina at Columbia, 1977.

Tagger, Barbara. "The Atlanta Race Riot of 1906 and the Black Community." Master's thesis, Atlanta University, 1984.

Thornbery, Jerry John. "The Development of Black Atlanta, 1865–1885." Ph.D. diss., University of Maryland at College Park, 1977.

Watts, Eugene John. "Characteristics of Candidates in City Politics: Atlanta, 1865–1903." Ph.D. diss., Emory University, 1969.

Wolcott, Victoria. "Remaking Respectability: African-American Women and the Politics of Identity in Inter-War Detroit." Ph.D. diss., University of Michigan, 1995.

Wrigley, Steven Wayne. "The Triumph of Provincialism: Public Life in Georgia, 1898–1917." Ph.D. diss., Northwestern University, 1986.